# HIP-HOP AND COMICS

Edited by Sheena C. Howard,
Justin D Burton, and Brea M. Heidelberg

Foreword by Patrick A. Reed

University Press of Mississippi / Jackson

The University Press of Mississippi is the scholarly publishing agency of the Mississippi Institutions of Higher Learning: Alcorn State University, Delta State University, Jackson State University, Mississippi State University, Mississippi University for Women, Mississippi Valley State University, University of Mississippi, and University of Southern Mississippi.

www.upress.state.ms.us

The University Press of Mississippi is a member of the Association of University Presses.

Any discriminatory or derogatory language or hate speech regarding race, ethnicity, religion, sex, gender, class, national origin, age, or disability that has been retained or appears in elided form is in no way an endorsement of the use of such language outside a scholarly context.

Copyright © 2026 by University Press of Mississippi
All rights reserved
Manufactured in the United States of America

∞

**Publisher**: University Press of Mississippi, Jackson, USA
**Authorised GPSR Safety Representative**: Easy Access System Europe - Mustamäe tee 50, 10621 Tallinn, Estonia, gpsr.requests@easproject.com

Library of Congress Cataloging-in-Publication Data

Names: Howard, Sheena C. editor | Burton, Justin D editor | Heidelberg, Brea M., 1985– editor | Reed, Patrick A. writer of foreword
Title: Hip-hop and comics / edited by Sheena C. Howard, Justin D Burton, and Brea M. Heidelberg ; foreword by Patrick A. Reed.
Description: Jackson : University Press of Mississippi, 2026. | Includes bibliographical references and index.
Identifiers: LCCN 2026004722 (print) | LCCN 2026004723 (ebook) | ISBN 9781496857910 hardback | ISBN 9781496861849 trade paperback | ISBN 9781496861856 epub | ISBN 9781496861863 epub | ISBN 9781496861870 pdf | ISBN 9781496861887 pdf
Subjects: LCSH: Hip-hop—In comics | Rap musicians—In comics | African Americans in comics | Rap (Music)—Social aspects
Classification: LCC ML3918.R37 H53 2026  (print) | LCC ML3918.R37  (ebook) | DDC 306.4/84249—dc23/eng/20260205
LC record available at https://lccn.loc.gov/2026004722
LC ebook record available at https://lccn.loc.gov/2026004723

British Library Cataloging-in-Publication Data available

To the visionaries who refuse to give up.
—Sheena

To Emmett and Evers, who keep me in fresh hip-hop and anime.
—Justin

To Amber and Grant, respectively my hip-hop and comics day ones.
—Brea

# CONTENTS

Foreword by Patrick A. Reed . . . . . . . . . . . . . . . . . . . . . . . . . ix
Introduction . . . . . . . . . . . . . . . . . . . . . . . . . . . . . . . . . . 3
SHEENA C. HOWARD, JUSTIN D BURTON, AND BREA M. HEIDELBERG

## Artistic Innovation and Resistance

Chapter 1: Eric Orr and the First Hip-Hop Comic Book:
Situating *Rappin' Max Robot*. . . . . . . . . . . . . . . . . . . . . . . . 11
SHEENA C. HOWARD

Chapter 2: DMC's Legacy:
Meaning-Making, Hip-Hop, and Comics . . . . . . . . . . . . . . . 29
SHEENA C. HOWARD

Chapter 3: Crafting an Alternate Reality Through Grassroots
Comics and Rap Music in India . . . . . . . . . . . . . . . . . . . . . 48
JAYANTI DATTA

Chapter 4: Wall (S)crawlers: Comics, Graffiti, and the Aesthetic,
Political, and Rhetorical Resonances of Public Visual Arts. . . . . . . 67
MICHAEL B. NORTON DANDO

## Marvel Comics and Hip-Hop

Chapter 5: "Sweet Christmas":
Luke Cage and Pulp Authenticity. . . . . . . . . . . . . . . . . . . . . 91
MATTHEW TEUTSCH

Chapter 6: Dynamic Duo: Marvel Comics and Hip-Hop Culture's
Innovations in Storytelling . . . . . . . . . . . . . . . . . . . . . . . . 110
STEPHEN J. TYSON JR.

Chapter 7: When Worlds Collide:
Hip-Hop Music and Superhero Movies . . . . . . . . . . . . . . . . 126
LAITH ZURAIKAT

Chapter 8: From Mic to Mask: Unveiling Hip-Hop's Impact
on Black Masculinity in Marvel Superheroes . . . . . . . . . . . . 145
JOHN P. CRAIG

**Cultural Expression, Impact, and Identity**
Chapter 9: Masked Marauders . . . . . . . . . . . . . . . . . . . . . . . 171
MICHAEL SALES

Chapter 10: To Murder the Hunger:
*The Boondocks*, the Exorcism and/or Beating of Tom DuBois,
and an Appeal to Black Male Solidarity . . . . . . . . . . . . . . . . 192
GEORGE WHITE JR.

Chapter 11: "I'm Michael Jordan, I'm Not Malcolm X":
Performing Black Masculinity in *The Boys*. . . . . . . . . . . . . . 209
COLLIN M. BRIGHT, KATHRYN HOBSON, LEA BEKA, AND DANIEL SILVER

Chapter 12: Remembering Daniel Dumile:
"The Classic Conception of Death" Through Dr. Victor Von Doom
née MF DOOM. . . . . . . . . . . . . . . . . . . . . . . . . . . . . . . . 228
JOHNNY JONES

Chapter 13: Hearing Comics in Hip-Hop:
Leikeli47 as Black Feminist Superhero . . . . . . . . . . . . . . . . 246
BREA M. HEIDELBERG AND JUSTIN D BURTON

Afterword . . . . . . . . . . . . . . . . . . . . . . . . . . . . . . . . . . . . 261
THE DARRYL MAKES COMICS TEAM (SPENSER NELLIS, AMY CHU, AND RIGGS MORALES)

About the Contributors . . . . . . . . . . . . . . . . . . . . . . . . . . 265
Index . . . . . . . . . . . . . . . . . . . . . . . . . . . . . . . . . . . . . . 269

# FOREWORD

PATRICK A. REED

Hip-Hop and comics are two of the most significant cultural forces to have emerged from the twentieth century—two forms that have progressed from being subject to marginalization and critical scorn to become driving forces in popular culture. Comics are now not only "cool," but ubiquitous, recognized by scholarly institutions, inspiring blockbuster film series, and underpinning a huge segment of the global entertainment economy. Likewise, Hip-Hop has grown from an underground movement to an ever-present aspect of society, its sounds and styles infiltrating every aspect of the modern media landscape. In order to discuss these subjects aptly, we need to acknowledge that we're dealing with terminology that is inherently flexible and open to interpretation. The terms themselves—hip–hop and comics—change meaning based on usage and context, referring at various times to forms of media, genres, cultures, and communities.

"Hip-Hop" is a term that's commonly used interchangeably with "rap," a descriptor of a genre of music based around beats and rhymes. And while music is an essential component of Hip-Hop, it is only a part of a much greater picture. Hip-Hop is a way of seeing the world. It's an attitude and an approach, a term that is often used in relation to music, but also can be applied to visual art, to dance and movement, to fashion. Hip-Hop is a viewfinder—a state of mind in which connections are made between different elements. It's a style, a rhythmic sense, and a method of lyricism, a culture that takes existing elements, combines them, and remixes them into something new and vital.

Even "Hip-Hop music" itself isn't just rap; it's a mindset that takes elements of many genres and fuses them into something greater than the sum of its parts. Hip-Hop music began with Kool Herc and other innovative DJs playing the funkiest, most percussive pieces of their favorite records—Babe

Ruth's *The Mexican*, Kraftwerk's *Trans-Europe Express*, the Monkees' *Mary, Mary*, James Brown's *Funky Drummer*, Jimmy Castor Bunch's *It's Just Begun*, Bob James's *Take Me to the Mardi Gras*, and countless others—assembling a patchwork structure of sound to create the foundation of a party, and keep the crowd dancing. Similarly, "comics" is a term that has multiple simultaneous definitions.

One can say comics and mean the specifically defined graphic medium that combines words and pictures in sequence. But "comics" is also a larger umbrella, that the comic medium itself is only one small part of. At a comic convention or in a comic shop, one can see a myriad of different pieces that feed into this wider definition. Comic culture includes not only comic books and strips but also animation and anime, manga, prose fiction, film, and TV; it spans fantasy, science fiction, superheroes, action/adventure, horror, romance, martial arts and action, humor, autobiography, and countless other genres. Each one of these pieces exists in communication with the others, passing inspiration back and forth: one can look at the way the comic books of the 1970s reacted to the Blaxploitation and Kung Fu crazes, how modern-day blockbuster films liberally adapt properties that originated in cartoons and comics, how western art styles have shifted and transformed over recent decades to interpolate the visual vocabulary of manga, how beloved franchises like Transformers and Robotech are quite literally forged from sampling and combining pieces of separate Japanese sci-fi and toy franchises. What this means, in both cases, is that because the core terms "Hip-Hop" and "comics" have equally applicable micro and macro definitions, conversations about these subjects require extra attentiveness from all parties—the meaning is equally dependent on the speaker's intention and the listener's interpretation. This, in and of itself, echoes Hip-Hop's concept of audience participation being an essential element of the art: The DJ's beats need to move the crowd, the MCs engage with call-and-response, the success of a dance move or a mural or a verbal freestyle is gauged by the effect it has on the spectators.

Hip-Hop and comic cultures are built around common impulses—the interwoven actions of consumption, collection, and creation. The most notable artists are fans themselves, drawing inspiration from that which has gone before, from their colleagues and peers, and from the outside media they enjoy, absorbing pieces of the world around them and transforming them into something fresh and different. Sampling sounds from the past, reinterpreting classic characters to tell new stories, building on what's gone before to create something vital and original. This hunger for input leads to the collecting mentality: you go out digging through boxes for that issue you need to complete a run, that rare LP with the perfect drum break, the old action figure, or the magazine with work by a particular graffiti artist. We end up tracing characters' appearances across different series and following MCs who we discover through a guest verse on someone else's single. We compile knowledge based on our passions and use it to determine which direction we're heading next. Through these shared enthusiasms, communities emerge. You can trade records or back issues with your friends, meet people at shows or conventions or DJ jams in the park, and form a bond with the other people who remember that one story or know every word to that one song.

At their heart, both Hip-Hop and comics are cultures of inclusion and amalgamation based around collaboration and community, synthesizing sometimes incongruous elements. Words and pictures, beats and rhymes, kung fu moves and dance steps, cartoon characters, and street-level narratives—people reinventing scattered pieces of the past through the lens of our own experiences and perceptions.

These forms and cultures exist in a constant state of evolution and revolution, incorporating outside input and pushing outward, expanding their reach as they go. More genres are folded in; new fandoms enter the scene, new technologies are employed and, adapted, and creatively turned inside-out. New generations of artists bring their own passions and frames of reference into play. These are worlds where the only limitations are those of imagination.

I've long felt strong connections between the fields of comics and Hip-Hop—listening to music while reading comics in my bedroom as a kid, finding a record store that also sold old comics when I visited a new city, seeking out the art that was often scorned by mainstream "arbiters of culture" but connected on a visceral level, feeling the undeniable impact of a well-crafted beat or a DJ creating a crescendo through cutting and scratching, thrilling to superheroics and graphic innovations that transcended the limitations of the four color printing process. These things seemed so intertwined that it took me years to consciously consider how they fit together.

Many connections were already clear-cut in my mind. I knew that Hip-Hop's South Bronx origins were steeped in what we now broadly think of as "comic culture," as the youth who we now recognize as cultural pioneers utilized iconography from the entertainment they had access to: the Kung Fu films that played in Times Square theaters, the sci-fi B-movies shown after school on local TV stations, comic books from the corner bodega. The sounds of funk underscored sequences on kids' shows such as *Sesame*

*Street, The Electric Company,* and *Fat Albert;* the *Jackson 5ive* animated series brought soul to the world of Saturday morning cartoons; Parliament's science fiction stylings were expanded into an entire cosmic mythology through the comic inserts and illustrations that Overton Lloyd contributed to their albums. The founder of Hip-Hop, DJ Kool Herc, took the name of his MC crew from Hanna-Barbera's *The Herculoids* cartoon. I also recognized that as Hip-Hop culture developed, growing around the four pillar disciplines of Graffiti, DJing, MCing and Rapping, and B-Boying/Breaking, the formative influences of comics became even more explicit, but this history was largely unwritten—a steady-building sequence of links that seemingly existed only as isolated instances and unique moments in time—and had never been viewed as related progressions toward a unified destination. The specific points of contact between Hip-Hop and comic books themselves were also evident, but not well-documented. Kid 'N Play and KRS-ONE starred in their own Marvel Comics, Wu-Tang Clan lent their name to a short-lived Image title in the nineties, and comic artists such as Bill Sienkiewicz and Denys Cowan had illustrated covers for rap albums, but there was a deeper, richer story beneath all that, just waiting to be uncovered. I set out to compile and document these connections and consider them as a single continuum. The formative influences of 1970s series like *Master of Kung Fu* and *Black Lightning,* and the underground works of Vaughn Bodé; the first incursions of Hip-Hop culture into mainstream comics in the eighties; the early nineties independent black-and-white titles that openly acknowledged their ties to Hip-Hop music and fashion; the modern works of Jim Mahfood and Ronald Wimberly and other comic creators. The lines that ran from graffiti artists through the Downtown New York club scene and ended up with a Marvel Comics staffer (who would later find fame as the cocreator of Nickelodeon's *Ren and Stimpy* cartoon) providing cover art for records by Soulsonic Force and Newcleus. The path that led from Archie Andrews encountering a crew of breakdancers at the Riverdale shopping mall to a team of teenage malcontents combating drug dealers and ninjas in the South Bronx, to world-famous musicians promoting stories with themselves as superheroes. In the process, I began sketching out a framework, a first draft of the history, looking for the clear-cut and concrete beats, the vital cornerstones of this narrative. As a historian of these forms, I acknowledge that no one event happens in isolation, yet there are certain fixed moments in time that one can cite as turning points—demarcations when prehistory ends and history begins. Everything I could find in all my research led to one conclusion: in 1986, the connection between Hip-Hop and comics finally became concrete when Eric Orr, a young artist known for collaborating with Keith Haring to design logos for rappers and DJs, self-published the first Hip-Hop comic book: *Rappin' Max Robot* #1. I found a copy of the comic itself and set out to track down its creator. And thanks to luck, happenstance, well-connected friends, and a lot of time and hard work, I found that Eric lived only a short subway ride away from my own apartment—and upon meeting him, got the story of how and why *Rappin' Max Robot* came to be, which you'll read about in chapter 1 of this book, in Eric's own words.

Having established the de facto starting point, it was off to the races. In 2009, comic creator/musician Adam Wallenta hosted a "Comic Books and Hip-Hop" panel at New York Comic Con, addressing the influence of superheroes on rap music and how rap had likewise impacted comic books. I had written a series of short articles covering the Hip-Hop and comics phenomenon, penning pieces for MTV News and other outlets that covered this topic, and in 2012, I organized and moderated the first *Hip-Hop and Comics: Cultures Combining* program at New York Comic-Con, bringing together panelists from both fields to swap stories to enthuse over their creative influences and illuminate just how many ways the worlds of Hip-Hop and comic cultures overlapped.

The following year, *Hip-Hop and Comics: Cultures Combining* debuted as part of San Diego Comic-Con's programming and has since been established as a fixture of that annual event. In 2015, I worked with an astonishing group of individuals to launch the first stand-alone *Hip-Hop and Comics* screening series as part of the Everything Is Festival in Portland, OR; in 2016, my colleague Professor Ben Saunders and I hosted a one-day *Hip-Hop and Comics* festival and academic conference at the University of Oregon; in 2017, I curated *The Hip-Hop and Comics Show* at New York's Wallworks Gallery, a retrospective exhibition showcasing more than 200 original artworks bridging the worlds of these two forms. We've held Hip-Hop and comics programs at the New York Public Library, at schools and festivals around the US, including taking part in the Louis Vuitton 200th Anniversary festivities in 2022. And while there's an increasingly vast library of great books covering each of these cultures individually—the Hip-Hop journalism of Hanif Abdurraqib, Jeff Chang, Sacha Jenkins, Joan Morgan, Danyel Smith, Greg Tate, and others; the essential comic writings of David Brothers, David Hadju, Sean Howe, Brad Ricca, Trina Robbins, Maggie, and Don Thompson, and countless other intrepid voices—this is the first volume to directly address the essential ties between comics and Hip-Hop, and I'm thrilled that Dr. Sheena Howard and her colleagues are the ones whose vision and efforts have brought it to fruition. I'm deeply grateful to be included and honored to be appearing in such prestigious company.

—Patrick A. Reed, July 12, 2024

\***Editors note:** In this foreword, we have capitalized Hip-Hop as we acknowledge Hip-Hop as a culture and as something more than simply a "genre." Throughout the book, however, we have gone with using lower case simply to stay in line with the APA citation guidelines.

# HIP-HOP AND COMICS

# INTRODUCTION

SHEENA C. HOWARD, JUSTIN D BURTON, AND BREA M. HEIDELBERG

As you'll come to learn in this book, the convergence of hip-hop and comics stands out as a compelling and culturally resonant intersection. This blending of the mediums, which might initially seem unlikely, has blossomed into a vibrant amalgamation of storytelling, vision, and cultural expression that extends beyond a tenuous or happenstance relationship. Both art forms serve as powerful mediums for self-expression, cultural commentary, and social critique not yet explored under one book cover—until now. This book demonstrates that their intertwined histories reflect a shared ethos of resilience, creativity, and transformation, much like the beats and rhymes of a classic hip-hop track.

Hip-hop, which emerged from the streets of the Bronx in the 1970s, has always been a voice for underestimated populations, offering a platform to express the struggles and aspirations of those often ignored by mainstream society. Comic books, too, have served as a vehicle for telling stories of those society has relegated as outcasts, rejects, or even heroes who battle against all odds and individuals who find strength in adversity. How do we know? This book shows, through interviews, historical analysis, and cultural critique, that the synergy between these two forms of expression is not a mere coincidence but a deeper cultural alignment that highlights their common roots in resistance and creativity.

The story of hip-hop and comics is one of mutual influence and inspiration. The range of analysis covered in this book offers us a unique compass for charting the parallels between hip-hop and comics. What do we mean? Well, even in the late 1970s to early '80s, the names of the hip-hop groups are strangely reminiscent of the titles of superhero groups—Grandwizard Theodore & the Fantastic Five, Grandmaster Flash & the Furious Five, and even the Stetsasonic. In the 1970s, as hip-hop culture took root, its visual arm, graffiti, emerged as a key element. Graffiti artists, such as Eric Orr, began using the city as their canvas, marking the beginning of a cultural revolution. Orr's transition from graffiti to comic books led to the creation of *Rappin' Max Robot* in 1986, the first hip-hop comic book.

Without giving too much away, this book explores the pivotal moments and key figures that have shaped this dynamic relationship. Take, for example, the emergence of hip-hop icon, Darryl McDaniels (DMC), who channeled his love for comics into groundbreaking records and performances, to the famous Wu-Tang logo created in the 1990s. The journey of these intertwined worlds is both fascinating and profound.

The 1990s was a turbulent and transformative time for both hip-hop and comics. Though, for different reasons, it's interesting to layer the two mediums on top of each other during this time period, especially considering the way hip-hop artists were embracing comic book culture. Of note, the backlash against rap in the 1990s has some curious parallels to things that were happening in the comic book industry. In the 1990s, hip-hop had evolved from its roots in the Bronx to become a global phenomenon. Artists like Tupac Shakur, the Notorious B.I.G., and N.W.A. dominated the airwaves, bringing gritty, unfiltered stories of life in urban America to the forefront of popular culture. However, this rise in popularity was met with significant resistance. Critics of rap music in the 1990s often pointed to its explicit content, which included themes of violence, drug use, and misogyny. Groups like 2 Live Crew faced legal challenges for their lyrics, with their album *As Nasty as They Wanna Be* being labeled obscene and subject to bans in several states. This led to high-profile court cases and significant media attention. There were unprecedented political and social reactions to hip-hop during this time period. Political figures and social organizations voiced concerns about rap's influence on youth. Then-Vice President Dan Quayle criticized the recording industry in 1992, blaming it for producing rap music that he claimed incited violence. Quayle specifically targeted Time Warner Inc.'s subsidiary, Interscope Records, demanding that they remove the album *2pacalypse Now* by rapper Tupac Shakur from stores. Similarly, Tipper Gore and the Parents Music Resource Center (PMRC) campaigned for parental advisory labels on albums with explicit lyrics, leading to widespread censorship efforts and debates over artistic freedom and free speech. The backlash also fueled negative stereotypes about rap artists and their audiences. Critics often depicted rap as a destructive force that glorified criminal behavior, reinforcing racial biases and stigmatizing the genre and its predominantly African American artists and listeners. This demonization had significant implications for how rap was perceived and consumed by the broader public. It's worth noting that comics went through similar public and social moral panic.

In the 1950s, outcry led to congressional hearings and the creation of the Comics Code Authority (CCA), a self-regulatory body established by the comic book industry to enforce strict content guidelines. This code effectively censored comic books, banning depictions of crime, horror, and any content deemed inappropriate for children. This functioned as a de facto censor for the entire United States comic book industry, with comics requiring a seal to be published. As you will discover in the pages of this book, both mediums had their fair share of moral panic, political frenzy, and public outcry. For comics in the 1990s, things were bleak, despite Milestone Comics publishing diverse and groundbreaking stories that challenged traditional narratives and showcased a broader spectrum of characters. The industry faced significant challenges, such as the burst of the speculative bubble leading to financial instability, the dominance of superhero fatigue, and ongoing debates about content and censorship. The creative renaissance offered by publishers like Image Comics and the push for greater diversity and representation were bright spots in an otherwise difficult era, highlighting the industry's resilience and capacity for reinvention in the face of adversity. Both mediums have been resilient. And yet, what was remarkable about the fusion of hip-hop and comics in the 1990s was that there continued to be notable hip-hop artists embracing comic book aesthetics and narratives, integrating them into their music and visuals. This decade solidified the presence of comic book influences in hip-hop culture, with artists like MF Doom adopting personas inspired by comic book characters, and of course, there's Ghostface Killah with his debut studio album named *Ironman*. As the new millennium dawned, technological advancements expanded the reach of both hip-hop and comics.

The 2000s saw hip-hop influences in iconic cultural comics like *The Boondocks* and graphic novels that encapsulated the essence of their music. This era also witnessed the emergence of books such as *Hip-Hop Family Tree*, which used the comics medium to document the history of hip-hop. As you read and refer to *Hip-Hop and Comics*, you will find that as we move through this millennium, the intersection of hip-hop and comics will continue to evolve, driven by a new generation of creators pushing the boundaries of both genres. The rise of digital platforms has democratized content creation and distribution, allowing more diverse voices to emerge. The twenty-first century and beyond promise even more innovative collaborations, with hip-hop and comic book culture continuing to inspire and influence each other profoundly. The fusion of hip-hop and comics is more than just a blending of art forms; it is a celebration of cultural resilience and the power of storytelling. This book invites you to explore the rich history of these two worlds, examining how they have come together to create a unique narrative that resonates globally.

As you'll learn in this book, the important and growing connections between the worlds of hip-hop and comics continue to be represented in films such as *Black Panther*, with Kendrick Lamar creating a musical Wakanda soundtrack to the film with collaborators across the African diaspora.

From pioneers like Eric Orr to contemporary creators who continue to push the envelope, the story of hip-hop and comics is one of endless creativity and boundless possibilities. As we delve into this dynamic relationship, this book highlights how these art forms have shaped and been shaped by each other, reflecting the ever-evolving landscape of cultural expression, social commentary, and even identity formation. With that said, welcome to *Hip-Hop and Comics*, where the elements of hip-hop culture and comics culture unite to tell stories that inspire, challenge, and transform. It's most exciting that this book is just the beginning of the conversation.

Before reading the chapters, it's helpful to know what to expect and how the sections of the book are divided. Each section represents a theme: Chapters 1–4 focus on *artistic innovation and resistance*, chapters 5–8 focus on *Marvel comics and hip-hop*, and chapters 9–13 focus on *cultural expression, impact, and identity*.

The first section, *Artistic Innovation and Resistance*, lays the groundwork for understanding the deep-rooted connections between the way both mediums have come together to create new works of art and how those works of art speak to cultural resistance and innovations. It explores the origins of the first hip-hop comic book to crafting alternate realities through rap music globally.

Chapter 1, "Eric Orr and the First Hip-Hop Comic Book: Situating *Rappin' Max Robot*" by Sheena C. Howard, focuses on Eric Orr's groundbreaking work, *Rappin' Max Robot*, which stands as the first hip-hop comic book. It discusses Orr's creative process and the cultural significance of his work, emphasizing its role in blending musical and visual storytelling to reflect and influence hip-hop culture. Chapter 2, "DMC's Legacy: Meaning-Making, Hip-Hop, and Comics" by Sheena C. Howard, examines the life and work of Darryl McDaniels (DMC) of Run-D.M.C. and his love of both hip-hop and comics. It highlights how DMC has used both art forms to create an alter ego for himself as well as empower underestimated communities through powerful storytelling. Chapter 3, "Crafting an Alternate Reality Through Grassroots Comics and Rap Music in India" by Jayanti Datta, draws parallels between grassroots comics and underground rap in India, exploring how these art forms challenge dominant narratives and offer alternative perspectives on society and culture. It highlights the role of these mediums in fostering community and cultural resistance. Chapter 4, "Wall (S)crawlers: Comics, Graffiti, and the Aesthetic, Political, and Rhetorical Resonances of Public Visual Arts" by Michael B. Norton Dando, rounds out this section. This chapter explores the cultural resonance and affinity of comics and graffiti along three threads: public marginalization, public accessibility, and public mediation.

The second section, *Marvel Comics and Hip-Hop*, comprising chapters 5 through 8, explores the broader cultural implications of the intersection between hip-hop and Marvel comics. It examines the relationship between Marvel and hip-hop, for better or worse, in influencing and reflecting societal narratives, identity formation, and the representation of underestimated communities. Chapter 5, "'Sweet Christmas': Luke Cage and Pulp Authenticity" by Matthew Teutsch, examines the creation of Luke Cage and its roots in Blaxploitation and pulp literature. It discusses how hip-hop has reclaimed and transformed these influences, turning them into powerful tools for social commentary and cultural critique. Chapter 6, "Dynamic Duo: Marvel Comics and Hip-Hop Culture's Innovations in Storytelling" by Stephen J. Tyson Jr., examines the collaborations between hip-hop artists and Marvel Comics, highlighting how technology has been used to enhance the comic book experience. It discusses projects like KRS-One's audio comic and will.i.am's augmented reality comic book, showcasing the innovative potential of these intersections. Chapter 7, "When Worlds Collide: Hip-Hop Music and Superhero Movies" by Laith Zuraikat, provides an overview of the use of hip-hop music in comic book adaptations, particularly in mainstream superhero movies. It analyzes the historical use of hip-hop in these films and its impact on the cultural landscape, highlighting notable examples such as the *Black Panther* soundtrack curated by Kendrick Lamar. Chapter 8, "From Mic to Mask: Unveiling Hip-Hop's Impact on Black Masculinity in Marvel Superheroes" by John P. Craig, explores the representation of Black masculinity in both hip-hop and Marvel Comics, focusing on how these narratives influence each other. It examines characters like Luke Cage and Black Panther alongside hip-hop figures such as Jay-Z and Kendrick Lamar, revealing the complex interplay between cultural expression and identity.

The final section, *Cultural Expression, Impact, and Identity*, encompasses chapters 9 through 13. These chapters focus on the innovative artistic practices and thematic intersections between hip-hop, comics, and identity, allowing us to deepen our understanding of both art forms. In chapter 9, "Masked Marauders" by Michael Sales, he recounts a transformative experience in Red Hook, Brooklyn, where he realized the harsh realities of urban life and the necessity of adopting a "mask" to survive. The chapter delves into the birth and evolution of hip-hop in the Bronx, highlighting its roots in systemic oppression and its role as a creative response to urban decay. Sales parallels his personal narrative with the story of Tony Stark/Iron Man and the Wu-Tang Clan, exploring themes of vulnerability, identity, and the masks Black men wear to navigate societal expectations and personal trauma. In chapter 10, "To Murder the Hunger: *The Boondocks*, the Exorcism and/or Beating of Tom DuBois, and an Appeal to Black Male Solidarity" by george white jr., he analyzes the role of hip-hop in *The Boondocks* comic strip and TV series, focusing on an episode that tackles themes of Black male solidarity and social justice. It examines how hip-hop serves as a critical lens through which the show addresses complex social issues. It showcases the ways these art forms push traditional boundaries and create new avenues for storytelling. Chapter 11, "'I'm Michael Jordan, I'm Not Malcolm X'; Performing Black Masculinity in *The Boys*" by Collin M. Bright, Kathryn Hobson, Lea Beka, and Daniel Silver, analyzes the depiction of Black masculinity in the TV series *The Boys* through the characters A-Train and Mother's Milk. It explores how the show critiques stereotypical representations of Black men, showing a shift from hypermasculine, image-driven portrayals to more nuanced and community-oriented identities. The authors argue that A-Train's character development, influenced by his relationship with Mother's Milk and hip-hop culture, offers a hopeful reconfiguration of Black masculinity that moves beyond traditional binaries of authenticity. Chapter 12, "Remembering Daniel Dumile: 'The Classic Conception of Death' Through Dr. Victor Von Doom née MF DOOM" by Johnny Jones, delves into the life and legacy of MF Doom, drawing parallels between his persona and Marvel's Dr. Doom. This chapter examines how both figures embody themes of transformation, resistance, and the artistic exploration of death and identity. Finally, chapter 13, "Hearing Comics in Hip-Hop: Leikeli47 as Black Feminist Superhero" by Brea M. Heidelberg and Justin D Burton, explores how Leikeli47's music video "OMC" creates an uncanny pocket dimension of New York City, characterized by disorienting visuals and sounds, symbolizing a space where Black feminist practices thrive and are protected. By blending theoretical concepts from hip-hop, comics, and Black feminism, the authors argue that Leikeli47's work transcends traditional boundaries, offering a new framework to understand the intersections of these art forms.

Through these chapters, the book you hold in your hands provides a comprehensive exploration of the unique and powerful relationship between hip-hop and comics. Each chapter offers an invitation to revel in the way these art forms have influenced each other and the broader cultural landscape, highlighting their significance as tools for artistic expression, social change, and the innovation needed for both art forms to thrive.

# ARTISTIC INNOVATION
# AND RESISTANCE

CHAPTER 1

# ERIC ORR AND THE FIRST HIP-HOP COMIC BOOK

## Situating *Rappin' Max Robot*

SHEENA C. HOWARD

### INTRODUCTION

In the chronicles of hip-hop culture, few individuals have bridged the gap between disparate art forms as effectively as Eric Orr. Known as the creator of the world's first hip-hop comic book, *Rappin' Max Robot*, Orr's legacy is a testament to the symbiotic relationship between hip-hop and comic books. This chapter explores Orr's groundbreaking contributions, examining how his work has influenced and reflected the broader cultural movements within these two dynamic spheres. There are numerous studies that use in-depth interviewing and ethnographic methods to examine graffiti writers, hip-hop, culture, and more (see Abram, 2024; Kramer, 2012; Malone, 2020). This study adds to the existing literature.

Eric Orr's journey is deeply rooted in the early days of hip-hop and graffiti in New York City. As a graffiti artist, Orr was at the forefront of a cultural revolution that saw young artists using the city as their canvas. His transition from graffiti to comic books was a natural evolution, driven by his desire to create a narrative that spoke to the hip-hop community. The creation of *Rappin' Max Robot* marked a significant moment in the history of both

**Figure 1.1** *Rappin' Max Robot.* Reprinted with permission from Eric Orr.

hip-hop and comics, blending the visual storytelling of comic books with the rhythmic and cultural essence of hip-hop.

This chapter features an in-depth conversation with Eric Orr, providing a first-hand account of his experiences and insights. We delve into the origins of his iconic character, the influences that shaped his artistic vision, and the challenges he faced in bringing his comic book to life. Orr's story is not just about creating a new art form; it's about the enduring power of cultural fusion and the role of individual creativity in shaping collective identities. By examining Orr's contributions, this chapter seeks to highlight the profound connections between hip-hop and comic books. It explores how these art forms serve as vehicles for self-expression, social commentary, and cultural transformation. Through Orr's lens, we gain a deeper understanding of the interplay between visual art and music, and how these mediums can inspire and empower individuals and communities.

The decision to include Eric Orr's interview in this book stems from his unique position at the crossroads of hip-hop and comic culture. Orr's pioneering work has not only influenced generations of artists but also provided a blueprint for integrating different artistic disciplines. His narrative offers valuable insights into the creative processes that drive cultural innovation and the importance of preserving and celebrating these hybrid forms of artistic expression.

In analyzing Eric Orr's discussion, this chapter will use Cultural Prism Theory (CPT) as the lens to examine the pivotal moments that gave birth to the first hip-hop comic. This includes examining relevant historical, economic, cultural, and political "impact moments" that bring the iconic comic book and Orr himself into focus. As mentioned by Patrick Reed in the foreword to this book, "No one event happens in isolation, yet there are certain fixed moments in time that one can cite as turning points—demarcations when prehistory ends, and history begins." You will read about these "impact moments" and turning points in Orr's recounting of his story. This sentiment reminds us of the relevance of Cultural Prism Theory, which seeks to better understand and situate culturally iconic works of art. As an artist, one knows all too well that timing can make or break an artist—sometimes the culture is ready for something, and sometimes it isn't. Sometimes, we are ahead of our time, and sometimes, artists do not get their flowers until they have passed away. I am always seeking to understand what that timing looks like as it relates to art—CPT helps us do that.

The following section will briefly explore the theoretical underpinnings of CPT and how these "impact moments" relate to Orr's work and its cultural longevity. Through this examination, I aim to illuminate the significance of Eric Orr's contributions and their lasting influence on the landscape of contemporary art.

## CULTURAL PRISM THEORY (CPT)

Cultural Prism Theory (CPT) offers a multifaceted lens to examine cultural artifacts by situating them within the complex interplay of "impact moments." Impact moments are key factors that influence the cultural artifact that is being studied within the context of history, culture, politics, and economics. I developed CPT in 2018 (see Howard, 2018) as a conceptual framework that provides a lens to understand how various moments and contexts give birth to and influence cultural creations such as Eric Orr's *Rappin' Max Robot*. The framework emphasizes the interconnectedness of different spheres of influence, positing that no cultural artifact exists in a vacuum but is rather a product of diverse and often overlapping influences through time and space. That is, the when, why, what, where, and who matter when looking at the success, acceptance, or even failure of a work of art in the cultural consciousness.

Cultural Prism Theory was first articulated in my article "Situating Cyberzone: Black Lesbian Identity in Comics," published in the *Journal of Lesbian Studies* (2018). In this work, I explored the comic book *Cyberzone*, focusing on how the comic was shaped by its historical, economic, cultural, and political contexts. The theory emerged from a need to comprehensively examine cultural texts beyond superficial analysis, acknowledging the complex matrix of factors that contribute to their creation and significance or even relevance in the eyes of the public. CPT builds on the premise that understanding a cultural artifact requires an examination of the "matrix" of historical, economic, cultural, and political moments that shape it. This approach allows for a deeper appreciation of how these factors interact to produce and influence cultural products. CPT challenges traditional methods of cultural analysis by advocating for a more integrated and contextual approach, allowing researchers to highlight how cultural artifacts can serve as sites of resistance, innovation, and reflection of broader societal trends.

Through the lens of CPT, the conversation with Eric Orr, and his book *Rappin' Max Robot*, we will be able to examine the artifact as not just a comic book in a vacuum but as a cultural artifact that embodies the historical, economic, cultural, and political complexities of its time. CPT will facilitate the connection of impact moments that Eric Orr's pioneering work illustrates so that we gain a deeper understanding of how cultural artifacts can serve as powerful tools for resistance, representation, and the blending of art forms, ultimately contributing to cultural expression.

The following conversation took place in the winter of 2024 over Zoom and has only been slightly edited for clarity.

**Sheena C. Howard:** Just to confirm for the readers, *Rappin' Max Robot* is the world's first hip-hop comic book, correct?

**Eric Orr:** I've been told so, yes. It's been confirmed through Cornell University.

**SCH:** For the people that may not have read it or ever even heard of *Rappin' Max Robot*, can you describe the comic book when someone opens the pages, what will they see in this book?

**EO:** The description of it, it, well, let me just back up a little bit about it, because it came to fruition because of the graffiti movement. I'm from the hip-hop era, the beginning of it, as they say. And I had graffiti friends that used to do *Black books. So my dive into comic books is through the Black books and graffiti art. In the early seventies, I noticed that graffiti artists here in New York City, in the Bronx and Queens and the other boroughs, that there were a lot of us borrowing from comic books and contemporary images at the time.

**SCH:** What is something memorable about this time for you?

**EO:** I remember when I first saw a graffiti artist's piece that had speech bubbles. That's one of my first recollections of a drawing from the comic book industry or from a comic book perspective. Because with the old Batman series with the bomb, the boom, the bang, all of that used to come up on the screen. A lot of graffiti artists used those elements in some of their works. You may know of the Cheech Wizard, comic book guy from the seventies. Graffiti artists borrowed his character and incorporated it into their works when they painted on the trains. So there was a lot of borrowing from contemporary culture, illustration, and comics back in the early, well, the mid-sixties, early seventies, and then really heavy into the eighties.

**SCH:** Is that where your love of comics came from?

**EO:** That's basically where my start for the love of comic books came from. I'm originally a graffiti artist, and I borrowed from comic books. How my comic book *Rappin' Max Robot* came about was also similar to that. But it goes back a little bit further because, in my family, we went to church every Sunday. Now, I don't know if they had that in Philly, where you're from, but every Sunday, they had this newspaper. It was the *Daily News* and it had everything in it. It had the sports pages, ads and all kinds of stuff. And it was wrapped with comic book pages, like Beetle Bailey, Dagwood, and Hagar the Horrible. And when we got to Sunday school, the way they kept us quiet inside the church after Sunday school was that they would allow myself, my brothers, and my cousins to read the comics so we could be quiet in the back of the pews. So that was one of the first introductions to comics for me, was in church.

**SCH:** How or when did you start to connect your artwork to hip-hop?

**EO:** It's 1984. The first record on Def Jam was "It's Yours" by T. LaRock and Jazzy Jay. There was a flip side record called *The Cold Rock Stuff* that Russell Simmons did. The label at the time was called Party Time. Jazzy Jay was the one who brought me into the music side of everything. I met Jazzy Jay in high school. We graduated from the Alfred E. Smith school.

I graduated in '78, he graduated in '79, or '80. I'm from Bronx River and we both graduated and went our separate ways. He went on to do that record. He did a record with Afrika Bambaataa. Planet Rock was on tour. I just moved from Bronx River to Parkchester, in The Bronx and it was the eighties. He was driving around the neighborhood, calling my name and driving

**Figure 1.2** Jazzy Jay logo (hand spinning). Created by Eric Orr.

up behind me. Music is blaring. That's when everybody had the booming systems in their car. Windows roll down, and it's Jazzy Jay. So we talked and he was like, "Oh, I'm into the music thing and I'm just off a tour." So he says, "Listen, I'm about to start a record label. I need a logo." He knew that I drew from back in high school. I was like, "Okay, cool," so I designed the logo, and that logo came from what I saw on the stage, with the turntables on top and all I could see was his hand. So, if you look at the actual Jazzy Jay logo, which he still uses today, his logo is just the hand scratching. So that was my first dive into graphic design in the hip-hop industry.

**SCH:** How did you get connected with Keith Haring early on?

**EO:** Jazzy Jay went on tour. He said that when he gets back, he's going to start all kinds of projects. Tours take a while. So he went away. I didn't see him for maybe six months because he was doing the record "It's Yours." It's now 1984. Swatch Watch was doing a break dance contest at the Roxy roller rink in New York City, I believe it was on 12th and 12th Avenue. I decided I wanted to go check it out, so I created a T-shirt with my robot head on it, and it was just a robot head, nothing else . . .

**SCH:** Okay. And when you say in your neighborhood, do you mean as graffiti art?

**EO:** Yes, as in graffiti, just the head. I was trying to be different. So I went with something more graphic. I did see some of the early Keith Haring chalk drawings in the subway, but I was already doing chalk drawings in the streets. So people thought that I was Keith. And I was like, "No, no, no, that's not me. That's not me." So when I ventured out, I was like, let me see who they talking about. So I went out, I saw his stuff, and I was like, shit, I could do that. So I got some chalk, and I started drawing in those black spaces in the subways. And one evening I drew on, I don't know, maybe fifty spaces from where I lived up in Parkchester all the way down to maybe, I don't know, 96th Street in Harlem, maybe further. And somehow he saw those drawings—the robot head.

So, jumping back to going to the Roxy roller rink. I go to the Roxy roller rink with my buddy to see this, Swatch Watch show. And Keith Haring happened to be a judge for that contest. Again, I got my shirt on with the robot head. Didn't think anybody knew other than people in my neighborhood knew what it meant and who it belonged to. So they [Swatch Watch] were filming. While they're filming, they take a break. Keith got up from the judge's table and walked around the Roxy. And my buddy said to me, "Yo, yo, cover that up. Cover that up." And he was talking about the image, the robot image on my shirt. He thought Keith looked like one of the guys from *the Vandal Squad. The Vandal Squad was a bunch of white policemen who dressed like us. But they were going around researching tags and trying to match tags with faces so they could bust you. So that's why he was telling me to cover up. I saw Keith, now, if you remember back in the eighties, pale white dude, short hair, rim glasses, look like a typical white dude. We don't know what's going on. So he started coming towards me, and I did one of these B-boy stances to hide my shirt, but he had seen it already. He walked up to me, and he was like, "Yo, you did that robot head." And I said, "Oh shit, I'm busted." He's like, "Nah, that's cool. I really like that. I saw it before." I was like, "Oh, okay." He's said, "Yo, I liked the way you did that and I saw you on some of the black spaces." So right then, I don't know what came over him, he was like, "Yo, let me have that shirt and I'll give you mine." He had one of the Swatch Watch T-shirts. I looked at my buddy, and he said, "Yeah, take it." So right there in the middle of the Roxy roller rink, we swapped T-shirts.

**SCH:** That was the first time you ever met him?

**EO:** That's the first time.

**SCH:** He had recognized this robot head from tagging it in different places in New York?

**EO:** Yeah. In the subway, in the spaces that he was already using as a means of putting up his iconic imagery. So like I said, that evening I went out, I did about fifty of 'em. So he probably went out and was going to draw on some of those spaces. And he saw that it was already taken up. Every station he went to, he was like, "Oh, somebody was here already." That kind of thing. It made an impression that much. So he was like, "Listen, I got to go back here and judge this. Most likely, you'll get some airtime because I'm a judge and the cameras are running." I'm like, "Yeah, that's pretty cool." And he says, "Yo, I would love to collaborate with you." I didn't know what 'collaborate' meant at the time, but I was like, "Yeah, okay." So we exchanged numbers.

**SCH:** And did you know his work at this point?

**EO:** I knew of it, but I didn't know how extensive it was. And at that time, it was '84, and it was just about to peak. I think he just had maybe two or three shows in some prominent galleries in New York City. And when we exchanged numbers, he said I'll give you a call when I get back in town. I didn't think anything of it. And I think it was maybe a week later, I got a phone call and it was on a Sunday. And I'm like, "Who's this?" And he said, "Oh yeah, this is Keith. I'm back, and if you want to go out, we can do that." And I said, "Yeah, okay. When do you want to go?" He said tomorrow, which was a Monday, and I said okay. On September 24, 1984, I met him at Bleecker Street, where his studio was. I met him in the front car on the number six train. We got on together, and we rode the train from Bleecker Street all the way down to the Brooklyn Bridge stop—the last stop on the six train, then back up to 125th Street in Harlem, and then back to Bleecker Street. In that time, I mean, we must have done at least seventy to eighty drawings together and some individually. And we got kicked out of the subway system twice. So at the end, he says, "Let's go have some lunch." We went up to the studio.

So here's how the robot came to *Rappin' Max Robot*, one of our last drawings in the subway. I was doing a robot head. And he's like, "Man, Eric put a body on that thing." I was like, "Okay." So that was the first time I put a body on *Rappin' Max Robot*. And if you look at that early drawing, you'll see that it looks like one of Keith Haring's bodies with the robot head. So that's how the robot came to be. And I say that to say this: he was the one who told me to put the body on it. And from there we became really good friends.

**SCH:** So, Eric, at this time, you were not necessarily reading comic books. You were doing your art in the hip-hop scene, but you were not an avid comic book reader?

**EO:** I never was. Never was. I'm more of a visual person. I love the visuals of comics. Yeah, I loved that. I wasn't a big reader, storyteller, or anything like that. Like I said, we were borrowing those visuals to put on the subway or wherever. So I said to myself, I'm going to make this comic book. I'm going to make a comic book that speaks to us. I had a zine I was doing with Strong City. If you ever get a chance to look inside it, you'll see that I talk about when Strong City Records was coming out and where the next show was going to be. And at that time, Andrew Dust was big and I'm big on antidrugs. So I made the first story about antidrugs, and that's how this whole thing came about.

**SCH:** So back then, Eric, publishing anything is totally different than it is today. So, how did you do it? What was the process of even just getting that first book done?

**EO:** I have educators in my family. My mother, sisters, and aunts are educators. So if you want to know something, you have to go to a book and read about it. And that's how I learned about creating my first silkscreen print. I made it myself with Shellac Wood, and that's how I made that first shirt. So I didn't know much about comic books and how to create comic books. So I went to my local library, thank God for that. And I found, I can't remember, there's a book, a very famous book, that most artists have on how to draw comics. I took that one out and that gave me the template on how to put this thing together. So that's how it came together.

**SCH:** Did you go to a local printing place? How did you physically print it somewhere?

**EO:** Remember the flyers from back in the day for concerts? That was what I was doing when I was working with Strong City and Jazzy Jay. I learned that you can make a book the same way you make a zine. Xerox the pages. Xerox, for lack of a better word. And then fold the pages in half. And that's it.

**SCH:** So once you had this first physical thing in your hand, what was your next thought process? Did you just print out a bunch and give them to people?

**EO:** No. What I did with putting this book together was add Strong City Records to it while designing for them, Jazzy Jay, and Rocky Buchanan. I put a dummy book together because the book I took out from the library mentioned doing that. I kind of knew where I was going to get it printed at. It was a place called Budget Printing in my neighborhood that did printings for the local businesses for their on-sale flyers. I didn't have the money for it at first. I went to my aunt, and she gave me some money. I went to my mom; she gave me some money too. It wasn't a lot of money. It might've been $20. So I looked at some comic books. They had ads on the back, the front, and inside. I was like, "Yo, I know Keith got money, Keith Haring." I decided to go to the studio to see if I could get him to buy an ad. Because at that same time, his Pop Shop was opening up. I went to a couple of local people and a pizza shop. You'll see it if you get a chance to look inside of it. There's a pizza shop ad in there for my buddy who owned the pizza shop in our neighborhood.

**SCH:** So you just went to them and you're like, "Hey, I got this book. Do you want to put an ad in here so that everybody that reads the book sees it?"

**EO:** That's what I did. I went to local shops.

**SCH:** I'm looking at the book ads now. OBM Records. I see one for Video World. Those?

**EO:** Yep. Those. They gave me $20 here, $20 there, whatever. And again, I was like, maybe I should go to Keith. So I went to Keith with the dummy and I showed it to him. Now this is early '86. He hadn't seen the drawings or the robots since '84 because he started traveling a lot and I hadn't seen him a lot. So when I presented him with the dummy book, he saw the progression of what we did in the subway to what I brought to him. And he's like, "Yo, you got something here and I want to be part of it." I was like, yeah, well, so if you want to buy a little quarter page, it's going to be $7. He said, "No, no, no. I got my Pop Shop. Open it up. I'll take the back page." That's how the Pop Shop ad got on the back, and the book was released the same year as the launch of the Pop Shop.

**SCH:** And how did you have distribution?

**EO:** I went to Budget Printing, which was right on Castle Hill Avenue in the Bronx, went to the guy, he's like, yeah, I can print this. He told me the prices. I was like, I want everything to be in color but I don't have a lot of money. He was like he couldn't do full color for the money I had, but he'd make it look like something. That's why it's only two colors. He printed up 500 of them. Now, back then, 500 looks like a lot of books. It's a lot of books for teenagers. So I'm like, damn, how am I going to get rid of all these books other than giving them out to friends in the neighborhood. Took a couple of stacks to the store owners and all that. Now I have, I don't know, maybe 450. What am I going to do now?

**SCH:** Yes, so what did you do next?

**EO:** There was a local comic bookstore. It was close by. I'd go in once in a while. I was like, listen, I got this book. It's *Rappin' Max Robot*. As soon they saw rapping, because of the hype of the music and the culture was starting to come up, they said, "Okay, we'll give it a shot." I put five there, went into another store in the neighborhood, put another five there. And that's basically how it went. Then I was told about St. Mark's, St. Mark's comic book store on Astor Place. That was the first place I went and was like, listen, I got this book, would you like it? And they said, "Oh, we're taking new consignments." So I left five there and when I got home, I got a phone call from St. Mark's, like, "Yo, we sold out. I need more." I said, okay, I'll bring five more next week. He's like, no, no. Can you bring 10 in the middle of the week?" So St. Mark's was one of the ones that really pushed it out there. So I was giving St. Mark's twenty and thirty books. And again, I'm a young kid, I don't know what the fuck is going on or what he was doing. He was actually doing the distributions for me.

So I had books in my neighborhood comic book stores. I took care of those downtown. Downtown, meaning in Manhattan, I had St. Mark's and I had Forbidden Planet. And most of the books were going to them. And now I realize, in retrospect, that they were taking so many from me. I'm like, all these people love my stuff. I'm thinking that all these people are coming and buying this. Wasn't that it? Actually, they were taking them in bulk and shipping it out. Yes. That's how it got out.

**SCH:** So what was it about the robot head originally that you were fascinated by? Why did you draw the robot head originally? What was it? Was it an alter ego?

**EO:** Because I loved the robot dance back in the day. That's why it was a robot. And I loved Charlie Brown. I was a big fan of Charlie Brown and Snoopy and all those guys. And Charlie Brown had the big head. So that's where that came from.

**SCH:** So when I talked to DMC, he said, quote, "Hip-hop would not exist if it wasn't no comic books in the form that exist because we all have alter egos." So Eric, what do you think about that relationship between hip-hop, comics and alter egos or being someone else?

**EO:** Well, I think we touched on it earlier. The rappers took on personas, different personas from comic book characters. But yes, Darryl was on point with that. And I guess my alter ego was *Rappin' Max Robot* because I loved the robot dance. I love robots. So yeah, I would say so.

**SCH:** So your work has been acquired by institutions like Cornell University and Columbia University?

**EO:** Yes. Yes, it has.

**SCH:** What does this recognition mean to you, and how do you think it reflects the cultural significance of hip-hop and comics?

**EO:** Well, I mean, I would say that because someone at an institution took the time and money to do the research to say, oh, this person did something significant to the culture. And not just the Black culture or the hip-hop culture, but American culture because hip-hop is an American thing. So for these two institutions to take the time, specifically Cornell University, took the time to listen to my story and take the book and actually do research and say, okay, yeah, he got something here. Because they're not going to just take anybody's word by, oh yeah, you're the first and start doing a curriculum behind it. They're not going to do that. So they did the research and it came back.

**SCH:** *Rappin' Max Robot* is only one issue, right, Eric?

**EO:** Actually, it's one physical issue that looks like a traditional comic book. There's three other foldouts that are actual zines. I didn't have the time to really put together a real comic book that looked like the first one. I was working, traveling, and like I said, if you knew anything about the tour life, the money was fast. The women were fast, and you were on the road a lot. And that's the only reason why I didn't put it to the side. I put the creating comic books to the side, but the character has always been with me on T-shirts.

**SCH:** Is there anything you would have done differently with the *Rappin' Max Robot* comic book, knowing what you know now?

**EO:** You know what? That's a really great question. And I don't know if I would change anything because if I would've changed anything, it might've taken a different direction.

**SCH:** It worked out.

**EO:** And it's still working out. And I only say that because again, in hindsight, the whole hip-hop move was organic. It was really organic. And so was the book. My book was really organic. It wasn't for the masses, it was for our community. Someone else pushed it out there, not me. I took it downtown NYC, thinking that, oh, we got eight million people. That should be enough. But no, someone else is like, let's push it. So if I changed anything, I wouldn't be where I'm at right now. I think I would keep it the way it is in hindsight and let it unfold the way it's unfolding.

**SCH:** What do you want to be remembered for?

**EO:** Creating the very first hip-hop comic book.

**SCH:** What advice would you give to young artists today who are inspired by both hip-hop and comics and they want to create something for their community? What advice would you give that young person?

**EO:** Be honest and genuine. And don't let anybody deter you because you never know. You never know what's going to happen.

**SCH:** This is amazing. Thank you for your work. Thank you for your time. We have to document this history. That's all that matters to me.

\* A graffiti Black book, or "piece book," is a sketchbook used by graffiti artists to draft designs and practice lettering before painting. It documents their artistic journey and can be shared with others for feedback and inspiration.

\* The Vandal Squad in New York City was established in the 1980s. While the exact years of operation can vary by city, the NYC Vandal Squad was notable for its efforts to combat graffiti.

## ANALYSIS AND CONCLUSION

Cultural Prism Theory provides a framework to understand how various dimensions like history, economy, culture, and politics influence and shape a cultural artifact—without these influences, a piece of art may never even exist. In this case, based on the conversation with Eric Orr and research found in and outside of this book, we will use this analysis section to situate *Rappin' Max Robot* within the matrix of impact moments that gave birth to and longevity to this culturally significant artifact. We will briefly discuss these moments in the following order: Historical moments, economic moments, cultural moments, and political moments. Then, we will conclude the chapter.

### Historical Impact Moments

Historically, *Rappin' Max Robot* emerges from the early days of hip-hop and the broader cultural revolution of the 1970s and 1980s in New York City. The time and place are critical to the existence of the first hip-hop comic as we know it today. Modern graffiti culture began towards the end of the 1960s in Philadelphia (Navitas, 2008). The center of graffiti innovation moved from Philadelphia to New York City in the 1970s, and 1966–1971 saw the invention of newer and much more creative writing techniques by the graffiti pioneers (Navitas, 2008). During the period between 1966 and 1989, when Orr created the robot, graffiti experienced prominent years where the act evolved in underground subways (Navitas, 2008). Graffiti, as a part of hip-hop culture, was not just about art but a political statement against urban neglect and a form of reclaiming public spaces. Orr's work is a product of the convergence of visual art (graffiti) and storytelling, reflecting the broader trend of the 1980s and 1990s, where hip-hop artists began to explore and merge different cultural forms. The cultivation of modern graffiti in New York City is a pivotal historical impact moment as it relates to the creation of *Rappin' Max Robot*, as Orr demonstrates in his retelling.

*Rappin' Max Robot*, looking back historically, is a trendsetter in terms of leading the pack in printing and distributing a physical self-published comic book without the assistance of a press or independent press. The comic book medium itself was undergoing significant changes with the rise of independent publishers (which really ramped up in the nineties) and the representation of diverse voices (again, really ramping up in the nineties) (see Costello & Whitted, 2012). For example, Dark Horse Comics emerged in 1986, followed by Image in the 1990s, which offered creators more control over their work and provided readers with alternatives to mainstream superhero fare. Similarly to an independent press, the way in which Orr published his work allowed for a more culturally specific narrative to emerge and find an audience both short-term and long-term. As Orr recounts his story, the roots and history of hip-hop are clearly an important aspect of his vision and ultimate creation of the robot. While historically, Orr was situated during a time period and geographical location that played a significant role in giving birth to the robot, economically, there is much to be said as well.

### Economic Impact Moments

Economically, the 1980s and 1990s saw significant changes in the comic book industry, particularly with the rise of independent comic book creators and the challenges posed by distribution monopolies and the direct market. Orr's decision to self-publish *Rappin' Max Robot* mirrors the broader trend of independent comic creators seeking to bypass traditional gatekeepers and reach audiences directly; however (as mentioned), he led the pack by at least four years or more before this trend exploded. This approach was partly due to economic barriers that limited opportunities and access for nonmainstream voices in the comics industry, as Orr alludes to in his recollection of distributing the hip-hop comic. The economic landscape of the comic book industry in the mid-eighties, when Orr published his work, made it difficult for new and diverse voices to find footing or be sold in comic book stores alongside Marvel and DC books. In the nineties and as we moved towards the twenty-first century, the rise of niche markets and the internet provided platforms for independent comic book creators like Orr to reach dedicated audiences who were seeking content that represented their experiences and interests. As technology advances, we see that *Rappin' Max Robot* continues to find new opportunities and collaborations for Orr, finding institutions such as Cornell University and other partnerships.

Orr, being scrappy and resourceful, incorporated ads into his comic, and had Orr had the financial means to publish and distribute his book on his own, we probably wouldn't have a hip-hop comic with ads in it from OBM Records, Video World, and other local shops. From an artistic perspective, this reminds us to be resourceful and scrappy in the face of funding our creative projects. It's interesting to think that Orr's need to actually talk to local shops and companies about his book so that he could get funding might have been just what he needed to get his book distributed outside of his small geographical area. Orr notes that these businesses were shipping and distributing the book far and wide, and this interplay between community and economics reminds us of how important working together to find an audience and fund creative projects is in the longevity and reach of our creative works. In addition, Orr lived in a matrix of cultural influences as well, which we will address next.

## Cultural Impact Moments

Culturally, *Rappin' Max Robot* is situated at the intersection of hip-hop and comic book culture, representing a unique blend that speaks to the experiences and identities of urban youth. The comic book serves as a political statement that challenges the mainstream narratives dominated by white male superheroes as well. By featuring a character with a hip-hop background, Orr's work confronts the underrepresentation of Black and urban youth in popular culture and the comic book industry at large in the seventies and eighties. *Rappin' Max Robot* acts as a form of cultural resistance, using the comic book format to empower its readers and provide a platform for voices that were often marginalized in both the comic book and broader cultural landscapes. The artist's struggles and triumphs can be seen as metaphorical reflections of the political and social challenges faced by the communities Orr represents. The robot character, which started as just a head, is also a reflection of hip-hop culture, especially the element of dancing. Orr reminds us that the character is a robot because he loved "the robot" dance when he was a youngster. This is a direct reflection of the cultural nuances that give birth to creative works. The beauty of these cultural influences is how they collide. CPT helps us uncover these nuances and examine how they work together. In addition, Eric mentions a number of people that he connected with, was aware of, and/or inspired by in the music industry, including but not limited to Afrika Bambaataa, Russell Simmons, Jazzy Jay, and more. These names are a part of the culture Eric grew up in and around. It is his connection to music and his talent as an artist that gives way to creating such an iconic symbol and character. As Orr notes, his cultural environment, from church on Sundays to his proximity to the Roxy and people like Keith Haring, gave way to the birth of *Rappin' Max Robot*, as CPT asks us to consider, time and space do matter in the art world. The robot aesthetic and the narrative style of the comic are deeply rooted in hip-hop culture, reflecting its themes of resistance, storytelling, and self-expression that only Eric Orr could have created at that time, in that space, in that aesthetic, surrounded by those people.

Hip-hop's emphasis on lyrical content and rhythm influenced the way stories were visually told in *Rappin' Max Robot*. The comic book serves as a cultural artifact that captures the spirit of an era where hip-hop was emerging as a powerful voice for marginalized communities. It uses the medium of comics to address issues pertinent to the hip-hop community, such as identity, creativity, and social justice. Orr's work embodies the principles of cultural convergence, blending elements from both hip-hop and comics to create a new, hybrid form of cultural expression. This fusion reflects a broader cultural trend towards the blending of disparate art forms to create something unique and relevant to contemporary audiences.

### Political Impact Moments

According to Lachmann (2002), New York in 1979 was a city just emerging from bankruptcy: youth unemployment was over 75 percent, the South Bronx was burning, and the subway system was about to enter its worst years of fires, breakdowns, and crashes. Nevertheless, the New York Times and the Koch administration were convinced that "the real cause of cynicism, sadness, and hopelessness . . . was the actions of young vandals, including those writing their names on the subways" (Austin, 2001, p. 144). Eric Orr was at the intersection of these trying times in New York City, specifically growing up in the Bronx.

Politically, the creation and reception of *Rappin' Max Robot* can be viewed within the context of the socio-political dynamics of the 1970s, '80s, and '90s, including the struggles for racial equality, cultural representation, antigraffiti policies, and the fight against systemic marginalization. In the 1980s, New York City's political culture surrounding graffiti was deeply polarized. Many City officials and law enforcement viewed graffiti as a symbol of urban decay and lawlessness, leading to aggressive policies and the formation of specialized units like the Vandal Squad to combat it. Orr notes his fear of the Vandal Squad when he first met Keith Haring, as he initially thought Haring was law enforcement. These efforts were part of broader "quality of life" campaigns aimed at restoring public order and reducing crime. Public perception, for some, often aligned with this view, seeing graffiti as a nuisance that contributed to the city's deteriorating infrastructure. However, within certain communities, particularly among marginalized groups, graffiti was celebrated as a form of artistic expression and resistance. Young artists like Orr used graffiti to voice their frustrations, creativity, and aspirations, transforming urban landscapes into vibrant art galleries. That is, *Rappin' Max Robot* likely wouldn't exist if Orr wasn't a graffiti artist at that time and in that space. Graffiti artists viewed graffiti as a legitimate form of urban art, challenging the mainstream narrative that sought to criminalize their activities.

Media coverage often reinforced negative perceptions of graffiti, linking it to the city's crime problem and legitimizing stringent antigraffiti measures (see Austin, 2001). Yet, there was growing recognition of graffiti's artistic value, leading to a more nuanced understanding in some circles. In fact, the more the city erased the graffiti art, the more it spurred new and emerging graffiti artists to use the subway as their canvas. Graffiti writers' code of honor prevented them from writing over the work of others, so when the available spaces for graffiti on the subways became filled, innovation slowed, and novice graffiti writers were unable to find the space to develop reputations for quantity or quality. Whenever the transit authority cleaned the outsides of subway cars, they inadvertently created new space for graffiti, which had the unintended effect of spurring artistic innovation and drawing new cohorts of writers into the subways. Full car murals were first created after a spasm of subway cleaning in the early 1970s (Lachmann, 2002). Orr notes tagging several subway spaces as the way his work was first introduced to Haring. Haring saw the robot head and was impressed by it before ever meeting Orr in person.

Community initiatives also played a significant role in shaping the political culture around graffiti. Activists and community groups advocated for alternative solutions, such as legal graffiti walls and youth art programs, aiming to balance the need for public order with the recognition of graffiti as a valid form of cultural expression. Today, we see the throughline of this with many cities adorned with mural arts programs and artists decorating walls through community outreach programs, with the City's approval.

The political culture of New York City in the 1980s, as it related to graffiti, was marked by a clear dichotomy between those who viewed it as a social ill to be eradicated and those who saw it as a vibrant and legitimate form of urban art. This conflict reflected broader debates about urban policy, social justice, and cultural recognition, making the story of graffiti in 1980s New York a microcosm of the city's complex efforts to navigate the challenges of urban life. Eric Orr lived right in the middle of these complexities, in both time and space.

In conclusion, using Cultural Prism Theory, this chapter was able to situate Eric Orr's *Rappin' Max Robot* within the context of impact moments that shed light on the birth and longevity of the cultural artifact. This chapter also situates itself within existing literature that includes interviews with graffiti artists to understand the nuances and complexities around the culture. For example, in *Painting with Permission: Legal Graffiti in New York City* (2010) by Ronald Kramer, he notes: "With this, my research opens up a variety of questions for further investigation. For instance, by consulting a greater diversity of graffiti writers, that is, those who paint with and without permission, one could work towards the development of a descriptive account that more adequately reflects the heterogeneity of contemporary graffiti writing culture in NYC." This chapter sheds light on the causes and choices Eric Orr made as an artist living and working in New York City during the 1980s and how that led to his ultimate success as a comic book creator.

In this chapter, we find nuggets of ingenuity that creatives can use today to turn their own work into a cultural icon by leveraging particular impact moments that make way for their creative endeavors. We learn the power of bridging gaps between different cultures that we interact with and engaging with our own surroundings and communities to create something innovative. Eric Orr shows us the possibility of what can be created when hip-hop and comics converge and when an artist continues to share their work with the world. *Rappin' Max Robot* can be understood as a culturally and historically significant work that intersects with economic and political dimensions to reflect and influence the broader socio-cultural landscape of its time and beyond. Eric Orr's pioneering efforts not only contribute to the fusion of hip-hop and comic book cultures but also highlight the importance of diverse and independent voices in shaping the narrative of popular culture. This analysis provides a comprehensive view of how *Rappin' Max Robot* serves as a powerful example of cultural convergence and resistance through art.

## REFERENCES

Abram, S. (2024). Graffiti, street art and murals against the neoliberal city. *SAUC-Street Art and Urban Creativity*, *10*(1), 54–71.

Austin, J. (2001). *Taking the train: How graffiti art became an urban crisis in New York City*. Columbia University Press.

Howard, S. C. (2018). Situating "Cyberzone": Black lesbian identity in comics. *Journal of Lesbian Studies*, *22*(4), 1–13. https://doi.org/10.1080/10894160.2018.1449992

Kramer, R. (2010). Painting with permission: Legal graffiti in New York City. *Ethnography*, *11*(2), 235–53. http://www.jstor.org/stable/24048062

Lachmann, R. (2002). [Review of *Taking the train: How graffiti art became an urban crisis in New York City*, by J. Austin]. *American Journal of Sociology*, *108*(1), 244–45. https://doi.org/10.1086/376284

Malone, T. (2020). Getting up: an ethnography of hip hop graffiti writers, their art, and perceptions of society's reactions [Doctoral dissertation, University of Louisville]. ThinkIR. https://ir.library.louisville.edu/etd/3524/

Navitas, P. (2008). 21st century graffiti. How authorities should deal with it in city centers. In A. Bergmann (Ed.), *Music-city. Sports-city. Leisure-city* (pp. 90–97). Bauhaus University Weimar.

Whitted, Q. J. (2012). Of slaves and other swamp things: Black Southern history as comic book horror. In B. Costello & Q. J. Whitted (Eds.), *Comics and the U.S. South* (pp. 187–213). University Press of Mississippi.

CHAPTER 2

# DMC'S LEGACY

Meaning-Making, Hip-Hop, and Comics

SHEENA C. HOWARD

## INTRODUCTION

In the annals of hip-hop history, few names are as emblematic and influential as Darryl McDaniels, better known by his stage name DMC, of the pioneering group Run-D.M.C. (we will refer to Darryl McDaniels as DMC going forward). This chapter delves into a conversation with the legendary artist, exploring the intricate interplay between two seemingly disparate worlds: hip-hop and comics. The rationale for this dialogue is rooted in a deeper understanding of how cultural artifacts, like music and comics, shape individual identities and societal narratives. As you will learn in this chapter, DMC is not just a hip-hop icon; he is a multifaceted artist whose passion for comic books has significantly influenced his musical persona and creative output. His journey from the streets of Hollis, Queens, to the pinnacle of hip-hop royalty and his subsequent foray into the world of creating comics offers a unique lens to examine the cultural and psychological impact of these art forms on individuals and how we engage with these creative mediums. The decision to interview DMC for this chapter stems from his unique position at the intersection of hip-hop and comic cultures. I've had the privilege to work with DMC over the last few years, writing several different projects, such as one of his graphic novel issues and a stage play about his life. DMC has navigated both arenas (hip-hop and comics) with remarkable success, and in this chapter, he offers invaluable insights into how these forms of expression have not only shaped his personal and artistic identity but also how they reflect broader societal trends and issues. This conversation will be grounded in the conceptual framework of Symbolic Interactionism.

## SYMBOLIC INTERACTION THEORY

This chapter uses Symbolic Interaction Theory as an interpretive lens to better understand the impact and meaning of comics and hip-hop on DMC's life. Specifically, this theory will be instructive in helping us better understand how we ascribe meanings to objects, and in this case, art forms, such as hip-hop and comics, through the lens of DMC. Lehn, Heath, and Hindmarsh (2001) have noted that experience of objects and artifacts emerges within and is constituted through interaction, an interaction that inextricably relies on a social organization that informs the very ways in which things are seen and experienced (p. 209). We are specifically looking at how hip-hop and comics shape individual identities and societal narratives, using DMC's experiences as the case study.

Blumer identified three basic premises upon which symbolic interactionism is built: first, people act toward things based on the meaning things have for them; second, meaning arises from social interaction with others; and third, meanings are handled through and modified by an interpretive process (Blumer, 1969). Both Blumer and Goffman have noted further that symbolic interactionism explains the way individuals establish meanings through interactions with other entities or objects in social contexts (Goffman, 1959). In *Symbolic Interactionism and Cultural Studies: The Politics of Interpretation* (1992), Denzin notes, "When a work of art enters an individual's or a group's field of experience, it is confronted by a preexisting set of cultural, personal, and political meanings. These meanings are woven into the individual or the group's taken-for-granted understandings of the world." They, in turn, transform the aesthetic object into an experience that passes through three stages: assessment and interpretation, the definition of how the object relates to the group, and interaction with the object as an experience. The aesthetic object thus becomes a part of the group's collective experience (Houser & Kwon, 2014). This will be instructive in this chapter's analysis of DMC's relationship between his identity and how he engages with each art form. Further, Symbolic Interactionism is a sociological perspective that emphasizes the importance of symbols and language in the formation of self-identity and

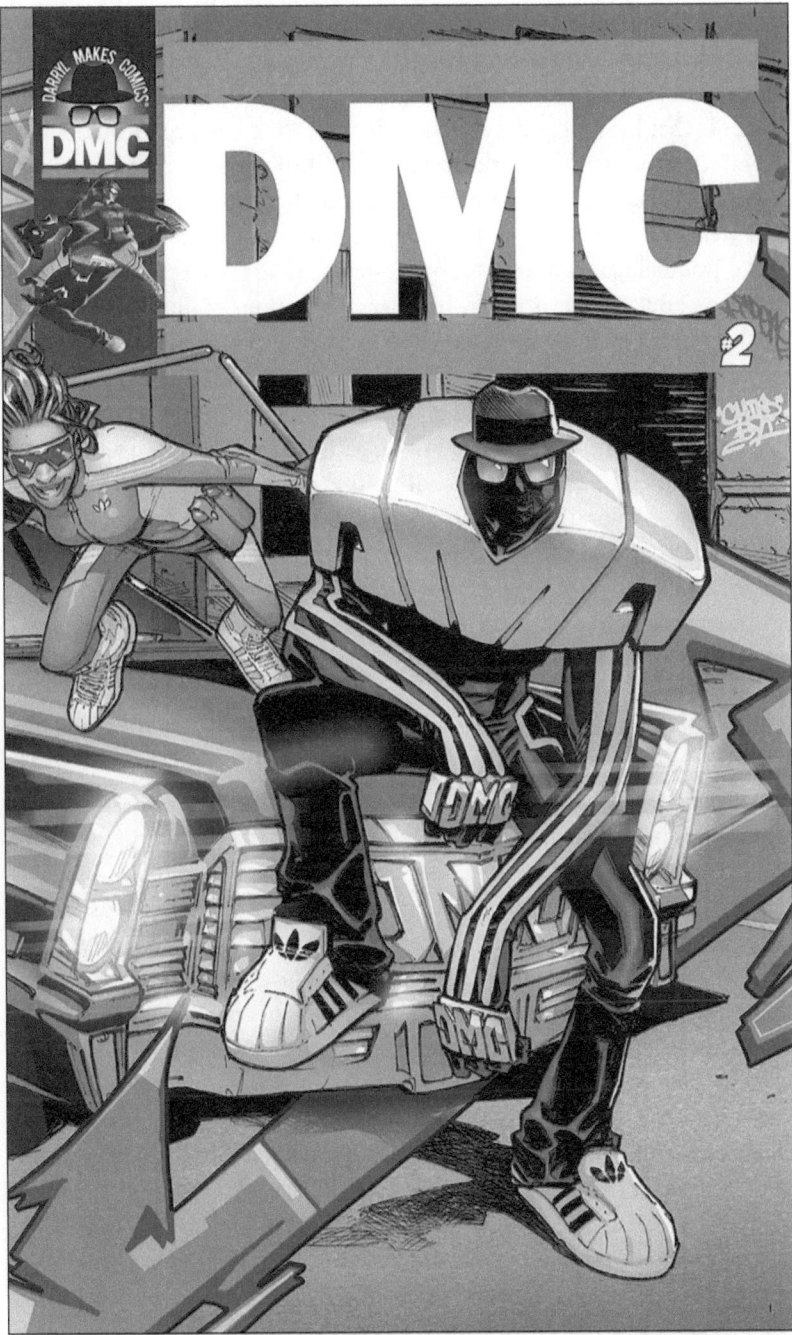

**Figure 2.1** *DMC* #2 graphic novel cover; art by Humberto Ramos. Reprinted with permission from Darryl McDaniels.

societal roles. It posits that individuals create meanings through their interactions with others, and these meanings are modified through interpretation. In the context of this discussion, hip-hop and comic books are seen as powerful symbols that have played a crucial role in DMC's identity formation and his interpretation of the world around him. Through this conversation with DMC, this chapter aims to uncover how the themes of heroism, adversity, and identity in comics are reflected in the ethos of hip-hop culture and vice versa. This dialogue is not only about understanding DMC's personal journey but also about appreciating the broader implications of how art forms like hip-hop and comics can serve as vehicles for self-expression, social commentary, and cultural transformation for the individuals who interact with them.

In short, this chapter seeks to explore the symbiotic relationship between hip-hop and comic books through the experiences and perspectives of DMC, a figure who embodies the fusion of these two vibrant cultures in complex ways. It is an exploration of how cultural expression shapes our understanding of ourselves and the world and how art forms can be used to challenge, inspire, and empower.

The following conversation took place in the winter of 2024 over Zoom and has only been slightly edited for clarity:

**Sheena C. Howard:** When did your love of comic books first start, and what was it about comics that you connected with as a child?

**Darryl "DMC" McDaniels:** My love for comic books started probably when I was in kindergarten. I saw a Batman cover, and I'm a kid. I can't read. But the way it looked, it did something to me physically, spiritually, and emotionally. So, first grade, straight-A student. By second grade, I was already reading these comic books. But by second grade, my brother introduced me to Marvel Comics. So the thing that sparked my love was Batman. But to have Superheroes in New York City! It was more real to me. And what attracted me to it was it was the only place where I saw geeky, nerdy, awkward people with problems who were super badass and educated. Growing up in Hollis, I wasn't selling weed, I wasn't in a gang. I wasn't doing what was powerful in my real world, but I was reading Tony Stark, Reed Richards, Spider-Man, and Dr. Bruce Banner.

**SCH:** Anything specific stand out about your love of comics back then?

**DMC:** Peter Parker was awkward, couldn't get it right with Gwen Stacy, getting teased and beat up, you know what I'm saying? But he was Spider-Man. When I saw that these guys were students in school, I was like, whoa. Most of my friends were playing hooky, robbing, stealing, and stuff like that. So the comic books were the only place I saw people with problems like these that were bad ass and educated. That was a connection for me. I would rather stay in the house and read comic books. I related to these people more than my friends on my block because my block was smoking cigarettes, cutting school, and not doing their homework. Plus, I was a kid that had to be in the house when a streetlight came on. So, I had to have an imagination.

SCH: Did you feel like you had to bury your love of comic books to be a hip-hop artist in the 1980s?

DMC: Nope. That's what made me so successful. My whole attitude is everything that I am, crash through walls, come through floors, bust through ceilings, and knock down doors. Rappers don't do that, superheroes do that. But I was just trying to be the most powerful entity in the hip-hop universe. I was a superhero on the microphone. That's what made me so different. And number one, I took positivity and made it harder than all the negativity everybody was rapping about. So to answer that question, if I didn't have comic books, I would've never had the confidence to get on a mic in the first place. I was a mild-mannered Catholic school kid. I was mild-mannered, straight-A student, Catholic school student, Darryl McDaniels, who transforms into the devastating mic controller. When I touched that mic, Thor had a hammer. Cap had a shield, I had my mic, and it was the same thing to me.

SCH: People need to hear that, to be yourself.

DMC: It gave me confidence. That was my confidence.

SCH: In what ways have creating comics and creating music helped you get through tough times in your life?

DMC: It was all my therapy. Even when I went to therapy, my therapist said, Dee, don't you know, listening back to all your music was all your therapy through all the tough times, adversity, and obstacles that life was bringing you, no matter if it was in the business, if it was the street, if it was in your neighborhood, if it was at home.

SCH: Can you give me an example of how comic books helped you define your identity?

DMC: I was scared to death because nobody in college was like in high school and elementary school, nobody helps you [in college]. You're on your own. But I was able to say I am DMC in the place to be. I'm DMC, I'm the king of rock. I'm the devastating mic controller. I'm those two words. I am hip-hop. And comic books allowed me to define that. And what's really key about that is Stan Lee was actually doing something that my culture and the so-called educational system wasn't doing.

I learned about this word called the adjective, which describes the noun. But think about it like this. I'm Darryl McDaniels, I'm DMC, but I'm not just DMC. I'm DMC, the King of Rock. I'm DMC, the devastating mic controller.

I'm DMC, the microphone master. Spider-Man isn't just Spider-Man. He's the Amazing Spider-Man. Hulk isn't just Hulk, he's the Incredible Hulk. Iron Man is the invincible. Thor is mighty. So I was looking at those things in the comic book because I could relate to them. So when it was time for me to go into my universe, I was pretending to be them. So when it was time for me to walk out that door or go on that stage or go to that studio, I was prepared with this confidence of who I am.

**SCH:** How has hip-hop culture influenced your approach to your *Darryl Makes Comics* (DMC) comic book line?

**DMC:** Oh, it's exactly the same thing. My comic book line is me, Daryl McDaniels, everything I am. And I tell other creators this, too. Take who you are. Everything about you, your flaws, the good things about you, your experiences, and put that into your work. Why? Because then the reader and people who come to your work, won't just see you anymore. They will see themselves. So for me, the only thing that is different from the DMC and DMC, the hip-hop guy, is it's a different universe.

It's Darryl McDaniel, the teacher with a superpower. And this universe here, my superpower is hip-hop and rock and roll. But in my DMC comic book universe, it's me, Darryl McDaniels, Hollis, Queens, all of that, except I never meet, RUN, and I don't become the rapper. I become a teacher. Because somebody asked me, Dee, if you never made music, what would you be doing? I said, I don't know. But I was a straight-A student. Only thing I knew was people kept telling me, Dee, you still teaching now when you ain't on stage and you ain't nowhere, where are you? I'm always at school talking to kids. If I'm not here with you, I'm at a school. When I'm off, I'm at a school talking to kids. But in that [comic book] universe, it's everything about me, but in a different manifestation.

**SCH:** It's like a world that you can create, too?

**DMC:** Exactly. Now, in my comic book, there's hip-hop, there's heavy metal, there's all the arts, everything that exists except that I'm not doing it. I'm the observer in my universe as opposed to being creative. But even in this universe, I was just an observer of Grandmaster Flash, Funky Four Plus One, the Cold Crush Brothers, Grandwizard Theodore & the Fantastic Five, and the Treacherous Three. So when it was time for me to go get on a microphone, I knew what to do. But then my advantage was, I don't come from the Bronx, I don't come from Harlem, I don't come from Manhattan. Hip-hop for me was to keep it real. So all I did was do the thing everybody was doing, but I added my ingredients to it.

**SCH:** How important is it for you to address social issues in your art? Or is that even important at all to you?

**DMC:** It's important for me to address social issues. It's not a so-called calling card or blueprint for me as a Public Enemy or for those where that was their agenda. That's why they do it. Mine comes from when I was a little kid, when I was reading Marvel comic books, for instance, Stan Lee didn't say, this book is about drug abuse. This book is about racism. He just told a story that would make you go, oh, I know what he's talking about. The X-Men were created to talk about discrimination, hatred, and bias. You know what I'm saying? You're different from me. So we're scared of you and afraid of you. So you must be the enemy. There must be something wrong with you. There were books with Spider-Man. It wasn't the drug issue, but Spider-Man was fighting drug dealers. And what I mean by that, if you listen to "Hard Times," if you listen to the avenue, if you listen to whatever records that we got, if you listen to "Rock Box," if you listen to King of Rock, we always talked about education, how you can make yourself better. But we just didn't label it as such. So the whole purpose of my creation is to address the social issues, but in a way that universally the kid from Compton and the gang can understand it. And that was my ability to come along with the big gold chain and the glasses, and then to start bragging about college the same way someone would brag about, how I got guns and I sell drugs and I'm in a gang.

**SCH:** This is going to liberate somebody out there.

**DMC:** I apply the same attitude that Chuck D would have, but I try to make it more universal. It's like that was about good and bad. And I never point a finger, saying you're wrong for doing anything. You know what I'm saying? And when you look at Captain America, when you look at certain superheroes, they try to tell these people there's another way before they bust their ass. So instead of me busting ass physically, I was busting ass mentally.

**SCH:** What are your biggest dreams for your DMC graphic novel line, and what would you like to see happen with it?

**DMC:** The first thing about it is, I'm not doing this for any return. I'm doing it because I enjoy doing it. Now that I see people like it, my dream is to do what? Marvel. I have big dreams, Star Wars, Disney. I want a theme park. I want movies. I want cartoons. I want books. I'm starting with the comic books. I want everything that DC and Marvel has, I want a Star Wars–level, Harry Potter–level thing. And people don't realize that once you take your creation, and once it's created thoroughly, it has all the potential to achieve all of those possibilities.

**Figure 2.2** *DMC* graphic novel panel; art by Rob Guillory. Reprinted with permission from Darryl McDaniels.

**SCH:** Any long goals for the comic book line?

**DMC:** It's not about now. Three hundred years from now, when they say Spider-Man, Superman, Bugs Bunny, Fred Flintstone, and the Powerpuff Girls, they're going to be talking about DMC. And here's what's cool, man. I don't even want people to like my character because it's me; I want to talk about all the other characters that I introduced.

**SCH:** Sounds like it's a legacy. It's part of your legacy that you could leave behind?

**DMC:** Yeah. And people can continually build on it. I want to achieve everything Marvel and Star Wars achieved.

**SCH:** In what ways do you believe hip-hop has impacted the comic book industry?

**DMC:** Everybody from Wu-Tang to MF Doom. And that being said, it has always been here. I spoke to Method Man about it. It has always been there. We had hip-hop. Hip-hop would not exist if there weren't any comic books in the form that exists because we all have alter egos. You know what I'm saying? Bruce Wayne is Batman, Darryl McDaniels is DMC. What had happened with hip-hop was we just wanted to be seen, and heard, and felt. And when hip-hop first started, let's start with the graffiti artists. It was like the colorful comic book pages jumped off the page and splattered all the trains on the walls in New York City, when you look at Ghostface Killah, he's Tony Stark. We all took nicknames and personalities from the comic book people that we grew up reading and studying. So, hip-hop is only attractive because we took from the comic book blueprint.

**SCH:** Can you say more about the alter ego theme?

**DMC:** It's an exact connection. If you look at early graffiti on the walls, there's always a Spider-Man or a Superman in there. There's always a character in the graffiti artist work that they connected with before they went out to create the art that they created. So we had to learn, okay, Bruce Banner is the Hulk. Melvin Glover is Melle Mel. People said that about the eighties rappers. Y'all guys were like superheroes because we were on MTV. But for us just seeing Melle Mel and DJ Hollywood and Grandmaster Caz walk down the block. This is before records. This is before *Video Music Box* and *Yo! MTV Raps*, this is before MTV. So the whole alter ego thing, the whole thing about what's your special power? You had Mel, he had his lane, Caz had his storytelling lane. KRS-One had Teacha. And not only do we have alter ego, we have nicknames. When I say, DMC in the place to be, *Darryl Makes Comics*, just like Stan Lee. Check this out. Like Peter Parker, I come from Queens, Peter Parker's from Queens and T'Challa, I am a king. I'm called the King of Rock. So hip-hop, the comic books has allowed us as hip-hop artists to become not just more than what we thought. We could be so much more than we even could imagine. A lot of our references to comic books is vocally and through audio, but a good visual is MF Doom wearing a Dr. Doom mask and making that his calling card. You know what I'm saying? He took it to a whole other level because he became the actual thing that inspired him.

**SCH:** Can you share your thoughts on how the themes of being a hero in comics parallel the themes of being a hero or overcoming adversity in hip-hop?

**DMC:** What's bad about hip-hop right now? We're in a bad position because it once was mandatory and an unwritten rule that with much power comes great responsibility. Now, a lot of hip-hop has all this power, and all the most irresponsible people on the face of the earth in all genres of entertainment. And it's a shame that the majority of them are all African American or Black or Latinos from the very places that this power can transform and save in a blink of an eye. And the responsibility was this. We had to write "The Message." We had to write "Planet Rock." We had to make records and tell the story. And then at the end say, but you young boy, you young girl, don't do what I do. There's another way. Now, none of our music does that. And the music that does do that, we are not fighting to get it played on radio. We are not fighting for it. We are not fighting to make it the only story that the media talks about because it used to be. We have that power somewhere along the way, a Joker and the Penguin and all the villains have quieted our existence. And what I mean by that was, here's a perfect example of power that transformed culture. When Rakim came along, he didn't rap. He said, I used to roll up, but now I learned to earn because I'm righteous. So when Rakim said that, as hard and street as he was, all the young G's were like, we don't have to do that. And there was a change. Now we are looking at the gods and heroes of our culture, and they're saying, drink and disrespect the women. Shoot each other, get the money by any means necessary. Something went wrong. Something went wrong.

So we have the power. We have the power tomorrow to make the radio change its format. They play the same four records over and over every twenty minutes. And all of those records is promoting destructive situations, circumstances, and behavior that is killing us. So for us, when we came along, when Run-D.M.C., LL Cool J, Public Enemy and De La Soul, A Tribe Called Quest, even Naughty by Nature, when we came along, we knew there was a responsibility with all of this power. So we made sure that we would never disrespect what the Zulu Nation and MC Sha-Rocks did before us, what they represented. They represented the transformation from death, destruction, and darkness to empowerment, education, uplifting, and enlightenment. Now, the top 10 records that are famous in hip-hop, there is no positivity. None.

**SCH:** That's real. Back to your DMC comic book and graphic novel line, I'm curious what challenges, if any, have you faced in the comic book industry and how have your experiences in hip-hop prepared you to tackle them?

**DMC:** Oh, it is synonymous with what happened in hip-hop when we came along. Nobody wants to hear it. It's a fad. It ain't real music. So everything with me and my comic book, no, it's just a hip-hop comic book. It's going to be going to be gone in three years. No, we don't want it. I think what they're really scared of is putting me next to Harry Potter and Star Wars, but it's the same exact thing, people who don't believe in it. People don't think it's relevant because people don't think it's necessary to see positive images of African American people of color or marginalized people in positions of power. Because once they allow that to happen, it reveals the truth of who and what we really are. So they are not ready for the images because it's like the teacher's salute. Oh my God, you're a teacher with superpowers. And this is no disrespect to my culture, but we had a habit. A lot of the hip-hop comic books in the past used profanity, and all of them used stereotypical characterizations of our culture. Everybody said, "Yo man, what's up, my n***a?" and this and that. And everybody's a drug dealer, a pimp, or a hustler. Everybody's coming from the ghetto. I'm like, no. Say, okay, you have gang bangers. In every Black neighborhood, I don't care if it was Compton or if it was Harlem, even at the worst times, it was kids playing Double Dutch. There were kids doing creative stuff. You always had that one kid on your block that was the scientist. He's always building experiments. These are the things that I'm putting in my book. The only time you see the negativity is when the bad guy shows up. I don't show it within my culture and community because we live it every day.

**SCH:** What types of images are in your DMC comics?

**DMC:** I'm trying to put images in my book that exist that people are overlooking, and we've been overlooked so long. We are scholars, we are educators. The graffiti artists are blessed now because somebody put artists on the name of it, before it was just graffiti. But today, an art person who really loved arts, knows these boys and girls are artists, was the game changer. So my book shows the baker, the tech wizard. My book shows the artist and the cook. My book shows positive African American police officers. All police officers ain't bad. I remember when I was growing up in Hollis, on my block, four of my friends' fathers were police officers. The reason why we continue to utilize negative images for financial gain is because these studios and these corporations and these organizations are quicker to write a check for me to be represented as that and won't put the same amount of money behind me to promote a good image of who we are. So we have to use our art to change it. I'm seven years in, I haven't given up. People laugh at me. I mean, all the other creators that I'm around, Sanford Greene, shout out to Sanford Greene, Damion Scott, great artists, all the makers of milestone comic books. They tell me, oh, people don't understand. You don't really make no money until they turn it into a series on Netflix or a series on the big network. But they're [big networks] quick to jump and give me a check if you're a crack dealer who turns into a superhero. You know what I'm saying? So I think what I'm trying to do with the DMC universe is change all of that, and not in a way where people say how great *Bill Cosby* show was because it showed Dr. Huxtable. What I'm trying to do is this: you have Shaft, Superfly, and you have the Huxtables, but it seems like Hollywood only takes one or the other. I'm trying to fill in everybody in between. That's when we become successful because we all have stories to tell.

**SCH:** In what ways do you think the collaboration between hip-hop artists and comic creators can further enrich both art forms today?

**DMC:** Perfect example is the Marvel Variant covers. When they did the Variant, they took superheroes and replaced all of them with hip-hop artists. They did. I remember that. Now, in the beginning, and this is what's crazy, so many comic book lovers were offended by it. What was that about? Because they don't respect our culture. Don't put this rap crap with our stuff, I grew up with. You know what I'm saying? They don't know that simultaneously, y'all just didn't know the same people. You don't want to use their art to represent your comic book culture, where the very same people are reading the books just like you. So the stories weren't getting told. So what I think is, I mean, they think we're a lesser class of being. That's why that happened. So many people hated the Marvel cover variants. But once people saw it, even the haters were like, yo, this is incredible. It took us to use the comic books to show other people who we really are. But the collaborations is the game changer because we are all products of pop culture. And it's like this, the same show, MTV, *Yo! MTV Raps* was a game-changer because it put our hip-hop culture in living rooms all throughout America. Even the living rooms that didn't want us in their house. But all those little white kids were sitting down. You don't know how many, but they couldn't stop it. So all of those little white kids from an Eminem to a Travis Barker, to all of them, to the Beastie Boys, once we get in people's lives, once our lifestyle becomes synonymous or equal in the presentations as everybody, nothing really happens until our culture is noticed, then transformation begins and we're seen as equal. You can make the movies, we make the best movies, and something happens. You can make the music. We make the stories. We are the best writers. We're the best fashion designers. So the collaboration of hip-hop and comics, what it does is it transforms society and it ever elevates humanity so that everything we were scared about or everything that had misinterpretations about us has all changed. Once we are represented, once we are artistically represented, things change. And that's what happens when comic books and hip-hop [come together], two different cultures, but have the same DNA.

**SCH:** What message do you hope readers take away from your comics, and how does that align with the ethos of your legendary hip-hop career?

**DMC:** Right, right. You have everything necessary to defeat whatever obstacle, whatever adversity, or whatever struggle is in front of you; you have it within you. You know what I'm saying? It's not alien. It's not supernatural. It's not foreign. It's there. It's the same thing that I've seen in Batman. No matter what the trauma is, there's something in you. It sounds cliché. You all have the power to overcome. And the other thing is everything that you want to be, you already are, because you wouldn't have ever had the desire to be it or see it or pretend to be it in the first place. I tell kids that all the time. When you say you want something, it's yours. It's done. But you got to go through it to get to it. You have to develop the creation that you are. You have to create the process and the navigation of the process. Every superhero goes through a discovery period, and nothing manifests for every superhero. Nobody wakes up on the good day and becomes the superhero. So if you can say, wow, Batman. Batman saw his two parents get murdered in front of him, imagine how that affected him. But even with that trauma, he says, I can't kill. Superman could crush everything. And he watches bad guys kill millions of people. He watched these people, but he says, I can't. And that's the painful thing. So what I want people to know is they have the power to defeat whatever it is they're struggling with physically, mentally, and spiritually. And second of all, when you say that you're something, you are!

**SCH:** Thank you so much. This was so inspiring.

## SYMBOLIC INTERACTIONISM, IDENTITY CONSTRUCTION, AND SOCIETAL NARRATIVES

In the dynamic intersection of music and narrative, the story of DMC unfolds as a testament to the power of cultural expression and identity formation, in which symbolic interaction theory can help us see those connections. This conversation delves into the heart of DMC's journey, revealing how the twin worlds of hip-hop and comic books shaped his persona, both as an artist and as an individual. This is where the conceptual framework of Symbolic Interactionism can help us unpack the interplay between art forms, identity, and the social context in which we live.

The theory of Symbolic Interactionism, proposed by Herbert Blumer, provides a compelling framework to contextualize this dialogue. At its core, Symbolic Interactionism posits that individuals construct their identities based on their interactions with others and the meanings they ascribe to those interactions. It emphasizes the role of society in shaping self-concept, where identity is not a static entity but an ongoing process of social negotiation and reinterpretation. DMC's narrative is a vivid illustration of this theory. Next, we will discuss identity construction as it relates to DMC's fusion of hip-hop and comics.

## Identity Construction

DMC's love for comic books, which began in his childhood, was not merely an escape but a foundational element in constructing his identity. Comics presented a world where the awkward, the nerdy, and the misunderstood not only found acceptance but also wielded power. This resonated deeply with DMC, growing up in Hollis, Queens, where he felt alienated from the prevailing street culture. The superheroes of Marvel and DC Comics, especially those set in the familiar backdrop of New York City, offered him a sense of belonging and a framework to understand his own potential, especially when it came to rapping. The interview with DMC illustrates how the constructs of the comic book narratives allowed him to become the superhero he was reading about when he stepped on stage as a performer. DMC integrated the ethos of comic book superheroes into his hip-hop persona. He did not conform to the conventional images of hip-hop artists of the time but instead carved out a unique identity that combined the bravado and social commentary of hip-hop with the moral and heroic qualities of the comic book characters he related to the most, such as Peter Parker. This is illustrated in the interview when he says:

> Peter Parker was awkward, couldn't get it right with Gwen Stacy, getting teased and beat up, you know what I'm saying? But he was Spider-Man. When I saw that these guys were students in school, I was like, whoa. Most of my friends were playing hooky, robbing, stealing, and stuff like that. So the comic books were the only place I saw people with problems like these that were bad ass and educated. That was a connection for me. I would rather stay in the house and read comic books. I related to these people more than my friends on my block because my block was smoking cigarettes, cutting school, and not doing their homework.

This synthesis was not only a personal coping mechanism but also a revolutionary act in the hip-hop world, challenging and expanding the genre's boundaries. Furthermore, DMC's venture into creating his own comic book line is a continuation of this identity exploration and construction. His comics are not just artistic expressions but are imbued with his life experiences, beliefs, and values. They are a medium through which he communicates with and influences his audience, particularly the younger generation, reinforcing the idea that personal narratives and cultural artifacts significantly shape our understanding of ourselves and the world around us. This is fitting for

Symbolic Interaction Theory. The superhero genre, became a part of personal narrative, that reminded him of the power of creating your own success, specifically becoming the hero of your own story. This narrative is a positive and important part of his identity, one in which he is trying to use to empower others. This is illustrated when DMC states:

> You have to develop the creation that you are. You have to create the process and the navigation of the process. Every superhero goes through a discovery period, and nothing manifests for every superhero. Nobody wakes up on the good day and becomes the superhero. So if you can say, wow, Batman. Batman saw his two parents get murdered in front of him, imagine how that affected him. But even with that trauma, he says, I can't kill. Superman could crush everything. And he watches bad guys kill millions of people. He watched these people but he says, I can't. And that's the painful thing. So what I want people to know is they have the power to defeat whatever it is they're struggling with physically, mentally, and spiritually. And second of all, when you say that you're something, you are!

Furthermore, the conversation with DMC is not just about a legendary hip-hop artist's career but a deeper exploration of how cultural elements like music and comics can be powerful agents in shaping one's identity, providing a creative outlet, and communicating one's identity to the world. It underscores the significance of Symbolic Interactionism in understanding the role of societal interactions and cultural artifacts in the ongoing process of identity formation. Comics gave him a visual and an outlet that was different than some of the things he was seeing and experiencing in his material life. This outlet that comics provided had a positive effect on him. This dialogue with DMC thus becomes a compelling narrative of personal growth, cultural resistance, and the power of art in our lives. Illustrating the power of art—specifically hip-hop and comics. As comics significantly contributed to the formation of his hip-hop identity. To drive this point home, DMC states:

> Hip-hop would not exist if there weren't any comic books in the form that exists because we all have alter egos. You know what I'm saying? Bruce Wayne is Batman, Darryl McDaniels is DMC. What had happened with hip-hop was we just wanted to be seen and heard and felt. And when hip-hop first started, let's start with the graffiti artists. It was like the colorful comic book pages jumped off the page

and splattered all the trains on the walls in New York City, when you look at Ghostface Killah, he's Tony Starks. We all took nicknames and personalities from the comic book people that we grew up reading and studying. So hip-hop is only attractive because we took from the comic book blueprint.

Through the lens of DMC's experiences with hip-hop and comics, we can vividly see the principles of meaning, language, the self, social interaction, and agency at work. Next, we will briefly explore my conversation with DMC by looking at a few core principles of the symbolic interactionism perspective—meaning and language, followed by the self, social Interaction, and agency.

## Meaning and Language

DMC's profound connection to comic books from an early age illustrates the process of meaning-making inherent in symbolic interactionism. DMC used comics to make sense of the world from his perspective. Comics provided DMC with narratives where individuals who felt out of place or underestimated found empowerment and recognition. This resonates with the concept that individuals act based on the meanings they ascribe to objects and experiences, meanings that are derived and continuously reshaped through social interaction. As we analyze DMC's experiences and relationship to the artforms of hip-hop and comics, we see the basic premises of symbolic interactionism play out. That is, objects have meaning ascribed by the individual, these are affected by social interaction, and that interaction can lead to joint action or reinterpretation by a group of people. This is supported by Smith & Bugni (2006), who notes that some art acts as agents to shape our thoughts and actions and invites self-reflection. The art forms of comics and hip-hop have allowed DMC to be self-reflective and, in turn, use the meaning he has made from the art forms, as a vehicle to shape the hearts and minds of others. This is revealed when DMC states: "So the whole purpose of my creation is to address the social issues, but in a way that universally the kid from Compton and the gang can understand it. And that was my ability to come along with the big gold chain and the glasses, and then to start bragging about college the same way someone would brag about, how I got guns and I sell drugs and I'm in a gang."

The role of language as a source of meaning is evident in DMC's transition from a fan of comics to a creator within the hip-hop sphere. His lyrical content in both art forms, influenced by the narratives and characters of comics, served as a medium through which he negotiated and shared his identity with the world. This underscores how language facilitates the interpretation and negotiation of meanings within one's environment. DMC believes in the power of language, in which he uses words through hip-hop music and his graphic novel to create meaning for his audience.

### The Self, Social Interaction, and Agency

Symbolic interactionism's emphasis on the self as a social product (see Lindsey, 2014) is mirrored in DMC's construction of his persona, blending elements of hip-hop culture with comic book heroism and the alter ego. The concept of the "looking-glass self" is relevant here, as DMC's identity was shaped in part by his perception of how others viewed him and his own reflections on these perceptions. His hip-hop persona, inspired by comic book heroes, showcases the dynamic nature of the self, developed through social interactions. DMC was able to look at himself through the lens of a comic book character, which in turn gave him power or agency to perform on stage. DMC states:

> I learned about this word called the adjective, which describes the noun. But think about it like this. I'm Darryl McDaniels, I'm DMC, but I'm not just DMC. I'm DMC, the King of Rock. I'm DMC, the devastating mic controller. I'm DMC, the microphone master. Spider-Man isn't just Spider-Man. He's the amazing Spider-Man. Hulk isn't just Hulk, he's the Incredible Hulk. Ironman is the invincible. Thor is mighty. So I was looking at those things in the comic book because I could relate to them. So when it was time for me to go into my universe, I was pretending to be them. So when it was time for me to walk out that door or go on that stage or go to that studio, I was prepared with this confidence of who I am.

In addition, other hip-hop artists were using comics as reference points, which reinforced DMC's connection with comics—that social interaction was key. On a deeper level, DMC recognized the alter ego mechanism used in comics as a device that other hip-hop artists used on stage. DMC himself essentially became someone else on stage, just as heroes in comic books transform into their superhero identities. DMC's engagement with the hip-hop and comic book communities highlights the centrality of social interaction in symbolic interactionism.

Through these interactions and experiences, DMC not only shared and reshaped his identity but also contributed to the broader cultural narratives of both communities. His experiences illustrate how social interactions are fundamental to the continuous process of interpreting and defining social reality. Finally, the concept of agency is vividly represented in DMC's active role in shaping his environment and contributing to cultural dialogues. His venture into creating his comic book line, aiming to reflect his experiences and values, exemplifies an individual's capacity to influence their social surroundings. This aligns with symbolic interactionism's view of individuals as active participants in their social worlds, capable of interpreting and acting upon their environments to effect change.

## CONCLUSION

DMC's journey from a hip-hop icon to a comic book creator serves as a powerful illustration of symbolic interaction theory's key concepts. His story highlights how individual identities are formed and expressed through the interplay of meaning, language, the self, social interactions, and agency within the cultural contexts of hip-hop and comics. Through this analysis, we gain deeper insights into the complex processes through which cultural expressions shape and are shaped by individual and collective identities.

It's clear that DMC's journey is not just about music or comics; it's about a profound transformation and a relentless pursuit of empowerment—both internally and externally, as he seeks to empower others. DMC's narrative, interwoven with themes of overcoming adversity and harnessing the power of art, offers a compelling reflection on the role of cultural icons in shaping societal narratives and individual identities. DMC's insights into the current state of hip-hop and his own experiences in the comic book industry reveal a profound understanding of the responsibility that comes with influence. His critique of the hip-hop industry's current trajectory, highlighting a shift from responsible messaging to glorification of negativity, underscores the need for a return to the roots of empowerment and enlightenment. This echoes the themes of heroism and responsibility that are central to both comic book lore and the essence of hip-hop culture. The parallels he draws between the struggles he faced in launching his comic book line and the early challenges of hip-hop underscore a recurring theme: the importance of persistence in the face of adversity and skepticism. DMC's determination to present multifaceted images and stories in his comics, especially of African American and underestimated communities, speaks to his commitment to using art as a tool for social change and empowerment. In his final words, DMC leaves us with a powerful message: the belief in the inherent capability within each individual to overcome obstacles and realize their true potential. His call for self-empowerment resonates deeply, mirroring the ethos of his legendary hip-hop career. DMC's narrative is not just about success in the face of adversity but about using one's platform to inspire, educate, and elevate.

## NOTE

**Darryl "DMC" McDaniels** is a seminal figure in hip-hop music as one-third of the groundbreaking group Run-D.M.C. Alongside Joseph "Run" Simmons and Jason "Jam Master Jay" Mizell, McDaniels revolutionized the industry in the 1980s with hits like "It's Tricky" and "Walk This Way." Beyond music, he's a vocal advocate for mental health awareness and education, sharing his own struggles to destigmatize these issues. McDaniels is also an accomplished author, known for his autobiography *Ten Ways Not to Commit Suicide*. He owns a graphic novel and comic book line called DMC (Darryl Makes Comics) and regularly attends comic book conventions around the world.

## REFERENCES

Blumer, H. (1969). *Symbolic interactionism: Perspective and method*. Prentice Hall, Inc.

Denzin, N. K. (1992). *Symbolic interactionism and cultural studies: The politics of interpretation*. Blackwell Publishers.

Houser, T., & Kwon, J. (2014). Connecting with observers, connecting with self: Symbolic interactionism and installation art. *SGEM2014 Proceedings*, 4(1), 113–20.

Goffman, E. (1959). *The presentation of self in everyday life*. Anchor Books.

Lehn, D.V., Heath, C., & Hindmarsh, J. (2001). Exhibiting interaction: Conduct and collaboration in museums and galleries. *Symbolic Interaction, USA*, 24(2), 189–216.

Smith, R. W., & Bugni, V. (2006). Symbolic interaction theory and architecture. *Symbolic Interaction*, 29(2), University of California Press.

CHAPTER 3

# CRAFTING AN ALTERNATE REALITY THROUGH GRASSROOTS COMICS AND RAP MUSIC IN INDIA

JAYANTI DATTA

This article wishes to show how the emergence of working-class voices in Indian hip hop and some recent Indian grassroots graphic narratives, taken together, are redefining structures of power and conceptions of history, society, and politics to shape an authentic language of resistance that arises out of knowledge coproduced within a community. The article will analyze the music of hip-hop groups Swadesi and 7Bantai'Z, as well as the graphic novels *Delhi Calm*, *Bhimayana*, and *River of Stories*. While *Delhi Calm* points to the potentiality of subversion, *Bhimayana* and *River of Stories* actualize protest. Swadesi and 7Bantai'Z interrupt the official narrative of progress to inscribe their own hitherto absent presence. Both the visual narratives and the hip-hop music highlight the suffering of the marginalized and desire to build a community of thinkers and creators who will challenge and interrogate neo—liberal and authoritarian discourses which seek to suppress the power and potency of the subaltern. This article will delve into experiments with language, form, and content; the use of both folk elements and modern urban idiom as a means of asserting identity over elitist modes of thought.

## OBJECTIVES

There are several commonalities between hip-hop music and graphic art. Both use multimodal forms of expression; both have the capacity to break down complex ideas into simple, easily comprehensible emotions; both focus on the lives of common men and women occupying specific localities, and their everyday concerns. However, what is of special interest to this article is the emergence of new counterhegemonic discourse in both these art forms in India in recent times and their ability to enter the mainstream and influence the masses, particularly in the case of rap, without losing their subversive potential.

## METHODOLOGY

The research method used is inductive. It does not begin with a fixed theoretical position, and primacy is given to the ethnographic material collected during the course of my investigations into Mumbai rap music. However, my position as a researcher may be said to fall within the broad ambit of Cultural Materialism, particularly as defined by Raymond Williams. Materialism is a constant and continuous response to new material conditions that are developing in all social processes. The relationship between the making of a work of art and its reception is always active. The work of art is to be viewed not as an object but as a practice (Williams, 2010). With regard to graphic narratives as well as rap, a set of artists have emerged who are noncanonical, who are writing from the margins of the cultural field. Their desire is to craft an identity through a kind of constitutive rhetoric which can be used aesthetically to create a new myth, to give form to something that either exists or for which there is a need in the community. The critic who uses the tool of constitutive rhetoric expands interior analysis to include examinations of how the text reaches out to its readers so that they rethink a culture's key terms. For this article, I have combined my extensive interviews together with material on music videos, material from online sites covering popular culture such as *Red Bull* and *Rolling Stone*, as well as examinations of graphic narratives and books and articles analyzing them.

## COUNTER HEGEMONIC DISCOURSES

In February 2020, the rap crew Swadesi released their first full album *Chetavani (Warning)* on Azadi Records. The official website states, "Chetavani explores a glacial, minimalistic soundscape, relying on guttural basslines and scattered Indian samples to drive the songs forward and paying homage to the crew's inspirations from the UK's grime and dub scenes" (Swadesi, 2020). The crew nurtures the kind of brotherhood and creative energy seen in pioneering collectives such as Wu-Tang Clan and Odd Future. It is a multilingual album, and there is the feel of a train journey, with the sound of wheels on the track, travelling through the country, listening in on and participating in numerous conversations among the people. "Salaam" is an ode to the working class; "Galliyan Bhool Bhulaiya" is on income disparity; "Stithi," in its unique *Bambaiya*[1] lingo blazes out bar after bar on everything, from the hard work of late-night *bhurji paav* sellers to religious partition to the unjust division of the rich and poor. "It even calls out Mumbai's double standards for giving slots to the LGBTQ community all the while ignoring the calls or stories of the eunuchs on the streets" (Nair, 2020, para 4). "Kranti Havi" is on the massive protests held by all cross sections of society against the Citizenship Amendment Act (CAA) and the National Register of Citizens (NRC). The act was the first time that religion had been overtly used as a criterion for citizenship under Indian law, and it carried with it the threat of discrimination against the Muslim community, already under attack in the current regime. "Kranti Havi" chronicles and commends the role of some of the key players in the protests, like Bhim Army chief Chandrashekhar Azad and activist politician Kanhaiya Kumar. It references historical figures like B. R. Ambedkar and the lakhs of students who gave up their lives in the Naxalbari revolutionary movement. The track spares no one: the media in cahoots with the ruling classes, the clamping down on freedom of speech, the conditioned hatred, and the autocracy. It does not back down from naming actual participants and actual cases of blatant injustice, such as the murder of Akhlaq and the suicide of Dalit (low caste) student Rohit Vemula. The rap works like the lashing of a whip, like the blasting of slogans. It would be interesting to compare the uncompromising stance of crews like Swadesi with the lyrics used in the Bollywood film *Gully Boy*, a film that admittedly popularized Indian rap and contributed to bringing it into the mainstream. Artist Dub Sharma had created a song in the wake of the Jawaharlal Nehru University student protests. Music was added to the vocals of students chanting "*Azadi* (liberation)!" "Azadi from *Manuvaad* (following the regressive scriptures of Manu); from *Brahmanyavaad* (Brahminism);

from *Sanghvaad* (the Hindutva politics of the Sangh); from *poonjivaad* (capitalism) and *samanthvaad* (feudalism)!" *Gully Boy* appropriated this song and the lyrics were changed to *bhukmari* (poverty), *bhedbhav* (discrimination), and *pakshvaad* (discriminatory politics). This was a considerable dilution of the original chant. This version was criticized for stripping the song of the subversive content that originally inspired it. "The filmic version does not merely water down, rather it cloaks dissent in garb that will be permitted within the dominant culture, it erases the 'original' definition of subversion and replaces it with its own negotiated construction" (Kulkarni, 2020). Swadesi cannot be accused of such subterfuge. During the course of the album, it adopts varied musical tones. But throughout the songs, there is one common theme, an admonition to the sleeping masses to come out of their holes, to quit chasing false bastards, celebrities, to be aware of those who are sucking their blood, to abandon fear and to speak up, to raise their *awaaz* or voices as it is their *haq* (their right) to do so.

Swadesi is politically conscious without following any definite ideology. They have acknowledged their sources of influence to be Rajeev Dixit, Chandrashekhar Azad, and Bhagat Singh, all of whom come from very different positions, the only link being their defiant stance against the status quo. Rajeev Dixit was doggedly opposed to the big multinational corporations trying to establish base in India. He launched the *Azadi Bachao Andolan* (Save Freedom Movement) in the early 1990s to protect Indian industries against the ravages of globalization. He emphasized the concept of "*swadeshi*" which promotes use of locally made products and boycotts foreign-made products. Chandrashekhar Azad is an ardent follower of B. R. Ambedkar and the anti-caste movement. He is the cofounder of The Bhim Army, whose mission is the emancipation of the Dalits through widespread education. And Bhagat Singh, of course, is the iconic revolutionary figure, a martyr of the Indian Independence Movement and, towards the end of his young life, inspired by Marx's ideas of equality and justice. What we have then, is a potpourri of ideas, which the rap crew has drawn from, without formulating them into any creed. We can say that this is a kind of sacrificial politics which brings politics in relation with ethics, willfully trying to create a different set of political norms in the face of a strong imperial structure. This is the imagining of a world without being in a position of power, yet without accepting defeat.

Many of the members of Swadesi come from the scheduled castes and tribes of India, who have been traditionally brutally disempowered, and who continue to be so. In my interview, the members stressed that the music industry is ruled by coteries and the concept of the *lok shayar*, the people's poet, is not in vogue. One can hardly find anything "local" played in the clubs of the big cities. As artists, Swadesi's main focus is on the issues facing working-class people. "What is required is a total cultural revolution. If my father was forced to be a gutter cleaner, should I too be forced to follow the same profession?" They say that they are connecting to the youth by speaking to them in their lingo about the actual day-to-day problems facing them. They believe that ground-level change can be achieved slowly, gradually, like a tree growing, which will take years. The transformation has to be psychological, internal, and that is why they term their artistic work "The Swadesi Movement." They believe that live audiences are more important than digital ones; their future desire is to travel more to the villages, but finding the finances is tough (Swadesi, personal communication, August 5, 2021).

While Swadesi is a politically conscious crew, there are numerous rappers who have risen or are trying to rise from the extensive slums and chawls of Mumbai, whose main motivation is to wrest a modicum of dignity for themselves from their lives. In this period of late capitalism, where large conglomerates direct every aspect of existence, the voice or the choice of identity is snatched away from a majority of the population by the material forces in control, so that the subaltern feels himself to be subhuman. In order to understand these rap artists who come from the ranks of the subaltern, it is important to understand the areas they inhabit and imbue with meaning.

Dharavi is one of the numerous slums of Mumbai. Over one million people both live and work here. Dharavi has several manufacturing industries, such as leather, food products, textiles, and pottery, that are the main source of Mumbai's export revenue. It has an annual turnover of one billion dollars. On my visits to Mumbai, I made several trips to the slums of Dharavi and Khar, where I met a number of struggling rappers who spoke to me about what their home means to them. They were all largely skeptical of the Dharavi Redevelopment Project, which has been in the pipeline for so long. Bunny showed me a dilapidated two-story house in front of us and said that he himself lived in a house like that. "Say, the top floor is occupied by me, my parents, brothers and sisters, and the ground floor by my uncles and their families. Would all of these people be accommodated in small 300 square foot flats?" I spoke to Aku, a b-boy dancer and the founder of the first school of hip-hop in Dharavi, which was later wrested away from him unfairly and commercialized. Undaunted, he has set up a parallel school in the same area. He felt offended by the name of the 2009 film *Slumdog Millionaire*. He and his friends formed the hip-hop group Slumgods. Their motive was not to enter the rat race, but to provide freedom of expression in the neighborhood. According to Aku, there is unorganized crime in Dharavi. There are young people's groups who can be manipulated by vested interests to indulge in violent activities, but there is no organized crime gang. Young people might celebrate *Navratri* in a grand manner or establish *Ganapati*, but their prime motive may not be religious. They primarily want to make an impact in the area. There is a recognition of community here, and *masti* (gusto, flamboyant merriment) is very strong. If anyone harms a member of the group, the others will dive in to support him. In this sense, the environment of Dharavi is vastly different from the inner cities of the 1970s Bronx—birthplace of hip-hop—which was largely controlled by organized rival gangs. Aku, too, scathingly dismisses the Dharavi Redevelopment Project as a mechanical one. "Has it taken into consideration the ground realities? You need open roofs for two of the major small industries of Dharavi, plastic recycling and leather. People not only live here, but work here as well." He wonders whether there is any imaginative projection at all of what the consequences might be. "Half the land will be taken away by Adani for his hungry commercial purposes" (Aku, personal communication, October 30, 2023).

This can be referred to as a kind of urbicide, which is a constituent feature of capitalist urbanization. It is not only about the destruction of certain physical structures, but also about the elimination of particular forms of social life: "Together, the destruction of built and social environments means the end of sensory experiences ('sights,' 'sounds') that may provide the affective foundations of socio-spatial identity ('home') and emancipation ('hope')" (Kipfer & Goonewardana, 2007).

Aku further goes on to say that the slum lifestyle is very important for them to experience fully as artists, because no matter wherever they go in future, they cannot change the fact of where they came from, where they originally belonged, even if they earn tons of money and reach the higher echelons of society. "Hip-hop has an ethics, stay true, keep it real. This is a rule which we cannot ignore. Hip-hop has given us the awareness, that no matter what, you will not be the slave of anyone, this sense is what many people lose, or do not develop." And in doing so, there is an alienation from their memories, an alienation from what has constituted them, a fractured identity.

In Dharavi, issues of religion and caste and even patriarchy seem to be less important than the issues thrown up by the everyday struggle for survival within the context of the congested and challenging urban spaces they live in. What comes to the forefront now is attention to everyday experiences where such fictions are released and ratified continuously. The banality of everydayness is released in a dynamic urban folklore. The routine is placed in dialectical opposition to the idea of special events. The routine is invested with the naturalness, the unpredictability, the practicality, the vulnerability and intimacy, the "piety" of everyday life. (Gencarella, 2009).

There are a number of rap groups functioning in Dharavi, and together they call themselves Dharavi United. I met several members of the 7Bantai'Z and they talked freely on various aspects of their lives in Dharavi, in response to a questionnaire I had framed for them. There were several key themes or recurrent topics in their talk. Firstly, they did not consider themselves poor or in the category of the lumpen proletariat. They did not want to project themselves as victims. They rather wanted to assert their fighting spirit and their readiness for struggle. The 7Bantai'Z and others felt that the laboring aspect of Dharavi, where hard work is valorized, is not shown in the Zoya Akhtar film *Gully Boy*. Rather, the seamy side of life has been romanticized in the film to focus on Ranveer Singh rising from it like a heroic figure. The paradigm of the single individual making it big by the dint of his resources is the archetypal capitalist rags-to-riches story that undermines the community structure of Dharavi as reflected in the lyrics below:

> Where there's danger, we're from there
> From the guts of Mumbai
> From its 17th part, from its 17th heart (the area code of the slum)
> We're from there, we're from there. (7Bantai'Z, 2018)

The rappers that I interviewed in Dharavi were mostly of the opinion that it was a part of their mission to educate and inspire the youngsters of the slums:

> We are rapping to teach people the state of politics in this country. We are rapping to teach the young boys of our hood. Many wanted to leave Dharavi and go because people called us *kachda* (garbage). Still there are boys who indulge in the thug life, in *humpateli*, the unnecessary brag. My friend got implicated in a false murder charge by the cops during a Ganapati *Visarjan* melee (the immersion in the river of God Ganesha). But things are gradually changing now, young girls and boys are no longer trying to hide the place of their origin, they are proud now, proud that they belong to Dharavi. I believe we did this, all of us rappers, we created it. We are creating *itihaas* (history). (Abhishek Kurme, 7Bantai'Z, personal communication, 2019)

They are creating history with their attitude, with their redefinition of the locus they inhabit, with the language that they use. Emiway Bantai, who has now become very successful, asserts in his song, "Classy Chapri" (Emiway, 2022), "they said this slang of mine wouldn't bring me fame; today these hacks line up behind me; I speak my lingo, I represent my city of Mumbai." *Chapri* is a cringey guy, a lowlife, a wannabe fuck boy; it is a very disturbing cultural usage, with roots in caste and class discrimination. Emiway proudly claims his identity with this song and cocks a snook at all the cultural gatekeepers (Cardozo & Waghule, 2023).

Like hip-hop, the comic genre has always carried the potential, through the carnivalesque, or mockery, or satire of the transgression of normative values. Traditionally, Indian comics have not played this role extensively. The popular Amar Chitra Katha series, for instance, solidifies the homogenization of Hindu culture and reinforces stereotypes. On the other hand, companies such as Liquid Comics and Graphic India deploy intensive research to investigate the latest market trends so as to be able to cater to a global audience (Singh, 2018). The emergence of oppositional narratives with postcolonial perspectives in recent times is therefore of particular significance. *Delhi Calm*, *River of Stories*, and *Bhimayana* are compelling examples of such narratives. They challenge the industrial model of comics production. Their desire is to craft community and social resistance through the medium of visual narratives. This desire and this discourse link them to the newly emerging hip-hop voices from the underbelly of society. The rap artists, like the grassroots graphic authors, maintain a certain degree of independence from the giant multinational music companies and do not surrender their autonomy to these labels.

*Bhimayana* is a direct attack on hegemonic structures and, like Swadesi, does not attempt to camouflage its strong anticaste political intent. While Indian hip-hop has witnessed the representation of working-class voices rarely heard before, the postmillennial anti-establishment Indian comic caters to a niche but influential audience. However, *Bhimayana* has a wider reach. Though originally written in English, it has been translated into six regional languages and has been included in the syllabi of schools and colleges. The name *Bhimayana*, published in 2011, instantly recalls the famous Indian epic *Ramayana*, but its protagonist is B. R. Ambedkar, the revolutionary Dalit leader, together with the millions of untouchables associated with the Dalit anticaste movement. The focus is not on a singular superhero, like Lord Rama. Rather, the focus is on a story that has not been told in the past, which has been repressed. According to P. K. Nayar, *Bhimayana* generates a postcolonial critical literacy; the reader-text relation is not of subject and object; it is in and through the process of reading the text that the reader is constituted. The readers are not just passive consumers of the text; they are constituted as potential activists. The same clarion call is given by Swadesi; in their music videos, we see hundreds of men and women taking to the streets despite police atrocities.

In *Bhimayana*, there are no images of unique, clear-cut individuals, but rather scores of identical faces representing Dalits, and scores of other identical faces representing the orthodox Brahmins. The entire narrative is punctured by accusatory fingers pointing at the oppressed. The narrative comes to an end with the impressive visual, spread over two pages, of a human chain, people holding hands in response to Ambedkar's inspiring words (Nayar, 2012). This redefinition of history, then this reconstitution of the past, is made to project into the future, for even today, the atrocities continue. The Dalits and other lower castes have been and are uniformly disenfranchised not only by Hindus but by a majority of the social, linguistic, and religious groups of India.

Colors and metaphors are used to create a space that is explicitly political in nature. In one of the first visuals, ten-year-old Bhim Ambedkar stands in front of his teacher with a fish in his stomach, asking for a drink of water. The teacher is annoyed with him and brusquely tells him to wait till the bell rings. But when it does ring, the peon, the man at the well, allows all the other students to drink except Bhim. The boy goes home thirsty. Little Bhim is dressed in blue, and the tubewell he struggles to reach is blue. This color, the color of the sky, and also of water, is the color linked with Dalit resistance. The Bhim Army of contemporary India uses it as its color. On the contrary, saffron, traditionally the color of Hinduism, has been used in the text to denote claustrophobic spaces (Pal, 2022). In Ambedkar's revolutionary Mahad speech, where he is exhorting the untouchables to take water from a public body of water, the root of his microphone is dipped within a water body while his voice reaches the audience through loudspeakers, which look like lotus seeds and act as sprinklers.

The narrative fuses magic realism with documentation of facts. It combines a personal story, the biography of Ambedkar, with a contemporary socio-political condition—the continuation of caste discrimination from the past into the present. Newspaper accounts of caste atrocities across India are placed in textboxes. At the same time, the narrative is dense with metaphoric and symbolic content. It is an inspired move by the writers of *Bhimayana* (Srividya Natarajan and S. Anand) to employ the Gond folk art of Madhya Pradesh, brilliantly executed by Gond Pardhan artists Durgabai Vyam and Subhash Vyam. The lake where Ambedkar agitated for access to water takes the shape of a giant fish; a winding road resembles a snake; the steam emitted by an engine is represented in the form of sinister, black flying locks of hair (Nayar, 2012). The entire village becomes a desert when Ambedkar is denied water, even as animals are shown drinking water from a pond. Animals are allowed what the untouchables are not. There are bird speech balloons for characters who are lovable and speech balloons shaped like a scorpion's sting for those who believe in caste.

Gond art is notable for its vivid colors. "Natural and earth inspired colours are used, taken from the clay or *matti* which is traditionally gathered by the Gond people as each season yields a different coloured clay from areas around the Narmada River" (Dawson, 2015, para 7). Originally, charcoal was used for black, cow dung for light green, and bean leaves for dark green. Gond artists are now using poster colors and oil paints, but the goal is to reproduce the hues of the original natural elements. Gond art is marked by dots, fine lines, curved lines, dashes, geometrical shapes, fish scales, seed shapes, and drops of water. The artists often portray abstract concepts, dreams, and imaginative constructs. They paint two-dimensional artworks where animals, birds, trees, mythical beings, and humans coalesce into one another (Pareek, 2022). The sense of movement is established through the curves and strokes of lines. The crisscrossing *dignas*, typical of this artwork, do not confine characters within boxes. It is a traditional geometric pattern that is painted on walls and floors. It is a way of connecting the human and natural worlds. There is a fluidity in the visuals, showing the mixing and merging simultaneously of many people, moments, and episodes. It is an open art form reflecting the ideological movement towards an open society with casteless equality. The Gond art form asserts its independence from any art form associated with the dominant culture, and is a fit container for the representation of Dalit aspirations.

Towards the end, Gandhi and Ambedkar are framed by a semicircle of people listening to their debate. The Ambedkar blue human chain spreads far beyond the semicircle, symbolizing its continuing resonance in areas of wider humanitarian activism.

*Delhi Calm* (published 2010) by Vishwajyoti Ghosh is another example of a narrative that focuses on the trauma of the disenfranchised. *Delhi Calm* deconstructs history and presents a biting critique of The Emergency enforced by Indira Gandhi in 1975 (the redefinition of history or the creation of new history is a motif common to working-class hip-hop and these graphic novels). The narrator's city is not the "Delhi of white ambassadors, leather briefcases, English speaking convent schools and stable salaries;" instead, "it is a city of pot-bellied enterprises and petty cash, fuelled by insecurity" (Ghosh, 2010, as cited in Singh, 2018, p. 3).

The first panel portrays the protagonist Vibhuti Prasad, VP, sitting on a chair, reading a newspaper, with a map of the world under his feet. The public conflict is viewed through private perspectives and the faithful recording of daily life. At the beginning of the story, VP is a radical poet, a journalist reporting on the Emergency, and a member of the activist group *Naya Savera* (New Dawn), which works in the villages and hopes to bring about revolutionary change in the form of a classless society. He is a representative of the middle-class intellectual who played a part in the ultimate failure of the "revolution" because of his readiness to compromise, finally, and settle for "security." He and his comrade Parvez act as pawns in the hands of political figures like Mother Moon (Indira Gandhi), her son The Prince (Sanjay Gandhi), and The Prophet of Revolution (Jayprakash Narayan). The narrative is not linear or sequential. It works in the form of a montage where a wide spectrum of viewpoints, voices, events are presented and critiqued simultaneously, creating a polyphonic effect. Government propaganda blaring through loudspeakers, excerpts from newspaper reports, legal reports, the people's own narratives of trauma, posters, truck art, bus tickets, and air balloons collectively form a multimodal register of expression.

The rhetoric of "beautification" and "development" is set against the terror and anguish of the ordinary and gagged citizens who are shown to dot the landscape of the city. The desire for beauty leads to massive slum demolitions, which the novel depicts in eight consecutive page-length panels. The eviction drive displaces and disorients more than 75,000 people. The bulldozers descend on the people in an arresting visual representation of "progress" imposed from above (Singh, 2018). Masked "smiling saviors" appear all over the city on the day after the Emergency; they are the puppet agents of the government and form an army. The visuals emerging from the music videos of the Dharavi rap artists focus on the narrow lanes and by-lanes of the slums; the houses heaped on one another; children sitting by the wayside. And in their vocals, they too point towards false ideas of development achieved by the official eradication of the poor through indifference.

Vishwajyoti Ghosh uses the representational strategy of an alternate mapping of the city by which the hapless citizens can try to place their subjective imprints upon the ruthless processes of urbanization. Two-page length panels depict a cutout of the topographical map of Delhi, which is dominated by the military touting guns and telescopes, looking down at the peasants as they seek to implement the goal of 50,000 forced sterilizations in the name of population control. A road runs through the map representing the division between the perpetrators of state-sanctioned violence and those who are the victimized. The pages have been digitally tinted sepia. The red-brown reminds us of dried blood, which is highlighted by ink splashes, especially in the scenes of violence. Countering the official discourse on space are the light pencil sketches showing alternative routes and places where characters like VP and Parvez can hide from the state, and which are embedded in subjective memories. Ghosh said in an interview that he wanted to do *Delhi Calm* completely in watercolors—"There is a certain illusion of easy-ness, in the sense that you can leave the paper white, that you can say things with just a stroke or two" (Holmberg, 2013, para. 47).

Ghosh draws attention to the deliberate silencing of the citizens. At a forced sterilization taking place inside a school, the speech bubble of the victim reads "spare me." However, the act of violence itself is not shown. Instead, the stem of the speech bubble points towards the blank space between the panels, the gutter. The gutter encourages the reader to notice what is included and what is left out in representations of suffering (Syposz, 2016). This lack of depiction highlights, through absence, the silencing strategies of the state. Often, the violence is not shown directly, but exists as a disorienting undercurrent, such as in the repetitive images of a syringe and a metal blade. The content of Ghosh's panels offers no clues as to its duration; sometimes borderless images "gives the events a sense of being suspended in time, as if the affliction is not anchored to any one historical moment" (Syposz, 2016, para. 14). The last page-length comic panel portrays, among the temples, mosques and bustling roads, a billboard welcoming people to New Delhi, proclaiming "Do Not Talk About—Emergency, 84 Delhi Riots, Babri Demolition, Gujarat riots . . ." (Ghosh, 2010, p. 246).

The presentation of the roguish character of Parvez is particularly interesting. During the Emergency, Parvez switches from a member of the resistance against the State (bringing about change in villages) to being a "smiling savior" even while continuing the work of underground resistance. His justification is that joining them was the only way to protect himself. A parallelism comes to mind with those rappers who are scathingly criticized by politically conscious crews like Swadesi as *naqli* or fake; those who feel that they have to compromise their art, cater to big labels, appear in MTV hustles, even as they rap about their slums, their gullies. This negotiation and interrogation of their authenticity is something that is forced upon them by the nonparticipative democracy of the neoliberal order. They rebel through sudden, disruptive moments through their art, even while remaining within the structure.

## ENVIRONMENTAL ACTIVISM AS A MEANS OF RESISTANCE

Through their activism and their music, the rap crew Swadesi, together with the many voices of resistance emerging from the tribal community, managed to get a stay order against the cutting down of trees in the Aarey forests for the construction of a Metro Shed in 2019, even though the order was later overturned. The struggle continues. This is a battle over Mumbai's green lung. The 1,300-hectare Aarey Forest is situated in Goregaon, on the northern suburbs of the city. It contains an entire eco system, many species of trees, birds and endangered animals: "MC Mawali: 'I've seen crocs, deer, snakes, beautiful butterflies there and experienced so many of nature's different colors and seasons there I can't tell you how blessed Mumbai is to have such a place, a forest right in the middle of the city'" (Valsan, 2017, para 8).

There are twenty-seven tribal hamlets known as padas in Aarey. The tribes are the original inhabitants of the land, and they sustain their livelihood by cultivating fruits and vegetables. One of the most vulnerable of these tribes is the Warli tribe, whose wall paintings have been appropriated by the music and fashion industry. In spite of repeated court orders in the past, they have been denied proper water supply, healthcare, and electricity, so that they are troubled enough to leave their land. The activists believe that the metro shed can easily be built on an alternative site. They fear that the metro shed is only part of a larger plan to increasingly encroach upon the forest land for commercial purposes, such as the building of a thirty-three-story Metro Bhavan with restaurants and shops surrounding it. Over the last five decades, local and state authorities have clandestinely parceled out hundreds of hectares of Aarey Colony to various development projects. The metro car shed project is the latest of these.

Swadesi has collaborated with the Warli leader Prakash Bhoir to compose "The Warli Revolt" (Swadesi Movement, 2019) track. The track is notable for the way it merges the frantic rhythms of tribal percussion and instruments with the hip-hop beat to create a unique war cry (Kundu, 2019). The music video begins and continues with impressive visuals of small figures playing traditional instruments, of people farming and gathering, with figures of rows of deer in the foreground, and the appearance, from time to time, of grand leopards as part of the ecosystem. The artwork is done in the trademark Warli style, and there is a seamless fusion of the rousing and lilting beats of the folk song with the more staccato rap. The song shows how nature is an integral component of culture. A rough paraphrase of the song would be as follows:

> This idea of development is tainted and corrupt; no faith can be placed on looters like you; you uproot forests to make metros; without forests how do you think you will breathe? You are evicting us today from our land, our place, the only place where we can find peace. You uproot us to drive us to our doom; I, an Adivasi, a poor man, I don't have charters to prove that this is my land; I till the soil,

I grow crops, and every living creature who inhabits this space is a member of my family. Do yourselves a favor, you evictors, save for your own sakes, this treasure of man.

Finally, Swadesi warns that "a massive revolution before you will stand . . . wake up and open your minds you fools, before it's all gone and there's nothing left to lose." Swadesi has held concerts in the rooted location of the Aarey Amphitheatre, because they wanted to let the rest of Mumbai know that people are living in these forests and they should not lose their home (Swadesi, 2019).

*River of Stories*, a graphic novel by Orijit Sen, also deals with the theme of environmental degradation. Both Swadesi and Sen make innovative use of folk idiom and aesthetics to constitute new urban and rural myths. They both point to a tradition that has maintained a nonviolative relationship with the environment they inhabit. *River of Stories* tells the story of a journalist, Vishnu, who decides to cover the story of the Rewasagar Dam over the Narmada River and the protests against its construction by urban activists, local villagers, and the tribal communities whose lands and very existence are at stake. Ranajit Guha, an Indian historian and one of the early architects of the Subaltern Studies Collective has focused in his varied writings on the need to read South Asian popular culture as part of the self-representation of those who saw in their own traditions, values which they were reluctant to change, who were not convinced by the binary posited between "development" on the one hand, and outdated primitivism on the other. In *The River of Stories*, a non-Western concept of totality is pitched against an imperialist concept of progress. The mythical narrative of Malgu Gayan, the bard, opens with the story of creation. Local mythology views the resources of nature with a sustainable and eternal lens as opposed to "rational" opportunism. The topographical map drawn in the novel is not an accurate cartographic depiction; it shows a cultural and ecological perspective of understanding a landscape. Malgu Gayan is shown sitting under a Mahua tree in a place where happiness and simplicity are considered more important than capital generation (Ghosh, 2021).

Amita Baviskar, anthropologist and Sen's collaborator observes: "Throughout the *gayana* flows the Narmada, bestowing life-giving gifts to all whom she meets, naming and making sacred the geography along her banks" (Sankar & Changmai, 2019, p. 114, para. 7). As far as the state is concerned, no official records exist as to the ownership of the land. It is only through the myths embodied in the *gayana*, the ritual song of the Bhilala tribe, that the tribals can stake their rightful claim to their ancestral lands. Malgu Gayan sits in the foreground, while the massive figure of a tribal woman behind him represents the universe.

The opening story is that of Kujum Chantu, who sacrifices herself so that the world she created may survive. Kujum Chantu is the selfless mother from a North Eastern myth, whereas the *River of Stories* is based in Central India. The motif of sacrifice is repeated through many ancient cultures of the world, and Sen's flexible usage universalizes the story of the Bhilala tribe. Further, we can see this fluidity in the choice of the artwork. The drawings on page 12 are based on Saora and Warli drawings, one from Odisha in Eastern India and the other from Maharashtra and Gujarat in Western India. The Warli and Saora paintings share a striking aesthetic similarity. Both use simple geometrical figures like circles, triangles, and squares to depict human figures, animals and elements of nature. The mythical narrative is structured in the manner of an epic, with leisurely digressions, such as when Malgu relates the extended story of how he came to possess the "rangai," the instrument which he plays. The very existence of such a world with its different conception of time and value in the backdrop of the narrative serves as a structure of resistance to ideas of modernity imposed by imperialism. This world calls out to the fragmented selves of cityscapes, hoping that "the river of stories which rises from the soul can flow out . . . to the far corners of the world, and people everywhere awake to its sweet music" (Sen, 1994). According to Diptarup Ghosh's striking argument—myth, memory, subjective mapping or cartography and finally a host of silent stories, taken together, present four pillars of resistance and a redeeming vision of futurity marked by ecological sustainability and humanity (Ghosh, 2021).

Soon after the creation myth, the narrative, portrayed in cursive ink drawings, becomes more contemporary. Vishnu's journey begins when he listens to the pitiful memories of his maid Relku, who was forced to move to the city when her house was burnt down and she was dispossessed of her land. But the very first panel presents the challenges of representing an oral culture in print. Relku is shown singing a song, yet the speech bubble contains no words. Instead, it shows a bird in flight. The English words that appear after that can be clearly identified as substitutes (Sankar & Changmai, 2019). Malgu Gayan instructs the reader to "listen well," not read. The author is suggesting, through these signs and symbols, that the book is inspired by oral and folk traditions. Earlier on, Relku is visualised in her natural habitat, picking Mahua flowers, while her brother, Somariya, tries to shoot down a bird with his arrow. This pastoral atmosphere is disrupted by the sound of a motor image, and Somariya is shown falling down through the panels, while the branch he was perching on breaks.

Impacted by Relku's memories, Vishnu decides to write a report on the resistance movement. He begins to listen to and respond to a host of stories which were hitherto silent, by men and women who had been invisibilized. This depiction is a rural counterpart to the urban stories of the Dharavi slums.

The tribals lament the fact that they were not consulted at all during the entire project, as though they did not exist: "An alternate way is one that does not benefit one person at the cost of the other. In which people are consulted and their ideas respected. . . . How beautifully our own methods of irrigation used to work. We went to some villages of Gujra district with Anand Bhai last year, where all the expertise of the engineer babus had been used to expand the old system of tanks and waterways by check dams, lift irrigation, windmills and so many things!" (Sen, 1994, p. 47).

In a newspaper report inserted in the novel, a tribal peasant from Umargaon is quoted as saying: "Our village will be submerged forever. . . . The government says they will resettle us. But our communities will be broken up . . . our music, our festivals, our gatherings, will all come to an end. Will there be any point in continuing to live after that?" (Sen, 1994, p. 51).

Change occurs in Vishnu slowly. When he runs into one of the supervisors of the dam, he denies being on any side of the story. Even when he hears all the stories of the protestors, Vishnu only lends a patient ear and hardly comments on anything. But we see his transformation in the report he ultimately prints.

The last pages show a group of young people reading and responding to Vishnu's article. And in the final panel, like in a musical composition, where the first note, after going through complex embellishments, is repeated at the end, we see Malgu Gayan sitting under his beloved Mahua tree with his timeless folk wisdom.

Within the book then, two distinct streams of story and style merge, in response to the crux of the questions on two developmental models—one indigenous and self-sustaining, the other modern and large-scale.

From the aesthetic point of view, the graphic narrative springs to life because of the meticulous care with which Orijit Sen presents the life and environment of the tribals. With just black and white, a magical atmosphere is created. Sen reproduces the topographical map of the Rewa Valley, drawn on a triple spread, covering the entire distance of the river Rewa to the dam site. This is not an accurate cartographic depiction with latitudes and longitudes. Sen believes in infusing the representation of fact with fictional understanding and imaginative depth. In a talk hosted by UNESCO Chair of Vulnerability Studies, Orijit Sen describes how he observed the people scrupulously and intimately; for instance, the way they dressed, the care they gave to presenting themselves with a certain amount of flair and style. He gave the example of a man combining a unique printed shirt with a lungi, and a turban decorating his head. He said that he observed the interiors of their houses carefully. For instance, if he showed a woman grinding millet in one corner of the room, he could not show anyone entering from there. (UNESCO Chair—Vulnerability Studies, 2023, 36:55). A lot of visual attention is given to the inhabitants of the valley, to their faces, to their expressions; faces seen against light that comes from a window or a night fire. This loving attention restores to them the visibility they have long deserved.

## CONCLUSION

Changes are taking place in the cultural field in contemporary India that are worthy of note, particularly in the realm of popular culture. While popular culture is often associated with populism and commercialization, unconventional trends are making their presence felt in the recent initiatives undertaken by comics artists, and the sudden entry of an entirely original form of urban folklore in the shape of rap music. Together, they are placing under the spotlight voices that were either never heard before or greatly underrepresented. They are offering oppositional critiques on neo liberal models of development that the global power centers tirelessly posit as the most superior model. Though the gully music has been criticized of late as being repetitive and nonexperimental, this is outweighed by the cultural significance of being able to listen to a myriad of working-class voices for the first time. This very fact is empowering that they have found a form where they can assert their identity as creative individuals, where they are no longer viewed as just a source of cheap labor. Equally significant is that both comics and hip-hop can reach out to the young masses with their simplicity, interactive performativity, and rootedness.

*Delhi Calm* deconstructs history to show a ruthless elitist version of "progress" that tramples upon the identities of countless gagged citizens; *Bhimayana*, through its forceful, colorful and metaphoric language indicts centuries of caste oppression and points the way towards future activism; *River of Stories* puts up structures of resistance against imperialist environmental degradation and presents a model of existence in alignment with the harmonies of nature; the rousing chants of Swadesi, the defiant presence of 7BantaiZ, and the persevering spirit of the Dharavi slums, all taken together point to a discourse radically different from state sponsored narratives of "India Shining" and the grandeur of India's mythological past. Here we have the people's narrative, which challenges the normalization of repressive politics and points to explosive possibilities that can disrupt the future for some other vision to rise like a phoenix from the ashes.

## NOTE

1. Bambaiya is the lingo often spoken by migrant slum dwellers, dock workers, daily wage earners, street thugs, travelers on the crowded local trains. It is a mixture of Hindi, Marathi, Gujarati, and sometimes other regional dialects, as well as English (for example, *bhot* hard, meaning extremely tough). It is a deliberately flamboyant and unpolished language marked by informality and freedom, with a number of exclamatory words such as *jhakaas*, derogatory words like *fattu* (coward), vulgar words like *gandu*. A word may have a surface meaning and a number of subtexts. For example, *ghanta* could mean impossible; it could also refer to the male organ. It is a racy and rhymable language, using words that are a condensed version of the original. Some examples are: *akela* (single), *thakela* (tired), *pakela* (bored), *satkela* (angry), *bhatkela* (lost), *chapri* (lowlife), *tapori* (street smart guy), *chikni* (good-looking gal).

## REFERENCES

Cardozo, E., & Waghule, P. (2023). "Haq se main chapri": Casteist slurs and cultural commentary in India. *Scaffold: Journal of the Institute of Comparative Studies in Literature, Arts and Culture*, 1(1), 21–33. https://ojs.library.carleton.ca/index.php/J-ICSLAC/article/view/4428

Dawson, E.V. (2015, June 15). Inequality and adversity in content and form: The Indian graphic novel "Bhimayana." Comics Forum. https://comicsforum.org/2015/06/15/inequality-and-adversity-in-content-and-form-the-indian-graphic-novel-bhimayana-by-e-dawson-varughese/

Emiway, B. (2022). Classy chapri [Song]. On *King of the streets* [Album]. Bantai Records, Mumbai.

Gencarella, S. O. (2009). Constituting folklore: A case for critical folklore studies. *Journal of American Folklore*, 122(484), 172–96.

Ghosh Dastidar, D. (2021). Material development and human regression: A decolonial reading of Orijit Sen's *River of Stories*. In A. Nirmal & S. Dey (Eds.), *History and myth, postcolonial dimensions* (pp. 87–97). Vernon Press.

Ghosh, V. (2010). *Delhi calm*. Harper Collins.

Holmberg, R. (2013, October 23). Inverted calm: An interview with Vishwajyoti Ghosh. *The Comics Journal*. https://www.tcj.com/inverted-calm-an-interview-with-vishwajyoti-ghosh/

Kipfer, S., & Goonewardena, K. (2007). Colonization and the new imperialism: On the meaning of urbicide today. *Theory and Event*, 10(2). https://doi.org/10.1353/tae.2007.0064

Kulkarni, D. R. (2020). Appropriation and articulation: Mapping movements in *Gully Boy*. *Cinergie - Il cinema e le altre arti*, 9(17), 87–96. https://doi.org/10.6092/issn.2280-9481/10508

Kundu, S. (2019, February 6). Watch: "The Warli Revolt" by Prakash Bhoir. thewildcity.com. https://www.thewildcity.com/news/11267-watch-the-warli-revolt-by-swadesi-ft-prakash-bhoir

MC, Altaf & D'Evil. (2019, April 25). *Wazan hai* [Video]. YouTube. www.youtube.com/@TheeevilyT

Nair, V. (2020, March 5). Theme music for the Indian revolution—"Chetavani" by Swadesi. The Indian music diaries. https://theindianmusicdiaries.com/theme-music-for-the-indian-revolution-chetavni-by-swadesi/

Nayar, P.K. (2012). Towards a postcolonial critical literacy: Bhimayana and the Indian graphic novel. *Studies in South Asian Film and Media*, 3(1), 3–21. doi: 10.1386/safm.3.1.3_1

Pal, P. (2022). Towards a visual literacy: Bhimayana and the caste problem of India. *International Journal of English Literature and Social Sciences*, 7(2). https://journal-repository.com/index.php/ijels/article/view/4856

Pareek, S. (2022). "We paint stories we heard from our ancestors": Intangible heritage of the Pardhan Gonds of Central India. *International Journal of Intangible Heritage*. https://ijih.org/volumes/article/1045

Sankar, R., & Changmai, D. (2019). Word, image and alienated literacies in the graphic novels of Orijit Sen. *Word & Image*, 35(2), 112–25. doi: 10.1080/02666286.2018.1547609

Sen, O. (1994). *River of stories*. Kalpavriksh.

7BantaiZ (2018, June 21). *Achanak bhayanak* [Video]. YouTube. www.youtube.com/@7BantaiZ

Singh, P. (2018). Graphic Delhi: Narrating the Indian emergency, 1975–77 in Vishwajyoti Ghosh's *Delhi Calm*. *South Asian Review*, 39(1–2), 86–103. https://doi.org/10.1080/02759527.2018.1509536

Swadesi. (2019, July 5). *This is my hood: Swadesi*. Red Bull. https://www.redbull.com/in-en/this-is-my-hood-swadesi

Swadesi Movement. (2019, February 1). *The Warli Revolt ft. Prakash Bhoir/Swadesi* [Video]. YouTube. www.youtube.com/@SwadesiMovement

Swadesi Movement. (2020, February 7). *Chetavani* [Album]. Azadi Records, Delhi.

Syposz, J. (2016, July 20). Exploring the potential for historical graphic narratives to challenge hegemony and empower the afflicted: Subaltern affliction in "Maus" and "Delhi Calm." Porridge. https://porridgemagazine.com/2016/07/20/exploring-the-potential-for-historical-graphic-narratives-to-challenge-hegemony-and-empower-the-afflicted-subaltern-affliction-in-maus-and-delhi-calm-jessica-syposz/

UNESCO Chair—Vulnerability Studies. (2023, April 3). *Drawing vulnerability | Form, function and fiction in my comics | Orijit Sen* [Video]. YouTube. wwwyoutube.com/@unesco-vulnerabilitystudies

Valsan, S. (2017, December 27). Swadesi: We're not faking anything here. *Rolling Stone India*. https://rollingstoneindia.com/swadesi-not-faking-anything/

Williams, R. (2010). *Culture and materialism: selected essays* (New ed.). Verso.

CHAPTER 4

# WALL (S)CRAWLERS

Comics, Graffiti and the Aesthetic, Political, and Rhetorical Resonances of Public Visual Arts

MICHAEL B. NORTON DANDO

## INTRODUCTION

Bright colors cover the sides of buildings and/or fill out spinner racks. Gigantic, bold murals seen from passing cars or on bookshelves at a local library or bookstore. Whether at the cinema or on a walk around downtown, these creative expressions, comics, and graffiti are ubiquitous indices of contemporary public life. It is almost as though graffiti and comics come from the same interconnected and interactive universe. The interchange of these two art forms includes but goes far beyond a character, Dr. Doom, appearing in a graffiti mural or a comic cover done in the style of a popular rap album. Graffiti writers and comics artists see words and the world differently and consequently approach making and thinking about art and public expression with attention paid to particular ways of rebellious thinking, knowing, and being. For many, visual art is both something you do and something you are.

This chapter's key contention is that comics and graffiti are intimately connected visual art forms that share similar aesthetic, political, and rhetorical inter and intra-actions, especially regarding their deployment as public visual media in cultural debate. Despite their historical marginalization, both creative forms still remain widely accessible and have significant connections to social movements, operating as sites for identity negotiation, resistance, and self-expression. Through three main dimensions—public marginalization, public accessibility, and public mediation—the study examines their compatibility and shows how each serves as a platform for social discourse and active participation. This chapter positions these complementary visual rhetorics as vital sites for public, creative, and social justice movements by examining the aesthetic and semiotic inter/intra-actions between comics and graffiti and by highlighting their roles in generating collective cultural narratives that promote substantive civic discussions concerning gender, race, and class.

Through three main dimensions (public marginalization, public accessibility, and public mediation) this chapter examines comics and graffiti's cultural resonances and affinities, and demonstrates what we mean when we speak about graffiti and comics in order to create a common framework. Then, we will consider how these art forms have been taken up, by whom, and where. Finally, we will consider how public audiences are drawn into meaningful conversation with these art forms, namely the interactive and shared approaches to visual rhetorics (communicated messages) that engage public discourse. Finally, this chapter explores the impacts that a more nuanced understanding of graffiti and hip-hop's shared DNA might have for cultural self-expression in the future.

There has been ample scholarship regarding both graffiti (Aiello, 2019; Avramidis & Tsilimpounidi, 2016; Ross et al., 2017; Stampoulidis & Bolognesi, 2023) and comics as discrete medium including their social, cultural, and artistic significance. Scholars have noted that both engage similar elements such as bright colors, the messages they portray and promote, and the tools and materials they use. Both comics and graffiti are visual art forms, but not every visual art form is mutually compatible. And, while it is clear that both are mutually compatible as they share aesthetic, ideological, and rhetorical commitments which afford them the opportunity to learn from each other, their mutual compatibility has been undertheorized and there has been a dearth of research examining the reasons why they are compatible.

By examining the interplay between graffiti and comics, we can gain deeper insights into the cultural significance of these popular artistic forms and their role(s) in shaping collective sociocultural and political identities. Understanding why these art forms are compatible invites us to consider where we have been as human beings, where we stand now, and what might lie on the horizon with regard to the intersections of art, popular culture, and social justice.

## HISTORICAL DEFINITIONS: WHAT WE MEAN BY . . .

### Graffiti

Graffiti can be understood as a form of visual expression that is usually painted on noncanvas surfaces, like walls, buildings, or bridges, which are usually unauthorized. Graffiti has become most visible in the late twentieth century, and associated with urban environments and the rise of counterculture movements. Although it may be legally considered an act of vandalism, many have come to recognize graffiti as a form of art and a strong channel for public expression social and political theme, for example, in the case of George Floyd Square in Minneapolis, where the graffiti that sprang up in the wake of the murder has become a semipermanent memorial/installation.

Graffiti is a key form of artistic expression that, in its broadest sense, encompasses the unsanctioned writing or drawing on public surfaces with words, symbols, or phrases, which differentiates it from other forms of street art. Graffiti is commonly believed to be more transgressive, while "street art" is understood to be a more commercialized and socially accepted art form as it is officially sanctioned by the authorities.

Graffiti writing itself is an ancient, artistic practice that can trace its roots back through the ruins of Ancient Roman city streets, to temples in long-abandoned Mayan cities, and on monuments built by Egyptian pharaohs. The markings (usually inscriptions or images painted on walls) had several purposes, so used for political propaganda, romantic messages to the beloved lover, or just the writer's name. Scratched into the city generations ago, these remain graffiti's central practices thousands of years later. The very word "graffiti" in fact stems from the Italian word, *graffiato* or scratched.

"Tags" are the simplest form and normally done in a hurry using marker pens or spray paint. A tag carries the same weight as a name badge for graffiti artists—or "writers." Among the most prominent taggers was Cornbread, one of the first graffiti artists from Philadelphia (White, 2018, p. 4), along with Taki 183, Stay High 149, and Fab 5 Freddy (later of the Furious Five). Throw-ups (also known as "throwies") are more complex pieces but don't take that much longer to paint. They often have two or three colors and bubble letters, making them among the fastest forms to write. And for many writers, time is of the utmost concern. Artists such as Futura 2000 have helped drive this style more into the mainstream.

"Slaps" are another type of sticker tagging, where designs (drawn or printed) are placed on stickers and put over various surfaces. This process provides a quick and easy way to apply. This approach was made perhaps most prominent by artists like Shepard Fairey and his "Obey" stickers before doing "HOPE" pieces for then-candidate Barack Obama. Pieces, short for masterpieces, are generally highly detailed, large-scale images that may take months to create due to complexity and size. Many of these works have intricate designs and vivid hues and are sometimes commissioned. Pathbreaking artists such as Seen and Dondi White are held in high regard for their contributions to this style.

A more complex and abstract form of graffiti called Wildstyle consists of intentionally difficult-to-read letters (for the uninitiated) intertwined in such a way that the general impression is both intricate and crisp. Artists like Zephyr and Tracy 168 are closely linked to this style. Stencil Art is essentially a spray-can version of screen printing, commonly associated with artists like Banksy, known for his outspoken political works. Similar to throw-ups or pieces, bubble letters are another style of graffiti writing with rounder and more inflated shapes. Cope2, a graffiti artist, has played a significant role in the proliferation of bubble letters. Character graffiti, a style dedicated to figures and scenes, and street art, which includes the creation of murals or installations, add to the ways graffiti writing can be considered a living, breathing culture with something important to say.

Overall, graffiti art embodies a complex interplay of creativity, rebellion, and social commentary. It continues to evolve, with cities around the world now hosting legal graffiti walls and street art festivals, reflecting its growing acceptance and recognition as a legitimate form of artistic expression. Graffiti's longevity and legacy illustrate that it is a living historical form of self-expression and social commentary. Like all art movements, graffiti has evolved over the years and, as it carries on into the twenty-first century, remains one of the most dynamic and influential forms of global visual culture.

## Comics

Comics are a unique form of visual storytelling that combines sequential art, written dialogue, and narrative structure to tell stories of all kinds with no limit as to subject or emotion. Definitions for comics as a medium are myriad, messy, and hotly contested. Some will turn to comics legend Will Eisner, who considered comics to be "sequential art" (1985, p. 5), meaning that there must be a story involved. For him, a single image was a picture. Comics scholar Scott McCloud (1993) defines comics as, "Juxtaposed pictorial and other images in deliberate sequence, intended to convey information and/or to produce an aesthetic response in the viewer" (p. 20). But this is

**Figure 4.1** Page from *The Adventures of Mr. Obadiah Oldbuck* (1849).

incomplete as it does not account for single-panel comics such as Far Side or Family Circus, animated films, or pictorial languages such as hieroglyphics (Meskin, 2007, p. 371). More recently, Hayman and Pratt (2005) define comics as a "pictorial narrative" (p. 419). There is no single definition for comics, and it ultimately may not be necessary. Like any form of art, many simply know it when they see it.

However, one may settle on defining it for discursive purposes, comics use both pictures and words to create a compelling reading experience so that it can stimulate the sense of image vision together with at least a perceived message or narrative. Comics have evolved from their traditional entertainment aspects, such as in newspaper strips, into a medium that cannot only tackle issues such as societal norms and complex themes, but also serves as critical, dialogue-inspiring, discursive artifacts.

Long associated with disposable or otherwise unserious entertainment, comics as a medium have evolved to flesh out complex themes and interrogate societal norms, fostering critical dialogue. Nineteenth-century publications of newspapers and magazines containing narrative illustrations are predecessors to the modern-day comic. Rodolphe Töpffer was a Swiss artist whose *Histoire de M. Vieux Bois* (*The Adventures of Mr. Obadiah Oldbuck*) has been called the first comic book. It was only in the late 1920s and early 1930s that comic strips and books gained wider popularity. Comics, at their base, are a type of reading art form that provides the reader with an exclusive method of interaction between image and text. Although formerly something exclusive for entertainment, comics have grown and can now be used to deal with certain themes, question society, or call up a critical discussion.

## PUBLIC MARGINALIZATION AND REFUSAL

Both graffiti and comics artists have been on the whole unwelcome by the general public or at least by those who would control dominant narratives in society. This shared marginal status affords them cultural proximity and often meant that their practitioners ran in similar social circles. It may be little surprise then that they began to borrow from and seep into each other.

Graffiti artists have been criminalized globally by the dominant culture, and writers are generally seen as a menace, criminal element, or threat. Graffiti art has been the object of derision and a public index of socio-cultural and economic decline for a given neighborhood or downtown area. For many in the public, graffiti is a crime, a blight, and a jailable offense for those who do it. Now disbarred lawyer and former New York mayor Rudy Giuliani cited graffiti writers among others as "the major enemies of public order and decency and the culprits of urban decline" (Smith, 1998, p. 3).

Likewise, comics as a medium have been consistently positioned as a threat and the social domain of the degenerate, undesirable, and corrupting elements. Shielding young people from purportedly harmful imagery, groups, or peoples was (and arguably remains) an instinct present in halls of power. From the development of the Hayes Code in 1934 to the institution of the Comics Code Authority (CCA) in 1954, based on the contested research of Dr. Frederic Wertham (Tilley, 2012), the status quo has endeavored to legislate or codify the "otherness" of both graffiti and comic books. At one point during the Senate hearings on comic books' links to juvenile delinquency, Wertham opined, "Hitler was a beginner compared to the comic book industry" (Carver, 2011, p. 12). For generations, these practices and cultures were widely vilified and publicly refused, and in some regard, continue to be today.

It is the historical, public marginalization, disregard, and disdain for these art forms that provide opportunities for solidarity and synergy between these two artistic communities. These affinity groups (comics readers and graffiti writers) occupy analogous if not equivalent positions culturally and to some degree physically, constituting a peculiar form of socio-cultural geography of what Cosgrove (1989) refers to as "excluded cultures" (p. 133). Their proximity can engender contact which affords opportunity for collaboration and exchange which cultural studies, especially perspectives offered by Hall (1989), hooks (Media Education Foundation, 1997) and de Certeau's concept of city as "a space of enunciation," (1980, p. 264) can begin to articulate these cultural practices' simple (but not simplistic) impact on being human with regard to notions of belonging and resistance.

Hall's concept of cultural identity as, "a sort of collective 'one true self'" (p. 69). This self, of course, is fluid and negotiated through public and social discourse, and Hall is an insightful theorist for analyzing how comic panels and graffiti help explain a writer and/or reader's cultural identity formation as a process of negotiated positioning influenced by a shared history rather than a fixed state of being. hooks' idea of "marginality as a space of resistance" and "radical possibility" is significant in understanding both how graffiti and comics position themselves as interlocutors despite the cultural subjectivities for writers. Creatives such as Basquiat and Bechdel (2008), as well as theorists such as hooks and Hall, continue to remind us of the ways these public spaces are key sites for cultural critique and for working towards greater inclusion and justice.

## PUBLIC ACCESS

There are three avenues of accessibility that are important to address with regard to the collaborative nature of these artistic forms: cash, camaraderie, and community. Another significant factor in the cultural interaction between these two forms is that of availability and accessibility. The cultural interaction between graffiti and comics includes one of democratic distribution and economic equity. Comics as an art form has historically been relatively affordable. Cover prices have continued to rise with inflation; however, in the era that graffiti was simultaneously ascendent, comics cost less than a dollar.

Further, comics readers are often social in nature. Many times, groups of readers would each purchase a single issue and circulate it among a peer group so that everyone in the collective could read and experience as many stories as possible each month. Edgardo Miranda-Rodriguez, current editor-in-chief of Darryl Makes Comics, recalls, "I wasn't even working class—I was poor. I grew up in the South Bronx and I used to collect bottles and cans. When I finally had enough loose change, I would go to the comic shop and buy myself a comic. It was affordable" (Lothian-McLean, 2015). The same held true for hip-hop. While many may not have been able to afford to purchase the newest records, although some did, many hip-hop aficionados would give a friend a blank cassette tape and, in short order, have a mixtape of the latest songs, securing social and cultural capital necessary for participation.

Much like comic creation, graffiti notebooks were modestly priced, sometimes being black and white composition notebooks. And, for many graffiti writers, securing paint cans illegally or "racking up" (Rahn, 2002), is a part of the culture, however one may feel about it ethically. For both forms, economic barriers are not a limitation when it comes to participation within comics or graffiti culture, echoing Jenkins's (2006) understanding of the necessity of "relatively low" barriers to participation (p. 221).

It is not only economic access but cultural forms of accessibility that are significant. For comics creators and graffiti practitioners, it is imperative to have access to the materials, but also to engage with particular "communities of practice" (Wenger, 1998, p. 2). While these are from the outside, perhaps exclusive and mysterious, and indeed have particular forms of discourse, norms, and practices, they are readily accessible to the public. For example, in hip-hop culture, a cypher is open to the public, and anyone can participate provided they have the requisite skills.

Likewise, graffiti writers will often share their notebooks, creative ideas, and collaborate in artistic jam sessions on paper or other readily available surfaces. More formally, graffiti writers will sometimes form a crew, a group of regularly collaborative writers and artists. Significantly, "crews are differentiated from gangs in that their main objective is to paint graffiti. Any group of friends can quickly and informally form a crew if they are interested in graffiti and want to start conspiring" (CMATO, 2021).

As comics scholar Scott McCloud using the metaphor of a campfire (2008, p. 229) notes that an indispensable facet of comic book culture is not (solely) attending conventions or festivals, or having a pull list at your local comic shop, but most importantly, comics culture is reliant of a group of individuals, or tribe that holds, "shared ideas, shared values, [and] shared goals." This is not to say that there is no exclusivity to comics culture, but rather that comics culture, contrary to public understanding, necessarily happens in concert with others.

Ultimately, the community, or spatial accessibility of these cultures, is significant in understanding the interconnected possibilities of these cultures. Both forms are openly democratic. A graffiti piece is written on the city. A membership to a museum or an invitation to an art gallery is not necessary. Graffiti is available to the public by a walk or a car ride. A famous, now tragically erased, example was 5Pointz, free and open twenty-four seven often called "the world's premier graffiti mecca" (Chused, 2017), where anyone could visit and write (provided you had the cultural skills). With a different perspective, waiting for a train becomes a pop-up, drive-by, no-cost art show.

For comics creators, anywhere was a studio. All a practitioner needed was pencils and paper to make a comic. Many public spaces, such as libraries or community organizations, offer comic art or reading clubs. Both graffiti writing and comics are incredibly democratic art forms where the entry required little more than a sheet of paper, a pencil or a spray can or marker, a friend or two, and a space to create.

## PUBLIC MEDIATION

The final public is that of the wider, general audience. Each of these artistic forms, from a semiotic and rhetorical perspective, demands visual, physical, and intellectual attention from their audiences, necessarily requiring an audience to engage in message transmission and reception using idiomatic techniques. Not only are they meant to engage from an aesthetic perspective, but they are also meant to engage with the creation of symbolic meaning (semiotics) and persuasion (rhetorics) in ways that can change the ways we interact with the word and the world, as what Collingwood (1958) calls "magical art" (p. 69). Both comics and graffiti are intended to physically stop the audience and demand their attention in this effort.

There is an intentional public discursive intent with the audience that makes it easy to borrow from one another. Both are intended to be seen, evoke, provoke, and induce thoughtful discussion regarding art, society, and our role(s) within it. Narrative theory, especially Bakhtin, recognizes their dialogism (Holquist, 2003). Comics are but one medium, the same way graffiti is a form of street art, reflecting and having a conversation with both its viewers and greater socio-cultural context. Comics are visual, often serial storytelling, usually published in ongoing series whose length is theoretically infinite with regard to number of issues and reissues. Because of their longevity, comics often develop alongside their social context with evolving perspectives that comment contextually and continually (re)leveraging perspectives to critique and comment on societal norms.

The dialogue between comics and graffiti writing reflects a common concern for sociopolitical expression as well as the visualization of cultural identity. This shared expectation of audience interactivity in a shared milieu engages public discourse in challenging and subversive ways. These forms are two of the most public-facing invitations for examining race, gender, and class through the lens of the counterpublic. These public-oriented mediums impact our daily lives like no other medium can by offering unescapable views (often viscerally embodied in their materiality) and perspectives that advocate for social change.

## RHETORICS IN PUBLIC

Both comics and graffiti traffic in visual rhetoric, or strategic use of texts to communicate messages effectively, and require that the audience engage directly with the message. Ultimately, visual rhetoric is more concerned with the effectiveness, persuasiveness, and communicative power of visual elements and their ability to convey meaning and influence the audience than perhaps the more subjective concerns of the aesthetic quality of the message itself.

Visual rhetoric refers to how people are persuaded by the things they see. It emphasizes images as sensorial expressions of cultural and contextual meaning, as opposed to purely or solely aesthetic consideration. Visual rhetoric is concerned with the study of communication in the art of persuasion through visual elements, such as images, typography, and layout, and how these elements convey meaning and influence the audience. Visual rhetoric theory explores the use of visual elements such as images, typography, and texts for effective communication. This involves developing visual literacy and analytic skills to think about both form and meaning.

Visual rhetoric, the study of how visual images communicate messages and influence viewers, is central to understanding both comics and graffiti. Theoretical principles from this field, particularly those discussed by scholars like Barthes and Scott McCloud, provide a framework for analyzing the ways these two art forms intersect.

Roland Barthes's (1964) concept of the "rhetoric of the image" is particularly relevant here as he posits that images carry a multiplicity of meanings, depending on cultural and contextual factors. In both comics and graffiti, the visual elements are loaded with cultural references and symbolism, allowing artists to convey nuanced messages.

Scott McCloud (1993), in "Understanding Comics," expands on this by discussing the idea of "closure," a process where the reader's mind naturally bridges the gap between panels, creating a sense of motion or continuity. Comics do this to tell the story and play with the timing or pacing of particular events, inviting the reader to fill in the blanks with their own mind almost automatically. Comics composition and layout, or the arrangement of how the elements appear on the panel and the overall page layout, is of immense importance. Composition requires reader participation as the page leads the reader's eye and lures attention to specific parts of the story, panel, or theme.

Comics use visual rhetoric to inform their audience via the ways images and text interact in its panels. There are few of the core principles that comics as a medium engage in that are particularly salient when analyzing messaging strategies. In comics, iconography and symbolism refer to the reliance on simplified, symbolic images as visual elements within the comic panels to convey something other than what can be literally communicated by the image in terms of the meaning. Simple symbols like these can be quickly discerned and communicate meaning more efficiently. This might be a color scheme for an antagonist or other readily recognizable icon. Comics also utilize juxtaposition, a strategy that includes organizing panels and parallels in order, leaving it to the audience to deduce meaning from their placement. In other words, it provides the requisite counterpoint to penetrate the clutter and produce narrative comics by affording opportunities for comparison, contrast, and self-construction of particular narratives through the sequencing of the images.

Another unique quality of comics as a medium is the concept of Text-Image Interaction. Words with images often work together quite naturally, one form of representation supporting or complementing another. Depending on the intent of the author, there may be more image or text in a given piece, which invites audiences to attend to the page in particular ways.

Pacing is the reader's experience of time and rhythm within the narrative. Panel width, height, and shape are intentionally varied to suit the intended tempo and amount of detail. Another crucial aspect is the individual style and craft that go into a comic's creation to compose the intended tone and mood for a comic. The original artwork (lines, colors, shading, art style) impacts the page flow and subjective engagement with the artists' message. Gutters, the spaces that separate the panels, demand that the reader process time and changes in action. The gutters connect time, space, and perspective shifts. All these complementary aspects require a participatory negotiation between the artist(s) and the audience.

Finally, typography and lettering refer to the way words are written and how they are rendered in a typeface, as well as where they are placed in the case of captions or speech balloons, in a way that makes them easily readable while also showing personality, emotion, and tone. Often, an antagonist will have a rhetorically sinister typeface or, in some cases, a completely black speech balloon with white font color. Other times, a word will be bolded or perhaps rendered in a different color or as a separate element altogether.

The medium of comics contains several artists who blur the lines of graffiti and comics. Artist Tradd Moore (Figure 4.2), known for his work on *Ghost Rider* (Smith & Moore, 2018) and *The Amazing Spider-Man* employs a gritty, exaggerated, almost geometric aesthetic alongside kinetic typeface to create a style reminiscent of graffiti art. Similarly, the work of Katsuhiro Otomo, particularly in *Akira*, showcases how graffiti's chaotic, expressive style can seep into comic storytelling, infusing it with a sense of urgency and rebellion.

Taken together, these principles work to form the cohesive, multimodal narrative experience that demonstrates the rhetorical efficacy of comics as a medium. It connects the literacy of visuals to that of prose, or to some other equally arranged text, resulting in a form of multimedia storytelling.

## GRAFFITI

Many of comics' major visual rhetoric elements are evident in graffiti art as well, functioning in analogous though not equivalent ways. Two artists, Jean-Michel Basquiat and Keith Haring, demonstrate the complementary exchange between graffiti and comics. Basquiat's work contains bold lines, iconic imagery, and vibrant colors, as well as various textual elements, which at times resemble comic art. Basquiat's frequent use of recurring symbols and textual elements mirrors, in some ways, the episodic structure of comics, creating a narrative across pieces that invites viewers to construct a story. Not only do Haring's symbolic figures, which usually take a sturdy, graphic form filled with bold colors surrounded by "aggressively fluid" lines (Gruen, 1992, p. 44), evoke comic book aesthetics, but they also invite audiences to engage narrative elements, commenting on social matters (Kolossa & Haring, 2002, p. 64) in a fashion akin to the critical allegory and satire found in many comics.

The visual rhetoric of comics and graffiti is deeply connected to their use of both space and form. Color usage, for example, is a significant component of the forms found in both mediums. Color carries emotion, message, and can provide contrasts that underscore specific semiotic aspects of a given image (Fehrman & Fehrman, 2004). When considering color, if we approach these works from a deconstructive or destabilized perspective (Derrida, 2020), we can observe how the use of color by artists disrupts conventional meanings and creates new interpretations. Retna, for example, uses bold script in rich color contrasts in ways that forge a cryptic yet iconic, pan-cultural visual language of indigenous cultural roots and modes of communication.

The spatial arrangement of graffiti—the location of the work, to its placement and size within the space—also serves to sell rhetorical batons. Related to this is Michel Foucault's heterotopia, which describes how graffiti converts ordinary urban sites into spaces of resistance and subversive histories. For one Brazilian artist, Os Gêmeos, this means not only creating large-scale murals that turn whole buildings into vibrant canvases that are both a reflection of the local culture and an expression of global issues. Often their works would interrupt the monotony of bland architecture, making its viewers reconsider the space around them.

Graffiti often ignores physical boundaries, spreading across walls and public spaces in an unrestrained fashion, creating, like comics, a sense of motion and closure. Both forms use their respective canvases to engage in creating gestalt understandings that guide the viewer's eye and convey meaning. The dynamism of graffiti can be seen in the work of comic artists who break away from rigid panel structures, using full-page spreads and irregular layouts to create a sense of movement and immediacy.

The connection between text and image is a significant aspect of visual rhetoric. Comics provide a layered narrative by combining conversation, captions, and visual aspects (such as line, composition, and color) to form a singular message. In graffiti, text is often more symbolic or aesthetic, where stylized lettering and tags are utilized to show identity and message. In this sense, the words in graffiti, similar to speech balloons or captions in comics, act as both an art form and a mode of communication.

A final piece in these shared strategies for visual rhetoric is kairos, or the opportune moment. Kairos has to do with the time and place that a message is given. Because graffiti is often placed in public, and often reflects current events by producing and situating graffiti in a timely manner it increases its rhetorical impact by touching on the immediate experiences and concerns of viewers. On another side of the same coin, comics can take up current or contemporary events to raise awareness and visibility to a degree that many other forms of protest may not be able to achieve, thereby making these narratives a tool of social and political reform.

Ultimately, these forms are uniquely suited in reaching a wide range of elements of visual rhetoric, including semiotics, multimodality, ethos, pathos, and kairos in order to convey their message prominently. These theoretical frameworks allow us to better understand graffiti as a multifaceted form of public discourse. By examining the works of key artists and the theoretical elements of visual communication, audiences can appreciate how these art forms use imagery and text to convey powerful messages. Whether through the structured narrative of comics or the bombastic self-expression of graffiti, both forms push the boundaries of visual language, creating a dialogue that resonates with a diverse audience. These strategies invite audiences to see

**Figure 4.2** Tradd Moore's work on Marvel's *Ghost Rider* and *Spider-Man* are graffiti pieces on the comic book page.

possible connections between graffiti and comics more broadly and thereby to consider understandings of self and society.

## PUBLIC NAVIGATION OF IDENTITY AND REPRESENTATION

### Knowledge of Self

Understanding how comics and graffiti use visual rhetoric to subvert norms and interact with a variety of audiences can help us understand how these mediums also serve as vital forums for sociopolitical discourse and identity construction. This convergence is especially clear when considering how both media have historically sprung from subcultural movements, providing a forum for underrepresented voices to express and negotiate their perceptions of society and themselves.

Though comics and graffiti writing are two separate avenues for expression in terms of form and medium, they have both served as significant sites of cultural and political engagement, especially regarding (re)considerations of race, gender, and class. Both forms emerged from subcultural movements around the late 1970s, early '80s, and were born out of communities set on rebellion against mainstream society and so have roots and particular ideological commitments that often lie outside the mainstream. The public facing, community-oriented relationship of these two complementary forms has resulted in opportunities for sociopolitical commentary and cultural identity, informed by hip-hop's principle of "knowledge of self" which might best be understood to mean that one must reckon with particular ideological commitments with regard social and cultural norms with respect to identity and the background of one's culture and the place where they come from an important facet in the navigation and creation of both graffiti and comics.

Although knowledge of self is central to both graffiti and comics, these "self" goals can differ. Marvel Comics' *Ultimate Spider-Man* series (Bendis et al., 2012) featuring the story of Miles Morales, an Afro–Puerto Rican youth who is also Spider-Man, is a high-profile example. And Miles's discovery of his identity and what it means to be Spider-Man is almost a mirror image of the same self-promotion seen in graffiti as an art form. For graffiti writers, their tags and murals are a form of asserting who they are to the world and telling their stories by literally painting their name on the city.

Many comic book characters go through the trials of self-discovery and/or finding their way back from or through hardship to their true selves, but in a much less public way. For example, Peter Parker/Spider-Man works through the interiority and tension of great power and responsibility very much behind the scenes. A secret identity is meant to keep things private. Conversely, what often makes graffiti so remarkable is the need to be seen and heard through their work. For many comics heroes, the interiority, the secret identity, is paramount and one that must be delicately navigated. This tension is forefront in the recent Sony Spider-Verse films, where Miles is quite literally creating a graffiti mural when he is bitten by a radioactive spider. Here, Miles begins to learn what is important to him, and that his power and responsibility are not just to himself but to the city itself as Spider-Man. Importantly, Miles continues to create slaps and keep a graffiti notebook throughout this process, even putting a sticker where only he, as Spider-Man, can see it. This incorporation of two desires, to create public art and to defend the private sense of self without abandoning either, demonstrates the synergy and resolution of the tensions between graffiti and comics beautifully.

**Figure 4.3** Bechdel's original comic and origin of the "Bechdel Test" in *Dykes to Watch Out For*.

## The Public Good

Through their unapologetic and assertive messaging and imagery, comics and graffiti afford viewers and audiences opportunities to articulate their stances and understandings of salient public issues in a very public way. How one feels and thinks about an issue is very much out in the open. These are very public commitments to the public. The ideological and cultural inclination toward social critique in comics and graffiti writing since the mid-twentieth century represents an artistic and aesthetic commitment to sociopolitical messaging and (re)consideration of cultural identity, resulting in increasingly nuanced discourses on race, gender, and class. Both art forms have historically served as vehicles for marginalized voices, challenging dominant narratives, and offering alternative perspectives through visual and textual storytelling.

Comics, especially underground and alternative comics, have long tackled issues of social justice, often intentionally resisting mainstream norms. For example, artists such as Art Spiegelman (1986) and Alison Bechdel have used the medium to address complex, often uncomfortable social themes such as the Holocaust in *Maus* and LGBTQ+ issues in *Dykes to Watch Out For*, respectively. *Maus*, often targeted for bans in libraries and schools, which speaks to the notion of public refusal, for example, expertly employs the graphic novel format to explore the intergenerational trauma of the Holocaust, using anthropomorphic characters to make poignant statements about identity and memory. Bechdel famously created the "Bechdel Test" in DWOF (Figure 4.3) as a means of critiquing the male gaze in contemporary culture.

Graffiti is often connected with African American and Latino cultures, as it has its roots in hip-hop culture. It became a means for young people from these communities to voice their identity and challenge the socioeconomic restrictions of that era. Writers like Jean-Michel Basquiat, who tagged as SAMO (Hoban, 2016, p. 12), were using graffiti as a form of socio-political commentary about race and class. Basquiat's graffiti contained elements of social commentary, most notably on the African American experience and racism. His work erased lines between street art and so-called high art, addressing in the process much of what was happening on the streets to an audience that crosses over into the mainstream art world (Belton, 2001, p. 1)

Still other artists, such as Shamsia Hassani, a leading, unapologetically female-identifying graffiti artist in the otherwise highly male-dominated graffiti world, resisted conventional gender expectations, not only proving that women did exist within hip-hop culture but that their lived experiences mattered. Hassani's work stands out for its emphasis on gender justice as for example, many of her murals depict women with no mouths, but expressing themselves in other ways. As one of the few prominent female graffiti artists in a male-dominated field, her work often addresses feminist themes and challenges gender norms, particularly with regard to women's rights in Afghanistan. Her pieces frequently depict strong, independent women, asserting female agency and presence in public spaces historically dominated by men.

Graffiti and comics invite communities that are often historically overlooked an opportunity to speak for themselves, express their own identity, on their own terms. While representation has changed in comics as more diverse characters and creators have been added to rosters over recent decades, stories from major comic imprints were rarely from, by, or for those directly impacted by systems of oppression.

This changed significantly in the 1990s when creators Dwayne McDuffie and Denys Cowan created Milestone Media in an effort to offer more diverse comic representations of African American characters. Milestone Comics created a stable of Black and brown characters (Brown, 2009), created largely by creators of color, which was a landmark shift in the world of comics publishing. Most of Milestone's characters dealt directly with contemporary issues of race, gender, class, and sexuality, often ignored or rendered metaphorical, with Milestone's most popular character, "Static" series, directly following a Black, teenage superhero fighting crime but also surviving in the United States.

Almost a generation later, G. Willow Wilson (2014), alongside Sana Amanat and Adrian Alphona, introduced Kamala Khan, a Pakistani American teen who acquires superpowers and takes over the Captain Marvel mantle in the summer of 2013. Marvel's *Ms. Marvel* has become renowned for its representation of a first-generation youth living in post-9/11 America, trying to navigate her cultural identities. Khan's storylines involve her Pakistani American background, her family, and her Muslim faith, as well as addressing common aspects of life when dealing with two identities (Chung, 2019, p. 5). This presentation of a Muslim female character is an important step in the direction of being truly inclusive for a medium that has historically struggled regarding the representation of communities and orientations other than male, cis-hetero, and white.

The synthesis of graffiti and comics is evident in a communal bond shared by both, following the way each can affect and inspire the other. The bold, graphic nature of graffiti has influenced comic art, and that narrative style employed in comics had a profound effect on the storytelling techniques to be found within graffiti. It intersects beautifully in Aaron McGruder's comic series *The Boondocks*. McGruder's unique graffiti-style characters visually provided an energetic, stylistically aligned aesthetic statement that complemented the strip's incisive political critiques on hip-hop culture (Howard, 2013, p. 157).

hooks is helpful once again as she notes the vital nature of cultural criticism and transformation by which she means the creation of representations that challenge racist and sexist stereotypes and the capacity to be "enlightened witnesses" (Media Education Foundation, 1997, p. 8). There are certainly further examples in both the fields of comics and graffiti; however, these are intended to serve as evidence that these publicly understood spaces of dominance are also contested terrain.

The interplay between comics and graffiti writing is a clear demonstration of the capacity of art as an effective weapon for public discourse (Gee, 1989) and cultural projection. Arguably, both platforms have been home to myriad marginalized voices creatively and effectively organizing, resisting, and calling for justice against destructive and oppressive societal norms. The tension in these spaces is that there exists both reinforcement and rethinking of cultural identities, subjectivities, and resistances. And this tension sits at the core of the "knowledge of self," the self-awareness, advocacy, and copowering of a common good. These are all commonplace trajectories within graffiti and comics, making a focus on issues of social justice/cultural representation essential to the practices and procedures of each.

## IMPLICATIONS

Research into why comic books and graffiti are so compatible can provide audiences with an understanding of how historically communities engage with notions of civil society as well as avenues for cultivating new kinds of speculative possibilities for public discourse. Graffiti and comics have been mobilized as instruments of social commentary, cultural expression, and political activism by examining these two contrasting artistic forms. Both comic books and graffiti writing have their origins in public acts of resistance, as spaces to critique what is and to dream other possibilities. Each does the work of challenging dominant narratives and making space for voices too often consigned to noise, expressing dissent but also hope. Kelley (2022) argues that we need to imagine what kind of world we are fighting for rather than simply rebelling against the notion that, "without new visions, we don't know what to build, only what to knock down. But we come away dizzied, rudderless, and with a hardened cynicism, failing to remember that, revolution is not simply about challenging the establishment but also who we become in the process" (p. 2). Here, we are reminded of the importance of dreaming as an act of speculative resistance that can create progressive political futures through public art.

## REFERENCES

Aiello, G. (2019). *Visual communication: Understanding images in media culture.* SAGE Publications Ltd.

Avramidis, K., & Tsilimpounidi, M. (2016). Graffiti and street art: Reading, writing and representing the city. In K. Avramidis & M. Tsilimpounidi (Eds.), *Graffiti and street art: Reading, writing and representing the city* (pp. 17–40). Routledge.

Barthes, R. (1964). Rhetoric of the image. *Communications,* (4), 40–51. https://doi.org/10.3406/comm.1964.1027

Bechdel, A. (2008). *The essential "Dykes to Watch Out For."* Houghton Mifflin Harcourt.

Belton, V. J. (2001). Racism, gender, ethnicity, and aesthetics in the art of graffiti. *Race and ethnicity in contemporary art and literature,* Yale-New Haven Teachers Institute, IV. https://teachersinstitute.yale.edu/curriculum/units/2001/4/01.04.01.x.html

Bendis, B. M., Hickman, J., Spencer, N., Pichelli, S., Larroca, S., & Crain, C. (2012). *Ultimate comics Spider-Man*. Marvel.
Brown, J. A. (2001). *Black superheroes, milestone comics, and their fans*. University Press of Mississippi.
California Museum of Art Thousand Oaks (CMATO). (2021, March 1). *Graffiti glossary: The more you know*. CMATO. https://cmato.org/exhibition/risk/graffiti-glossary/
Carver, S. (2016). *More weird tales from the vault of fear: The EC legacy*. Ainsworth & friends. https://ainsworthandfriends.wordpress.com/2016/02/16/more-weird-tales-from-the-vault-of-fear-the-ec-legacy/
Chung, E. (2019). Ms. Marvel: Genre, medium, and an intersectional superhero. *Panic at the Discourse: An Interdisciplinary Journal*, 1(2), 5–16.
Chused, R. (2017). Moral rights: The anti-rebellion graffiti heritage of 5Pointz. *Colum. JL & Arts*, 41, 583.
Collingwood, R. G. (1958). *The principles of art* (vol. 11). Oxford University Press.
Cosgrove, D. (1989). Geography is everywhere: Culture and symbolism in human landscapes. In D. Gregory & R. Walford (Eds.), *Horizons in human geography* (pp. 118–35). Palgrave Macmillan.
de Certeau, M. (2010). Walking in the city (1980). In I. Szeman & T. Kaposy (Eds.), *Cultural theory: An anthology* (pp. 264–73). Wiley-Blackwell.
Derrida, J. (2020). *Deconstruction in a nutshell: A conversation with Jacques Derrida, with a new introduction*. Fordham University Press.
Eisner, W. (1985) *Comics and sequential art*. W.W. Norton & Company.
Fehrman, K. R., & Fehrman, C. (2004). *Color: The secret influence* (2nd ed.). Prentice Hall.
Gee, J. P. (1989) Literacy, discourse, and linguistics: Introduction. *Journal of Education*, 171(1), 5–17.
Gruen, J. (1992). *Keith Haring: the authorized biography*. Simon and Schuster.
Hall, S. (1989). Cultural identity and cinematic representation. *Framework: The Journal of Cinema and Media*, (36), 68–81.
Hayman, G. & Pratt, H. (2005). What are comics? In D. Goldblatt, L. B. Brown, & S. Patridge (Eds.), *Aesthetics: A reader in philosophy of the arts* (2nd ed., pp. 419–24). Routledge.
Hoban, P. (2016). *Basquiat: A quick killing in art*. Open Road Media.
Holquist, M. (2003). *Dialogism: Bakhtin and his world*. Routledge.
Howard, S. C. (2013). Gender, race, and The Boondocks. In S. C. Howard & R. L. Jackson II (Eds.), *Black comics: Politics of race and representation* (pp. 151–267). Bloomsbury Publishing.
Kelley, R. D. (2022). *Freedom dreams: The Black radical imagination*. Beacon Press.
Kolossa, A., & Haring, K. (2004). *Haring* (vol. 3). Taschen.
Lothian-McLean, M. (2015, March 27). *From Run DMC to Run the Jewels, this is how comic books influenced hip-hop*. VICE. https://www.vice.com/en/article/rgbae9/hip-hops-relationship-with-comics
McCloud, S. (2008). *Making comics storytelling secrets of comics, manga and graphic novels*. Harper.
McCloud, S. (1993). *Understanding comics: The invisible art*. Harper Perennial.

Media Education Foundation. (1997). *bell hooks: Cultural criticism and transformation [transcript]*. Media Education Foundation Transcripts. https://www.mediaed.org/transcripts/Bell-Hooks-Transcript.pdf

Meskin, A. (2007). Defining comics? *The Journal of Aesthetic and Art Criticism*, 65(4), 369–79.

Rahn, J. (2002). *Painting without permission: Hip-hop graffiti subculture*. Bloomsbury Publishing USA.

Smith, F. & Moore, T. (2018). *All-new "Ghost Rider" vol. 1: Engines of vengeance* (T. Moore, Illus.). Marvel Entertainment.

Smith, N. (1998). Giuliani time: The revanchist 1990s. *Social Text*, (57), 1–20.

Spiegelman, A. (1986). *Maus: A survivor's tale*. Pantheon Books.

Stampoulidis, G., & Bolognesi, M. (2023). Bringing metaphors back to the streets: A corpus-based study for the identification and interpretation of rhetorical figures in street art. *Visual Communication*, 22(2), 243–77.

Tilley, C. L. (2012). Seducing the innocent: Fredric Wertham and the falsifications that helped condemn comics. *Information & Culture*, 47(4), 383–413.

Wenger, E. (1998). Communities of practice: Learning as a social system. *Systems Thinker*, 9(5), 2–3.

Wilson, G. W. (2014). *Ms. Marvel, vol. 1: No normal*. Marvel Worldwide, Inc.

# MARVEL COMICS AND HIP-HOP

CHAPTER 5

# "SWEET CHRISTMAS"

Luke Cage and Pulp Authenticity

MATTHEW TEUTSCH

Marvel's Luke Cage debuted in June 1972 at the confluence of Holloway House's dominance in pulp fiction publishing and in the era of Blaxploitation cinema, each of which went on to influence hip-hop. Birthed at the intersection of Holloway House's capitalistically exploitative publishing of authors such as Iceberg Slim and Donald Goines and the subversive commercial success of Blaxploitation cinema, Marvel sought to financially capitalize on a cultural moment that presented audiences with what Jason Lee Oakes and I (2018) term "pulp authenticity," a framework that "incorporates the sensational on one hand and varying forms of genuineness on the other," working to address "cultural and social issues by espousing a constructed 'keeping it real' ethos" (para. 5). While Luke Cage does not purport, on any level, to "keeping it real," his debut relates to the "pulp authenticity" that writers such as Slim and Goines employed by working to engage readers in an examination of structural issues of white supremacy, notably mass incarceration, while at the same time presenting stereotypical caricatures of Black individuals and the urban environment. Since Luke Cage's initial appearance within this framework, artists and writers have remixed Cage in numerous ways over the subsequent decades in the pages of comics, on television, and in art exhibits by visual artists such as Black Kirby. Each creator remixes Luke Cage by taking the original and reimagining it, adding to it, forming a new iteration in the process. Eduardo Navas (2014) points out that "[r]emix is meta—always unoriginal," but in the same moment, "when implemented effectively, it can become a tool of autonomy," expanding upon the original (p. 4).

Steve Englehart makes Marvel's desire to exploit the Black cultural moment through Luke Cage abundantly clear. Englehart (2015) writes that while Luke Cage adhered to Marvel's position as "pro-human rights," Cage's creation really came down to the fact that "Marvel's corporate bottom line wanted some of that genre money" because Blaxploitation films were "a saleable genre, to whites as well as blacks" (para. 12). Ultimately, as Englehart puts it, the decision came down to the "[n]ature of capitalism," a way to increase profits (para. 11). Englehart points out that all of Luke Cage's creators, starting with Archie Godwin and editor-in-chief Roy Thomas, were white, apart from inker Billy Graham, one of the first Black illustrators at Marvel, known for his work on *Jungle Action featuring the Black Panther* (1972–1976). This set-up, of course, did not differ from Jack Kirby and Stan Lee's creation of T'Challa (Black Panther) in 1966, but the makeup of Luke Cage's early creative team reinforces the underlying capitalistic and exploitative nature of Cage's creation. Jim Owsley (Christopher Priest) served as Luke Cage's first Black writer with *Power Man and Iron Fist* in late 1984, addressing—along with Mark Bright (who illustrated and cowrote Priest's run) and Dwayne McDuffie—Cage's problematic publication history and remixed Cage by having him analyze the psychological impacts of white supremacy on his psyche and actions.[1] Blaxploitation cinema, while being "open to accusations of complicity because of its reliance on white mainstream resources," Jonathan Munby (2011) argues, "also opened up other possibilities" to critique systemic oppression and capitalism (p. 131). Tracy Bealer (2017) points out that we need to think about Luke Cage in relation to "other blaxploitation (super)heroes before him, produced by and in resistance to white institutions" because his narrative in early issues, even amidst the stereotypes, exposes "the systemic racism structuring those institutions," notably the prison industrial complex (p. 171). William Svitavsky (2013) points out that although creators modeled Cage on Shaft, the Blaxploitation hero played by Richard Roundtree, Cage "rarely comments on racial tensions or inequalities" and instead becomes "a nonconfrontational, noncontroversial Shaft" (p. 155). Priest and Bright have Cage confront these tensions in their *Power Man and Iron Fist* run, and McDuffie and Bright do the same through the satirical Buck Wild in *Icon*.

Marvel's craving for a piece "of that genre money" mirrors not just Blaxploitation cinema but also Holloway House, the publishing company that released books such as Iceberg Slim's *Pimp: The Story of My Life* (1967) and

Donald Goines's Kenyatta novels. The cover of *Luke Cage, Hero for Hire* #1 directly plays into the Blaxploitation cinema and Black pulp narrative images of mass-market stereotypes of individuals in an urban setting, depicting Cage in the foreground, hands balled into fists, looking at the reader. Semiotic images of the "ghetto" and criminality surround him with a Black woman smoking a cigarette beneath signs that read "Girls" and "Bar," a Black man firing a gun at someone, a scene in prison with one officer restraining another officer who has attacked Cage, and images of cards and dice directly behind Cage. The initial splash page depicts a similar layout: Cage angrily screaming in the center, a Black teen shooting at someone, a seductive Black woman, a police officer, a police car underneath Cage's legs, and again cards and dice behind Cage. The narration reads, "Look closely at the figure before you, study him, study his costume. This is Luke Cage now. A super-hero . . . yet unlike any other before him, but he was not always as you see him. Before the super-hero, there was the man" (Goodwin, 1972, p. 1). As Blair Davis (2015) notes, audiences read these pages semiotically before they even encounter Cage's origin story and do so at the command of the narrator. These images become "linked in the reader's minds with scenes that are implied as being criminal and/or morally questionable given the entrenched presence of the law among the visual milieu" (p. 196).

Space occasionally opens up to challenge the connotations that arise from the visual images, yet these moments appear and then fade away without any examination. Two instances appear in issue #2 when Cage rents an office above a movie theater to house his business and when he goes to a costume shop for his costume. Arriving at the cinema, Cage meets a white, blonde-haired teenager who introduces himself as Dave Griffin. The teenager tells Cage, "My movie freak friends call me D. W. . . . After the director, y'know?" (Godwin, 1972, p. 13). Griffin's friends refer to him as "D. W." based on D. W. Griffin, the infamous director of *Birth of a Nation* (1915), the first blockbuster film in the United States and one filled with white supremacist stereotypes, praise for the Ku Klux Klan, and blatant misinformation about Black individuals and Reconstruction. Cage merely responds, "I'm Cage, D. W. You got a grand tour, I'll take it" (p. 13). The reference to Griffin ends there, and Cage moves forward with renting the space and setting up his office. At the costume shop, the proprietor shows Cage some escape artist's props. The owner produces a chain and dismisses the possibility that Cage would want it for his costume; however, Cage tells the man that he wants the chain because it will serve "as a kind of reminder" (p. 7). Cage does not expound upon this. Rather, it lingers in the air between Cage and the costume shop owner. The unspoken implication points to the chain, reminding Cage of

**Figure 5.1** Luke Cage, *Hero for Hire* splash page.

his wrongful incarceration. Davis points out that "the steel chain (along with his bracelets, which resemble shackles), also serves as a reminder of the heritage Cage carries with him, as a black male, signifying the chains that bound those who were loaded onto slave ships to make the forced journey from Africa to foreign lands" (p. 198). Yet, neither Cage nor the owner nor any other characters make these semiotic connections for the reader; rather, they float along in the air, becoming nothing more than a fleeting reference to Cage's time at Seagate, devoid of the historical and racial symbolism that the chains embody within themselves. Each of these interactions pushes right up against progressive storytelling to dismantle stereotypes like issue #1 does with incarceration, but each refuses to address the stereotypes and white supremacist depictions of Black men, such as Cage.

The command to "look closely" from issue #1 implies that the comic will take the reader on a tour of the "ghetto" and specifically "Harlem," which appears in big letters on the page. This command recalls the promotional material for Iceberg Slim's *Pimp*, a memoir written by Robert Beck (a.k.a. Iceberg Slim) and published by Holloway House. Bentley Morris, the owner of Holloway House, promoted *Pimp* to his white readership, and as Kinohi Nishikawa (2018) argues, we must read and engage with *Pimp* through this lens, specifically in relation to how Morris promoted the book as a voyeuristic ghetto safari and "showed how his appropriation of street culture was an essentially pornographic undertaking" (p. 56). Slim presents *Pimp* as a moral tale in the hopes of keeping just "one intelligent valuable young man or woman . . . From the destructive slime," and the backmatter plays upon the ethnographic and voyeuristic desires of white male readers to experience the "ghetto" and learn how to manipulate women (p. 17). The backmatter informs the reader that it contains "no pretense of moralizing" and exceeds other books because none of them "comes anywhere near this one in its description of the raw, brutal reality of the jungle that lurks beneath the surface of every city."

Initially geared towards white readers, *Pimp*, along with Slim's other novels and his 1976 album of pimp toasts *Reflections*, would go on to have an impact on the rise of Blaxploitation cinema and gangsta rap, with artists like Ice-T, Ice Cube, and Kendrick Lamar directly citing Slim as an influence on their work.[2] Artists such as Killer Mike elevate "Slim to more than just a raconteur of the urban experience," they place him alongside individuals such as W. E. B. Du Bois and James Baldwin as someone "who chronicles the urban experience and presents his audience . . . with both release and escape" (Teutsch & Oakes, 2020). The artists reappropriate and remix Slim for a new moment. Black Kirby, a collaborative artistic project between John Jennings and Stacey Robinson that takes the work of Jack Kirby and reimagines it through an Afrofuturist lens, uses Luke Cage in a similar manner to bring to light issues surrounding Black masculinity, cultural appropriation, medical racism, mass incarceration, and other institutionalized issues through the remixing of Luke Cage. Writing about the impetus behind Black Kirby, Jennings (2013) notes that he and Robinson "are both children of the Hip-hop Generation," the generation immediately following the civil rights movement, and that their project specifically uses comics, a medium many identify as "low" and "uncultured" as a way to use art to address both the unfulfilled promises of the movement and the "increasingly problematic issues around poverty, education, social justice, and access to health care" (p. 9). Expanding upon this, Jennings told Raymond Morales in 2012 that Black Kirby's remixing of Kirby's work draws the connections between characters such as the X-Men and the civil rights movement even tighter; he told Morales, "So we [Black Kirby] just made those more explicit and just started remixing things. We put in a lot of hip-hop. We put in a lot of science fiction. We put in all kinds of stuff, you know, just black power politics and looking at how those things have been depicted" (p. 6–7).

In 2018, Black Kirby debuted *Uncaged: Hero for Higher*, an art installation that remixes and "aims to unpack the possible multiple meanings of Luke Cage in media culture as a symbol for the many tensions regarding the black male body and the historically negative meanings projected upon it" (Robinson & Jennings, 2019, p. 209). Along with the visual exhibit, Jennings and Robinson created an interactive "illabus" (a play on syllabus, illustrated, and Nas's 1994 *Illmatic*). The "illabus" provides teachers with resources and questions for a ten-week class, and the title and themes for each week come from a song by Mos Def.[3] Through this, Black Kirby bring together hip-hop, comics, history, literature, and more to "delve into expressions of black respectability politics, the great migration, black patriarchy, black sexuality and subjectivity, the prison industrial complex, gentrification and cultural appropriation, medical apartheid, and black fatherhood" (Robinson & Jennings, 2019, p. 209).

For week five of the "illabus," Black Kirby provide teachers with "Mr. N\*\*\*a" (1999), presenting Luke Cage in relation to Black respectability. They ask the audience to think about the ways that Cage pushes audiences to examine how stereotypes create a "hypocritical and class-based monolithic idea around black identity in our country" and the ways that audiences can counter this thinking (Robinson & Jennings, 2019, p. 213). Mos Def's song details the ways that even when a Black man becomes successful, society still views him as nothing more than "Mr. N\*\*\*a." Economic success and artistic success do not lead to the dismantling of white supremacy because, as Mos Def raps, even someone with "two assistants, two bank accounts, two homes" gets pulled over by the police for being Black because even though they "say they want you successful," they deny that success because "your skin is dark." Even in first class on a plane, the flight attendants "stay on n\*\*\*a patrol," policing the space to make sure Black individuals do not interlope on white spaces. Like Mos Def, Priest confronts stereotypical representations and caricatures that impact how whites perceive Black men, and he breaks them down by addressing these issues in relation to Luke Cage's publication history.

Near the end of his *Power Man and Iron Fist* run, Priest directly addressed the ways that white creators had relied on stereotypes of "Black culture as

Figure 5.2 *Power Man and Iron Fist* #122 (1986).

represented by Sherman Hemsley or Jimmy Walker or Richard Roundtree.... [creating] a list of rules and hair styles and speech patterns, invented for the game, but bearing little resemblance to any actual culture" (*Ducks!!*). Issue #122 (1986) focuses on the relationship between Misty Knight and Danny Rand (Iron Fist) and Misty's new romantic partner, police sergeant Tyrone King. After King stops a robbery, he goes into a diner to eat, and Cage confronts him, telling King, "You're doing my partner wrong" (p. 9). Cage points his finger in King's face, letting his anger get the better of him. When an officer comes in and calls King outside, Cage stays in the diner and contemplates the exchange. He sits in the booth, left hand under his chin and thinks, "What does Misty see in that guy?! . . . My 'loud angry Negro' bit didn't phase him. Gotta move into 'Plan B'" (p. 10). This moment, one panel in a twenty-two-page issue, encapsulates the ways that "pulp authenticity" and publication work, producing stereotypical images of Black characters for mass consumption and passing them off as a somehow "authentic" representation of "Black culture." Priest states that Cage's thoughts in the issue are "ground-breaking" because he admits to the reader that his persona and speech "is a put-on," a code switch. He continues, "Many whites are shocked to see Queen Latifah or Usher or the late Tupac Shakur in film or on television shows speaking in complete sentences with a calm, even voice. It seems many whites don't realize the gregarious street voice is something we can turn on and off" (*Ducks!!*).

Perceived authenticity lies at the core of Cage's thoughts in the panel and in Priest's comments. After joining Marvel as an intern in 1978, Priest became the first Black editor at one of the big two in 1979. Priest understood Cage's publication history and the presumed "authenticity" it portrayed. Writing about Cage's early days, Priest states that as a consumer reading Black characters written by white writers, "most of that work seemed disingenuous, having not much in the way of anything that was true to my experience as a black youth in America" (*Ducks!!*). Continuing, Priest points out that during the 1970s, and into the 1980s and 1990s, much of Black characters' dialogue "is an appropriation of black culture and voice; it seems to be what white people *think* black people are" (*Ducks!!*). Even some of the staffers in the office approached Priest about his depiction of Cage in the series. While Priest and Bright toned down Cage "a bit from the very loud, histrionic hair-trigger Hulk Smash guy, and gave him a wider vocabulary," some of the staffers told Priest that he wrote "lousy black dialogue" and made fun of him, saying he was not "'really black' because none of [his] characters 'sounded black'" (*Ducks!!*). Priest's comments highlight the ways that staffers perceive him as not racially authentic because he does not adhere to the constructed stereotype of a consumer market that they themselves perpetuate through the propagation of caricatured representations of Black characters in their publications.

At the end of issue #122, *Chiantang*, a large flying dragon with the ability to disguise himself in mortal form takes Iron Fist and Luke Cage captive. Chiantang lures Misty Knight, Colleen Wing, and King into a trap at the docks. In the form of Cage, he sends Misty Knight toward the boat where Iron Fist and the real Cage remain captive. King realizes the ruse and points a gun at Chiantang's temple, explaining how he figured it out. Chiantang begins to change into his dragon form, and King pulls the trigger, shooting him in the head. The three-panel sequence correlates to Cage's earlier thoughts about the mask he puts on for others. In the first panel, Chiantang's face becomes monstrous as it morphs from Cage to his dragon form. The next panel shows a close-up of Chiantang's face with the barrel of King's gun pointed right at it. Here, Chiantang looks like Cage, no metamorphous appears to occur. The final panel shows us Chiantang's point of view as King pulls the trigger. Chiantang's hands frame King as the gun fires. King, in essence, shoots us as well as Chiantang. The sequence reinforces Cage's earlier statements about his façade by having Chiantang take on the façade, acting like Cage, and that façade falls away when King shoots him. As well, the sequence addresses us as readers, telling us, through the positioning in the last panel, that we need to let go of the fabricated images that Cage embodies. This movement and concluding positioning of the audience as the imposter Cage serves as a symbolic death of Cage's constructed persona, something that McDuffie and Bright make more explicit through Buck Wild in their *Icon* series.

Following *Power Man and Iron Fist* #122, Priest calls the next issue, *Getting Ugly* (1986), "the shot not heard round the world [because] nobody seemed to notice the examination of racial issues and the implied indictment of the comics industry" embedded within the issue's narrative, which saw Cage, King, and "Sam Wilson (the Falcon) tracking down William Blake, a radioactive man who attacks Black individuals in the city" (*Ducks!!*). *Getting Ugly* explores the psychological impact of white supremacy on oppressed individuals. Priest and Bright, through Cage, highlight the ways that rhetoric and stereotypes dehumanize and cause individuals to internalize ideas of inferiority. The issue opens with a newscaster reporting on an event at a military facility where Cage, as the reporter says, "almost singlehandedly invaded a midtown United States armory" (p. 1). The reporter skews reality through his use of "invaded," painting Cage as a villain who sought to attack an armory instead of as the hero who went to the armory to apprehend Blake for the murders of a Black mother and child and Black police officers.

The bulk of the issue moves into the past, tracing Cage's pursuit of Blake, which begins when he goes to the police station after Blake murders the Black mother and child. Outside of the station, a group of individuals protest the police response, as the newscast states, because if the murdered officers were white, "a suspect would've been in custody by the following evening" (p. 4). As Cage enters the precinct, a Black man in the crowd calls out to him and says, "I remember when you was Black!" (p. 4). Cage stares at the man, then enters the building. The police records identify Blake as a "male Caucasian," and we learn that during his time in the Marines, Blake volunteered for a medical experiment that sought "to recreate the super-soldier serum that created Captain America!" (p. 5). Blake's record indicates that he had issues with "the Black guys" he served with and that he told his therapist that "his upbringing in the deep South" made him grow up "to believe Blacks to be inferior to whites," thus causing him to develop "a pathological disorder" (p. 5). Blake's record details the impact of white supremacy on the psyche, and his actions stem from deep-seated feelings sparked by the system.

Blake strikes again outside of Wilson's office when he attacks two college students, focusing on the Black college student. Cage, Wilson, and King foil Blake's attack and arrest him; however, Blake gets remanded to military custody at the armory. When King goes to the armory and produces an arrest warrant, the guards deny him access to Blake, so King, Cage, and Wilson, "[b]acked by a court order," storm the armory (p. 13). During the skirmish with military personnel, Cage thinks to himself, "The dudes on the TV . . . talkin' about me . . . sayin' I don't care. Saying I ain't Black. Too busy bein' a hero . . . well . . . we'll have to see all about that" (p. 14). The protesters' rhetoric towards Cage begins to affect him, and he thinks, as he moves towards Blake's cell, that he needs to prove himself by reasserting his "authenticity" within the eyes of the community. When Cage gets to Blake's cell, a fight ensues, and as Cage smashes Blake through the floor, he thinks, "I gotta prove somethin' to all those people who are sayin' I sold out . . . I gotta prove somethin' to myself!" (p. 17). Blake's actions cause Cage to care about what people think about him, when he has never cared about their thoughts before, and as he punches Blake, Cage tells him, "If I don't put you down, they'll label me an Uncle Tom" (p. 18). Cage feels the perceptions of others on him, either calling him a thug or an assimilationist Uncle Tom who has turned his back on the community.

The fight culminates with a five-panel sequence with each panel spreading horizontally across the page and diminishing in size as Cage and Blake battle over the course of the panels. Each panel shows Blake and Cage fighting as a busted pipe fills the scene with water. Cage repeatedly hits Blake and screams, "I don't know right from wrong anymore, Blake. I hate that. But I'm a man! And I'm Black! And I'm just as good as you!" (p. 19). Cage's proclamation calls attention to the historical representation of Black characters in mainstream comics, specifically their relegation to the urban environment or to the role of supporting characters for the Avengers or Captain America. This history causes Cage's proclamation to push back against the "White patriarchal universalism," as Sheena Howard and Ronald Jackson (2013) put it, of comics that "tell a story of White heroes and minority villains, White victors and minority losers, White protagonists and perhaps a minority sidekick" (p. 2).[4] Cage's statement also brings to mind the "I Am a Man" signs that Memphis sanitation strikers carried in 1968 and Josiah Wedgwood's abolitionist image of a shackled enslaved man kneeling and asking, "Am I not a man and a brother?" that became an abolitionist symbol in Britain and the United States.

After Cage knocks Blake out and water fills the room, Cage pulls Blake to safety. Cage looks at Blake in astonishment because the radiation has disappeared from Blake's body, revealing he is not white but Black. Blake internalizes what white supremacy says about him, and that belief manifests itself in his actions. When King and Cage seek an answer to why the police classified Blake as white, the technician asks Cage why it even matters. Cage

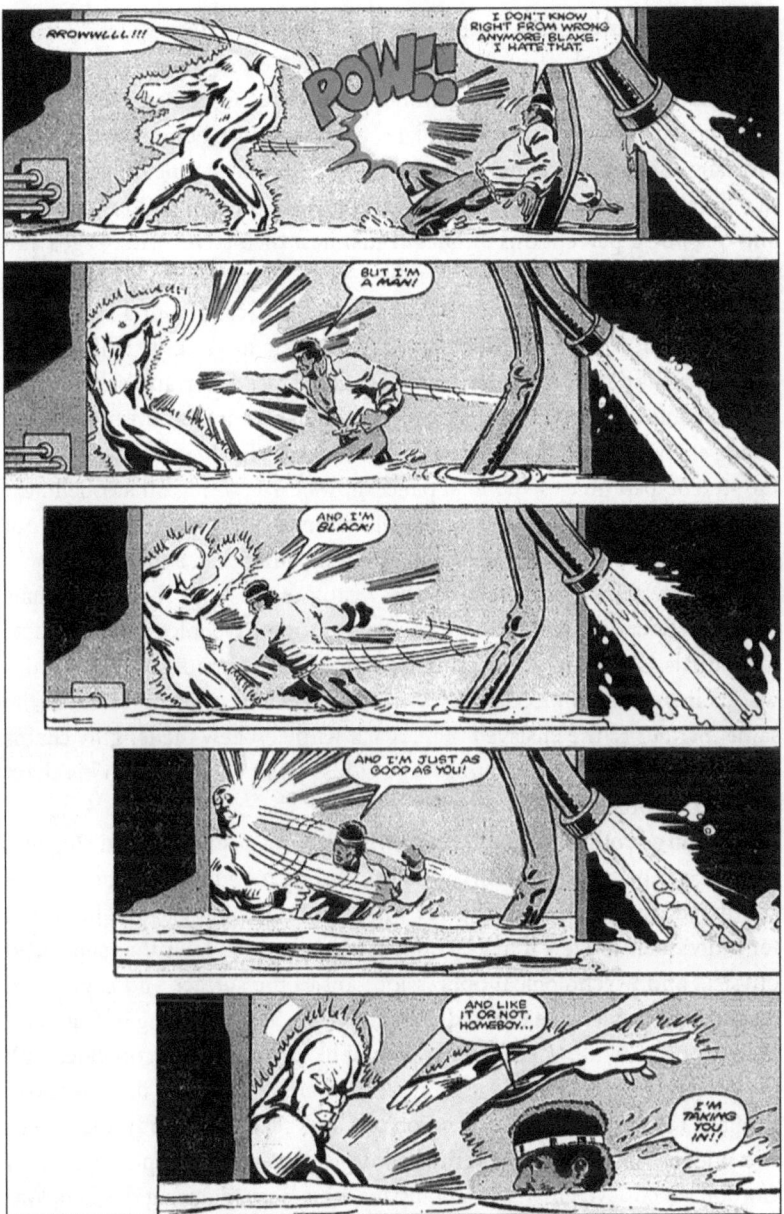

**Figure 5.3** *Power Man and Iron Fist* #123 (1986).

turns to King, asking him to answer the question, but King replies, "Explain what? I'm not Black. I'm not a cop. I'm a man. Period. This 'Black' thing is your hang-up" (p. 21). King's comments reinforce Cage's assertion of his humanity during the fight with Blake, but they differ because while Cage proclaims himself a man first, then Black, King ends by stating he is not Black or a cop but merely a man. The conflict between the perceptions of others and one's own perceptions of oneself manifest themselves with Cage's and King's differing views of their identities. While King asserts his humanity, society will view him as not just a man but as a Black man or a Black male cop. The final page drives this point home as the news cast highlights the shifting terms describing Blake from "'psychotic race-killer' and 'super bigot'" when people thought he was white to "'victim of society' and 'misunderstood young soldier'" when people learn he is Black (p. 22). However, even amidst the stereotyped images, the final panel shows Cage, sitting on a couch next to King and Wilson, reaching for the television to turn it off, thus tuning out the voices that seek to define him as anything other than a man.

Like Priest and Bright, Black Kirby explore the ways that individuals and society craft identity and how that crafting psychologically impacts individuals. One example of this is when Black Kirby remix Cage and Wedgwood's image into a piece that shows Cage kneeling, arms upraised, in the same manner as the enslaved man. Black Kirby eschew the lengthy chains of Wedgwood's image, depicting Cage in his classic costume with his chain belt and his bracelets that resemble manacles. The caption reads, "Am I not a Cage and a brother?" Along with this, Black Kirby print Langston Hughes's poem "Harlem" (1951) beneath the image, causing the audience to ponder the continued psychological impact of white supremacy on Cage as he pleads for individuals to view him as a human being and the ways that continued physical and psychological oppression boil to the surface and explode in reaction to the violence enacted upon a person. This remixing of Cage and Wedgwood reiterates Cage's declaration of his humanity and coincides with the perceived threat that Cage represents when he "invaded" the armory.

Black Kirby address the perception of Cage's Black male body and speech as a boogie man threat in a series of images that remix the photograph of Gordon, an enslaved man from Louisiana who escaped during the Civil War and was photographed baring his whip-scarred back for the world. Black Kirby present Cage in five images that remix the photograph. Each shows Cage in the same position as Gordon, and unlike the Wedgwood remix, broken chain links dangle from Cage's wrist bracelet, signifying his psychological enslavement to the perceived images he encounters as well as his escape from those preconceptions. However, biases remain with him, scarred into his back and

Figure 5.4 "Am I not a Cage and a brother?" Reprinted with permission from Black Kirby.

psyche because five different words appear on Cage's back over the images: "Scary," "Thug," "Evil," "Monster," and "Buck." Each of these words carries connotations of Cage as a threat, as a predator, because he is a Black man. These words have historical connotations, and through their placement on Cage's back, Black Kirby use the words to "reimagine the absurdity of the stereotypes as subliminal texting of scripting Black masculinity through repetitive text on the same Black man" (Robinson & Jennings, 2019, p. 224).

Mos Def's "The Boogie Man Song" (2004) resides at the intersections of the commodification and fear of Black male bodies that Cage, Slim, and Goines represent. By playing on "boogie," a term associated with music and dancing, specifically a blues or R&B groove pattern, and the fear of the "boogeyman," a stereotype of a Black man seeking to do harm to white children and families, Mos Def uses the song to address these dual images that audiences place onto him, Cage, and others. Musically, "The Boogie Man Song" moves forward sensually, instruments meandering underneath the vocals as he raps about being "the most beautiful boogie man" who wants to "be your favorite nightmare" that you will "feed," "fuck," "love," and "trust." The interplay of "beautiful" and "nightmare" creates an image both of lust and fear, two juxtaposed emotions that play into the stereotypical fears about Black men preying on white women. Weaving together desire and horror, Mos Def encapsulates, in less than two and a half minutes, the tensions that appear in Cage's early publication history and the narrative that Priest and Bright work to dismantle.

From his earliest appearances in the 1970s, Luke Cage played into stereotypical images of Black masculinity, specifically as reflected through Blaxploitation cinema. As stated earlier, Englehart points out that these images arose from the capitalistic foundation that lay beneath Cage's creation, and this foundation, partly laid atop the success of Blaxploitation cinema, led to appropriations of Blackness that future comic creators such as Priest, Bright, and McDuffie pushed back against. McDuffie (2016) writes about how he never identified with Cage, "the bastard child of 10,000 blaxploitation movies, a super-strong 'angry black man' who wore chains by choice, didn't seem particularly bright, and spoke in a bizarre version of street slang that didn't remotely resemble the speech of any black people I knew (lol!!!). Spider Man made sense to me, Cage? What can I say? I just couldn't relate" (p. 325).

McDuffie calls Cage "the bastard child of 10,000 blaxploitation movies," and Englehart even admitted as much. As well, McDuffie states that Cage "wore chains by choice," and here McDuffie points out that Cage, historically, plays into stereotypes and is confined within those stereotypes. Countering this history, McDuffie and Bright introduced Buck Wild, a parody of Luke

Cage, in *Icon* #13 (1994).⁵ Meant to be a one-off, fans embraced the character as a satirical commentary on Cage's problematic history, leading him to come back for multiple issues, culminating in an entire issue devoted to his funeral. The cover of Buck Wild's initial appearance harkens back to the splash page from Cage's debut. It shows Buck Wild, front and center, breaking the chains that bind him. Without any words, the image shows how McDuffie and Bright "challenge [the] visual histories" that Cage embodies (Wanzo, 2015, p. 316).

From the cover and the initial splash page, *Icon* #13 directly confronts Luke Cage's publication history up to that point. The issue opens with Buck Wild jumping through a window as bullets buzz past him. He thinks to himself, as he spouts Cagesque phrases, "There's this old played-out record that I can't get outta my head" (p. 1). That "played-out record" connects Buck Wild to Cage's history. One attacker shoots Buck Wild point-blank, stunning him. The next panel shows a close-up of Buck Wild holding a hand to his eye. Still pondering the "played-out record," he thinks, "And I can't get it outta my head. The music or the pictures" (p. 2). The next panel shows a tear descending from Buck Wild's right eye, the one that took the bullet. Teeth clenched, eyes ablaze, he continues his thoughts, this time about Blaxploitation stereotypes: "Pimps in platform shoes. Big black studs. Fat, sloppy, rag-headed mammies" (p. 2).

While these panels show Buck Wild enduring physical harm, the perspective and narration also ask readers to think about the psychological aspects of his narration. The stereotypes he mentions continue to impact him, mentally, and by grabbing his head as he mentions that he cannot get the song out of his head, the panel highlights the ways that he has internalized them. The close-up panel of his face presents an image of a man ready to fight back against the "played-out record." The sequence concludes with Buck Wild telling the shooter, "Things is sho nuff about ta get UGLY!" (p. 3). Buck Wild's statement, and the panels themselves, contain visual references to the panels in *Power Man and Iron Fist* #122, and his words reference the title of #123, *Getting Ugly*. Through these references, Bright and McDuffie link Buck Wild directly to the ways that Priest and Bright interrogated Cage's history. The key difference, though, is that instead of ending with a panel that positions the reader as the recipient of the gunshot, the sequence begins with that positioning, then transitions to Buck Wild's reaction to that moment. The panel with the tear in his eye echoes the panel from *Power Man and Iron Fist* #122, where Chiantang's disguised face looks angry and menacing. Anger appears in Buck Wild's face, but the tear streaming down his cheek,

**Figure 5.5** *Power Man and Iron Fist* #122 (1986).

**Figure 5.6** *Icon* #13 (1994).

coupled with his internal dialogue, signifies the psychological effects of the representational history he exists within.

Again, Black Kirby highlights the psychological impact of the social construction of race through caricatures in pieces such as "Luke Cage: Man Thang," a work that merges Cage with Man-Thing, pointing to medical experimentation on Black individuals as well as the social fictions of race that continue to flow throughout society. Notably, they choose Mos Def's 2006 song "Fake Bonanza" to counter "the lie that we are different because of our skin, eyes, and hair" (Robinson & Jennings, 2019, p. 212). Black Kirby points out, "Race is a type of science fiction" and that "Black speculative fiction is a powerful technology to bend those cages and maybe even break them" (p. 212). Priest, Bright, and McDuffie use speculative fiction to break the cage of internalized racism that impacts Cage and Buck Wild, and "Fake Bonanza" echoes the characters' internalized conflicts as they struggle to reconcile their identity with preconceived notions that society uses to shackle them. In the outro to "Fake Bonanza," Mos Def raps that he woke up in the morning with his mind on his "state of freedom," but he "had the baddest feeling." The contradiction of feeling free while also having a bad feeling about what lies ahead plays upon the tensions of the speaker's view of themselves compared with society's view of them. Mos Def ends the song by rapping, "Said, woke up this morning and my mind stayed on freedom/It makes no difference what people say." Instead of worrying if others view him as a "boogieman" or a threat, the speaker knows who they are, and the perceptions that white supremacy places upon them do not matter. Likewise, Cage and Buck Wild, through conflicts within themselves, come to the same point, knowing themselves apart from the noise and perceptions of others.

Cage's history remains inconsistent. Creators such as Priest, Bright, and McDuffie challenged and remixed Cage's initial publication history, while others, such as Brian Azzarello and Genndy Tartakovsky, fell back on stereotypes, dragging Cage backwards. However, others, such as David Walker, Sanford Greene, Mike Benson, and Adam Glass pulled in the other direction, using their time writing Cage to challenge racial disparities in medicine and to link Cage to badman figures such as Stagolee, bringing Cage into a longer historical arc. Due to the nature of comics' production, what one artist does, another changes. Comics continually move forward, drawing partly from the past but always reinventing and remixing. Priest, Bright, McDuffie, and Black Kirby all work within this context, taking the past and remixing it for the present and future, much like hip-hop taking the past and remixing it through song. In this manner, they pay homage to what came before while also looking ahead to the future.

## NOTES

1. Throughout this chapter, I will use Christopher Priest in reference to Jim Owsley. Also, Priest was the first Black writer to write characters such as Black Panther, which he took over in 1998, thirty-two years after the character's debut.

2. Jason Oakes Lee and I detail Slim's influence on hip-hop in "For Those in the 'Ghetto Torture Chambers': Iceberg Slim, Pulp Authenticity, and the Noir Tradition in Hip-hop" in the *Oxford Handbook of Hip-hop Music*.

3. Since Black Kirby uses Mos Def's music for the "illabus," I will focus primarily on some of the songs that they incorporate into *Uncaged: Hero for Higher*.

4. Notably, Cage's partner, Iron Fist (Danny Rand), is absent from "Getting Ugly." The issue focuses solely on Cage, Wilson, and King—three Black men—pursuing Blake together and Cage confronting Blake on his own at the end of the issue. This fact makes Cage's comments important in relation to his publication history and the publication histories of other Black characters in the Marvel Universe up to that point.

5. While I focus on Buck Wild's initial appearance in this chapter, it is worth looking at his role as Icon and his funeral in issue #30. For this, read Rebecca Wanzo's "It's a Hero? Black Comics and Satirizing Subjection" (2015) as well as my posts "Buck Wild, the New Icon" and "The Death of Buck Wild" on my blog *Interminable Rambling*.

## REFERENCES

Bealer, T. L. (2017). The man called Lucas: Luke Cage, mass incarceration, and the stigma of Black criminality. *Inks: The Journal of the Comics Study Society*, 1(2), 165–85.

Davis, B. (2015). Bare chests, silver tiaras, and removable afros: The visual design of Black comic book superheroes. In F. Gateward & J. I. Jennings (Eds.), *The blacker the ink: Constructions of Black identity in comics and sequential art* (pp. 193–212). Rutgers University Press.

Englehart, S. (2015). *Marvel masterworks presents Luke Cage, hero for hire, volume 1*. Marvel Comics.

Goodwin, A. & Tuska, G. (1972). Out of hell—a hero. *Luke Cage, hero for hire*. (1). Marvel Comics.

Howard, S. C., & Jackson, R. L. (2013). Introduction. In S. C. Howard & R. L. Jackson II (Eds.), *Black comics: Politics or race and representation* (pp. 1–8). Bloomsbury Academic.

Jennings, J. I. (2013). Connections. In J. I. Jennings & S. Robinson (Eds.), *Black Kirby: In search of the Motherboxx Connection* (p. 9). Cedar Grove Books.

McDuffie, D. (2016). Afterward. In *Marvel masterworks presents: The Black Panther*. Marvel Comics. pp. 325–26.

McDuffie, D., & Bright, M. D. (1994). It's always Christmas. *Icon* (13). DC Comics.

Morales, R. (2012). Fantastic Blackness with John Jennings. In D. Washington (Ed.), *John Jennings: Conversations* (pp. 3–20). University Press of Mississippi.

Mos Def. (2004). The Boogie Man Song [Song]. On *The new danger* [Album]. Geffen Records.

Mos Def. (2006). Fake Bonanza [Song]. On *Preservation* [Album]. Geffen.

Mos Def. (1999). Mr. N***a [Song]. On *Black on both sides* [Album]. Rawkus.

Munby, J. (2011). *Under a bad sign: Criminal self-representation in African American popular culture.* University of Chicago Press.

Navas, E. (2014). *Remix theory: The aesthetics of sampling.* Ambra Verlag.

Nishikawa, K. (2018). *Street players: Black pulp fiction and the making of a literary underground.* University of Chicago Press.

Owsley, J. & Bright, M. D. (1986). What's Eating Misty . . . ? *Power Man and Iron Fist.* (122). Marvel Comics.

Owsley, J. & Bright, M. D. (1986). Getting Ugly. *Power Man and Iron Fist.* (123). Marvel Comics.

Priest, C. (2000, December). *Ducks!!* Digital Priest. http://digitalpriest.com/legacy/comics/powerfist.html.

Robinson, S. A., & Jennings, J.I. (2021). Teaching Black masculinity through the uncanny Black Kirby. *Journal of Curriculum and Pedagogy, 18*(2), 208–29.

Slim, I. (1967). *Pimp: The story of my life.* Holloway House.

Svitavsky, W. L. (2013). Race, superheroes, and identity: Did you know he was Black?" In J. Chambliss (Ed.), *Ages of heroes, eras of man: Superheroes and the American experience* (pp. 153–62). Bloomsbury Academic.

Teutsch, M., & Oakes, J. L. (2020). For those in the "Ghetto Torture Chambers": Iceberg Slim, pulp authenticity, and the noir tradition in hip-hop." In J. D. Burton & J. L. Oakes (Eds.), *Oxford handbook of hip-hop music.* https://doi.org/10.1093/oxfordhb/9780190281090.013.38

Wanzo, R. (2015). It's a Hero? Black comics and satirizing subjection. In F. Gateward & J. I. Jennings (Eds.), *The Blacker the Ink: Constructions of Black identity in comics and sequential art* (pp. 314–32). Rutgers University Press.

CHAPTER 6

# DYNAMIC DUO

Marvel Comics and Hip-Hop Culture's Innovations in Storytelling

STEPHEN J. TYSON JR.

Hip-hop and comic books share a well-documented connection spanning over fifty years. A recent example is Marvel's incorporation of hip-hop into its comic book universe by creating "variant" covers for traditional comics, which began in 2015. On these alternate covers, Marvel superheroes and villains are reimagined as remixes of famous hip-hop album covers. However, the interconnected history of hip-hop culture and comic books dates back much earlier.

Some of the most recognizable examples come from early rap artists and graffiti writers referencing comic book characters in their music and incorporating many of the same characters into their work on walls, billboards, trains, and other prominent locations, respectively. Rappers have often drawn inspiration from superheroes and comic books for their names and personas, such as Grandmaster Flash & the Furious Five, the Treacherous Three, MF DOOM, Ghostface Killah's alter ego "Tony Starks," and Method Man's alter ego "John/Johnny Blaze." Comic book artists also began embracing the emergence of hip-hop culture as early as the 1980s.

In 1983, when Marvel Comics illustrator Bob Camp independently designed the album artwork for Afrika Bambaataa and the Soul Sonic Force's "Renegades of Funk," it was an iconic moment for the culture (De Paor-Evans, 2018). But it took another decade for comic book publishers to recognize hip-hop and collaborate more regularly. Marvel Comics, arguably the most popular comic book publisher in history, was the first major publisher to empower numerous hip-hop artists to fulfill their comic book dreams. The most significant being collaborations that enabled hip-hop artists to create their own comic book series or single-issue specials with the publication. This has allowed many artists to develop their own fictional universes or even achieve childhood dreams of teaming up with legendary superheroes.

Since the early 1990s, hip-hop artists like Kid 'N Play, Eminem, Fat Joe, Twista, Lil' Kim, T.I., Fabolous, Trick Daddy, Onyx, and the Black Eyed Peas have all been featured as comic book characters in various partnerships with Marvel Comics. While some of these publications were quite popular, and others came and went with minimal attention, most of these traditional collaborations did not expand beyond the pages of the comic books themselves. However, in 1994 and 2017, Marvel took risks to create two innovative comic book experiences through respective collaborations with hip-hop artists KRS-One and will.i.am.

In these two collaborations, their respective creative teams used technology to enhance the reader's comic book reading experience. They set up the opportunity to change how future fans of the art form experience comic books. In this chapter, we will explore a timeline of Marvel Comics' endeavors into hip-hop culture and take a deeper look at how hip-hop artists have helped to push the boundaries of creativity in storytelling, helping to pioneer the innovation and inclusion of new technology into the comic book reading experience.

## *KID 'N PLAY* GET IT STARTED

The earliest documented collaboration between Marvel Comics and hip-hop culture was in 1992, with the rap group Kid 'N Play (Kearns et al., 2015). Kid 'N Play are rappers and dancers from New York, NY, who had an incredible hip-hop career kick-started by the success of their first two albums. They built a significant following through several hit songs, but they were most well-known for their choreography and signature dance moves. Eventually, Kid 'N Play leveraged the success of their music career into acting.

In the 1990s, they starred in the hit movie series *House Party 1, 2, and 3* (1990, 1991, and 1994, respectively) and the cult-classic *Class Act* (1992). The success of the first two *House Party* films led to the group securing a deal for a self-titled Saturday morning children's cartoon television show. Their cartoon led to the commissioning of the Marvel Comics series *Kid 'N Play* (Cronin, 2013). This nine-issue collaboration marked the first time a major publication collaborated with hip-hop culture to produce a comic book.

Written by Dwight Coye and illustrated by Chuck Frazier, *Kid 'N Play* follows the duo's adventures as they navigate seemingly random circumstances in each issue. The story seems to be set in the same universe as the *Kid 'N Play* cartoon, which was based on the characters in the movie *House Party*, but not all the elements were the same (Coye, 1992a). What made the *Kid 'N Play* comic book feel relatable to me and many other kids at the time was its authenticity to the fictional world of the characters in the *House Party* movies. Coye and Frazier intentionally immersed hip-hop culture into the comic's storytelling and illustrations. It highlights nineties era hip-hop fashion, slang, and cultural expressions in a stylized manner that avoids cultural misappropriation. The attention to detail in the characterizations of Kid 'N Play resonated with young hip-hop fans like me and helped showcase the culture to a broader audience.

Collaborating with Marvel Comics provided Kid 'N Play with an opportunity to tap into the immense popularity of the characters from their movie and expand their already massive brand. The ninth and final issue in the series features Play encountering various well-known Marvel characters as he travels through a dream. In this dream, he meets the Hulk, the X-Men, the Punisher, Ghost Rider, She-Hulk, Captain America, Iron Man, and the Thing, among others. Additionally, this issue includes one of the earliest appearances of the notorious Spider-Man villain Venom (Coye, 1992b).

The *Kid 'N Play* comic book series was a creative vision realized by Kid 'N Play, Dwight Coye, and Chuck Frazier. It exemplified the importance and value of cross-cultural collaboration in entertainment publications, paving the way for a new era in comic book storytelling that was finally embracing hip-hop. Though their nine-issue run was brief, their influence was longstanding. Kid 'N Play's partnership with Marvel Comics inspired future Marvel executives to expand the boundaries of creativity and cultural expression within the company. The series established the conceptual foundation for Marvel Music, an initiative by Marvel Comics to create a comic book production line and record label for collaborations with musicians across various genres (Grossman, 2015). Two years later, KRS-One became the first rapper to sign a deal with Marvel Music when he cocreated *Break the Chain* in 1994. This collaboration also introduced technology into the hip-hop comic book experience.

**Figure 6.1** *Kid 'N Play* #9, photo by Stephen Tyson Jr. (Coye, 1992b).

## BREAKING GROUND WITH *BREAK THE CHAIN*

In 1994, hip-hop comic books were taken to a new level through the establishment of Marvel Music and its collaboration with rapper KRS-One. He, artist Kyle Baker, and Marshall Chess, founder of Chess Records, created an audio-supported comic book experience for young audiences entitled *Break the Chain*.

The story is a social analysis of Black youth culture in the early 1990s, which tries to promote education and knowledge of self while encouraging a broader appreciation for learning Black history through hip-hop (One, 2017). The project is a thirty-two-page "psychosonic comic," as described by the side panel of the read-along cassette, which also includes three songs by the comic's main character Big Joe Krash (portrayed by KRS-One). Krash attempts to teach his younger sister and her friends the value of going to school and seeking an education. He also reminds her friend's grandmother of the value of appreciating younger generations and how they choose to enjoy themselves through hip-hop.

The story begins with Big Joe Krash looking for his younger sister, Minasha, who has been skipping school. When she and her friends dismiss him, he admonishes them for listening to his music through headphones rather than a boom box. He then plays the first accompanying song of the project, "Who Am I" (Parker et al., 1994). She and her friends love his music, but he's more focused on making sure they have a desire to learn their history as Black people in America. When they visit her friend Malcolm's grandmother, they want to keep hearing his music in her living room and play the project's lead single, "Break the Chain," through a boom box. At first, the grandmother hates how loud the music is and refuses to pay attention to the lyrics until Krash performs his third song, "So Much Greater." This song convinces her that hip-hop music can be uplifting and enjoyable while inspiring Minasha and her friends to take greater value in attending school.

*Break the Chain* is complete with KRS-One's signature message of self-empowerment. Although Marvel Music provided the platform for this project, KRS-One, Kyle Baker, and Marshall Chess were responsible for the project's writing, production, and direction. Marshall Chess, who created the concept of *Break the Chain*, wanted to develop a hip-hop-themed educational comic book. The most obvious person for him to reach out to would be KRS-One, and he did precisely that (Baker, 1994).

KRS-One is one of the most prominent hip-hop artists of the 1980s. He immersed himself in the culture at an early age and eventually mastered the art of MCing. Throughout his career, he has continually encouraged and promoted the necessity of critical thinking in hip-hop music. This is why KRS-One is one of the most respected MCs in the culture. He is known for his socially conscious music and his passion for advancing hip-hop through educating people worldwide about its history and origins. Always an advocate for social justice and political change, his reputation of being an educator and entertainer is what he likes to call being an edutainer. *Break The Chain* became another opportunity for him, as the character Big Joe Krash, to continue educating and entertaining by using the story's narrative to challenge readers to reflect and analyze social issues in new ways.

At its core, *Break the Chain* addresses issues still affecting young Black Americans today and urges intergenerational reconciliation between youth and adults. In addition to its entertainment value, the comic was intended to inspire meaningful conversations among young readers, help them learn and appreciate history through each song's lyrics, and help them see themselves as so much greater than how society may represent them. It also challenges adults and elders to listen to young people and learn from their experiences (Baker, 1994).

*Break The Chain* was primarily appreciated by fans of KRS-One, like myself. The comic book had a provocative message in its storytelling and was illustrated with dynamic colors and textures to make kid-friendly yet sophisticated artwork. Although the only commercially released single, "Break the Chain," did not make it onto the *Billboard* charts, it did lead to the creation of the first fully animated hip-hop music video (Baker, 1994). The music video for "Break the Chain" premiered on *Yo! MTV Raps* and features Kyle Baker's illustrations as the basis of the animation.

Baker's artistry is one of the most influential aspects of *Break the Chain*. His colorful, vibrant, textured illustrations capture the size and bombastic energy of the Big Joe Krash character. They convey the meaning and impact of KRS-One's lyrics and the vibrancy of the music as you listen to the audio cassette. *Break the Chain* was an essential opportunity for Baker to showcase how his artistic talents can help carry the reader through the story's narrative (Parker et al., 2012).

Whenever you are expected to turn the page, you hear Big Joe Krash's voice exclaim "WORD!" between the dialogue. However, because it is an audiobook, some of the text and dialogue are also the song lyrics. This means the panels of the comic book had to be constructed precisely so the words on the page match the pace of each song, and the "WORD!" indication to turn each page was also accurately placed within the songs as ad-libs. Kyle

Figure 6.2 *Break the Chain* #1, photo by Stephen Tyson Jr. (Parker et al., 1994).

Baker's attention to detail and visual storytelling immerses readers into the world of *Break the Chain*, and combined with the music and narrative on the audio cassette, it only enhances the experience.

*Break the Chain* remains an important work today because it combines the worlds of hip-hop and comic books with the intention of education and social uplift. Marshall Chess is credited with the idea for this project. However, KRS-One and Kyle Baker's creative collaboration with the team at Marvel Comics led to an artistic, thought-provoking experience that can resonate with audiences across generations.

After the release of *Break the Chain*, hip-hop's collaboration with comic books also became less innovative in their use of music, technology, and voice acting. It became less intentional in promoting messages of social awareness and cultural upliftment. KRS-One's status as one of the most influential figures in hip-hop will continue to be relevant, as you will read later, because the precedent set by *Break the Chain* to educate and entertain will be seen through his involvement in a future Marvel collaboration.

However, as the late 1990s and early 2000s approached, hip-hop culture became increasingly influenced by the broader entertainment industry. It started to move away from its founding principles of peace, unity, love, and having fun, with many of the positive messages once highlighted in comic books no longer being published. New storylines emerged in collaborations between Marvel Comics and hip-hop artists.

## TRYING SOMETHING NEW

In an effort to expand its reach into hip-hop culture and connect with new audiences, Marvel Comics took advantage of the opportunity to collaborate with the Queens, NY, rap group Onyx. Veering away from the feel-good energy of Kid 'N Play and the positive messages of KRS-One, Marvel tapped into Onyx's aggressive aesthetic and rebellious persona. The group signed a deal with Marvel Music in 1995 to bring their idea for a science-fiction comic to life.

*Fight* is set in a fictional postapocalyptic New York City in 1999. Onyx has formed an underground rebellion called Bal Hedz, who use the controlled anger of their music to destroy invader aliens named the No-Madz. Writer Karl Bollers collaborated with Onyx to craft the forty-eight-page adventure, which was illustrated by artist Larry Lee in a cyberpunk style intended to fit the postapocalyptic theme of the story (Unknown, 2019).

The collaboration between Onyx and Marvel was innovative in its combination of sci-fi, music, and comics in the storyline. In addition to the comic, Onyx recorded a promotional single, also titled "Fight," to support the comic book's release (Montana, 2017). By continuing to bridge the gap between comic book fans and hip-hop audiences, Marvel demonstrated the ability to take risks to increase creative collaboration. But when those risks are taken at the expense of sacrificing artistic integrity for commercial marketability, it can lead to less innovative comic book experiences. This was seen in some of Marvel's collaborations in the early 2000s, where the marketing of artists and products took center stage.

## MARKETING MAKES ITS WAY IN

*The Heist* was a 2005 comic from Marvel Comics that was not published under the Marvel Music brand but was a formal partnership between the comic book company and Atlantic Records. *The Heist* showcased a collaborative effort among hip-hop artists, including Fat Joe, Lil' Kim, Twista, Trina, Trick Daddy, Fabolous, and T.I., who were depicted as fictional, heroic versions of themselves.

The comic book follows this crew, the Joint Chiefs, as they attempt to recover a character named the Check Writer's stolen diamond. Each rapper has unique skills necessary to defeat an army of enemies sent by a villain named Clone (Watkins, 2005). The diamond the group was searching for was ultimately the rapper Trina. What sets *The Heist* apart from previous comic book publications was its distribution in connection with the direct sales of the artists' albums and the commercial marketing placed within it. The creators of *The Heist* filled the comic with appropriate depictions of hip-hop fashion at the time, creating a visually entertaining and stylistically authentic experience for readers.

While *The Heist* featured contributions from some of the biggest names in hip-hop, the fact that it was released with a limited distribution model might have been a misstep in helping to market the comic book effectively. The only way to obtain a copy was to purchase an album by any member of the Joint Chiefs, located at exclusive stores during the limited promotional campaign. The comic also featured extensive product placement within it, such as the logo for Rockstar Games' *Midnight Club 3 Dub Edition* video game featured on the windshield and headrest of each team member's vehicle. The Rockstar Games logo was also included on every license plate (Jones, 2021).

The publication of *The Heist* marked a significant moment in the history of hip-hop and comics. By intentionally marketing toward two distinct cultural movements on the rise, hip-hop and video games, Marvel Comics demonstrated its commitment to innovation and diversity while appealing to new audiences who seek entertainment over education.

## EMINEM MEETS THE PUNISHER

In 2009, *Eminem/The Punisher* was released as a special one-issue comic book published in collaboration with XXL Magazine that brought together rap superstar Eminem and the Marvel antihero, The Punisher. Written by Fred Van Lente, with art from Salvador Larroca and colors by Frank

D'Armata, the comic adventure combines the violent world of The Punisher with the raw, angry energy of Eminem's persona.

It opens with Frank Castle, also known as The Punisher, in Detroit, tracking down a notorious drug dealer named Barracuda. Barracuda hides out at a concert where Eminem is performing, and as the story unfolds, Eminem is thrust into the middle of the action. He and The Punisher are captured by Barracuda and are forced to put aside their differences to team up to defeat him.

One of the strongest aspects of *Eminem/The Punisher* is the integration of Eminem's music and Slim Shady-like persona into the narrative. Throughout the comic book, Eminem's lyrics from his song "Kill You" are woven into the dialogue, adding a sort of "easter egg" moment for fans of his music. However, these moments could become heavy-handed in the product placement. Like when Eminem gets thrown onto a patch of ice in the middle of the ocean, gets up, and walks until he finds a man who happens to be his biggest fan, ice fishing while listening to *Relapse* on his phone (McGuire, 2019).

One of the best aspects of the comic book is the artwork by renowned Spanish comic book artist Salvador Larocca. His style and D'Armata's coloring complement The Punisher's dark, violent world. Van Lente's writing captures Eminem's dry humor while highlighting the absurdity of his character's existence in the storyline in the first place. Although *Eminem/The Punisher* was intended to be well-received by their respective fanbases, the comic book did not lead to any future collaborations between Eminem and Marvel Comics. However, it built upon the type of storytelling and narrative established by earlier collaborations like *The Heist* while lessening the amount of in-your-face marketing and product placement.

## *MASTERS OF THE SUN*

In 2017, technological innovations began to reemerge in the collaboration between hip-hop artists and Marvel Comics when will.i.am of the rap group Black Eyed Peas collaborated with writer Benjamin Jackendoff and artist Damion Scott to create *Masters of the Sun*.

*Masters of the Sun* is an Afrofuturistic sci-fi tale about a hip-hop group known as the Blast Masters, who are attempting to protect Earth from an ancient alien god named Apep who is turning drug dealers and gangsters into a zombie army. The Blast Masters are led by Zulu-X, a hip-hop artist who possesses extraordinary powers that allow him to combat the army. Alongside his teammates, Zulu-X uncovers the history behind Apep's destructive behavior, stops the zombie invasion, and saves the city (Williams, 2018).

*Masters of the Sun* is the first hip-hop comic book to include both augmented reality (AR) and virtual reality (VR) technology in its storytelling. With AR and VR technology, readers can see 3D-animated illustrations that connect to the comic book. AR comics overlay digital content onto the physical pages of a comic book using a smartphone or tablet, allowing readers to interact with characters and objects in real-time (Pierrisnard, 2024). The use of AR in Marvel Comics was announced in 2012 with the release of the Marvel Unlimited app for smartphones (Unknown, 2014). To use the AR function, specially marked panels of any comic book could be scanned in through Marvel Unlimited to unlock exclusive content for readers.

With AR, fans of comic books can access unique animations, behind-the-scenes footage, commentary, and interactive games. AR added a new dimension to comic book reading, allowing everyone to dive deeper into their favorite stories and connections with iconic characters in new and exciting ways. In addition to AR, *Masters of the Sun* was supported by groundbreaking VR technology at the time. VR allows readers to go beyond simply seeing an image pop up on their smartphone, as with AR, and fully immerse themselves in a 360-degree computer-animated adaptation of the comic book. The VR version of *Masters of the Sun* consists of twelve episodes lasting ninety minutes, bringing readers into a virtual environment where they can interact with characters and engage with the story's narrative in a more sophisticated manner than the AR version (Williams, 2018).

*Masters of the Sun* falls in the direct lineage of prior Marvel collaborations. Its blend of hip-hop culture, art, and storytelling as a vehicle for learning about and gaining an appreciation for Black history is similar to KRS-One's effort to do so back in 1994 with *Break the Chain*. This time, instead of being set in a twentieth-century urban city, it is presented through an Afrofuturistic sci-fi storytelling narrative that can be experienced through a technology that was only dreamed of nearly twenty-five years prior.

The *Masters of the Sun* AR and VR experience also features a notable cast of voice actors, including Marvel Comics creative leader Stan Lee. Hip-hop legends Rakim and KRS-One portray the main characters' voices, Master Sun and Zulu-X, respectively. Other prominent figures in hip-hop who voice characters in *Masters of the Sun* include Common, Slick Rick, Raekwon, Redman, Pete Rock, Snoop Dogg, Ice-T, Flavor Flav, and Queen Latifah (Manalo, 2017).

The comic book also has a companion album from the Black Eyed Peas, released in 2017, which bears the same title. The album comes across like a

**Figure 6.3** *Masters of the Sun* vol. 1, photo by Stephen Tyson Jr. (will.i.am & Jackendoff, 2017).

soundtrack that was inspired by the graphic novel, with songs like "RING THE ALARM (Pts. 1, 2, and 3)" and "CONSTANT (Pts. 1 and 2)" that feel like they were created to accompany the action-packed scenes and socially conscious message found within the story. For example, "RING THE ALARM (Pts. 1, 2, and 3)" begins with a horn sample reminiscent of a 1970s superhero cartoon theme and "CONSTANT (Pts. 1 and 2)" starts with a traditional laid-back 1990s hip-hop vibe, which switches into futuristic electro-funk halfway through the song.

Outside of music, will.i.am has explored an interest in technology through various entrepreneurial and philanthropic ventures. Over the past decade, he has launched several tech companies and has been involved in multiple charitable organizations that empower young people through STEAM (science, technology, engineering, arts, and mathematics) education programs (Howarth, 2015; Unknown, 2022).

The setting, characters, and action of *Masters of the Sun* are brought to life by illustrator Damion Scott and colorist Sigmund Torre (will.i.am & Jackendoff, 2017). The artwork takes inspiration from classic hip-hop albums, Egyptology, video games, and regional Los Angeles culture. Scott and Torre's art captures the reader's attention, and the AR and VR capabilities bring their artwork to life in 3D, making the reader feel like fiction and reality are blending into one.

*Masters of the Sun* received significant hype during its initial press run, and fans seemed to appreciate the depth of the story's concept and the experiences offered by the immersive AR and VR technology. The artwork and technology within the comic book and the AR experience are so terrific that they play a crucial role in overshadowing some of the weaker aspects of the comic, such as the dialogue. For instance, when a character saves Zulu-X's life, he is rewarded with the promise that Zulu-X will listen to his mixtape. Not an equal exchange in my opinion.

Beyond its entertainment value, *Masters of the Sun* celebrates hip-hop culture and its Afrocentric roots. It intentionally includes names, themes, and characterizations based on African and ancient Egyptian cultures and pays homage to the pioneers of hip-hop. This project stands on the shoulders of previous efforts like *Break the Chain*.

## TRANSFERRING THE ESSENCE OF A COMIC BOOK INTO THE DIGITAL AGE

One of the most significant innovations in the comic book industry over the last decade has been digital storytelling. While many of us think of TikTok, Instagram, and other social media platforms for digital storytelling, there is still a market for supporting print media that has made its way into the digital landscape. The most practical benefits are that you can take hundreds of comics on the go with minimal effort, access rare and out-of-print issues, and reread any issue as many times as you want without inevitably damaging the pages or cover.

More comic book fans than ever own smartphones, VR headsets, and tablets, providing us with more opportunities than ever to access comic books through digital means. Today, the Marvel Unlimited AR app is a monthly subscription that gives comic book fans the technology to access over 30,000 digital comics published throughout the last eighty years (Unknown, 2024b). While this innovation may be helpful for those readers who want to experience a specific comic book for many years without fear of destroying it, it also means digital comics have no resale value. As a result, the digital model has yet to be readily accepted by many comic book enthusiasts who still find joy in the traditional model of collecting, preserving, and reselling physical comic books (Harth, 2023).

Our society's need to seek out the most convenient method of enjoying something has led to relying on technology in almost every aspect of our lives, especially when it comes to reading. Today, we consume more digital text and images than ever on devices like tablets and smartphones rather than through physical media such as newspapers and magazines. In a soft poll of the university students I teach, the vast majority consume their information through social media. This has necessitated publishers like Marvel to figure out how to translate the essence of what makes a comic book unique: its storytelling, artwork, colors, and text, onto a digital platform.

In recent years, Marvel has relied on fans' desire for new ways of consuming stories, such as AR and VR, to keep fans' attention. But as innovations in AR and VR continue to develop, comic book creators will need to adapt their storytelling techniques and artistic styles to take advantage of what new technology is created. This provides an opportunity for the creators and consumers of comic books to perpetually be open to things like new storytelling formats, experimenting with new layouts and text styles. This gives way to potentially building new collaborative partnerships with creators and innovators inside and outside the comic book world.

The future of comic books is full of new possibilities, as is the future of hip-hop, through focusing on the inclusion and advancement of technology. Even though digital devices have increased our access to comic books, they have also raised concerns about the impact digitization has on the professional sustainability of comic book creators who are still creating in the physical medium. Using AR and VR may be part of the future of physical comics. Still, the more we rely on digital subscription models like Marvel Unlimited to sustain the industry, the fewer physical copies will need to be published (Harth, 2023).

If comic book creators stay up with all the new technology that seemingly comes out daily and can embrace these innovations, they have the opportunity to push into new territory for storytelling to engage and sustain readers beyond traditional print media. The industry must also keep up with any threats to artistic integrity, like digital piracy, copyright infringement, and the emergence of artificial intelligence programs.

Comic books have the potential to thrive in the digital environment through future collaborations with hip-hop innovators like will.i.am, who can continue innovating the comic book experience for new readers in future generations. *Masters of the Sun* is the most complete example of the comic book industry's willingness to embrace collaboration and creativity to be innovative and reach new audiences through collaborating with hip-hop culture. *Masters of the Sun* would not exist without the various predecessors along the way that were discussed in this article, starting with *Kid 'N Play*, then being taken to a new level through an interactive experience with a social message in *Break the Chain*, and expanding through the creative storytelling of comics like *Fight*, *The Heist*, and *Eminem/The Punisher*.

*Break the Chain* and *Masters of the Sun* used multimedia to enhance the comic book reading experience. What sets these two projects apart from others is their consideration of how technology can deeply immerse readers into the story, seeking not only to sell comic books but also to educate while entertaining audiences. As hip-hop continues to evolve and influence various aspects of global culture, its role in comic books will continue to push new boundaries for years to come and create new opportunities for future creators to build upon their work.

## REFERENCES

Baker, K. (1994, August). *That's edutainment: Kyle Baker and KRS-One talk hip-hop comics*. VIBE.

Bollers, K. (Ed.). (1995). *Onyx: Fight vol. 1*. Marvel Comics.

Coye, D. (1992a). *Kid 'N Play: Kid 'N Play in Kung Fools*. Nicieza, F. (Ed.). Marvel Comics.

Coye, D. (1992b). *Kid 'N Play: Dream A Dream*. Nicieza, F. (Ed.). Marvel Comics.

Cronin, B. (2013, March 11). *I love ya but you're strange—How did it take until 1992 for Kid 'n' Play to have their own comic book?* CBR. https://www.cbr.com/i-love-ya-but-youre-strange-how-did-it-take-until-1992-for-kid-n-play-to-have-their-own-comic-book/

De Paor-Evans, A. (2018). The futurism of hip hop: space, electro and science fiction in rap. *Open Cultural Studies*, 2(1), 122–35. https://doi.org/10.1515/culture-2018-0012

Grossman, D. (2015). Marvel music's strange, brief, and totally doomed rock-comics revolution. *SPIN*. https://www.spin.com/2014/03/marvel-music-rock-comics-revolution-1994-billy-ray-cyrus-onyx/

Harth, D. (2023, August 7). *Are digital comics or print comics better?* CBR. https://www.cbr.com/whats-better-digital-comics-or-print-comics/

Howarth, D. (2015, March 6). *will.i.am launches Ekocycle products made from waste*. Dezeen. https://www.dezeen.com/2015/03/06/will-i-am-coca-cola-ekocycle-products-sustainable-materials-harrods/

Jones, K. (2021). *Marvel x Atlantic "The Heist" comic book starring Lil' Kim, Trina, Fat Joe, Twista, Trick Daddy, T.I., and Fabolous. (2004).* [Post]. X (formerly Twitter). https://x.com/LilKimMedia/status/1468944241934147591

Kearns, S., Bernstein, E., Caraan, S., Eng, E., Huynh, D., Montes, P., Davis, J., Tan, S., Witte, R., & Yeung, G. (2015, July 30). *A look into Marvel Comics' collaborations with hip-hop*. Hypebeast. https://hypebeast.com/2015/7/a-look-into-marvel-comics-collaborations-with-hip-hop

Manalo, G. (Ed.). (2017, November 24). *Black Eyed Peas' comic "Masters of the Sun" gets AR/VR treatment* [Video]. YouTube. https://www.youtube.com/watch?v=OB70AtsoGR4

McGuire, L. (2019, December 20). *Eminem once tried to kill the Punisher in Marvel Comics*. ScreenRant. https://screenrant.com/eminem-punisher-insane-comic-crossover-marvel/

Montana, F. (2017, October 15). *Onyx—Fight (unreleased) (1995)* [Song]. SoundCloud. https://soundcloud.com/felixmontana/onyx-fight-unreleased-1995

One, D. S. (2017, May 31). *KRS-One aka Big Joe Krash "Break the Chain" (1994)*. Hip-hop nostalgia. https://www.hiphopnostalgia.com/2017/03/krs-one-as-big-joe-krash-break-chain.html

Parker, K., Baker, K., & Chess, M. (2012, July 28). *Big Joe Krash (KRS-One)—"Break the Chain" 1994 (HQ)* [Video]. YouTube. https://www.youtube.com/watch?v=313sTto2SyE

Parker, K., Baker, K., & Chess, M. (1994). *Break the chain*. Marvel Comics.

Pierrisnard, P. (2024, February 26). *The future of comics: Digital comics, augmented reality, and beyond*. Toons Mag. https://www.toonsmag.com/the-future-of-comics-digital-comics/

Unknown (2014, April 23). *Experience the new Marvel AR app*. Marvel. https://www.marvel.com/articles/comics/experience-the-new-marvel-ar-app

Unknown. (2019, September 5). *Onyx: Fight (Marvel music) comic book—VF/Good (1995)*. Adventures Into Mystery Collectibles. https://www.aimcollectibles.com/2019/09/onyx-fight-marvel-music-comic-book.html

Unknown. (2022). *i.am STEAM*. i.am.angel foundation. https://www.iamangelfoundation.org/programs/i-am-steam/

Unknown. (2024a). *The temple of hip-hop*. Temple of Hip-Hop. https://www.thetempleofhiphop.org/

Unknown. (2024b). *Marvel Unlimited: Over 30,000 comics. One all-new app!* Marvel Unlimited. https://www.marvel.com/unlimited

Watkins, G. (2005, June 2). *Atlantic rappers land specialty comic with Marvel*. AllHipHop. https://allhiphop.com/news/atlantic-rappers-land-specialty-comic-with-marvel/

will.i.am, Jackendoff, B. (2017). *Black Eyed Peas present "Masters of the Sun."* Marvel Comics.

Williams, G. (2018, February 5). *Marvel & will.i.am brings Rakim & KRS One to VR, "Masters of the Sun"* [Video]. YouTube. https://www.youtube.com/watch?v=mswJHDOKymM

CHAPTER 7

# WHEN WORLDS COLLIDE

Hip-Hop Music and Superhero Movies

LAITH ZURAIKAT

## INTRODUCTION

On March 10, 2018, Marvel Studios' *Black Panther* crossed the $1 billion global box office mark after just twenty-six days in theaters (Rubin, 2018). That same week, eight of the top ten songs on the Billboard Hot 100 chart were either by, or featured a hip-hop artist, including the number ten song, *All the Stars* by SZA featuring Kendrick Lamar, the lead single from the *Black Panther Soundtrack* (Billboard, 2018). Within the next year, both the film and its soundtrack, which was curated by hip-hop superstar Kendrick Lamar and consisted of the original score of the film as well as a series of original songs inspired by the movie, would be nominated for and win multiple Grammy, Golden Globe, and Academy Awards. The financial, cultural, and critical success enjoyed by *Black Panther* and its hip-hop dominated soundtrack served as a standout intersection between two art forms, which have been on surprisingly similar trajectories over the past forty years. While unrelated at first glance, a closer look at hip-hop music and superhero movies reveals a surprisingly similar rise to prominence in the United States, with various points of intersection. Both genres came into public consciousness at similar moments in history, faced public skepticism at first, eventually grew to dominate their respective fields, and continue to battle for acceptance from critics. The histories of hip-hop music and superhero movies are the stories of underdogs and outcasts, and much like the comic books that serve as the inspiration for these movies and often this music, when there is a crossover event (to borrow a phrase from the comics industry), the results can be truly spectacular.

Throughout this chapter, I will examine the parallel historical rises of these mediums, examining how the progression of the mainstream popularity and acceptance of hip-hop music mirrors that of the superhero movie. I will discuss how hip-hop music fits into the wider application of sound in film, look at some of the memorable intersections of hip-hop and superhero movies, and examine what the future holds for these two mediums as they approach a potential cultural and financial crossroads.

## BACKGROUND AND CONTEXT

### The Superhero Film

While there are a variety of different visual media whose source material comes from the pages of comic books and graphic novels, the most visible (and lucrative) form of these media over the past several decades has been the superhero movie. In 2022, superhero movie adaptations yielded $1.75 billion in domestic box office ticket sales, and while that number dropped to $1.02 billion in 2023, that was still over $300 million more than the combined domestic earnings of video game adaptations of comic book material (its nearest genre competitor) (Lammers, 2024).

As with many entertainment genres, determining what qualifies as the first "superhero" movie raises a variety of answers and debate. Some would point to the 1920 silent film *The Mark of Zorro* as technically the first film in this genre (Bradley, 2022), while others would identify Richard Donner's *Superman* (1978) as the first major superhero feature film (Gigool, 2023; Koole et al., 2014). There is also an argument for 1966's *Batman* as the originator of the genre. I have chosen to use Donner's *Superman* as the "first" film in the genre for several reasons. First, most comic scholars assert that the "first" true superhero comic was created in 1938 with the introduction of Superman in *Action Comics* #1 (Chalasani, 2016). This timeframe eliminates the 1920s Zorro films. Secondly, *Superman* was a stand-alone film, whereas the earlier *Batman* movie served as an extension of an existing television show and is viewed by some as just a marketing tool to help sell comics and toys tied into the show (Russell, 2023). This is not meant to discredit these other films, but rather to help provide a definitive starting point for the examination of the superhero film genre for this specific chapter.

Hip-Hop Music

First and foremost, it is important to acknowledge that, as with most musical genres, attempting to create an immutable definition of what hip-hop is would require a simplification of an incredibly complex idea. It is imperative to recognize that hip-hop is not merely a style of music, but an artistic, cultural, political, and social phenomenon (Aldridge & Stewart, 2005). Hip-hop culture has expanded beyond music to influence the language, clothing, aesthetics, and worldview of millions (Aldridge & Stewart, 2005). It has also become commodified, appropriated, and commercialized to appeal to that audience. Hip-hop, like many other genres, has its roots in a wide range of musical styles and traditions. The genre of music that we recognize today as hip-hop is believed to have originated out of the diverse minority communities of the South Bronx in the 1970s (Aldridge & Stewart, 2005; Leach, 2008). Hip-hop quickly spread from the Northeast of the United States to the rest of the country and overseas, leading to the development of numerous hip-hop styles and subgenres. Thanks to a confluence of factors, including the rise of MTV and other music-focused television, portable music options like the CD and MP3 players, and the internet and social media, hip-hop eventually became one of the dominant cultural movements in the United States (Kitwana, 2004). Some point to the evolutionary nature of the genre as a key reason for its spread and subsequent musical and cultural dominance (Vadukul, 2023). Regardless of how or why it became so popular, within around fifty years of its recognized emergence, hip-hop has become a major force in the US music and cultural landscape. With the diversity of this genre in mind, I have chosen to use a broad definition of hip-hop music when looking at how it has intersected with superhero movies.

## HEROES OR VILLAINS?

One of the major similarities between the two mediums is how many experts, critics, and even members of their art form have judged them. Since its inception, hip-hop has faced pushback and criticism. Some of the most prominent criticisms relate to the gangsta rap subgenre of hip-hop due to "concerns over the content of the lyrics, particularly the glamorization of violence" (Fried, 1999, pp. 705–6). These concerns over the potential negative effects that hip-hop lyrics and music videos can have on children, and how hip-hop is "responsible" for increased crime have persisted despite a wealth of research which has pointed out that other genres of music like country and heavy metal have also focused on similar subject matter but have not faced the same levels of scrutiny (Fried, 1999; Hansen & Hansen, 1990). So why does this stigma remain attached to hip-hop to this day? One potential reason lies in the role that race plays in the perception of the hip-hop genre, which, "because of its association with African American culture, is judged through the tainted lens of a Black stereotype which includes such traits as violence, hostility, and aggression" (Fried, 1999, p. 707). This is not to say that critics of the genre are completely baseless, as there are many hip-hop songs that contain violent, explicit, and misogynistic material. The reason I bring this up is to provide context for some of the criticism of the genre of music, and while the focus of this chapter is not to examine the role that race and prejudice play in critiques of hip-hop, it is important to recognize this when addressing how the music and its artists have been judged.

As the genre has developed and grown, divisions within the community have also grown, leading to internal critiques as well. One of the most prominent internal debates of recent note has centered around the perceived "quality" of the art form. This divide has become most visible in the back and forth between the older generation of hip-hop artists and the newer artists making their mark in the industry today. Seminal members of the genre like Snoop Dogg, Ghostface Killah, and Rakim have all complained about a perceived lack of lyrical and storytelling quality amongst the new generation. These critiques tend to focus on the art form more than anything else, and mirror those leveled superhero movies by members of the film community.

Superhero movies have also faced criticism for their content (especially violence). Like the critiques of hip-hop, some of these condemnations contain aspects of truth to them, as some studies have found that despite the prosocial behaviors usually associated with superheroes, "the prevalence of negative themes, especially acts of violence, outweighed positive themes" (Muller et al., 2020, p. 2). Other studies have noted that the so-called "good guys" in these films often commit even more acts of violence than the antagonists, which could negatively influence children (Muller et al., 2020). While the influence that race may play in the critiques of these films has been less explored than that of hip-hop music, it is very interesting to see that external criticism of both has focused a great deal on their content, with a particular emphasis on violence.

Despite their popularity and commercial success, superhero films have not been universally embraced by all the members of the film community. Acclaimed director Martin Scorsese famously asserted that the movies of the Marvel Cinematic Universe "weren't cinema" (Sharf, 2019), while director James Cameron has criticized both DC and Marvel for what he perceives as a lack of character development and complexity in their films (Nugent, 2022). Francis Ford Coppola has even gone as far as to call them "despicable" (White, 2019). Once again, the parallels between the criticism of the two are quite striking. Just as the older generation of hip-hop artists feels that the new generation lacks skill and talent in their craft, a common aspect of the criticism that is leveled at superhero movies by other filmmakers is that they fail to honor the "art" of the genre. While the generational divide within the film community is not as obvious, it is interesting to note that all the previously mentioned filmmakers are established older members of the industry. While I will leave it to others to dive into the motivations behind these assessments, I will point out that the pushback that both mediums have faced is strikingly similar and speaks to a common aspect of their journey to cultural dominance.

## PARALLEL JOURNEYS

### Superhero Film Growth

To get a better picture of the parallel trajectories of superhero films and hip-hop music, we first need to determine what exactly a superhero film is. For starters, what is a superhero? Comics legend Stan Lee defines them thusly, "a person who does heroic deeds and has the ability to do them in a way that a normal person couldn't . . . and you need to use that power to accomplish good deeds" (Lee, 2013). Since there are a multitude of films that contain characters that could fit this description, for the purposes of this examination, I have added the requirement that a "superhero" film must also feature a character(s) whose origins can be found in a comic book. To limit this examination to films that had a "tangible" impact, I have chosen to only include movies that grossed at least $100 million at the box office when adjusted for inflation. Analysis began with 1978's *Superman* (the "first" official superhero movie) and ended with 2024's *Blue Beetle*. These criteria produced a total of 104 films over that forty-six-year period. Figure 7.1 shows a timeline of when these 104 films were released. Until 2000, there were anywhere from zero to two of these films produced per year. However, starting in the year 2000, there is clear growth in the number of superhero films produced per year, peaking during a three-year span from 2016–18, which saw seven released each year. Although the growth has not been linearly consistent, some of the drops can be tied to specific events. For example, the dip in the number

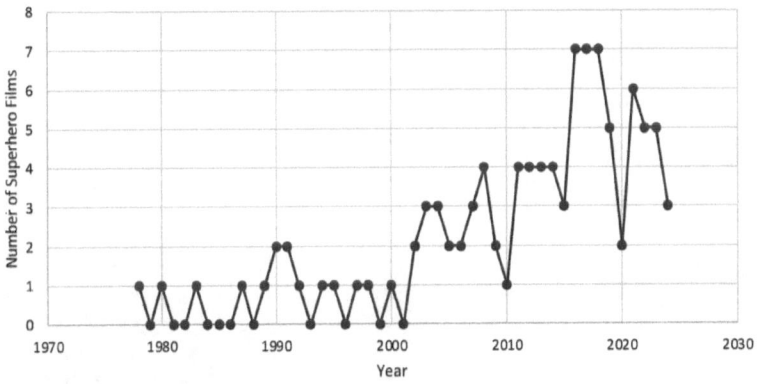

**Figure 7.1** Chart of the number of superhero films per year.

of movies released in 2020 can be traced to the COVID-19 pandemic and shutdown of the movie industry. Other occasional dips can likely be tied in part to the nature of the film industry and the fact that it usually takes years to produce a film, leading to fewer superhero movies being produced in some years than others. Regardless of these dips, when looking at the overall picture, it is clear to see that in the past twenty-plus years, there has been an increase in the number of financially successful superhero films produced.

Not only has the number of these films increased over time, but so has the amount of money that they have made. As Figure 7.2 shows, there is a clear increase in the individual box offices of these films (adjusted for inflation) over time. A closer examination of these trends shows that there is clear, nonlinear growth in individual films' box office earnings from 1978 to 2024, thanks to films like *The Dark Knight* (2008) cracking the top ten with its $1.48 billion adjusted box office haul. Notable earlier films earning large box offices when adjusted for inflation include *Superman* (1978), which placed twelfth overall with a box office of $1.42 billion, and *Spider-Man* (2002), which placed eleventh with a box office of $1.41 billion. The year 2018 is worth special consideration, as seven superhero films made over $100 million, including two of the top five grossing superhero films of all time: *Avengers: Infinity War* ($2.54 billion) and *Black Panther* ($2.06 billion). Of course, these are just a few of the numerous examples of how this genre has increased in both number and profitability over time, but they do help to illustrate how dominant and popular the superhero film has become over time.

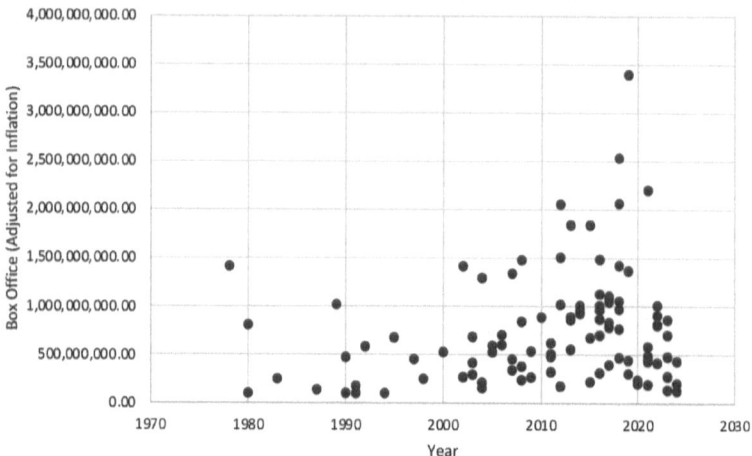

**Figure 7.2** Chart of superhero film box office.

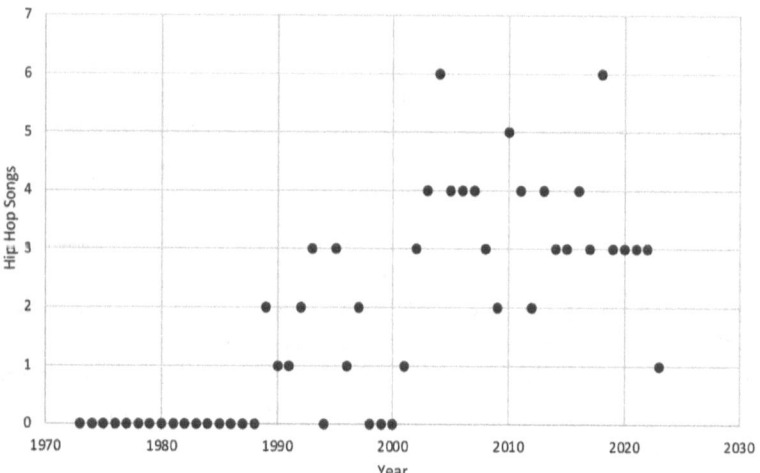

**Figure 7.3** Chart of year-end Billboard Top 10 singles.

## Hip-Hop's Path

What makes the comparison of hip-hop music and superhero films so interesting is how similar their growth and progression have been. When attempting to quantify hip-hop's growth, a focus was placed on more quantifiable data like album sales and song charts rather than more nebulous impacts like social and cultural growth and influence. To that end, year-end *Billboard* top ten singles from 1973 (the "birth" year of hip-hop) to 2023 were examined, to see how many songs by, or featuring a hip-hop artist, made it into the top ten played songs of the year (Figure 7.3).

This analysis showed that it was not until 1989 that a hip-hop song or artist was able to crack the year-end top ten. Even then, the two songs which made it into the top ten ("My Prerogative" by Bobby Brown and "Girl You Know It's True" by Mili Vanilli) were not pure hip-hop songs, but rather borrowed aspects of hip-hop and combined them with jazz, gospel, and soul elements as part of the New Jack Swing genre of music (Maultsby & Lewis, 2021). Regardless, these songs making the top ten are the first indication of the gradual progression of hip-hop into mainstream cultural acceptance. The first "purely" hip-hop songs to enter the top ten did so in 1992, thanks to Sir-Mix-A-Lot's "Baby Got Back" and "Jump" by Kris Kross, but even with these songs, some fans of hip-hop would likely point to the music put out by artists like EMPD, UGK, Eric B. & Rakim, and Too $hort as "better" representations of the genre. This difference in perspectives speaks to the challenges the genre faced when attempting to break into mainstream radio, as hip-hop artists were often at the mercy of the industry's gatekeepers (Coddington, 2023). Nevertheless, these entries represent another step of progress for the genre. This progress would explode in the next decade, as the 2000s would see multiple years where hip-hop songs made up almost half of the *Billboard* top ten. This domination would continue through the 2010s, with an average of 3.7 hip-hop songs on the *Billboard* top ten per year.

The growth and success of hip-hop can also be seen in the album sales generated by hip-hop artists over time. It's important to look at album sales data because while many artists have been able to craft a popular song which can get airtime or streams, creating a comprehensive album which generates enough interest to convince millions of people to buy it, speaks to an even greater level of social acceptance and popularity. Figure 7.4 shows how many hip-hop albums were amongst the top five selling albums each year from 1973 to 2023.

Once again, it took time for hip-hop to achieve success, as it was not until 1990 that a hip-hop album made it into the top five selling albums of the year. That honor went to M.C. Hammer's third studio album, *Please Don't Hurt 'Em*. After a few years of no hip-hop albums making the chart, we start to see gradual growth from 1994–1997, with one album making the chart each year. While none of these albums made it higher than fourth on the chart, this consistency shows that hip-hop was starting to find popularity and relevance. The early 2000s once again seem to mark a shift in hip-hop's growth. From 2000–2005, hip-hop albums were amongst the top five

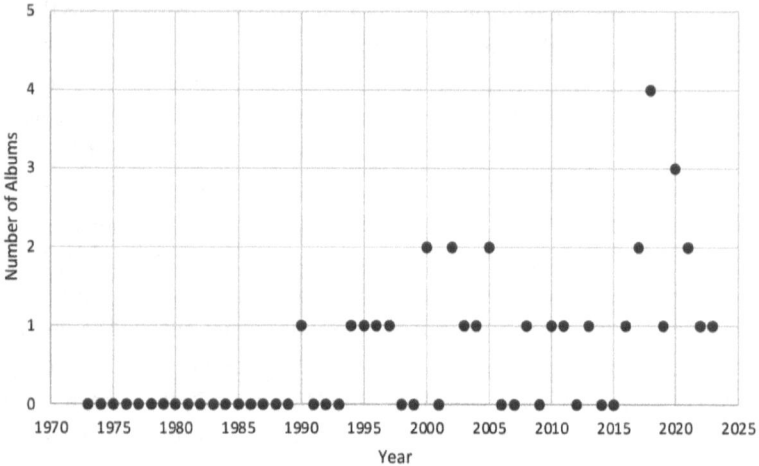

Figure 7.4 Chart of Top 5 selling albums each year.

best-selling every year bar one, and in three of those years, a hip-hop album was the top-selling album. This was thanks to the one-two punch of rappers Eminem and 50 Cent, who claimed the top spots in 2002, 2003, and 2005 with *The Eminem Show*, *Get Rich or Die Tryin*, and *The Massacre*. Interestingly, it took longer for hip-hop to dominate the album sales charts than it did to own the singles charts, with the late 2010s being the most successful years for album sales. From 2017–2021, hip-hop artists averaged 2.4 albums in the top five best-selling albums per year (almost half of the chart). Hip-hop also enjoyed a three-peat from 2018–2020 when albums by Drake, Post Malone, and Lil Baby topped the charts for three straight years. The high point of this dominance undoubtedly came in 2018 when four of the five top-selling albums of the year were from hip-hop artists, with Drake's *Views* at number one, followed by *Beerbongs & Bentleys* by Post Malone at two, *Invasion of Privacy* by Cardi B at four, and Tavis Scott's *Astroworld* rounding out the top five.

While the growth of hip-hop album sales and chart dominance are certainly excellent indicators of hip-hop's move into the mainstream, as noted previously, hip-hop is a multifaceted cultural movement. While music is at the forefront of this movement, to base hip-hop's relationship with mainstream pop culture on pure numbers alone would discredit its' true impact. To quote former Billboard Vice President of Content Ross Scarano, "Rap has been the most dominant force in American culture for years" (Bruner, 2018, p. 3). To become "mainstream," your music needs to be heard. However, early generations of hip-hop artists often found breaking into the mainstream a challenge due to gatekeepers in the record and radio industries: "The tastes of a few-radio titans and record-label kingpins of the predominately older, white and male variety-often ruled distribution, and in turn popular success" (Burner, 2018, p. 3). The development of streaming and online music platforms like SoundCloud, Spotify, etc., provided hip-hop artists with a new way to engage the fans directly, and many hip-hop artists have taken advantage of these channels to spread their music to the masses thus overcoming these barriers (Burner, 2018). Furthermore, it is often the younger generations who help to decide what is "cool" and "popular," so hip-hop's embrace of new channels has allowed it to speak directly to the technologically adept younger generation. It is not surprising to learn that "Once the Billboard charts began taking all streaming data into consideration in 2013, hip-hop gained ground" (Bruner, 2018, p. 4). Streaming has provided hip-hop artists with the ability to expand beyond previous limitations and reach a wider audience, which has in turn helped the public to realize that rap has always been in the mainstream; it just has not been given proper acknowledgement (Bruner, 2018). As with most relationships, hip-hop has not only influenced mainstream culture, but has itself been changed by its acceptance by the public. Most notable of these changes is how the literal structure of hip-hop songs has been affected as, "Over time, the formal structure of hip-hop music has become consolidated in the verse-chorus image of mainstream popular music" (Duinker, 2020, p. 93). This change in structure can be traced again to the impact of radio gatekeepers who played the hip-hop songs that they felt would be most popular, and tolerated by mainstream audiences (Duinker, 2020). To maximize their airplay (especially during the 1990s and early 2000s, prior to the rise of streaming), many hip-hop artists thus felt compelled to incorporate some of the elements of pop music into their music, leading to more radio-friendly, chart-topping songs and wider mainstream airplay. After that, it was a relatively short time until hip-hop soon came to dominate other avenues of pop culture, from movies to TV shows, video games to toys, even cereal and children's shows, hip-hop music and hip-hop artists have become ubiquitous in modern culture.

Comparing the Two

After looking at the growth of these two mediums separately, the question that naturally arises is how similar are their journeys? If we start by comparing the growth of the number of hip-hop songs on the *Billboard* singles chart with the number of superhero films produced each year, we can see how the popularity of these mediums has followed remarkably similar trajectories (Figure 7.5).

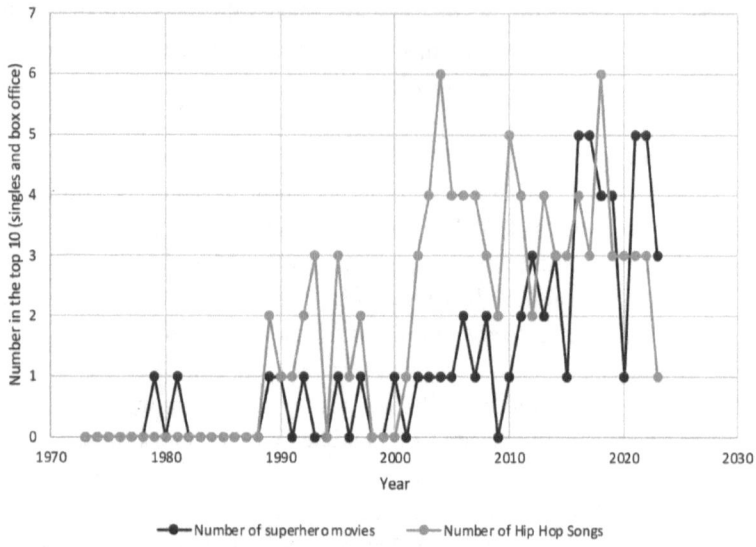

**Figure 7.5** Chart of year-end Billboard Top 10 singles versus number of superhero films per year.

As noted previously, both genres struggled to break into the top ten (with limited exceptions) until the late 1980s. From the 1990s to the 2000s, both genres rose and fell, with hip-hop achieving slightly higher peaks (more songs on the top ten chart). In the next decade, hip-hop saw a massive spike in success before regressing in 2009, while the number of superhero movies increased at a steadier pace before also seeing a significant drop-off in 2009. The two genres continued along similar patterns to the present (consistent overall growth with occasional drops and periods of stagnation), with both seeing a sharp drop in 2023. The similarities in the growth patterns of hip-hop music and superhero films are reinforced when comparing the percentage of superhero movies making up the box office top ten each year since 1973 with the percentage of hip-hop albums comprising the top five best-selling albums each year since 1973 (Figure 7.6).

Neither superhero movies nor hip-hop albums made much of an impact on the charts through most of the 1970s and 1980s, but interest in both increased in the late 1980s into the 1990s. While both genres fluctuated in popularity during the 1990s, unlike the previous comparison (Figure 7.5), the peaks and valleys of the two stay much closer. When looking at the overall trends of the two, the first decade of the 2000s shows hip-hop albums grabbing a greater share of their respective market, with this trend flipping in the early 2010s. Interestingly, in the last few years of the decade, both genres experienced major growth, with the massive spike in hip-hop album sales in 2019 really standing out. Both genres seem to have entered another valley in

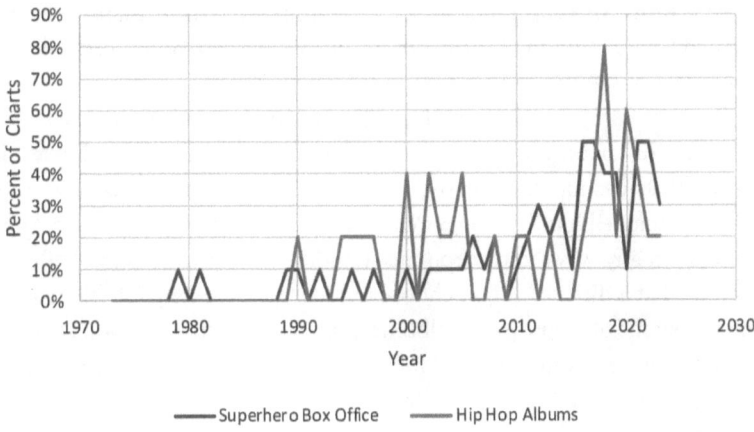

**Figure 7.6** Chart of percent of superhero movies in year-end box office Top 10 versus percent of hip-hop albums in Top 5 year-end sales.

2023, with hip-hop albums dropping from 60 percent of the top five selling albums in 2020 to only 20 percent in 2023. Likewise, superhero movies went from having 50 percent of the top ten highest-grossing movies of 2022 to only 30 percent in 2023. Whether this dip is merely temporary, or an indicator of a larger, more persistent trend remains to be seen, the similarities in the paths of the two remain clear.

## INTERSECTIONS AND CROSSOVERS

### Superhero Movies and Hip-Hop

As fans of comic books will know, a common trope of the genre is for two superheroes to start out as opponents before eventually teaming up. Having just looked at these two genres in comparison to each other, the next logical step is to look at how they have worked with each other. Early superhero films tended to rely on orchestral scores, which were "designed to inspire and evoke a sense of awe in the audience" (Harris, 2023, p. 1). In the 2000s, the use of popular music started to become more prominent as filmmakers sought to use these songs as part of their storytelling and studios looked for new avenues for marketing and profits. Several of the superhero movies of the 2010s advanced this trajectory even further by developing soundtracks comprised entirely of existing and original popular songs. These songs not only served as background music for the story, but also, "as a character-driven storytelling device" (Harris, 2023, p. 1), which directly contributed to "the narrative and emotional arc of these films" (Harris, 2023, p. 1). Unsurprisingly, the evolution of the use of music in superhero films eventually led to interactions with hip-hop.

When it comes to the use of hip-hop music in superhero movies, the question that naturally arises is, what does that relationship look like? To answer this question, 104 superhero movies were examined to see how many of them included hip-hop songs or songs that featured a hip-hop artist. Since there are many ways to incorporate sound into a film, and many different reasons that a director might choose to incorporate a song into their story, the film's official soundtracks/albums and the times that hip-hop was presented as diegetic sound (sound that exists in the film world) were analyzed to determine when hip-hop music was used in each film.

While the overall totals of hip-hop music in each superhero movie were gathered, the greater focus was on how often hip-hop music was used at least once. Unlike singles charts, album sales, and box office totals, which have a clear correlation between more (rankings, songs, sales, etc.) equaling "better," including music in a film tends to be a subjective one that is often narrative-based. With this context in mind, the choice to include even one hip-hop song indicates that the production felt that there was something about that song and the hip-hop genre that fit the movie. Furthermore, because there is no set standard for the number of songs in a movie and/or a movie soundtrack, one film having more hip-hop songs than another does not necessarily indicate any sort of greater appreciation for the genre. In total, there were 2,113 songs in the 104 films, 184 of which were hip-hop songs or featured a hip-hop artist. As can be seen in Table 7.1, of the 104 superhero films, 43 of them featured at least one hip-hop song, meaning that a little over 41 percent of the most financially (and arguably culturally) successful superhero films featured a hip-hop song.

Table 7.2, on the other hand, provides a more detailed look at these 104 films over time. This breakdown provides clarity into the number of films that featured hip-hop songs in each decade. When looking at the inclusion of hip-hop in superhero movies over time, we can see that in both the 1990s and 2020s, most superhero films featured at least one hip-hop song. This integration is in stark contrast to the twenty years between these two decades, when only about a third of the superhero movies featured a hip-hop song. While this may seem like a major decrease, I would argue that given the sheer number of superhero films produced during this time, combined with the number of potential song genres and choices, having a hip-hop song in a third of these films is quite impressive, and speaks to the strong ties between these musical and film genres.

**Table 7.1** *Superhero Films With and Without Hip-Hop Songs*

| Superhero Films | Number of Films | Percent of Superhero Films |
|---|---|---|
| With Hip-Hop Songs | 43 | 41.35 |
| Without Hip-Hop Songs | 61 | 58.65 |
| Total | 104 | 100 |

**Table 7.2** *Number of Films With and Without a Hip-Hop Song*

| Time Period | Number of Films With a Hip-Hop Song | Number of Films Without a Hip-Hop Song | Percent of Films in Decade with a Hip-Hop Song |
|---|---|---|---|
| 1978–79 | 0 | 1 | 0.00 |
| 1980–89 | 0 | 5 | 0.00 |
| 1990–99 | 5 | 4 | 55.56 |
| 2000–09 | 7 | 15 | 31.81 |
| 2010–19 | 17 | 29 | 36.95 |
| 2020–23 | 14 | 7 | 66.66 |

## Notable Team-Ups

There are several notable milestones in this relationship that are worth pointing out. The first superhero movie to feature a hip-hop song was 1990's *Teenage Mutant Ninja Turtles*, which featured three hip-hop songs (fittingly, this movie was set in New York City). The next film is 1998's *Blade*, which starred Wesley Snipes as the titular vampire hunter and was the first of the superhero films examined to feature a soundtrack comprised entirely of hip-hop music. *Blade* also happens to be the first superhero movie examined to feature a Black lead hero. Moving into the 2000s, Fox's *Fantastic Four* not only featured four hip-hop songs, but also highlighted a prime example of using the content and lyrics of a song to reinforce the visual and narrative information provided. In one scene, the impulsive Johnny Storm (a.k.a. the Human Torch) defies the orders of his sister and soon-to-be brother-in-law to lay low, and instead enters a BMX contest, only to end up bursting into flames and flying for the first time when a stunt goes wrong. After crashing to the ground in front of the stunned audience, Johnny eventually gets to his feet and rips off his motorbike gear to reveal the new Fantastic Four costume. As the crowd cheers, "On Fire" by rapper Llyod Banks swells in the background, serving as both a literal representation of his powers and a metaphorical reinforcement of his brash personality.

While 2008's *Iron Man* is heavily associated with the iconic classic rock songs used throughout, it did also include a hip-hop track. In this case, it was the upbeat and bombastic sound of Ghostface Killah's "Slept on Tony," which played in the background of Tony Stark's private jet as he and his best friend, Colonel James Rhodes, get drunk and party on their way to the Middle East. The inclusion of this song was by no means a coincidence, as Killah is a noted comics fan and even filmed a cameo in *Iron Man* (which was later cut) (Weiner, 2014). In fact, "Slept on Tony" was written specifically about the comic book character Tony Stark (a.k.a. Iron Man), and Killah's debut solo album was not only titled *Ironman* (1996), but also featured several tracks influenced by Marvel comics.

Undoubtedly, one of the high points of this relationship occurred with 2018's *Black Panther*. We have talked about the critical and financial success that both the film and its soundtrack experienced, but the relationship between the film and the soundtrack (curated by rapper Kendrick Lamar) goes further than monetary success and awards. According to Lamar, the themes of the film were what convinced him to overcome his initial hesitancy to create the album, "[The film's themes] reminded me of why I made *To Pimp a Butterfly*. It was survivor's guilt" (Atkins, 2024, p. 1). The film also fulfilled a dream that he hadn't even thought was possible. "It was something I dreamed of as a kid," Kendrick marveled. "A superhero who looked like us, talked like us and liked the same music" (Atkins, 2024, p. 1). The resulting album provided Lamar and his collaborators with a chance to create tracks like "Black Panther" and "King's Dead," which spoke from the viewpoints and perspectives of some of the main characters in the film, like T'Challa (a.k.a. Black Panther) and his cousin and rival Erik Killmonger. What made the album so unique is that it stands on its own as a work of hip-hop and yet takes on even greater appreciation when listened to with the context of the film's plot and storylines considered. It is a rare example of the genres working with each other in a truly symbiotic manner.

Another iconic collaboration between hip-hop and superhero movies occurred near the end of 2018 when the animated film *Spider-Man: Into the Spider-Verse* introduced the cinematic world to Miles Morales (a biracial Spider-Man introduced in the comics in 2011). With an innovative mix of animation styles and a wild storyline featuring numerous Spider-Man variants from several different forms of media, *Into the Spider-Verse* became a surprise box office hit and won the 2019 Academy Award for Best Animated Feature. The film also featured a hip-hop heavy soundtrack, which produced one of the songs of the year in "Sunflower" by rappers Swae Lee and Post Malone. Not only did the song play a prominent role in the marketing of the film, but it also served as the background music for Morales's onscreen introduction to the audience. The first time the audience meets him, he is singing along to the song as he gets ready for school, creating an enduring connection between the song and the character. Another iconic moment from the film occurs near the climax of the story when Miles makes the decision to fully embrace his role as Spider-Man. After donning his costume, Miles explodes off the side of a New York City skyscraper into the night to face his enemies and save the day, while the song "What's Up Danger" by Black Caviar and Blackway echoes in the background as a literal challenge to his foes. These are but a few of the examples of the symbiosis between hip-hop music and superhero movies, but they help to illustrate the interconnected relationship between these two mediums.

## AREAS FOR GROWTH

When examining the contributions of female hip-hop artists to superhero films, a notable disparity becomes apparent. In the 104 films studied, there were only 23 songs that were either by or featured a female hip-hop artist. This disparity is mirrored when looking at year-end Billboard top 10 singles charts from 1974–2023, with only nine songs in the entire period by or featuring a female hip-hop artist. Sadly, these results are not too surprising given the history of both genres. As has been touched on earlier in this chapter, hip-hop music has a long history of being criticized for being misogynistic (both justified and not) and has been dominated by male artists. While some female hip-hop artists have managed to gain both critical and commercial acclaim, like Missy Elliot, Nicki Minaj, and Megan Thee Stallion, far too often these women prove to be exceptions to the rule rather than the norm. The superhero genre is by no means immune from this issue as well, as it too has tended to focus primarily on male characters with female superheroes filling in supporting roles, or romantic interests. For example, the character of Catwoman has served primarily as the object of Batman's affections in numerous movies, including Tim Burton's *Batman Returns* (1992), Christopher Nolan's *The Dark Knight Rises* (2012), and Matt Reeves's *The Batman* (2022). These criticisms are reinforced by the data from this study, which found that only twenty-eight films featured a female superhero in a leading or coleading role. However, even these numbers are a bit deceptive, as in twenty-one of these movies, female superheroes were part of a larger ensemble of leading characters. For example, Storm in the various *X-Men* movies, Black Widow in the main *Avengers* films, and Sue Storm in the different iterations of the *Fantastic Four* on film. What is interesting about this lack of representation is that all seven of the films that featured a female superhero as the sole main character made it into the top ten grossing movies of the year, and several even broke the $1 billion box office mark. This disparity becomes even more noticeable when compared to the successful integration of female hip-hop artists and their music into several superhero-focused television series. For example, the Marvel show *She-Hulk: Attorney at Law* (2022) not only featured multiple songs by female hip-hop artists like Eve, Megan Thee Stallion, and Saweetie but also cast Megan Thee Stallion in a cameo role, further integrating the music into the show. While this degree of integration is not necessary for every single superhero film and TV show, it does show that it can be executed effectively and contribute to the overall narrative of the story.

## LOOKING FORWARD

While the history of both hip-hop music and superhero movies is one that has been defined by steady growth since their inception, there are warning signs on the horizon that bring into question how long their dominance will last. The past few years have seen the decline of hip-hop's dominance of the musical charts. The same holds true for both the box office grosses and the number of superhero movies as well. Critics of the superhero film genre point to superhero movie "fatigue" to explain this decline, blaming audience overexposure to the genre for the fall. The hip-hop community has blamed a perceived lack of substance, writing skill, and the focus on creating music that will go viral on social media for the decline of the genre. While there certainly is reason for concern should these trends persist, it remains to be seen if this is just another dip or something more permanent.

# REFERENCES

Billboard. (2018, March). *Billboard Hot 100*. Billboard. https://www.billboard.com/charts/hot-100/2018-03-10/

Bradley, D. (2022, July 7). *The superhero film: A guide for superfans*. The Beat: A Blog by PremiumBeat. https://www.premiumbeat.com/blog/superhero-film-guide-for-superfans/#:~:text=Arguably%2C%20the%20first%20superhero%20film,a%20talking%20picture%2C%20in%20color!

Bruner, R. (2018, January 25). Kendrick Lamar to Migos: How rap became sound of mainstream. *Time*. https://time.com/5118041/rap-music-mainstream/

Chalasani, R. (2016, January 22). The birth of comic book superheroes. *CBS News*. https://www.cbsnews.com/pictures/superheroes-in-gotham-comics-exhibit-new-york-historical-society/

Coddington, A. (2023). *How hip hop became hit pop: Radio, rap, and race*. University of California Press.

Duinker, B. (2020). Song form and mainstreaming in hip-hop music. *Current Musicology*, (107), 93–135. https://doi.org/10.52214/cm.v107i.7177

Fried, C. B. (1999). Who's afraid of rap: Differential reactions to music lyrics. *Journal of Applied Social Psychology*, 29(1), 705–21. https://doi-org.ezproxy.hofstra.edu/10.1111/j.1559-1816.1999.tb02020.x

Gigool, D. (2023, April 19). *The history of superheroes in cinema: From comics to the big screen*. MovieWeb. https://movieweb.com/history-of-superhero-movies/

Hansen, C. H., & Hansen, R. D. (1990). Rock music videos and antisocial behavior. *Basic and Applied Social Psychology*, 11(1), 357–69.

Harris, A. (2023). *The evolution of music in superhero movies: From classic scores to modern anthems*. Beat. https://vocal.media/beat/the-evolution-of-music-in-superhero-movies-from-classic-scores-to-modern-anthems

Kitwana, B. (2004). The state of the hip-hop generation: How hip-hop's cultural movement is evolving into political power. *Diogenes*, 51(3), 115–34. https://doi.org/10.1177/0392192104043662

Koole, S. L., Fockenberg, D., Tops, M., & Schneider, I. K. (2014). The birth and death of the superhero film. In D. Sullivan & J. Greenberg (Eds.), *Death in classic and contemporary Film* (pp. 135–50). Palgrave Macmillan. https://doi.org/10.1057/9781137276896_9

Lammers, T. (2024, April 2). Video game adaptations give superhero movies run for their money in 2023. *Forbes*. https://www.forbes.com/sites/timlammers/2024/04/01/video-game-adaptations-make-big-gains-on-superhero-movies-in-2023/?sh=2cd04c0d3eda

Leach, A. (2008). "One day it'll all make sense": Hip-hop and rap resources for music librarians. *Notes*, 65(1), 9–37. https://link-gale-com.ezproxy.hofstra.edu/apps/doc/A183449235/AONE?u=nysl_li_hofs&sid=bookmark-AONE&xid=351f2b6b

Lee, S. (2013, November 17). *Stan Lee on what is a superhero*. OUPblog. https://blog.oup.com/2013/11/stan-lee-on-what-is-a-superhero/

Maultsby, P., & Lewis, S. (2021). *"New Jack Swing": A history of African American music*. Timeline of African American Music. https://timeline.carnegiehall.org/genres/new-jack-swing

May, A. (2013). Phil Spector and the new movie soundtrack. *Media International Australia incorporating Culture and Policy*, (148), 127–34. https://link-gale-com.ezproxy.hofstra.edu/apps/doc/A345694551/AONE?u=nysl_li_hofs&sid=bookmark-AONE&xid=c2fb061b

Muller, J. N., Moroco, A., Loloi, J., Portolese, A., Wakefield, B. H., King, T. S., & Olympia, R. (2020). Violence depicted in superhero-based films stratified by protagonist/antagonist and gender. *Cureus*, 12(2), 1–7. https://doi.org/10.7759/cureus.6843

Nugent, A. (2022, October 26). James Cameron calls out Marvel and DC characters: "That's not the way to make movies." *The Independent*. https://www.independent.co.uk/arts-entertainment/films/news/avatar-marvel-james-cameron-b2210451.html

Rubin, R. (2018, March 10). "Black Panther" crosses $1 billion at Global Box Office. *Variety*. https://variety.com/2018/film/news/black-panther-billion-global-box-office-1202723326/

Russell, A. (2023, February 27). *"Batman" 1966 found enduring success by embracing its iconography*. CBR. https://www.cbr.com/batman-1966-iconography-created-success/#:~:text=Batman%3A%20The%20Movie%20was%20released,%2D%2D%20increased%20comic%20book%20sales.

Sharf, Z. (2019, October 4). *Martin Scorsese compares Marvel movies to theme parks: "That's not cinema."* IndieWire. https://www.indiewire.com/features/general/martin-scorsese-marvel-movies-not-cinema-theme-parks-1202178747/

Vadukul, A. (2023, August 17). Old-school fans celebrate that hip-hop didn't stop. *The New York Times*, D5. https://link-gale-com.ezproxy.hofstra.edu/apps/doc/A761144414/AONE?u=nysl_li_hofs&sid=bookmark-AONE&xid=1d3003a8

Weiner, S. (2014, December 10). *How a comic book writer helped Ghostface Killah create his new album*. Fast Company. https://www.fastcompany.com/3039309/how-a-comic-book-writer-helped-ghostface-killah-create-his-new-album

White, A. (2019, October 20). Godfather director Francis Ford Coppola calls Marvel movies "despicable." *The Independent*. https://www.independent.co.uk/arts-entertainment/films/news/marvel-movies-francis-ford-coppola-disney-martin-scorsese-a9163816.html

CHAPTER 8

# FROM MIC TO MASK

Unveiling Hip-Hop's Impact on Black Masculinity in Marvel Superheroes

JOHN P. CRAIG

## INTRODUCTION

This chapter examines how hip-hop directly informs the portrayal of Black masculinity in Marvel Comics, particularly through characters like Luke Cage, Miles Morales, Black Panther, and Blade. More than just sharing thematic parallels, hip-hop's aesthetics, storytelling techniques, and cultural ethos actively shape the ways Black superheroes are written, depicted, and understood. The influence of hip-hop extends beyond music, embedding itself into the visual, linguistic, and ideological framework of these characters. By analyzing this intersection, this chapter reveals how hip-hop serves as both a creative and ideological foundation for modern representations of Black masculinity in superhero media. Hip-hop has long been a site of both resistance and contradiction in its depictions of Black masculinity. It oscillates between hypermasculinity, procapitalist individualism, and exclusionary attitudes on the one hand, and Afrocentric, community engagement, and self-reflection on the other. These same tensions emerge in the narratives of Black superheroes, who often grapple with the expectations placed upon them as figures of both power and oppression. The entrepreneurial prowess and resilience of Jay-Z parallel the unyielding determination and street-level heroism of Luke Cage and Blade. Tupac's socially conscious lyricism and activism reflect the themes of identity and responsibility central to both Luke Cage's fight for his community and Black Panther's role as a leader. Kendrick Lamar's introspective storytelling mirrors the complexity of Black Panther, particularly in his navigation of legacy and power, while Drake's emotional range and vulnerability align with Blade's internal struggles as he grapples with his dual existence between humanity and the supernatural. These artists do not merely represent different archetypes of Black masculinity; their artistic personas actively shape the ways Black superheroes are imagined, received, and interpreted by audiences.

Although Kendrick Lamar and Drake's ongoing rap beef has sparked widespread cultural debate, this chapter does not seek to analyze their personal rivalry. Instead, it focuses on how their artistic personas contribute to broader discussions of Black masculinity, a conversation that extends beyond diss tracks and industry competition. The nuances of their lyrical feud offer a rich area for further academic exploration, and other scholars can continue to examine how competitive dynamics in hip-hop intersect with larger questions of identity, power, and masculinity. However, the primary concern of this chapter is how hip-hop, as a cultural force, informs and shapes the representation of Black masculinity in superhero narratives. While much of the discussion in this chapter focuses on Black male figures, it is also important to acknowledge the profound contributions of Black women in both hip-hop and superhero media. Female artists such as Lauryn Hill, Queen Latifah, and Missy Elliott have challenged gender norms, redefined artistic expression, and pushed back against hypermasculine narratives in hip-hop. Similarly, female superheroes like Storm, Misty Knight, and Shuri have played vital roles in shaping Black representation in Marvel Comics, providing nuanced and powerful portrayals of Black identity. By recognizing these contributions, this chapter aims to provide a more comprehensive understanding of how hip-hop and superhero media work together to construct Black identity in all its complexity.

Two key analytical frameworks guide this discussion: the "Cool Pose" and the "Badman" trope. The Cool Pose, a stylized and composed demeanor often adopted as a defense mechanism in Black American life, is evident in both hip-hop culture and superhero narratives, where controlled exteriority is crucial for survival. The Badman trope, a rebellious and defiant figure who operates outside societal norms, is equally significant, informing the portrayal of antiheroes and morally complex Black characters in both mediums. These frameworks help to further establish the direct relationship between hip-hop's construction of Black masculinity and its super heroic representations. Marvel serves as the focal point of this analysis due to its profound influence on comics, films, and television, with its Black heroes shaping cultural discourse in significant ways, particularly over the past two decades. Likewise, the selection of these four hip-hop artists is intentional, as they each represent distinct facets of Black masculinity, reinforcing that Black identity is not monolithic but a dynamic spectrum of performances and self-conceptions. By intertwining hip-hop's cultural language with Marvel's Black superheroes, this chapter demonstrates how hip-hop has been a driving force in shaping contemporary portrayals of Black masculinity in the realm of comics. Ultimately, this analysis moves the conversation forward, questioning the rigid definitions of Black manhood and advocating for broader representations that acknowledge and embrace the diversity of Black male expression while also acknowledging the integral role of Black women in shaping these narratives.

## I. EXPLANATION OF THE SIGNIFICANCE OF EXAMINING THE INTERPLAY BETWEEN HIP-HOP AND COMICS

The influence of Black popular culture, especially hip-hop, has profoundly impacted the development of Black superheroes in the Marvel universe. When Jack Kirby and Stan Lee introduced the Black Panther in 1966, they were inspired by the socio-political climate of the time, marked by African independence movements, the American civil rights struggle, and Black Power ideology, which informed the creation of the character and the rich lore surrounding him (Nama, 2011). This is exemplified in the depiction of Wakanda, a fictional African nation symbolizing resistance against colonial forces, reminiscent of Ethiopia's historical defiance against colonization (Hine et al., 2014). In the 1970s, Marvel expanded its roster with diverse Black characters, drawing inspiration from the era's popular Blaxploitation films. These characters embodied the cultural aesthetics of the time, characterized by their distinctive appearance and use of vernacular. Their narratives often depicted personal journeys of redemption, transitioning from past lives marked by crime to assuming roles as community defenders. This narrative trope resonated with audiences seeking representation and empowerment amidst systemic challenges. As hip-hop became a dominant cultural force in the 1990s and 2000s, its influence permeated the portrayal of characters like T'Challa, Blade, and Luke Cage. Blade, for example, underwent a significant transformation from his 1970s depiction. He shifted from his iconic Afro, oversized peacoat, and distinctive attire to a look that reflected the aesthetic of 1990s New York City. This era, characterized by the New Jack Swing (NJS) style, saw Blade sporting a high-top fade, black trench coat or bubble jacket, and a style that blended white goth and urban Black fashion. Artists like Bobby Brown, Guy, and Teddy Riley epitomized this NJS aesthetic, which Blade's updated look mirrored, blending their influence with his own unique flair (Intelexual Media, 2024).

Similarly, T'Challa's representation, while always exuding confidence, notably reflected the influence of hip-hop culture and fashion among Black men. T'Challa sported a bald head with a goatee, a look that became ubiquitous among Black men in the 1990s and early 2000s, popularized by figures such as Michael Jordan, Charles Barkley, and Tupac Shakur. This trend extended into hip-hop culture, with artists like DMX and L.L. Cool J adopting the bald aesthetic. While not every Black character adopted this appearance, it symbolized the integration of hip-hop's visual elements into comic book narratives. Furthermore, this evolution was not limited to male characters; it also influenced the portrayal of Black female characters like Misty Knight and Storm. In the 1990s, these characters received modern updates, drawing inspiration from prominent figures such as Robin Givens, Halle Berry, Lauryn Hill, and Angela Bassett. Their hairstyles ranged from voluminous curls, reminiscent of the era, to the popular short haircuts sported by Halle Berry to the short locs of Lauryn Hill and Erika Alexander, reflecting the diverse beauty standards embraced within hip-hop culture (Intelexual Quickies, 2024).

In examining comic narratives, it becomes evident that they extend beyond the superficial portrayal of characters' appearances. They delve into the linguistic intricacies present in the dialogue of diverse Black characters, often characterized by African American Vernacular English (AAVE). This linguistic exploration is woven into examining how these characters interact with one another and how they present themselves within the societal fabric. One noteworthy instance of such exploration emerged in 2003 with the introduction of "The Crew" by Marvel Comics. This superhero ensemble, spearheaded by James Rhodes, a.k.a. War Machine, was predominantly comprised of Black characters (Marvel Database, n.d.-a). The formation of this group was not merely to combat external threats; instead, it was rooted in addressing a specific community concern—a murder investigation—underscoring the significance of community empowerment within the narrative. Building upon this foundation, *Black Panther and the Crew* emerged over a decade later, expanding upon the thematic depth established by its predecessor. This iteration, led by the Black Panther, featured iconic characters such as Storm, Manifold, and Luke Cage grappling with many societal issues, most notably police brutality (Marvel, 2024b). Set against the vibrant backdrop of Harlem, these narratives provide a platform for exploring the complexities of race, identity, and social justice in a manner that resonates with audiences of diverse backgrounds.

Hip-hop has a fascinating relationship with the comic book industry, tracing back to the genre's early days. Graffiti, one of the five elements of hip-hop and a key visual expression of the culture, links hip-hop to the world of comics. Graffiti was fundamentally about personal expression, with each artist striving to showcase their unique style. In her text *Black Noise: Rap Music and Black Culture in Contemporary America*, Tricia Rose highlights the evolution and importance of graffiti within hip-hop culture. She explains that by the mid-1970s, graffiti took on a new focus and complexity. No longer a matter of simple tagging, graffiti began to develop elaborate individual styles, themes, formats, and techniques, most designed to increase visibility, individual identity, and status. Themes in the larger works included hip-hop slang, characterizations of b-boys and b-girls, rap lyrics, and hip-hop fashion. Using logos and images borrowed from television, comic books, and cartoons, stylistic signatures, and increasingly difficult executions, writers expanded graffiti's palette. Bubble letters, angular machine letters, and the indecipherable wild style were used in larger spaces with more colors and patterns. Advances aided these stylistic developments in marker and spray paint technology, which included better spraying nozzles, marking fibers, paint adhesion, and texture, enhancing the range of expression in graffiti writing. Small-scale tagging developed into the top-to-bottom format, covering a section of a train car from the roof to the floor. This was followed by the top-to-bottom whole car and multiple car "pieces," an abbreviation for graffiti masterpieces. Graffiti art found its way onto album covers, hip-hop fashion, music videos, and eventually comics.

In 1986, during what many consider the golden age of hip-hop, Eric Orr released the first hip-hop comic, *Rappin' Max Robot*. Orr's protagonist was a robot hero fully immersed in hip-hop culture, participating in rap battles, graffiti art, and breakdancing, all set against a fictionalized version of the Bronx. This comic, produced in a four-issue run and sold for fifty cents, was distributed by Orr to local music store patrons and fellow hip-hop fans throughout the city (Marvel Database, 2024). DJs, MCs, and breakdancers crafted fantastic identities, resembling costumed crimefighters, while graffiti artists incorporated elements from the comic books they had grown up reading. Flyers for hip-hop parties and gigs early on often utilized superhero iconography. These visuals grabbed attention and resonated with the youth who were fans of both comic books and the emerging hip-hop scene. By incorporating vibrant and dynamic images of superheroes, the flyers helped establish a cultural bridge between the two worlds, making the events more appealing and relatable to a broader audience. As hip-hop grew beyond the confines of NYC neighborhoods and rap records became an industry, these bonds strengthened: groups were depicted in exaggerated poses, artists' names were embellished with superlatives, and outlandish, colorful identities became a hallmark of the burgeoning hip-hop culture (Burroughs, 2018).

Throughout the following decades, the relationship between hip-hop and comics continued to flourish when some comic book artists began creating album covers for prominent hip-hop musicians such as Outkast, GZA/Genius, RZA, Public Enemy, Pete Rock, and T.I. (Taylor, 2020). This connection extended beyond album art, with some rappers adopting direct superhero/villain personas. British rapper MF Doom, for instance, took his name from the Marvel villain Dr. Doom, frequently referencing comic book characters in his lyrics and wearing a Dr. Doom-inspired mask on stage. Members of the legendary group Wu-Tang Clan would also reference comic book characters, with some members referring to themselves as Johnny Blaze and Tony Stark/Iron Man, with these names often having a double meaning (Williams, 2023). For many in the community and younger generations, these rappers were already seen as superheroes and antiheroes, accomplishing the impossible against all odds. Their ability to be authentic, represent their neighborhoods, start their own businesses, gain endorsements, achieve high levels of popularity and financial success, and, at times, push back against systems of white supremacy made them iconic (Williams, 2023). Even "gangsta" rappers, frequently criticized for their perceived glorification of violence, were often regarded as folk heroes. Their unconventional lives and decisions to live outside mainstream white American norms and values were seen as aspirational, akin to the "Badman" tradition in Black American folklore. In *Who Got the Camera?* Eric Harvey delves into the complex role of hip-hop, particularly gangsta rap, in the media's portrayal of African Americans. He examines how "gangsta rap" contributed to a media battle over Black stereotypes, highlighting its dual capacity to perpetuate negative stereotypes while simultaneously serving as a powerful platform for Black expression. Despite these contributions to Black culture, Harvey notes significant pushback from some African Americans who viewed concerns over stereotypes as a form of respectability politics. They argued that regardless of African Americans' behavior, racists would continue to hold racist stereotypes about Black individuals. This tradition includes stories of figures like Stagolee and real-life personalities such as Bumpy Johnson and Demetrius "Big Meech" Flenory.

Over the following decades, hip-hop and comics continued to intersect. Marvel, for instance, created a series of variant comic book covers inspired by classic hip-hop albums. These covers featured numerous characters from the comic world, such as the X-Men, Wolverine, Miles Morales, and Kamala Khan, mimicking artists from the hip-hop world like DMX, Lauryn Hill, Ghostface Killah, and Jay-Z (Taylor, 2020). Comic book artists began slowly incorporating breakdancers and rappers into their titles before fully embracing the concept of a hip-hop comic book. This evolution eventually led to rappers such as Method Man, Lil Uzi Vert, and 50 Cent having their own comic books. Atlantic Records even featured some of their most prominent artists—Fat Joe, Twista, T.I., Fabolous, Trick Daddy, and Lil' Kim—as a group called the "Joint Chiefs" in a comic book narrative where they attempted to steal a diamond from a villain named "The Checkwriter." This comic could only be read by purchasing Fat Joe's 2005 album *All or Nothing* (Williams, 2023).

## II. HIP-HOP'S INFLUENCE ON BLACK MASCULINITY

Building upon the fusion of music and storytelling pioneered by artists like Method Man, Jay-Z, 2Pac, and Nas, the influence of hip-hop extends far beyond the realms of music itself. Transitioning from the creative realm of comic books where rappers became superheroes, hip-hop's impacts on Black masculinity emerged as a dynamic force, shaping perceptions and expressions within urban communities worldwide. Undoubtedly, hip-hop music and culture have exerted a profound global influence, shaping the outlooks and behaviors of entire generations. Founded in the Bronx of New York, hip-hop emerged towards the end of the Black Power and the Black Arts Movement (Gladney, 1995). Originating from marginalized communities in Black America, particularly in urban areas, this genre provided a platform for the disenfranchised, disillusioned by the unmet promises of the post–civil rights era.

While hip-hop has been heavily associated with the construction of Black masculinity, female hip-hop artists have played an equally significant role in challenging and redefining gender norms within the genre. Early pioneers like MC Lyte, Queen Latifah, and Monie Love used their music to push back against misogyny while asserting their presence in a male-dominated industry. Lauryn Hill's introspective lyricism broke barriers by fusing rap and soul, while Missy Elliott redefined artistic expression with her futuristic aesthetics and genre-bending style. More recently, artists such as Megan Thee Stallion, Cardi B, GloRilla, and Doechii have unapologetically embraced themes of power, sexuality, and financial independence, subverting traditional narratives of femininity in hip-hop. Their contributions have expanded the scope of hip-hop culture, proving that women are not just participants but central figures in shaping its evolution. As hip-hop gained popularity, particularly with the rise of "gangsta rap," it profoundly influenced both societal perceptions of Black men and Black men's self-perceptions. Often regarded as the Golden Age of hip-hop, the mid-eighties to the mid-nineties witnessed the emergence of a diverse array of artists. During this time, Black men were portrayed in various roles, including thugs, gangsters, players, and revolutionaries. These depictions had a direct impact on young Black men in urban communities, influencing their attire, language, and attitudes toward life and women. Consequently, hip-hop significantly shaped the urban landscape, fostering a sense of identity and empowerment among Black men while also perpetuating certain stereotypes (Gladney, 1995).

### III. THE MULTIFACETED NATURE OF BLACK MASCULINITY AS DEPICTED IN HIP-HOP

By the 1990s, hip-hop had evolved into a significant musical art form, with the "gangsta rap" subgenre dominating its image. This influence was driven by figures like Ice-T, Dr. Dre, Snoop Dogg, and groups such as N.W.A. and the Ghetto Boys. "Gangsta rap" emerged as the dominant narrative, growing particularly popular among suburban white youth. However, this portrayal of Black masculinity as aggressive, violent, and hypersexual troubled many middle-class African Americans who valued other aspects of the genre (Rose, 2008). Nonetheless, hip-hop's appeal among young Black men persisted, with hip-hop's bravado symbolizing a potent form of masculinity. Despite this, hip-hop also showcased diverse portrayals of Black masculinity, with artists like Tupac Shakur expressing both positive and negative aspects. Tupac's lyrics highlighted social issues and personal struggles while also exhibiting misogyny and violence, reflecting the complexities of Black masculinity (Belle, 2014). Similarly, artists like Jay-Z, Nas, and Snoop Dogg displayed contradictory behaviors, critiquing capitalism and racism while promoting wealth and drug dealing. This bravado influenced young Black men, who aspired to emulate these successful figures. Although the commercialization of hip-hop has perpetuated harmful stereotypes, it has also allowed Black men to explore and express diverse aspects of their masculinity (Belle, 2014).

## IV. A BRIEF HISTORY OF BLADE, BLACK PANTHER, LUKE CAGE, AND MILES MORALES

Debuting in 1966 in *Fantastic Four* #52, Black Panther (King T'Challa) was Marvel's first Black superhero. As the ruler and protector of the fictional African nation Wakanda, T'Challa's dual role reflects themes of tradition, community, and Black identity. Wakanda's wealth of Vibranium enabled it to become the most scientifically advanced nation on Earth, untouched by European colonization. T'Challa's leadership and struggles to maintain sovereignty against external threats mirror real-world African nations' battles against colonialism. His interactions with characters like Shuri and the Dora Milaje highlight the essential roles Black women play in his life. Luke Cage, Marvel's first African American superhero, debuted in 1972. Wrongfully imprisoned and subjected to experiments, Cage gained unbreakable, bulletproof skin. His character was heavily influenced by 1970s Blaxploitation films, incorporating exaggerated jive talk and a persona akin to Shaft. Cage's narrative often includes his struggle with financial instability and his role as Harlem's protector, fighting systemic racism and local criminals. His relationships, particularly with Jessica Jones, reflect broader stereotypes and dynamics within the portrayal of Black superheroes. (Marvel Database, n.d.-a).

Cage's heroism mirrors the street-level valor seen in artists like Tupac and Jay-Z, balancing his responsibilities as a hero and a family man, illustrating the tension between personal aspirations and community obligations (Marvel, 2024b). Blade, introduced in 1973 in *Tomb of Dracula* #10, is another product of the Blaxploitation era. As a vampire hunter immune to vampire bites, Blade blends elements from films like Blacula and Shaft. More popular in movies than comics, Blade has seen significant character development, including the introduction of his daughter, Brielle Brooks. Blade's cultural style, language, and mannerisms reflect a Black man's cultural identity, contributing to his "cool" persona—a defense mechanism seen in Black American life, which will be examined in greater detail later in the chapter. His character's evolution from a Blaxploitation figure to a nuanced hero reflects broader societal changes, symbolizing the ongoing struggle for identity and acceptance within the Black community and broader society (Marvel Database, n.d.-c). Miles Morales, who debuted in 2011 in *Ultimate Fallout*, is a biracial teenager of Puerto Rican and African American descent and the second Spider-Man in the Ultimate universe. His stories explore the balance between his superhero duties and his life as a teenager. Miles's cultural heritage is a significant aspect of his character, making him a proud Afro-Latino. His popularity surged with Sony's *Spider-Verse* films (2018–2023), which emphasize cultural authenticity and the complexities of Black and Brown identities. Miles represents modern intersectionality, highlighting the challenges of young Black individuals navigating multiple cultural spheres (Marvel Database, n.d.-d).

## V. BLACK MASCULINITY IN HIP-HOP AND MARVEL

In both hip-hop and the Marvel Universe, we find rich and complex portrayals of Black masculinities, each contributing uniquely to the cultural narrative. Figures like Tupac Shakur, Kendrick Lamar, Drake, and Jay-Z in hip-hop, alongside Marvel characters such as Black Panther, Luke Cage, Blade, and Miles Morales, embody diverse aspects of Black manhood, reflecting the intricacies and resilience of Black experiences. The intersection between hip-hop and comics is most evident in how both mediums construct and deconstruct Black masculinity. Hip-hop artists, much like superheroes, create larger-than-life personas that reflect personal and collective struggles. The way Tupac Shakur embodied both a revolutionary thinker and a street-savvy poet mirrors the duality of T'Challa, who balances his identity as a warrior-king and a diplomatic leader. Similarly, Kendrick Lamar's deeply introspective and politically charged lyrics, such as those in *To Pimp a Butterfly*, parallel the complexity of Luke Cage's character in Marvel comics and television. Both figures navigate spaces where their strength is both a necessity and a burden, challenging traditional notions of masculinity. By engaging with narratives of survival, resistance, and vulnerability, hip-hop and comics work in tandem to redefine Black manhood outside of narrow, Eurocentric ideals. These connections highlight how both mediums function as tools for storytelling and cultural affirmation, reinforcing the idea that Black identity is fluid, layered, and shaped by historical and social forces.

Tupac Shakur and Black Panther (T'Challa) both serve as pivotal figures in articulating Black masculinities. Raised by Black revolutionaries, Tupac's music embodies his Black nationalist roots, addressing systemic oppression and the struggles of Black women (White, 2011). Similarly, T'Challa's uncolonized sovereignty of Wakanda symbolizes a powerful, unyielding Black identity untainted by colonial influence (Marvel Database, n.d.-a). Both figures use their platforms to challenge stereotypes and highlight the strengths and complexities inherent in Black masculinities. Kendrick Lamar and Luke Cage offer nuanced portrayals of Black male identity through their respective mediums. Kendrick's work addresses contemporary issues, internal conflicts, and systemic oppression, offering a portrayal that challenges toxic masculinity while celebrating the multifaceted nature of Blackness (Majors & Billson, 1992). Luke Cage, a street-level hero in Harlem, similarly navigates themes of identity and resilience, embodying the Cool Pose—a repertoire of behaviors and attitudes adopted by African American men to assert their identity in response to socio-economic challenges and racial discrimination (Marvel, 2024b). Drake and Miles Morales represent a more emotionally vulnerable side of Black masculinity. Despite criticism for being perceived as "soft" and "whiny," Drake's willingness to express genuine emotions defies traditional notions of Black masculinity (White, 2011). As a biracial teenager balancing his superhero responsibilities with everyday struggles, Miles Morales mirrors this duality and vulnerability, offering a fresh perspective on Black identity in a genre often dominated by hypermasculine archetypes (Marvel Database, n.d.-d). Jay-Z's evolution from street hustler to business mogul parallels the transformation seen in characters like Blade. Jay-Z's music traces his journey from glorifying gangsta rap themes to engaging with race, class, and personal growth issues, embodying the "Homeboy Cosmopolitan" concept—a blend of authenticity and fluid identity (Majors & Billson, 1992). Initially a vampire hunter defined by his supernatural battles, Blade has evolved through contributions by Black creators to reflect more nuanced aspects of Black masculinity, including resilience and the fight for justice (Marvel Database, n.d.-c).

Drake, Tupac Shakur, Jay-Z, and Kendrick Lamar all embody the Cool Pose in distinct yet overlapping ways, reflecting broader themes of Black masculinity and resilience. In both hip-hop and superhero narratives, origin stories play a crucial role in shaping the protagonist's character. Just as Spider-Man's origin is defined by loss and responsibility, hip-hop artists often craft their narratives around personal trauma and resilience. Jay-Z's transition from street hustler to business mogul, chronicled in albums like *Reasonable Doubt* and *The Blueprint*, mirrors the journey of Blade, who evolves from a rogue vampire hunter into a more introspective and strategic leader. Similarly, Miles Morales's struggle to embrace his superhero identity while navigating his Afro-Latino heritage aligns with how rappers like Drake wrestle with their dual cultural backgrounds in their music. In both cases, the tension between personal authenticity and external expectations shapes their growth. The superhero origin trope thus finds a direct parallel in hip-hop's emphasis on "coming up"—overcoming systemic obstacles to carve out a distinct and powerful identity. By incorporating these narrative structures, both mediums amplify the realities of Black experience, positioning their protagonists as cultural symbols of perseverance and evolution.

Drake's persona exemplifies the Cool Pose through his emphasis on emotional control and introspection, often juxtaposed with a suave, confident exterior (Majors & Billson, 1992). His music frequently explores themes of love, success, and personal struggles, maintaining a balanced portrayal of vulnerability and strength. Tupac Shakur, on the other hand, epitomized the Cool Pose through a potent blend of defiance and sensitivity. His work highlighted socio-political issues, personal pain, and a profound sense of justice, all while maintaining a charismatic and rebellious image. Tupac's lyrics and public appearances were marked by a seamless integration of toughness and emotional depth, challenging stereotypes and offering a multifaceted view of Black masculinity (Knight, 2023; Shakur, 1995). Jay-Z and Kendrick Lamar also utilize the Cool Pose in ways that reflect their unique artistic and cultural contexts. Jay-Z's embodiment of the Cool Pose is characterized by his meticulous portrayal of success, resilience, and self-assuredness (White, 2011). His narrative often revolves around his rise from the streets to the pinnacle of the music industry, emphasizing themes of perseverance, strategic thinking, and unshakable confidence. This portrayal reinforces the notion of the Cool Pose as a mechanism for navigating and overcoming systemic obstacles (Majors & Billson, 1992). Kendrick Lamar, meanwhile, incorporates the Cool Pose into his work through a blend of introspective lyricism and social commentary. His music delves into complex issues such as racial identity, inequality, and personal growth while maintaining a poised and reflective demeanor. Kendrick Lamar's Cool Pose is evident in his ability to convey profound messages with calm assertiveness, offering a powerful commentary on the Black experience in America (Majors & Billson, 1992). Collectively, these artists demonstrate how the Cool Pose serves as both a cultural expression and a strategic response to the challenges faced by Black men, enriching the discourse on Black masculinity through their distinct yet interconnected narratives. The influence of Cool Pose extends beyond the music industry into the realm of comic book and cinematic heroes.

Blade's characterization, for instance, incorporates this concept as a central aspect of his identity. As a half-human, half-vampire, Blade understands that losing his cool could trigger his bloodlust, endangering innocent lives. Similarly, Black Panther, as the leader of Wakanda, cannot afford to be governed by his emotions, given his responsibility for the welfare of an entire nation. This portrayal underscores the stoic and composed demeanor necessary for leadership and the safeguarding of his people. Miles Morales, a young Black teenager navigating the complexities of life in New York City, embodies Cool Pose through his awareness of the potential repercussions of losing his composure, particularly in interactions with law enforcement. His vigilant control over his emotions is a protective strategy in a society where Black youth are often unjustly scrutinized. Luke Cage, who strives to protect his neighborhood, similarly recognizes that emotional restraint is crucial, as the stability and safety of his community depend on his steadfastness and resilience. These characters collectively illustrate how Cool Pose defines individual behavior and serves as a critical strategy for navigating complex social landscapes. This concept reinforces the broader cultural narrative of resilience, strength, and adaptability within the Black community. By maintaining their composure and control, these characters provide a powerful counternarrative to prevalent stereotypes, showcasing the multifaceted nature of Black masculinity and its expression in both real and fictional realms (Majors & Billson, 1992).

When discussing Black masculinity and hip-hop, no Marvel project or comic embodies these themes more centrally than Luke Cage. The character has always exuded a gritty resilience, and as hip-hop rose to mainstream prominence in the 1980s and 1990s, Luke Cage's narrative evolved alongside it. The Netflix series places hip-hop fashion, music, and vernacular at the forefront, even featuring appearances by hip-hop legends like Fab Five Freddy and Method Man. This blend creates a rich tapestry that merges modern hip-hop aesthetics with the storytelling style of 1970s Blaxploitation films. The lyrical content of hip-hop and the dialogue in superhero narratives both serve as powerful vehicles for exploring racial injustice and systemic oppression. Kendrick Lamar's "Alright" became an anthem of resistance, much like how Isaiah Bradley's story in *Truth: Red, White & Black* critiques America's history of medical experimentation on Black bodies. In the *Luke Cage* Netflix series, Method Man's freestyle in season 1 explicitly ties Cage's heroism to the Black Lives Matter movement, reinforcing how hip-hop serves as a direct commentary on contemporary social issues. Likewise, the philosophical debates between T'Challa and Killmonger in Black Panther reflect the ideological clashes found in hip-hop, where artists like Nas and Jay-Z have long debated the best path to Black empowerment. By integrating these themes, both hip-hop and comics provide a necessary counternarrative to dominant cultural myths, challenging the erasure of Black resistance and resilience in mainstream storytelling.

More significantly, Luke Cage explores the complexities of being a bulletproof Black man within the sociopolitical context of the Black Lives Matter movement and widespread protests against police brutality. The show poignantly engages with historical injustices, particularly through Luke's involuntary subjection to scientific testing and his wrongful imprisonment, drawing direct parallels to the exploitation of Black communities throughout American history. This theme of forced experimentation and systemic oppression finds an even more explicit parallel in the character of Isaiah Bradley, introduced in the miniseries *Truth: Red, White & Black*. Like Luke Cage, Bradley is a victim of unethical government experimentation, yet his story carries even broader implications for understanding America's history of exploiting Black bodies for scientific and military gain. As the sole survivor of a secret US government project that subjected 300 Black men to dangerous trials in an effort to recreate the Super Soldier Serum, Bradley's fate stands in stark contrast to that of Steve Rogers. While Rogers was heralded as a national hero, Bradley was imprisoned on fabricated charges of treason and subjected to further experimentation against his will. His narrative serves as a powerful metaphor for the long-standing medical and military exploitation of African Americans, evoking real-world atrocities such as the Tuskegee Syphilis Study. Bradley's story not only exposes this painful history but also highlights a recurring pattern of systemic disenfranchisement—where African Americans contribute to the nation's progress yet remain denied full citizenship, equal rights, and recognition. While this chapter focuses on Black masculinity, it's essential to recognize that medical experimentation, involuntary medical intervention, and police brutality also profoundly affect Black women. These issues are shaped by social and cultural ideologies that often sideline or ignore the experiences of Black women. These narratives echo real-life systemic injustices and resonate with contemporary social issues (Marvel, 2024b).

Moreover, Luke Cage celebrates the richness of the Black experience by referencing pivotal cultural movements like the Harlem Renaissance and the civil rights movement. The show also explores the personal and societal struggles of Black men, particularly ex-convicts, who face significant challenges in securing steady employment. This aspect highlights the broader implications of economic disenfranchisement and societal reintegration. Additionally, Luke Cage tackles the pressing issue of gentrification, focusing on the efforts to maintain Harlem's cultural and historical identity amid rapid urban development. By portraying these multifaceted themes, the series offers a comprehensive and nuanced exploration of Black masculinity, community, and resilience within the framework of contemporary and historical struggles (Marvel, 2024b).

In the comics, numerous social issues have been explored, notably through the character Luke Cage, who has encountered racist police officers and bigoted citizens, with storylines deeply rooted in the Black experience in America. William Jones, in his seminal work *The Ex-Con, Voodoo Priest, Goddess, and the African King*, highlights the origins of Luke Cage's super strength and unbreakable skin, positing that "Luke Cage's acquisition of enhanced strength and steel skin may be based on the very real history of experimentation on inmates, and Black people in particular" (Jones, 2016). Harriet A. Washington's *Medical Apartheid* meticulously documents the history of medical experimentation on Black women in America, from colonial times to the present. Washington dedicates an entire chapter to experiments on inmates, drawing eerie parallels to the fictional narrative of Luke Cage, underscoring the tragic reality of such historical events. The *Luke Cage* television series delves further into themes of Black liberation, a recurrent motif in hip-hop music and African American cultural discourse. By the conclusion of season 2, Luke Cage assumes the role of the Boss of Crime, aiming to regulate and enforce the unwritten rules of Harlem, while his confidante and ally, Misty Knight, upholds the written laws. This narrative tension is poignantly captured when Misty questions Luke's new role as the boss of crime, asking, "And what about the law, Luke?" to which he retorts, "When has the law ever really protected us?" (Coker, 2018, season 2, episode 13). This dialogue encapsulates the broader societal view where Black heroes and freedom fighters are frequently perceived as antagonists by mainstream white America. The thematic exploration of Black liberation and the complexities of being a Black superhero in a racially prejudiced society extends beyond Luke Cage. For instance, *The Falcon and the Winter Soldier* addresses similar issues, examining the legacy and responsibilities of a Black Captain America. Moreover, Marvel's animated show *What If...?* episode "What If... Killmonger Rescued Tony Stark?" offers a nuanced examination of alternative narratives within the Marvel universe (Andrews, 2021, season 1, episode 6). The film *Black Panther* also grapples with these themes, mainly through the character Erik Killmonger, who advocates the use of Wakandan technology to empower Black communities and dismantle oppressive structures. These narratives collectively contribute to a richer understanding of Black identity, resistance, and the quest for justice within the superhero genre.

The implications of Cool Pose in character development extend to a broader understanding of cultural identity and representation. The deliberate portrayal of these characteristics in Black superheroes and hip-hop artists serves to challenge monolithic perceptions of Black masculinity, offering nuanced and diverse representations (Majors & Billson, 1992). The aesthetics of hip-hop culture also leave an indelible mark on superhero representations, reinforcing the Cool Pose as a performative yet deeply meaningful strategy. Hip-hop artists have long used fashion as a means of self-expression and resistance, much like Black superheroes' iconic costumes serve as both armor and identity markers. Luke Cage's hoodie, a tribute to Trayvon Martin, and

Miles Morales's Jordan sneakers in *Into the Spider-Verse* align with the way hip-hop artists like Run-D.M.C., Tupac, and Jay-Z have used specific clothing styles to construct their personas. Moreover, the signature stances of Black superheroes—whether Blade's stoic, arms-crossed pose or T'Challa's Wakandan salute—echo the body language of hip-hop artists who project confidence, power, and defiance. These visual parallels between the two mediums underscore the ways in which hip-hop and comics function as platforms for self-definition, where aesthetics are as much about survival as they are about style.

This deliberate narrative choice promotes a deeper appreciation of the complexities inherent in Black cultural expressions and the strategies employed to navigate systemic challenges. Furthermore, the portrayal of Cool Pose in media reflects existing cultural dynamics and contributes to shaping societal perceptions and attitudes. By foregrounding the theme of emotional control and resilience, these narratives encourage a reevaluation of how Black masculinity is understood and represented. This ongoing dialogue between cultural production and social reality underscores the transformative potential of media in fostering more inclusive and accurate representations of marginalized identities. The concept of the Cool Pose extends beyond behavior and attitudes to encompass the characters' physical appearance and personal style. A significant aspect of Black masculinities involves maintaining an impeccable appearance and carrying oneself with confidence. This theme is also deeply rooted in hip-hop and is a frequent topic of discussion among Black men. The emphasis on appearance and personal style is mirrored in the portrayal of characters within various media. The notions of being "so fresh," "looking good," and "appearing sharp" are crucial in hip-hop, where fashion and personal style are paramount. This cultural expression has evolved over decades, from the Adidas shoes and tracksuits of the 1980s, the Kangol hats, Air Jordans, and Timberland boots of the 1990s, to the oversized white tees and throwback jerseys of the 2000s. Fashion lines such as FUBU, Cross Colours, Rocawear, and Phat Farm have been instrumental in shaping this aesthetic. Additionally, distinctive Black hairstyles, ranging from afros, flat tops, and bald heads to a fade with parts, contribute significantly to this cultural identity.

This aesthetic sensibility is prominently showcased in comics, movies, and television shows. For instance, in the film *Blade*, Wesley Snipes sports a stylized fade with multiple parts in his haircut, enhancing his character's rugged and sleek image (Marvel Database, n.d.-a; Norrington, 1998). Similarly, Mike Colter, who portrayed Luke Cage in the Marvel Netflix series, adopts a bald head and frequently wears an HBCU hoodie, which was popular in the 1990s. This choice of wardrobe serves a dual purpose: it not only aligns with the character's cultural background but also acts as a tribute to Trayvon Martin, the young Black teenager unjustly killed in 2012, thereby adding a layer of social commentary (Coker, 2016–2018). In the film *Black Panther*, T'Challa, the titular character, maintains a standard Black man haircut, whereas the antagonist, Killmonger, opts for short locs braided hair, a style that has inspired numerous cosplay interpretations (Coogler, 2018). This contrast in hairstyles between the hero and villain subtly highlights their differing ideologies and cultural connections. In the animated films *Into the Spider-Verse* and *Across the Spider-Verse*, Miles Morales initially dons his Jordans, baggy jeans, and a hoodie with his costume before transitioning to a more traditional superhero outfit. This sartorial choice reflects his youthful exuberance and cultural roots, making his character relatable and authentic to the audience (Marvel Database, n.d.-b; Persichetti et al., 2018).

## VI. THE BADMAN

The "Badman" trope, which refers to a rebellious, defiant figure who often operates outside the law and societal norms prevalent in African American folklore and culture, also significantly influenced the development of these four superheroes. Although it is unlikely that Stan Lee, Jack Kirby, Brian Michael Bendis, and Marv Wolfman were directly acquainted with the Badman trope, they were undoubtedly influenced by the portrayal of Black masculinity in the movies, music, and literature they consumed. Blade, Black Panther, and Luke Cage emerged in the context of the civil rights movement, the Black Power Movement, and the Blaxploitation era of the 1960s and 1970s (Nama, 2011). Conversely, Miles Morales was conceived within the hip-hop generation of the 2000s and, from the very beginning, had a hip-hop aesthetic (Burroughs, 2018). Across these various movements and decades, the Badman trope was evident and prominently displayed in numerous forms. Activists participating in the civil rights movement through marches and sit-ins embodied the Badman trope as they endeavored to reform an unjust system, often being perceived as troublemakers and criminals (Quinn, 2005, chap. 5). Similarly, the activists of the 1970s who advocated for a more aggressive and militant approach to confronting white supremacy and called for a cultural renaissance epitomized the Badman trope by seeking either to overthrow existing systems or to emigrate from America. The Blaxploitation era further depicted Black men and women as quasi-superheroes who combated systemic oppression and operated outside conventional legal boundaries. While the Badman figure was not invariably political, their aspiration to live autonomously and assert their Black identity without compromise was a quality admired by many African Americans, who regarded them as heroes within their communities. This trope, prominently featured in Blues music, continues to exert substantial influence in hip-hop. Rappers frequently reference the Badman archetype in their work, portraying it positively and negatively (Quinn, 2005).

Tupac Shakur, Jay-Z, Drake, and Kendrick Lamar each manifest aspects of the Badman trope. Tupac, with his raw and unfiltered lyrical content, often highlighted social injustices, systemic racism, and the struggles of African American communities. His persona combined political activism with a rebellious spirit, challenging authority and mainstream norms, epitomizing the Badman as both a social critic and a cultural renegade. Similarly, Jay-Z's rise from the streets of Brooklyn to becoming a business mogul reflects the Badman's journey of self-determination and defiance against the odds. His lyrics often discuss his early life of crime and subsequent success, portraying a narrative of resilience and the relentless pursuit of autonomy and respect. Although often seen as less militant, Drake embodies the Badman trope through his nuanced exploration of identity, relationships, and personal success within a society that frequently marginalizes Black voices. His introspective lyrics and ability to navigate both commercial success and artistic integrity underscore the Badman's adaptability and depth. On the other hand, Kendrick Lamar directly channels the Badman's spirit in his profound critiques of institutional racism and his advocacy for Black empowerment. His music, rich with historical and cultural references, positions him as a modern-day griot, using his platform to educate and mobilize his audience. Kendrick's work often delves into themes of systemic oppression, resilience, and the quest for justice, aligning closely with the traditional Badman's role as a voice of resistance and change within the community (Roberts, 2010).

The intersection of the Badman trope with the superhero genre underscores a broader cultural narrative. As a vampire hunter, Blade exemplifies the outsider status and the relentless pursuit of justice characteristic of the Badman. Black Panther, as a king and a superhero, merges regal authority with the revolutionary spirit of the Badman, challenging both internal and external threats to Wakanda. With his indestructible skin, Luke Cage symbolizes resilience and defiance against systemic oppression, resonating with the ethos of the Badman in urban environments. As a more contemporary figure, Miles Morales reflects the evolution of the Badman trope within the framework of modern-day struggles and cultural expressions. His story integrates the themes of identity, community, and resistance, all central to the Badman trope but reinterpreted through the lens of the hip-hop generation.

This ongoing adaptation highlights the dynamic nature of cultural tropes and their capacity to address contemporary issues while retaining core elements of historical significance. The sustained presence of the Badman trope in various forms of African American cultural expression underscores its role as a symbol of resistance, resilience, and self-determination. Its influence on superhero narratives enriches the genre and provides a critical lens through which to understand the broader socio-political and cultural dynamics at play.

## VII. THE BADWOMAN

Just as the Badman archetype has shaped representations of Black masculinity in hip-hop and comics, the Badwoman trope has also emerged as a powerful counterpoint, embodying defiance, autonomy, and resistance against societal constraints placed on Black women. Figures like Foxy Brown, Pam Grier's Coffy, and Cleopatra Jones from the Blaxploitation era showcased Black women who navigated and challenged oppressive systems much like their male counterparts, asserting agency in ways that defied both racism and sexism. In hip-hop, female artists have embodied the Badwoman trope by unapologetically asserting their power, sexuality, and independence in a male-dominated industry. Lil' Kim and Foxy Brown broke barriers by embracing hypersexuality on their own terms, turning a space of exploitation into one of empowerment. Missy Elliott, Queen Latifah, Lauryn Hill, Megan Thee Stallion, and Cardi B further expanded this archetype, challenging restrictive gender norms while carving out their own space in hip-hop culture. Their music, fashion, and public personas embody a form of rebellion against traditional notions of Black womanhood, paralleling the Badman's resistance to dominant social expectations. Similarly, female superheroes in Marvel Comics embody the Badwoman trope by operating within or outside the law to fight oppression. Storm, one of the most influential Black superheroes, embodies both regal authority and defiance, frequently leading the X-Men and confronting oppressive power structures. Misty Knight, a street-level hero much like Luke Cage, navigates law enforcement and vigilante justice, often taking justice into her own hands. Shuri, as a technological genius and warrior, redefines leadership in Wakanda, proving that intelligence and innovation can be as revolutionary as brute strength. The Badwoman and Badman archetypes go hand in hand, both representing figures who resist systemic oppression and redefine what power looks like within Black identity. Their presence in hip-hop and comics underscores a broader cultural shift, demonstrating that rebellion, agency, and defiance are not exclusive to Black men but are essential to understanding the expansive narratives of Black resistance and self-determination in popular culture. Their continued evolution ensures that both hip-hop and superhero media will reflect the complexities of Black identity for generations to come (Roberts, 2010).

## CONCLUSION

In conclusion, the representation of Black masculinity in both hip-hop and superhero media plays a crucial role in shaping cultural perceptions, self-identity, and societal expectations. These narratives not only reflect historical and contemporary struggles but also serve as powerful vehicles for reimagining Black identity in ways that challenge dominant stereotypes. The monumental success of the *Black Panther* films has catalyzed a cultural movement, inspiring a surge of academic discourse, literary explorations, and the continued expansion of Afrofuturist and Black sci-fi projects, such as *Lovecraft Country*, *Wakanda Forever*, *The Blade* reboot, *Noughts and Crosses*, and *Malika: Warrior Queen*. These works broaden the cultural landscape, offering audiences a richer, more nuanced appreciation of African heritage while positioning Black excellence at the forefront of speculative storytelling. Beyond their entertainment value, politically conscious superheroes like Luke Cage and Black Panther function as deeply symbolic figures at the intersection of heroism and social justice. They embody the resilience, complexity, and multifaceted nature of Black masculinity, resonating with audiences who see their own struggles, triumphs, and aspirations reflected in these characters. Their stories serve as a direct response to systemic oppression, illustrating how Black men in both hip-hop and superhero media navigate power structures that often seek to contain, exploit, or erase them. As the cultural landscape continues to evolve, the question remains: how will future representations of Black masculinity in these mediums adapt to shifting social and political realities? While hip-hop has traditionally been a space that oscillates between reinforcing and resisting dominant narratives of masculinity, contemporary artists such as Kendrick Lamar, J. Cole, and Tyler, the Creator are pushing the boundaries of vulnerability, self-reflection, and emotional depth. Similarly, superhero media is beginning to explore more complex and diverse portrayals of Black male identity, moving beyond the archetypes of hypermasculinity and trauma to depict a fuller spectrum of experiences. The future of these representations depends not only on creators within the industry but also on the audiences who demand more expansive and authentic narratives. As both hip-hop and superhero media continue to redefine the possibilities of Black storytelling, they offer a unique space for reclaiming agency, reimagining heroism, and expanding the cultural imagination of what Black masculinity can be. Whether these portrayals will fully embrace the breadth of Black identity, including queerness, tenderness, and nontraditional forms of strength, remains to be seen. However, the growing demand for authenticity and representation suggests that the next wave of Black storytelling will push even further, continuing to challenge outdated paradigms while forging new paths for future generations.

## REFERENCES

Andrews, B. (Director). (2021, September 15). What if . . . Killmonger rescued Tony Stark? (Season 1, Episode 6) [TV series episode]. In A. C. Bradley (Executive Producer), *What If . . . ?* Marvel Studios.

Belle, C. (2014). From Jay-Z to Dead Prez: Examining Representations of Black masculinity in mainstream versus underground hip-hop music. *Journal of Black Studies, 45*(4), 287–300. https://doi.org/10.1177/0021934714528953

Burroughs, T. D. (2018). *Marvel's Black Panther: A comic book biography, from Stan Lee to Ta-Nehisi Coates.* Diasporic African Press.

Coker, C. H. (Executive Producer). (2016–2018). *Luke Cage* [TV Series]. Marvel Television.

Coogler, R. (Director). (2018). *Black Panther* [Film]. Marvel Studios.

Gladney, Marvin J. (1995). The Black Arts Movement and hip-hop. *African American Review, 29*(2), 291–300. https://doi.org/10.2307/3042308

Hine, D. C., Hine, W. C., and Harrold, S. (2014). *The African American odyssey* (6th ed.). Pearson Publishing.

Intelexual Media. (2024, March 22). *What was life like for Black Americans in the 90s* [Video]. YouTube. https://www.youtube.com/watch?v=n1wbJRUM45A&t=13s

Intelexual Quickies. (2024, March 25). *1990s Black film* [Video]. YouTube. https://www.youtube.com/watch?v=n3iKfxLmbcI

Jones, W. (2016). *The ex-con, voodoo priest, goddess, and the African king: A social, cultural, and political analysis of four Black comic book heroes.* Blue Artists LLC.

Knight, S. (2023, October 31). *30 years ago Tupac Shakur shot two off duty police officers.* Medium. https://medium.com/@ShamarieKnight/30-years-ago-today-tupac-shakur-shot-two-off-duty-police-officers-f4a73531ca0b

Majors, R., and Billson, J. M. (1992). *Cool pose: The dilemmas of Black manhood in America.* Lexington Books.

Marvel Database. (n.d.-a). Eric Brooks (Earth-616). *Marvel Database.* Fandom. https://marvel.fandom.com/wiki/Eric_Brooks_(Earth-616)

Marvel Database. (n.d.-b). Luke Cage. *Marvel Database.* Fandom. https://marvel.fandom.com/wiki/Lucas_Cage_(Earth-616)

Marvel Database. (n.d.-c). Miles Morales. *Marvel Database.* Fandom. https://www.marvel.com/characters/spider-man-miles-morales

Marvel Database. (n.d.-d). T'Challa (Black Panther). *Marvel Database*. Fandom. https://www.marvel.com/characters/black-panther-t-challa/in-comics

Marvel Database. (n.d.-e). Isiah Bradley. *Marvel Database*. Fandom. https://www.marvel.com/characters/isaiah-bradley

Nama, A. (2011). *Super Black: American pop culture and Black superheroes*. University of Texas Press.

Norrington, S. (Director). (1998). *Blade* [Film]. New Line Cinema.

Persichetti, B., Ramsey, P., & Rothman, R. (Directors). (2018). *Spider-Man: Into the Spider-Verse* [Film]. Sony Pictures Animation.

Quinn, E. (2005). *Nuthin' but a "G" thang: The culture and commerce of gangsta rap*. Columbia University Press.

Roberts, J. W. (2010). *From trickster to badman: The Black folk hero in slavery and freedom* (1st ed.). University of Pennsylvania Press.

Rose, T. (2008). *The hip-hop wars: What we talk about when we talk about hip-hop—And why it matters*. Basic Books.

Shakur, T. (1995). *Me against the world* [Album]. Interscope Records.

White, M. (2011). *From Jim Crow to Jay-Z: Race, rap, and the performance of masculinity in American popular culture*. University of Illinois Press.

Williams, J. T. (2023, June 20). Exploring hip-hop's relationship with comic books. Okayplayer. https://www.okayplayer.com/hip-hop-comic-books

## WORKS CONSULTED

Brown, J. (2001). *Black superheroes, milestone comics, and their fans*. University Press of Mississippi.

Chrysostomou, G. (2024, April 30). Marvel is forgetting the most important thing about Blade. CBR. https://www.cbr.com/blade-marvel-forgetting-gothic-horror/

Clark, T. (2023, June 23). A Marvel comic writer apologized after a Miles Morales story received backlash over racial stereotypes. Business Insider. https://www.businessinsider.com/marvel-miles-morales-comic-writer-apologizes-for-racial-stereotypes-2022-6

C. M., E. (2016, October 7). Here are the great hip-hop moments in the "Luke Cage" series. XXL Mag. https://www.xxlmag.com/luke-cage-hip-hop-moments/

Davidson, B. (1985). *Modern African history*. Routledge Books.

Deggans, E. (2016, September 29). Hip-hop and superheroes inspire "Luke Cage" showrunner Cheo Coker. NPR. https://www.npr.org/2016/09/29/495807648/hip-hop-and-superheroes-inspire-luke-cage-showrunner-cheo-coker

Diawara, M., & Kolbowski, S. (1998). Homeboy cosmopolitan. *October, 83*, 51–70. https://www.jstor.org/stable/779070

Drake. (2010). *Thank me later* [Album]. Young Money Entertainment, Cash Money Records, Universal Motown.

Drake. (2011). *Take care* [Album]. Young Money Entertainment, Cash Money Records, Republic Records.

Draven, D. (2020, September 26). *BLADE: The 10 biggest differences between the comic & film characters.* CBR. https://www.cbr.com/blade-marvel-comic-movie-character-comparison/

Graves, S. (2022, June 22). *The author of Marvel's problematic Miles Morales "What if . . . ?" comic has apologized.* Gizmodo. https://gizmodo.com/marvel-miles-morales-what-if-thor-comic-writer-apologiz-1849096096

Guerra-Recinos, H. (2020). Miles Morales as influence or influencer: Marvel Comics' "Ultimate Spider-Man" in diversity discourse. *Washington College Review*, XXVII(W3).

Hamilton, V. (1993). Introduction. *The people could fly: American Black folktales.* Penguin Books.

Harte, C. (2023, November 24). *How "Spider-Man 2"'s Miles Morales represents community, Black culture, and me.* Game Informer. https://gameinformer.com/opinion/2023/11/24/how-spider-man-2s-miles-morales-represents-community-black-culture-and-me

HipHopDX. (2018, February 24). *Real hip hop vs. fake hip hop part 2: Viewers choice edition* [Video]. YouTube. https://www.youtube.com/watch?v=ZuaoZSKEEC8

Jay-Z. (1996). *Reasonable doubt* [Album]. Roc-A-Fella Records, Priority Records.

Jay-Z. (2001). *The blueprint* [Album]. Roc-A-Fella Records, Def Jam Recordings.

Jay-Z. (2017). *4:44* [Album]. Roc Nation, Universal Music Group.

Lamar, K. (2015). *To pimp a butterfly* [Album]. Top Dawg Entertainment, Aftermath Entertainment, Interscope Records.

Lamar, K. (2017). *DAMN* [Album]. Top Dawg Entertainment, Aftermath Entertainment, Interscope Records.

Makaveli (Tupac Shakur). (1996). *The Don Killuminati: The 7 day theory* [Album]. Death Row Records.

Mathé, N. (2019). Representations of Black masculinity in the 2010s hip-hop. *Studia Universitatis Babeș-Bolyai Philologia*, 65–80. https://doi.org/10.24193/subbphilo.2019.1.06

Neal, M. A. (2013). *Looking for Leroy: Illegible Black masculinities.* NYU Press.

Newby, R. (2022a, March 12). *What happened to "Blade"?* The Hollywood Reporter. https://www.hollywoodreporter.com/movies/movie-news/blade-started-a-revolution-was-abandoned-by-marvel-1135703/

Newby, R. (2022b, July 15). *Controversial Miles Morales story shows limits of Marvel Comics.* The Hollywood Reporter. https://www.hollywoodreporter.com/movies/movie-news/miles-morales-spider-man-marvel-1235174852/

Platon, A. (2016, September 30). *The unexpected hip-hop crossover in new Netflix series "Luke Cage": Everything you need to know.* Billboard. https://www.billboard.com/music/rb-hip-hop/netflix-luke-cage-hip-hop-7525526/

Rivera, J. (2016, October 3). *How "Luke Cage" got its Gang Starr–influenced episode titles.* GQ. https://www.gq.com/story/luke-cage-cheo-hodari-coker

Shakur, T. (1996). *All eyez on me* [Album]. Death Row Records/Interscope.

Shakur, T. (1998). *Greatest hits* [Album]. Death Row Records, Interscope Records.

Spellman, M. (Creator). (2021). *The Falcon and the Winter Soldier* [TV Series]. Marvel Studios.

Taylor, P. (2024, February 26). *16 times comic book artists absolutely rocked hip-hop album cover art*. Medium. https://pacotaylor.medium.com/16-times-comic-book-artists-absolutely-rocked-hip-hop-album-cover-art-522aad4151df

Tyler-Ameen, D. & Madden, S. (2018, February 6). *Here's how "Black Panther" the album came together*. NPR. https://www.npr.org/sections/therecord/2018/02/06/582841574/heres-how-black-panther-the-album-came-together

# CULTURAL EXPRESSION, IMPACT, AND IDENTITY

CHAPTER 9

# MASKED MARAUDERS

MICHAEL SALES

The first time I saw it, I was walking through Red Hook.
It was 1990 somethin'. I was on summer break from college and me and my boy were hanging out in New York. One day, his sister from Brooklyn called, asked if he could come stop by and visit. So early one morning, we took a train and went down.

I was just out of Georgia and 'bout as country as an outhouse. My boy was from Northeast DC, on the rough side of the Anacostia River. Since the day we met, he was my Hood Sherpa, the guide who taught me how to move in the big city.

So when we got there, he looked me dead in the eye. "See that?" he said. "That's Red Hook. They don't play up in there." He pointed to this tall apartment complex across the street. "So when we go up in here, just follow me and don't talk."

I might be country, but I did not fear *us*. In my hometown, I'd been around every variant of Black Man in the known Multiverse—working class hood, boughie suburban, old, country, and everything in between. Kinfolk or not, they looked out. So, I could go anywhere and never feel afraid.

"Whatever, dawg," I said. "Let's go."

We hit the courtyard. I saw this one rough-looking guy, but I knew just what to do. I looked him right in the eye and gave him The Nod™. Then I just waited. *Once he hit me back*, I thought, *I'm good*.

See where I'm from, The Nod™ is a universal sign of recognition, like when people from Wakanda pull their lip down. It says, "I see you and I acknowledge you. And no matter where we are or how far we get separated, you're still one of us."

I was a fool. The Nod™ didn't mean shit up in Red Hook and when he looked back at me, I felt a cold knot in my chest. When I looked at this man, I saw . . . nothing. Not one ounce of recognition, just a face cold and hard like a cinder block in the winter, with eyes vacant and absent of all emotion. It was the look a bug sees before some bored kid stomps it into mush. *I don't know you*, the look said. *So you mean nothing to me. I could kill you right now in front of all these people and sleep like a baby.*

Five seconds earlier, I was in a courtyard with *my brothers*. Now I was trapped in a cage full of strangers. My chest got tight, and I remember thinking, *I could die up in here today.*

My boy asked one of 'em if they knew "Miss So and So." Somebody mumbled something back then they all parted like the Red Sea. We slid through the crowd, found the elevator and went on up. After we got done, we walked back out the same way we came in—but this time, nobody bothered us.

Thirty years later, and I still remember that moment. That was the day my fairy tale ended, and real life began. *This ain't Georgia*, I told myself. *Everywhere ain't safe and every Black man don't know you.* There was something between us in Red Hook that day, something terrifying and deadly.

It took me years to name it. It was The Mask. And we all had one. Even me. I just didn't know it yet.

Hip-hop was born on August 11, 1973 (Jones, 2023). The delivery room was just a random rec center in the South Bronx, an area so poor *The New York Times* said it had "the largest proportion of poor families among all 62 counties of New York State" (Burks, 1972). It was delivered right there on that sweaty dance floor, and from the very first time DJ Kool Herc played the beat and Coke La Rock spit the rap, the crowd fell in love.

But if New York City was the Daddy and the five boroughs were his children, the Bronx was the bastard Daddy never claimed. So hip-hop grew up neglected, shaped by poverty, poor housing, and deep unemployment. But to understand why, you gotta go back to Robert Moses.

Considered the most powerful builder of modern times, Moses was the city planner who directed the Cross Bronx Expressway (Gubaydullin, 2013). From 1948–1972, this seven-mile highway was the first large-scale freeway ever built in America and kicked off what would later be called the Urban

Renewal Movement. But what they called "urban renewal" was more like medical malpractice, as the freeway sliced through neighborhoods like an ugly c-section cut with a rusty ax. By the end, over 60,000 people were displaced and thousands of apartments demolished. (Susaneck, 2024). As Tricia Rose notes in her book *Black Noise*, Moses and his allies never wanted to acknowledge the harm they caused or how the expressway "supported the interests of the upper classes against the interests of the poor and intensified the development of the vast economic . . . inequalities that characterize contemporary New York" (Rose, 1994, p. 30).

Property values dropped, and white residents fled to the suburbs. Meanwhile, Black and Brown residents were stuck—redlining policies barred them from white neighborhoods. Through cruel public policy, Moses transformed these once thriving communities into bombed-out war zones, with 80 percent of the housing destroyed and 250,000 people displaced (Ndiaye, 2024).

After decades of abuse, The Bronx wasn't pretty like she used to be, but she still had a creative spirit. She wasn't rich or well-connected like her siblings, and it would have been easy for her to suffer in silence. Instead, she used hip-hop to speak for herself and, through art, both visual and sonic, found a way to keep her own spirits alive.

When the city cut art in schools, she grabbed spray paint and bombed graffiti on every public surface she could find. If you rode the subway, you'd see her garish, brightly covered art plastered all over the train.

When they cut music, they took turntables and old records and made their own.

When they cut police, the Black Spades and Black Panthers created safe spaces for her around the way. She brought all her art into those safe spaces and turned them into one big party, where—just for a night—they could dance, sing, and clap her cares away. Where she could shout back from her segregated corner of the world and tell them all:

"I AM somebody!"

But here's the thing—a party might last for a night, but racism never sleeps. Music can mask your troubles for a night, but you still gotta wake up and deal with racist ass New York City the next morning. The government can pressure wash your beautiful graffiti, and cops can lock up the Black Panthers. Block crews might fill the void for a while. But when unemployment stays high and schools stay wack, sooner or later those crews turn into gangs. And the gangs treat her just as bad as her daddy.

When kids get older, their voices change. Hip-hop was no different. "Rapper's Delight" (1979) and "Planet Rock" (1982) were cool party songs, but it's hard to keep rapping about silly shit surrounded by burnt-up projects and doped-up fiends. There was more going on and *somebody* had to rap about it. That would be Melle Mel and Duke Bootee, from the group Grandmaster Flash & the Furious Five. The song was "The Message" (1982).

It took seven minutes and twelve seconds for hip-hop to grow up. With vivid language over a funky groove, Melle Mel describes a place filled with homeless people who eat trash, kids who smoke dope in school, and parks so dangerous he has to "keep his hand on his gun, 'cause they got me on the run." There's constant stress, and he struggles every day just to keep it together.

"Don't push me," he warns, "'cause I'm close to the edge. / I'm trying not to lose my head."

The last verse is not just poetry. It's prophecy. In it, God smiles when a young child is born, but then frowns at the future ahead. The child falls to the street life and eventually commits suicide in jail. When the song fades, "the message" is clear: the inner city is a jungle that turns people into animals and eventually puts them in a cage to die. Over and over through this song, Melle Mel wonders "how I keep from goin' under?"

There's no answer. And as urban renewal spread like cancer, things got worse. Between 1972 and 1982, joblessness among blacks increased 140 percent. By 1990, the unemployment rate for Black males was more than double the rate for white males, according to the Bureau of Labor Statistics. But the statistics for black teenage joblessness, especially for males, were even more alarming. In 1987, the unemployment rate among black youths was 34 percent—twice the rate of 17 percent for teens of all races combined (Major & Billson, 1992, p. 15).

If you are trapped in the jungle, you live with expectations—to be providers and examples in your communities—without any means or opportunity to meet them. What does that do to a man? How does he manage the anger, the frustration, and the hopelessness you feel when you realize your own country went to war against you—not with bombs and bullets, but with policy and politics. And you lost.

Scholars Richard Majors and Janet Mancini Billson wrote a book to answer those questions. In their seminal work entitled *Cool Pose—The Dilemmas of Black Manhood in America* (1992), they set out to understand the mind state of Black men in urban America. In their book, they say Black men, in response to the unrelenting pressure they faced in these big cities, took on a "cool pose" as a mask to "hide deeper vulnerabilities."

They define "cool pose" this way. First and foremost, it is ". . . a facade to ward off the anxiety of second-class status. It provides a mask that suggests competence, high self-esteem, control and inner strength. It also hides self-doubt, insecurity and inner turmoil" (Major & Billson, 1992, p. 5).

In war, emotions get you killed. Better to just hide your feelings and soldier on. You know there's a cost, but first, you gotta stay alive. *If there's a cost,* you think. *I'll pay it back later.*

If urban renewal was a horror movie, The War on Drugs was the sequel. You could watch it for free, every night on the local news. Mug shot after mug shot, they'd show you, of young Black men on their way to jail. Melle Mel's prophecy had become reality, but now the same white folks who fled to the suburbs suddenly had questions. "How could this be?" they'd ask. "And what does it mean?"

The answer came from a conservative magazine called the *Weekly Standard*. They published a story called "The Coming of the Super-Predators," and they put the blame squarely on the Black community (DiIulio, 1995).

The story was written by John J. DiIulio Jr. He came up with the term, and he warned that by the year 2000, "30,000 young murderers, rapists, and muggers" would be running wild and committing crime left and right. And if that wasn't terrifying, he added this little tidbit: ". . . they place zero value on the lives of their victims, whom they reflexively dehumanize as just so much worthless 'white trash' . . ." (DiIulio, 1995).

The words "housing discrimination" and "racist lending practices" don't appear anywhere in his article. Instead, he claims super-predators came from "the abject morals . . . in homes where unconditional love is nowhere but unmerciful abuse is common."

The article blew up like a nuclear bomb and "super-predator" spread everywhere, like deadly fallout. *Newsweek* and *Good Morning America* ran segments on it. Elected officials, always ready to use the Fear of a Black Criminal like a political football, took that thang and ran with it.

Bob Dole, the Republican candidate for president, had this to say: "Unless something is done soon, some of today's newborns will become tomorrow's super-predators—merciless criminals capable of committing the most vicious of acts for the most trivial of reasons" ("Dole Seeks to Get Tough," 1996). He even implied that these super predators gave up the right to be considered children and should be tried like adults.

Dole lost, but the message stuck. When it came to super predators, it was better to lock them up now and ask questions later. States all over the country

**Figure 9.1** Hide the women and the children—the superpredators are coming!

began removing protections for juveniles caught up in the criminal justice system. The feds released millions of dollars to beef up police presence. To quote Ice Cube, they took that to mean "Serve. Protect. And break a n***a's neck" (Ice Cube, 1990).

So right around the time I was headed to the big city, America declared war on another generation of Black boys. When I got to DC, I found a city that was hard and violent. Crack was running wild in the streets, and "gun control" meant holding a pistol with two hands when you shot.

Every time I left the house, I felt like Gomer Pyle trying to Double Dutch through a minefield. I was "scared to death" and "scared to look." Especially that day, a few months later, when my boy took me to Red Hook. After that, I copied all the other Black men I knew up there. I played it cool and made a mask. Not literally, of course. More like a new persona I took on to protect myself from this harsh, new environment.

My face was the first problem. I was always the guy people would find when they got lost. "Ask that guy," they would say. "He looks friendly." That had to change.

I built a Face of Stone. In public, I remove any look of compassion or warmth out of my eyes and set my mouth in a hard, rigid line. Now, when people looked at me, they couldn't tell what was going on. In the city, sometimes that's all you need. Better to be a question mark than a mark period.

I began to see people differently. It's like I had a third eye that let me view the world through a filter of distrust and skepticism. It could peep danger from any angle, a huge benefit when crackheads stay lurking and desperate people might have to jack you so they can eat.

I was always the one Black kid in white spaces, so I knew how to code switch before I left Georgia. In DC, I hacked my system, disconnecting my words from my heart. Without thinking, I could censor my genuine feelings, filter out any wasteful emotions, and calibrate my words for any situation. Empathy, kindness, and soft, graceful language were all removed, replaced with aggression, and mean vulgarity if necessary. In a city filled with dawgs, I was always set to *bark*.

There came a voice in the back of my mind, warning me. *How much is this mask changing you?* I heard. *Is anything you even say or do even real anymore?* I lived in a place where a sudden movement in the club could turn into a shootout on a dime. Or a random Crown Vic might follow me in my new car, waiting for me to run a stoplight so the cops could find a reason to take me to jail. I had one concern.

Survive.

But they say to a man with a hammer, everything looks like a nail. For a man with a mask, everything is a performance. Especially a mask designed to shield you from the truth in your own heart. And maybe that's why I loved Tony Stark. Maybe because deep down, I thought we were just the same.

*Super Friends* introduced me to superheroes.

I'd get up early every Saturday morning to watch this show. Superman was in it, along with a couple more characters from DC comics like Wonder Woman, Batman, and the Flash. Their headquarters was called The Hall of Justice, and it looked like a giant museum. They spent most of their time fighting the Legion of Doom, a bunch of villains who lived in a giant black dome in a swamp somewhere. I dug it at first, mostly because it was all I had.

But then I found Spider-Man. The Super Friends looked corny and wack after that. See, Spider-Man was a real dude who lived in an apartment around the way. He had to go to work every day to pay rent, but he still tried to find ways to use his power to help people. He always had to ask, "Should I be sel*fish*? Or sel*fless*?" I could relate—even as a kid.

Also? The theme song had a funky, jazzy feel, and every episode felt cinematic. The action was more dramatic, and the violence felt real. *Super Friends* was a kiddie cartoon. *Spider-Man* felt like a minimovie.

I found out Spider-Man came from a whole different company—Marvel, not DC. There were shows with guys like Captain America, the Hulk, and one about a dude in a metal suit called Iron Man. I got up with Marvel, and I never looked back, and a lot of my friends did the same. Especially my Black friends who were all into hip-hop.

There was just something about DC we couldn't stand. Maybe the heroes were just too corny and the stories too lame. By that point, I was all into LL Cool J, Rakim, and Big Daddy Kane—bold, confident characters who were brash, aggressive, and super cool. Nothing like *dry ass* Superman. He was as far from hip-hop as you could get.

Matter fact, one of the most iconic rap songs ever spent damn near a whole verse clowning that guy. And, of course, it starts with a brother trying to holler at Lois Lane.

It goes down in "Rapper's Delight," the first rap song I ever heard (and the first rap song to be laid down in a recording studio). In it, rapper Wonder Mike approaches Lois Lane and begins with the wildest display of Dirty Mackin' ever. He calls Superman a "fairy" who "flies through the air in panty hose." She'd be better off with a man with "finesse" who "has his whole name across his chest."

Hip-hop had spoken. Superman, and all the noble, white bread heroes like him, were out. If you wanted to rock with us, you had to be cool. And wasn't na'an hero in the whole Marvel Universe *cooler* than Tony Stark. He might have been white, but he had style and finesse. He was Elon Musk and James Bond, all rolled into one character—he commanded the boardroom and charmed any woman he wanted. And when it came to clothes, Anthony Stark was gon' stay fly!

When he wasn't running his tech company—Stark Enterprises—he was Iron Man, a high-flying superhero with a flashy red and gold suit of armor that made him super strong and gave him the ability to soar through the air and shoot laser beams from his hands. The only people who knew his true identity were the Avengers, the super team he financed to help him deal with threats he could not handle alone. They were also the only people who knew his history and where the armor came from in the first place.

Early in his career, he found himself in the jungles of Asia, testing a prototype for the US military. He was nearly killed when the weapon malfunctioned, sending hot shrapnel into his chest. He was soon forced to make

Figure 9.2 Tony Stark—the flyest superhero ever.

weapons by the enemy army. With the metal shards slowly damaging his heart, Tony had to secretly build the armor to keep himself alive, repurposing weapons and circuitry he found on the enemy base. Eventually, he escaped and used the technology in his armor to lay the foundation for his high-tech empire.

Tony never fully recovered from being a prisoner of war. He drank too much, especially when the stress of running a multinational company and saving the world got too heavy. I still remember when I read "Demon in A Bottle," the classic storyline from his early Iron Man years.

This dude kept liquor on deck *at all times!* It didn't matter where he was— private jet, corporate office, or just chilling in his penthouse apartment. *Ol' boy just drank four martinis!* I remember thinking. *How you gon' fight crime* **drunk?!**

When it came to women, he was even worse. He could be arrogant when he felt wronged and dismissive of any woman who could not match his intellect.

Tony was a rolling stone, the type of guy to come through "for a good time, not a long time." He avoided any deep relationship that might make him grow up and confront his demons.

According to historian Robert Genter, everything about Tony Stark—his money, his armor, and *especially the women*—were all a cover, a way to mask his deeper pain. Stark, Genter says, needed to conquer women because he never fully recovered from his time in the jungle. His intellect was his greater power, and while he was a prisoner, it was taken away and made to serve others. He goes on to say: ". . . he is emasculated by his loss of autonomy as

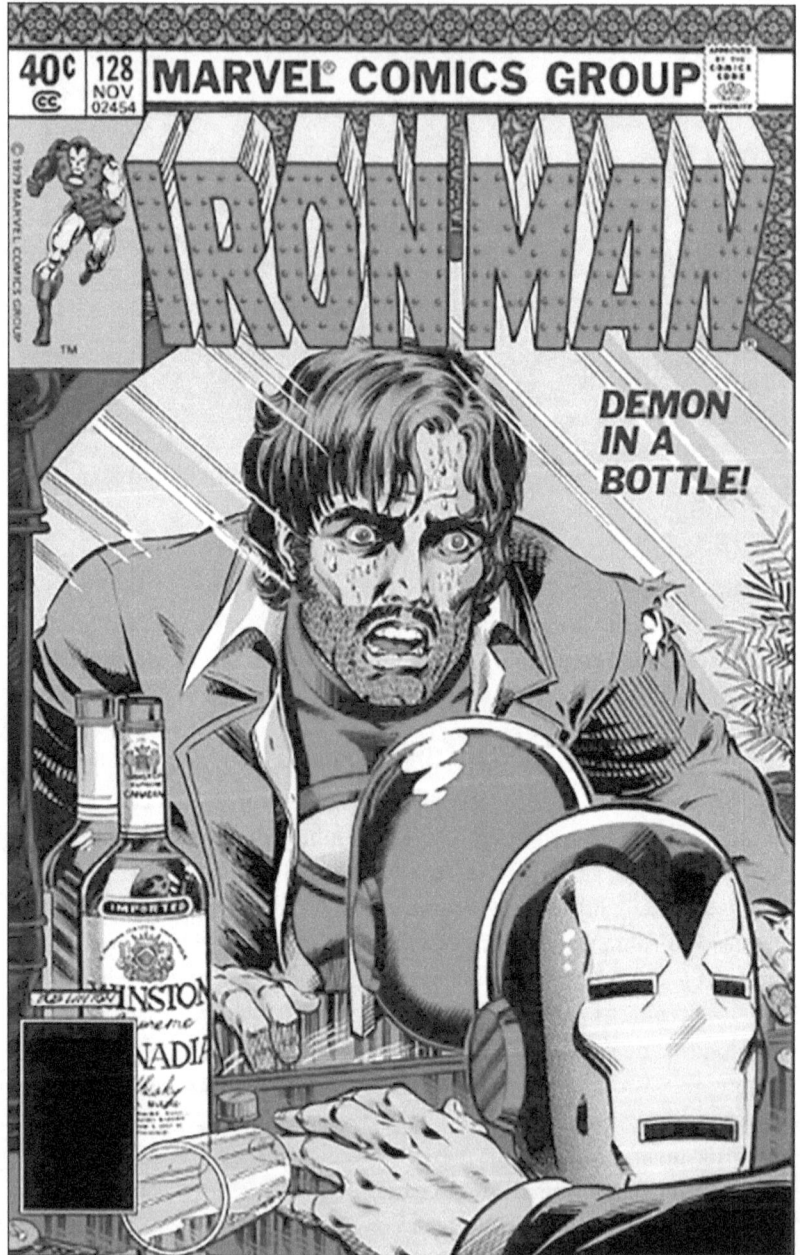

**Figure 9.3** "Demon in a bottle" puts a human face on a superhero.

**Figure 9.4** Stark used women to cover his deeper pain.

an inventor—a blow to his manhood symbolized by his chest wound—and Iron Man centers on Stark's inability to reconcile with this wound to his masculinity" (Genter, 2007).

After a while, the armor became an escape, the place he ran to when the world got too crazy or his drinking sent him spiraling. What does it mean when a man would rather face Thanos than face his own trauma? Or save the world instead of saving his own soul?

Money, status, and women carry top dollar in the gutter currency of hip-hop. Tony had all three, and maybe deep down, that's why we liked him. We finally found a guy who did exactly what we did, whether we could fully articulate it or not—bought a mask to cover up that helpless feeling, when his enemy used him like a slave and then put him on a leash like a dog. And if he overdid it a little bit with liquor and the ladies?

Hell, we did, too.

Maybe that's what struck a certain young boy, way back when he was living in Stapleton projects, an urban jungle "where the ambulance don't come." This kid would help start Wu-Tang Clan, one of the greatest rap

**Figure 9.5** Did saving the world make Tony a hero? Or a coward?

groups in history. At the beginning, he would call himself Ghostface Killah. But when he blew up and reached the peak of his career, he took a nickname.

Tony Stark. Also known as Iron Man.

Just like Marvel had the Avengers, hip-hop had the Wu-Tang Clan. Rolling nine deep, this supergroup from New York burst on the scene in 1993. They were mysterious and stylish on the cover of their groundbreaking album *Enter the Wu-Tang* (1993), wearing purple robes and white masks over their faces. Beyond introducing Asian martial arts and Eastern philosophy, no group ever produced so many solo stars. When they became celebrities and the masks came down, the world saw a roster full of Black men, with different personalities and styles:

Method Man—the sensitive thug who could drop a lyrical banger and a love ballad with Mary J Blige in the same year.

Ol' Dirty Bastard—the wild, chaotic street dude who sounded half drunk but could hop on a track with Mariah Carey and make a classic like "Fantasy" (1995).

The GZA—a lyrical beast whose album *Liquid Swords* (1995) is still considered one of the best Wu-Tang projects ever.

Raekwon the Chef–part hoodlum, part businessman, the visionary behind what many consider one of the best albums in the history of hip-hop—*Only*

**Figure 9.6** Wu Tang burst on the scene like the hip-hop Avengers.

*Built 4 Cuban Linx* (1995). The album was a unique blend, half Italian mobster movie, half Asian action flick. Rhyming over some of the best beats RZA ever made, Raekwon told lurid stories about drug dealing, jet setting, and street life, set against backdrops that go from glamorous to gritty and back again. The album made him a legend and created a whole new genre called Coke Rap. Jay-Z, 50 Cent, Rick Ross, and Pusha T all point to this album as the one that inspired their work.

But he could not have done it without his partner in crime, his former classmate from junior high school—David Coles, a.k.a. Ghostface Killah. If RZA was Lebron, Ghost was D-Wade, the indispensable Yin to his Yang. He popped up on over half the songs and to this day, *Only Built 4 Cuban Links* is seen as the ultimate collaboration in rap music.

"It felt good," Raekwon said, "to have my boy next to me, Ghostface, who basically comes from the same lifestyle as I come from. And we were able to sit down and concoct an idea that we both were able to respect and basically get everybody in the crew involved" (Eustice, 2020).

Ghost went for a new direction when it was time to drop his first album. You can hear a more soulful sound and comic book references that would define his work here and there. He called it Ironman because he was inspired by Tony Stark. "Being a powerful thinker alone makes me Iron Man," Ghostface told *SPIN* in 2000. "It's not always just the muscle tip—'cause I ain't got no muscles and shit" (Jenkins, 2000).

When Ghostface rhymes, the booth becomes a laboratory and the song is a science experiment, with crazy metaphors thrown together like chemicals in a Petri dish. On "Daytona 500," he says he can "slap box with Jesus" and "kick shots with Joseph," but before he eats meat, he'd "slap blood out of Perdue." Since he's Iron Man, he's no cheap metal, but more like "steel alloy," and his "true identity is hidden inside secret tabloids."

The similarities don't end there. In real life, Coles also struggled with drinking and sickness—in his case, diabetes. So when he dropped his next album, *Supreme Clientele* (2000), you hear Iron Man out the gate. The very first note steals the same smooth intro from the cartoon:

> Tony Stark makes you feel
> He's a cool exec with a heart of steel
> As Iron Man, all jets ablaze,
> he fights and smites with Repulsor Rays!

As the song fades, a narrator—sounding like a news reporter from the fifties—warns us that Tony Stark, the renowned superhero, may be doomed to die. There is a mini component in his heart that contains a strange secret, and it's the only thing keeping him alive.

This new persona—the troubled street superhero—adds a new level of depth to the thugged-out raps from Ghostface's early work and turns *Supreme Clientele* into a masterpiece. On "One," he refers to his crew as the "masked Avengers" and in story after story, he shows up draped down, drugged up, and pimp tight—just like Tony Stark in the comics. On "Ghost Deni," he comes through in a "Booger green pacer, velour down like the sheik of Iran." On "Stroke of Death," he's high out of his mind on "Dust and Alize," rocking three-quarter Timbs and a burgundy mink.

Let Ghost tell it, no woman can resist him. Game too strong. Style too fly. On "Cherchez La Ghost," he tells a lady straight up, "No girl can freak me, I'm just too nasty." Is it a warning or a welcome? In this hood fantasy they're both the same.

Majors and Billson understand these emotional games. In their study, they found that some women were attracted to the cool, suave qualities these men exhibit. (Major & Billson, 1992, p. 43).

Is it true and genuine? It doesn't matter. Especially on the street, where a corny brother can easily become a mark for bad guys trying to break his jaw or women trying to break his heart.

Take a song like "Wildflower." Ghost comes off tour, only to learn his woman cheated. Just like that, all that playboy energy disappears. He flies into a rage, calling her a "dumb bitch" and a "ho." He is clearly hurt, saying it feels like "somebody died" and not just because of all the great sex they had. He tried to bring her blessings, "earth lessons," but she clearly did not appreciate anything he did.

No matter how cool they try to appear, Majors and Billson sympathize. To them, the rage is just a mask to cover up feelings of inadequacy. "If he feels rejected," they say, "the black male may reject a woman rather than admit his hurt feelings" (Major & Billson, 1992, p. 44).

"If she complains about his inadequacy . . . he may strike out in anger to cover up his anguish. It may appear that he is emotionally drained or dead." Like Tony Stark's armor, that cool facade becomes a stumbling block over time. "The games and masks, the highly stylized expressions of self that makes the male attractive, are the very same artifices that inhibit intimacy and genuine companionship" (Major & Billson, 1992, p. 43).

Where Majors and Billson are sympathetic, author bell hooks is much more critical. For her, the creative genius that makes hip-hop powerful cannot outweigh the harmful white supremacy and toxic patriarchy baked into the music. Clever metaphors and hot beats are not worth the vulgar language directed at women, and she says it "reveals the extent to which patriarchal black males, like males in general, see sexuality as a war zone where they must assert dominance" (hooks, 2004, p. 73).

For hooks, sexism is not just a part of hip-hop. It's so pervasive, it might as well *be* hip-hop. If social consciousness even still exists, it can't erase the bitter taste that comes from listening to Black men "bragging about their sexual violence" (hooks, 2004, p. 73). It's "frightening" to her, not just because of the harm it does to women, but because we've internalized the same toxic patriarchy that dehumanized our whole race for centuries. No matter what he calls himself, Ghostface cannot be the hero in this story if he talks about Black women the same way "massa" did. He's actually the villain, stuck in the same emotional trap, reliving "Wildflower" over and over again. He just can't see it because of his mask.

If songs like "Wildflower" represented the misogynistic *call*, rappers like Queen Latifah had the feminist *response*. The New Jersey–based MC was a powerful voice in the conscious rap movement, and her single "Ladies First" reminded us that rap songs could center women and still bang. Throughout the song, Latifah and Monie would showcase iconic black women like Harriet Tubman and deliver rap braggadocio with a feminist twist, with Latifah claiming to be "divine" with a mind that "expands throughout the universe."

"Ladies First" was a jab. Her next great release would be the knockout blow that left no doubt where she stood. Released on her very next album,

"U.N.I.T.Y." would become her most well-known song and eventually win a Grammy for Best Rap Solo Performance. This time, Latifah was not content to just celebrate women—she would celebrate Black love fully, while at the same time directly addressing the sexism in hip-hop. Only a master like Latifah could hop from affection to correction in a single break, on one hand asking "Who you callin' a BITCH?!" and then declaring "Love a Black man from infinity to infinity." To angry rappers, throwing a sexist tantrum like a child, Latifah responds like a wise mama with a forceful yet loving rebuke over crazy bars and a hot beat. The fact that "U.N.I.T.Y" turned out to be one of the greatest songs of that era made it even better.

If Latifah was a sovereign queen *above* the streets, Lil' Kim was part of a royal court *in* the streets. Also known as "The Queen B," she would coreign over the charts with Notorious B.I.G. and their group Junior Mafia. On their best songs, they told stories rooted in fame and fortune through street hustling, and Lil' Kim stole the show on their hits, taking the cocky, over-the-top style we expected but adding a new level of sexual sass. On "Get Money," she asks her main squeeze if he "wanna lick between her knees" and when he threatens to get violent, she warns that if he pulls out his nine, she can "cock on mine." And on another song called "Crush On You," she tells her man to go get a bag of the lethal and she'll be "undressed in the bra all see through."

Both Queen Latifah and Lil' Kim see and accept the reality Ghost portrays in Wildflower. But while Latifah imagines a new reality through empowerment and liberation, Lil' Kim accepts the current reality and carves out a space for herself with what's available to her right now: money, sex, and violence. For women like her, you did what you needed to do to be safe *today*. If there was a price, you paid that later.

Majors and Billson had the receipts. The same behaviors that gave us some "social competence and control," they say, "are the very same things that run our relationships into the ground" (Major & Billson, 1992, p. 43). The mask protects, but it also separates. But if we wear it too long, we won't even care.

I know from experience.

One time, when I was back home in Georgia, my cousin pulled up on me. She helped raise me, so she knew me pretty well. Maybe I was more aggressive that day. Or cussin' too much. Whatever it was, something was off, and she had to let me know.

"Michael T?" She used the nickname only kin folks knew. "Something's wrong? You different since you been gone."

I could have told her about the stepshows. About guns barking after the crowd let out, folks screaming and running in every direction, all of us hiding, hoping the bullets couldn't find us behind the bushes and the trash cans.

I could've told her about the police. How we were posted up at the McDonald's parking lot one homecoming, the year we played Central State. How the cops came through with tear gas and horses and chased us up and down Georgia Avenue like slaves in a cotton field. They treated us like criminals for having too much fun.

I came home one random Friday night and my roommate was on the couch, popping bullets into a magazine. A jet black .380 sat right next to a Tecmo Bowl cartridge on the coffee table. "My cousin in some beef," he said. "Gotta go handle that, young'un." I went back to my room, closed the door, and went to bed.

I bought a house one time, right next to a boarding house where they rented rooms by the hour. One time, some guy ran his car into my fence, cracked one of the slats wide open. By the time I got over there, dude was gone. So now I gotta run up in the boarding house to deal with it. Alone.

I barked at the old man behind the counter. "I'ma need you to fix that ASAP!" He looked at me for a minute, then he reached under the counter and picked up the phone. Somebody fixed the fence the next day, but later it occurred to me—old buddy could have had a pistol under that counter, too. And then what could I do?

I could've told her about all that stuff. But instead, I said, "yeah, you probably right." Then I changed the subject and finished my potato salad. She was just concerned, but I really didn't care. Why take my mask off if I didn't need to?

Eventually, corporate America and marriage made me change. Put too much bass in your voice and watch how quickly "Karen from accounting" reports you to HR. Hide your true face from your spouse and notice how hard it is to love her right. My mask was built to handle threats in the street. But like Tony Stark in that very first issue of Iron Man, what happens when the threat is in my heart?

Somewhere along the line, Kendrick Lamar figured out he had a "heart" problem, too. At some point, between the breakout hits, the sold-out tours, even becoming the first rapper ever to win a Pulitzer Prize, he lost his ability to write. Now he was a broken demigod, like Samson when they cut off his hair. And just like Samson, the power did not come back until he asked God to use him. The result? His fifth studio album—*Mr. Morales and the Big Steppers* (2022).

From the first bar, we know this one is different.

"I been going through something," he says. "Be afraid." And for the next hour and eighteen minutes, he takes us on a tour, and every song is like a stop along the way where we get to look through a window and peek into his soul.

In "Mother I Sober," he remembers the guilt he felt as a five-year-old son listening to his mother cry after she got beat and the pain brought on by his own family when they suspected he'd been abused by his own cousin. Kendrick says it never happened, but he goes down a spiral of self-doubt when they don't believe him. He starts rhyming to try to cope, but by now his self-esteem is shot. The refrain, delivered by Portishead's Beth Gibbons, provides a devastating look at his psyche: "I wish I was somebody," she sings. "Anybody but myself."

On "Father Time," Kendrick says, "man should never show feelings, being sensitive never helped." So what do you do with all the sexual and physical trauma that's infected every generation of your family? If you're Kendrick Duckworth, you find a loophole. You put on a mask and transform into Kendrick Lamar, and make *him* say the things you can't. You use his brilliant curiosity to find meditation and the teachings of Eckhart Tolle, more medicine to help you heal. And you use his incredible imagination to take your mind to new realms, so you can escape the violence and death all around you, if only for a little while.

That's what he does on "The Heart Part 5," the last track on the album. He envisions himself in the afterlife, looking back on his hood and all the people in his community. He is in a place of peace now, and this is his final message.

To his killer, he offers forgiveness.

To his children, he offers love. And to his hood he offers advice:

"You can't help the world until you help yourself."

He should know. That's what the whole album was about.

That's probably why I like it so much. Christianity—all by itself—did not always help me with the questions I wrestled with as a Black man in America. When I was young and arrogant, I blamed simple, down-home faith of my elders.

*I need a more "sophisticated" religious space*, I thought. *Something with a more "well-reasoned" and "intellectually rigorous" theology.* So of course, I ended up in a mostly white space, full of well-meaning people who encouraged me to bring my questions. We'd work through them together. Equally. Before God.

It didn't work. We met at the feet of Jesus, but we all took different paths to get there. Mine was a Black man in America. "I am angry about the injustice I see every day," I would ask. "What does God say to that?" My

**Figure 9.7** To become a true hero, Tony has to take off his mask.

white friends didn't even think about God that way. He's supposed to save us from sin so we can *leave* here and go to heaven. They couldn't understand why I was obsessed with the starter home on Earth when God already promised a mansion in the sky.

I left. Eventually, I found a physical yoga practice. I loved it from the beginning, because on my yoga mat, there is no sin and no heaven. There is only cause and effect, observation, and choice. Our "preacher" guides us through different physical poses, and we do them. Or not. She tells us to breathe. Either we do or we don't. And whatever happens, we are called to simply pay attention to what we feel. And then, based on that, listen for the next call from the teacher. And choose again. And again. And again. Until the practice is over and we can rest.

My mat has become a safe space, free from guilt and shame. I can bring the most authentic version of myself, flaws and all, and feel perfectly safe. On the mat, I can take off my mask and practice what it feels like to move through the world—if only for an hour—without hiding. And on my good days, when I'm brave, I actually leave it there. And move out into the world liberated and free.

I'm not the only one. Creators in hip-hop have become more willing to reexamine what it means to be a man, and what it costs to be a fake version of yourself. In "Take Your Mask Off," rapper Tyler, the Creator looks at two men living false lives and sings, "I hope you find yourself, I hope you take your mask off." On *4:44*, Jay-Z raps that he has to "Kill Jay-Z," as a way to put aside his old, hypermasculine street ways to be a better husband to his wife Beyonce and his new children. And on the cover of his Jeffery mixtape, Young Thug even wore a dress.

In comics, writers are using *fatherhood* to explore characters like Superman, Wolverine, and Batman in new ways. Once a brooding loner, Batman was shocked to discover he had a son named Damian, who'd been raised by an assassin. Without him, his son would most likely become a villain, but that was not something Batman could easily fix. Martial arts and high-tech gadgets would not make him the type of father his son would respect. The Dark Knight had to take off his mask and show the other side of his personality—Bruce Wayne. He could only connect with Damian when he was willing to show up in a real way.

Ecclesiastes says, "there is an time for everything." Maybe there was a time when these masks served us, but maybe now it's time to "put away childish things." Our lives demand more from us, and the only way we can show up properly is to stop hiding who we really are and work to finally be truly free.

## REFERENCES

Burks, E. (1972, November 4). Bronx rate of poverty is highest. *The New York Times*. https://www.nytimes.com/1972/11/04/archives/bronx-rate-of-poverty-is-highest.html

DiIulio, J. (1995, November 27). The coming of the super-predators. *Washington Examiner*. https://www.washingtonexaminer.com/magazine/1558817/the-coming-of-the-super-predators/

Eustice, K. (2020, August 1). *Raekwon announces "Only Built 4 Cuban Linx 3" album as original turns 25*. Hip-hop DX. https://hiphopdx.com/news/id.57118/title.raekwon-announces-only-built-for-cuban-linx-3-album-as-original-turns-25

Genter, R. (2007). "With great power comes great responsibility": Cold War culture and the birth of marvel comics". *The Journal of Popular Culture*, 40(6), 953–78. https://doi.org/10.1111/j.1540-5931.2007.00480.x

Gubaydullin, M. (2013, September 26). Robert Moses and the Cross-Bronx Expressway. *Politics and Society Since Vietnam*, Fall 2013. https://blogs.baruch.cuny.edu/his3460fall2013/?p=217

hooks, b. (2004). *We real cool—Black men and masculinity*. Routledge, Taylor and Francis Group.

Ice Cube (1990). Endangered species—Tales from the darkside [Song]. On *Amerikkka's most wanted* [Album]. Priority Records, Capitol Records.

Jenkins, S. (2000). The return of Iron Man. *SPIN*. https://books.google.com/books?id=Lupf_ZdXF98C&pg=PA125&dq#v=onepage&q&f=false

Jones, O. (2023, February 21). Inside the block party where hip-hop was born. *Essence*. https://www.essence.com/entertainment/the-block-party-where-hip-hop-was-born-1973/

LA Times Archive. (1996, July 7). Dole seeks to get tough on young criminals. *Los Angeles Times*. https://www.latimes.com/archives/la-xpm-1996-07-07-mn-22017-story.html

Majors, R., & Billson, J. (1992). *Cool pose: The dilemmas of Black manhood in America*. Simon and Schuster.

Ndiaye, D. (2024, September 14). *How the Bronx burned*. Bronx River Alliance. https://bronxriver.org/post/greenway/how-the-bronx-burned

Rose, T. (1994). *Black noise: Rap music and Black culture in contemporary america*. Wesleyan University Press.

Susaneck, A. P. (2024). *The Bronx: The Cross Bronx Expressway*. Segregation by Design. https://www.segregationbydesign.com/the-bronx/the-cross-bronx-expressway

CHAPTER 10

# TO MURDER THE HUNGER

The Boondocks, the Exorcism and/or Beating of Tom DuBois, and an Appeal to Black Male Solidarity

GEORGE WHITE JR.

## I. INTRODUCTION

Those of us who are the direct targets of white supremacist capitalist patriarchy face important decisions every day about how we will shape ourselves. Our oppressors prefer to deny us our basic humanity, instead shaping us into arch caricatures of fully actualized people. We lose this battle when, among other things, we surrender to the identity of "monster" or "animal," and, ironically, we often do so in a spirit of self-defense. The fantasies and caricatures of our oppressors come bearing an insatiable hunger for completion that rests on self-abnegation, impatience, and the concomitant contempt for the world and others who dwell in it, particularly others who look like us. Consequently, one path to self-realization is to murder that hunger, to assert our humanity, and to defend it by defending the humanity of all others. Through his hip-hop-inflected storytelling, Aaron McGruder attempts to chart such a path.

This chapter explores the cultural tools that McGruder deployed in an effort to create a vision of Black solidarity that can murder this hunger. It will situate the animated version of *The Boondocks* within the Black comedic tradition, while homing in on a specific episode of the television series. Finally, the chapter will offer a gendered critique of that episode by examining the absence of Black women from this subversive vision, suggesting that the exclusion of Black women is a fatal flaw in the artist's scheme to free Black people. By unintentionally reinforcing Patriarchy, McGruder's artistic quest ultimately will create a different hunger.

In season 2, episode 4 (aired October 29, 2007) of the animated TV show *The Boondocks*, a scene opens on a typical suburban mall parking lot in which mild-mannered Tom DuBois is looking for a parking spot. After he activates his turn signal, another driver races into the spot. Tom voices his displeasure at the driver: "What the.... Oh come on, you ... nincompoop! ... Hey, that was my space. I had my blinker on and everything!" The other driver, an adult Black male, retorts in withering fashion: "Fuck you, punk ass, bougie ass n***a. I beat yo' mo'fuckin', saddidy ass, n***a. Don't ever in yo' life try to holla at me, n***a." As the other driver punctuates his statement with a finger to Tom's chest, Tom stands transfixed, unable to respond. The other driver mumbles, "Fuck wit me, n***a, and I'll be done popped a trunk on yo bitch ass," as he walks away.

Feeling angry and disrespected, Tom's body quakes and suddenly surrenders to the demented soul of the deceased enemy of the Freeman family, Colonel Stinkmeaner. As the other driver continues walking away, Stinkmeaner/Tom exclaims, "What did you say, n***a?" The other driver turns around to say, "You know what, motherfucka? Eat a dick, n***a!" As the other driver returns, Stinkmeaner/Tom leaps in the air and kicks the other driver in the chest, knocking him to the ground. Stinkmeaner/Tom lectures the other driver: "Look atcha! You was poppin' all that good shit a minute ago. Then you got kicked in yo' chest! You eat a dick, n***a. You eat a dick!" As the other driver writhes in pain on the ground and tries to crawl away, Stinkmeaner's spirit exits Tom's body, and the audience hears Tom plaintively cry: "Oh my God! Sir, are you okay? Who did this to you? What did he look like? Did anyone see who accosted this man?"

This scene fully sets the stage for the episode entitled "Stinkmeaner Strikes Back." The episode explores the rivalry between Granddad Freeman and his nemesis, Colonel Stinkmeaner, while playing along the social fault lines of Blackness. The episode satirizes toxic masculinity and the ways Black people can harm each other, all while excluding Black women from the discourse. Its appeal to a form of Black male solidarity is noteworthy and, perhaps, a reflection of constricted, pre–Black Lives Matter (BLM) efforts to "save" the Black community.

*The Boondocks* television show (which aired on Cartoon Network from 2005–2014) is an example of contemporary storytelling and social critique that is central to the tradition of Black comedy in the United States. Part of what makes *The Boondocks* unique is its hip-hop flavor, sometimes reflected in the characters but even more so in the mélange of visual and aural references at work in each episode. Thus, McGruder's use of skilled comedians, celebrities, and mash-ups of political and pop culture icons helps *The Boondocks* stand out from live-action dramas or other satirical series.

*The Boondocks* comic strip (1999–2005) and, later, TV series centers on the lives of the Freeman family—Robert "Granddad" Freeman, ten-year-old Huey, and eight-year-old Riley—as they navigate the complicated social terrain of contemporary American suburbia. Like the comic strip, the TV show has examined a wide range of topics, from climate change and police brutality to hypermasculinity in hip-hop or the superexploitative effects of unregulated capitalism. Creator Aaron McGruder eschews easy binaries of "good" versus "evil," and his team of writers and voice actors help to complicate audiences' view of social phenomena while playing up the insecurities and shortcomings of the show's central characters, Granddad, Huey, and Riley. Indeed, some regular readers/viewers might assert that *The Boondocks* does its heaviest lifting when exploring the myriad ways in which post-traumatic stress disorders inflect the behaviors of Black Americans. Even as McGruder and his crew delight in satirizing and critiquing contemporary political, social, and cultural icons (whether Black or white), they never lose sight of a core question: what is the truth of the relationship between Black men and America, their ostensible home? (Howard, 2013).

In keeping with the best aspects of the Black comedic tradition in America, *The Boondocks* provides a way of describing and coping with the realities of persistent racial fascism. In a Season 1 episode that I routinely play for students, *The Boondocks* proffered a critique that continues a tradition exemplified by intellectuals and leaders like bell hooks, Malcolm X, Angela Davis, and Martin Luther King, who linked America's savage projections of violence overseas to racial oppression at home. By casting two well-known Black entertainers, Charlie Murphy and Samuel L. Jackson, as voice actors portraying the lawless white characters, Ed the III and Gin Rummy, McGruder and his team call attention to white privilege, and the show exposes the commonplace operation of whiteness through witty writing, parody, and visual cues. The episode, "A Date with the Health Inspector," (season 1, episode 5; aired December 4, 2005) explores which behaviors American society sanctions and privileges, and examines the methods by which media, state actors, and "peer pressure" work to create a "fog of war" that obscures reality.

The episode that is the primary subject of this chapter, "Stinkmeaner Strikes Back," turns McGruder's analytical lasers inward. What follows will be a contextualization of the animated series within the realm of Black comedy and television, including an examination of the layered influence of hip-hop on the show. The analysis builds upon my prior scholarly work that addressed the use of *The Boondocks* to facilitate the discussion of difficult historical topics in a classroom, as well as the power of racialized violence in US foreign policy (white, 2013). Ultimately, this exploration will highlight the fact that McGruder's art offers a path to freedom that is clear but unnecessarily circumscribed.

## II. A BRIEF HISTORY OF *THE BOONDOCKS* AND ITS PLACE IN THE BLACK COMEDIC TRADITION

Aaron McGruder created *The Boondocks* comic strip while he was an African American Studies major at the University of Maryland. The strip became syndicated in 1999 and ran in newspapers across the nation. Given its penchant for racial satire and social commentary, *The Boondocks* received mixed reviews. Many readers and critics dismissed it as "angry," while some objected to what they perceived as the reinforcement of racist stereotypes (Braxton, 2004; Bruchey, 1999, p. 1). Others chastised it for its open mocking of cultural and political elites. In fact, the comic strip was censored in some newspapers for its critique of then-President George W. Bush and many of his advisors. The hip-hop references that peppered the comic strip were manifest on the cover of the second compilation of comics, a tome entitled *Fresh for '01, You Suckas: A Boondocks Collection* (2001). The title of the compilation paraphrases the "Outro"—"*Fresh for '88, you suckers*"—on KRS-One's smash hit "My Philosophy," the lead single on the album *By All Means Necessary* (Boogie Down Productions, n.d.). Lost on most critics is the fact that McGruder's sharp wit takes aim at Blacks and whites, rich and poor, Left/Liberals and Neo-Conservatives, alike (Braxton, 2004; Bruchey, 1999, p. 1). Much like socially conscious rappers Immortal Technique and the Disposable Heroes of Hiphoprisy, McGruder aimed to slay many a sacred cow. At least five of the episodes in the show's inaugural season almost exclusively examine self-inflicted wounds within the Black community (episodes 2, 4, 6, 9, 13).

*The Boondocks* animated television show, featured on Cartoon Network's Adult Swim block of programming, debuted in 2005, and its fourth season aired in 2014. The theme song for the show marks the most obvious influence of hip-hop on the series, a song called "Judo Flip" by the artist Asheru. The lyrics that McGruder deploys for each episode tell us: "I am the stone that the builder refused / I am the visual, the inspiration / that made Lady sing the blues" (Asheru, 2006).

As a framing device, the theme song is a wonderful reflection of the influences on McGruder and his male characters. Although technically a reference to Psalm 118:22, the opening line calls to mind Bob Marley and the song "Cornerstone" on the Bob Marley & the Wailers 1970 album *Soul Rebels*. The seventh line—"I am the ballot in your box"—a call back to Malcolm X's famous speech, also serves to demarcate the line between Granddad and his grandsons, Huey and Riley. Finally, in a particular nod to the dilemma at the heart of "Stinkmeaner Strikes Back," the song urges a Black man to acknowledge another Black man as his "brother" and call him "son," as opposed to some derogatory term like "n****r." As a whole, the theme song centers Black men as the foundation of the community and the source of its actions. The collection of references also speaks poignantly to the African American and Afro-Caribbean influences that created hip-hop, as well as to the passive positioning of Black women in the cultural phenomenon (Chang, 2005).

Although the comic strip and show existed simultaneously only for a year, the expansion of the strip into a different medium signaled McGruder's effort to reach a wider audience, slightly different from the steady consumers of the comic strip. "According to McGruder, younger adults . . . are the target market for his Adult Swim series, and older adults who read the daily newspaper were the target market for his former comic strip" (Whaley, 2013). It bears mentioning that the first collection of McGruder's comics was titled *The Boondocks: Because I Know You Don't Read the Newspaper* (2000). In the book's Dedication, McGruder thanks a number of people, including "the hip-hop artists who used to teach Black people to love themselves . . . and the few who still do." The transition from print to television expanded McGruder's "commitment to candor in comedy," as Harry "Media Assassin" Allen noted in his forward to the compilation (McGruder #1). Much like "the Bomb Squad" did for Public Enemy's records, the move to television allowed McGruder to add layers to his storytelling that would have been impossible in the three-frame limit of a syndicated political cartoon (Forman & Neal, 2004).

At the heart of the comic strip/animated show is the Freeman family: Robert "Granddad" Freeman, and his grandsons, Huey and Riley. The story centers on Granddad's relocation of the family to a predominantly white suburb—the fictional "Woodcrest"—of Chicago and the "shock of arrival" felt by each member of the family (Alexander, 1996). In the TV show, comedian John Witherspoon portrays Granddad, and Emmy Award–winning actress Regina King voices both Huey and Riley. The family members represent three different iterations of the multifaceted Black male experience in America. Equally important is the disappearance of Huey and Riley's parents, creating a negative space in the family that implicitly makes room for the corrosiveness of Mass Incarceration, foster care, and the New Jim/Jane Crow, among other phenomena, on Black families.

On the surface, it appears that Granddad and ten-year-old Huey represent the competing and complementary aspects of the modern civil rights movement—nonviolent civil disobedience and Black Power—while eight-year-old Riley represents the overweening contemporary icon of the "Gangsta" (McGruder #1). The hairstyles drawn for each character reinforce this notion, with Granddad's conservative low-cut, clean-shaven style standing in stark contrast to Huey's spiky Afro and Riley's ever-present skull cap and (later) cornrows. Some observers see the brothers as markers of competing poles of Black culture and Granddad as their mediator (Whaley, 2013). However, on deeper reflection, the Freeman men seem to mark something other than political strands in contemporary Black history. Granddad is the respectable, aspiring Black man who is relatively well-educated, has worked hard all of his life, and aims to achieve satisfaction (if not comfort) by breaching the color barrier imposed by white privilege through the purchase of a home in a white enclave. Granddad is a "striver," representing a cohort of Blacks like Paul Cuffee, T. Thomas Fortune, Madame C. J. Walker, Oprah Winfrey, and the Obamas, who consistently struggled to build wealth within an antagonistic environment. In many ways, Granddad reflects the power and limits of the politics of respectability. In turn, Huey represents the activist, militant strand of Black masculinity through his overt critiques of power, his revolutionary manifestos, and his forays into direct action protest. Riley, on the other hand, represents the pragmatic element of Black manhood that does not believe it is possible to redefine the power relations that capture him and, thus, seeks a face-saving accommodation while simultaneously challenging Huey's idealism. Although Riley invokes analysis, styles, and idioms associated with "Gangsta Rap," his actions and rhetoric reveal a "mother wit" common to generations of Black people who have struggled to survive a society that does not welcome them. Riley sneers at both activism and white privilege, since he is neither a wide-eyed dreamer nor a quiet integrationist. His comments, wrapped in the "cool pose" of young Black men, often underscore a sharp understanding of how the world actually exists, even if he feels powerless to change it (Allen, 2000, p. iii; Howard, 2013, pp. 160–63).

*The Boondocks* fits neatly into longstanding traditions of Black humor. For some Black intellectuals, humor (especially the type that plied racial stereotypes) was a way of coping with the pain of slavery and the anguish of stubborn racialized privilege (Howard, 2013, pp. 151–56; Watkins, 2005; Williams, 1995). To the extent that *The Boondocks* seeks redress of injustices, it fits into the tradition of Black comedy as a form of resistance. As one scholar has written: "By conceding to the possibilities that black comics are doing more than telling jokes, entertaining us, or are otherwise there for our consumption, we endow them with agency so that we can begin to consider ways that analyzing said performances yields new and insightful commentary about race, class, gender, sexuality, and a host of other conditions endemic to life in America, indeed to life everywhere" (Bailey, 2012, p. 257).

McGruder knows that his art is about more than "just jokes" and, as such, effortlessly glides into line behind other Black comedic greats.

In addition to the therapeutic or redemptive paths in Black humor, another possibility exists in a world of "color-blind racism" (Bonilla-Silva, 2006). Glenda Carpio proposes an "incongruity theory" through which artists as diverse as Kara Walker, Ishmael Reed, and Dave Chappelle "do not so much protest against the sociological manifestations of this racism as probe into the subtle and sometimes difficult-to-define ways that the concept of chattel slavery, especially the stereotypical imagery that it produced, influences individual identity, social relations, and artistic production of African Americans" (Carpio, 2008, p. 7).

Black comics like Jackie "Moms" Mabley and Richard Pryor used comedy in therapeutic ways, but they also employed comedy to help people understand the social world. Sometimes their comedy was not just about redeeming Blackness, easing pain, or teasing out absurdities; sometimes their comedy acted as a machine that stripped the mask from the claims of white American nobility, innocence, and primacy to reveal a much less appealing face.

Because so much of the humor of *The Boondocks* comes as the lead characters interrogate each other, one can understand the easy conclusion that the show is simply another "hootin' and hollerin'" comedy in the vein of *Amos 'n' Andy*. For instance, episodes like season 1's "Granddad's Fight" (the prequel to "Stinkmeaner Strikes Back") involve the Freemans criticizing or teasing each other. However, the story offers a critique of a very narrow definition of Black masculinity that requires a Black male to violently respond to any show of disrespect by another Black person. Ultimately, the episode mocks these showings of machismo and mourns the consequences of reflexive action. Of course, the prolific use of "n****r" only seems to drive home the point that the show's humor rests on the plying of negative racial stereotypes. If *The Boondocks* were in less deft hands, this argument might be persuasive. However, much like the paintings and sculptures of Kara Walker, the comedy of *The Boondocks* deploys racial stereotypes and stretches them to their ludicrous, logical conclusions in order to undermine the culture that birthed them. Moreover, the characters' use of "n****r" appears to be a means by which the artists make clear the persistence of white supremacy while also pointing to the ways in which Black people can be complicit in our own oppression. Another fear that critics may hold is the fact that the Freemans are not a "nuclear" family and, thus, reflect a supposedly pathological Black culture. The absence of Huey and Riley's parents may not be a symbol of Black family dysfunction as much as a reflection of the multigenerational families that have always been a part of the Black experience. McGruder and staff never explain the absence of Huey and Riley's parents, but repeatedly demonstrate the love between the generations and refuse to pass judgment on the clan. Finally, like many of the comedies from the 1970s, a great deal of the noteworthy discussions on race emerge from the mouths of Huey and Riley. Yet, unlike the elders in those pioneering shows, Granddad and other adults weigh in on these matters as well, often in equally outrageous ways.

Like Moms Mabley and Richard Pryor, McGruder and his team of artists seek to voice that which remains silent, the willfully forgotten chasms and obstacles between Blacks and the American Dream. McGruder's characters show us that the differences (and differing levels of awareness) between people of color and whites are stark and have a tangible effect on everyday life. Pryor's Long Beach concert performance exposed one of the great aspects of white privilege: that things white people do not even know about often kill Black Americans. The Freeman boys learn this in "Stinkmeaner Strikes Back."

## III. "STINKMEANER STRIKES BACK" AND THE INFLUENCE OF HIP-HOP ON *THE BOONDOCKS*

In season 1, episode 4 (aired November 27, 2005), the audience is introduced to Colonel Stinkmeaner. In short, Granddad gets lost in the blistering heat of a "n***a moment" and accidentally kills Stinkmeaner during a "cage match" set up by Riley. "Stinkmeaner Strikes Back" begins with highlights from the episode "Granddad's Fight" and a voiceover by Wu-Tang Clan member, Ghostface Killah:

> Now, if y'all was payin' attention to last season, y'all know what a "n***a moment" is. A "n***a moment" is when the mind of a perfectly logical Black man is overwhelmed by some stupid n***a shit. Like when a n****r steps up on ya sneakers and fucks up your kicks, or hits your car and some shit. And the n*****r get mad like it's your fault, like you fucked up. So his ignorance makes you act crazy. And the next thing you know, n*****s is beefin', shootin', fightin' and someone ends up dead. But, yo, not even death can stop a n***a moment.

The audience then sees Colonel Stinkmeaner engaged in martial arts training in Hell. As the Devil compliments Stinkmeaner's ferocity and wickedness, Stinkmeaner fights and defeats a "swarm" of demons. This demonstration of martial arts prowess prompts the Devil to agree to send Stinkmeaner back to the mortal realm "to exact vengeance on the Freeman family and . . . spread ignorance and chaos in the Black community." When Stinkmeaner returns to Earth, he possesses the body of Tom DuBois during the aforementioned altercation over a parking spot.

As Granddad is taking pictures to post on his online dating profile page, Huey confides that he had a dream that Stinkmeaner was returning from Hell to terrorize the family. Granddad tries to calm Huey by dismissing the idea that anyone can return from the dead to hurt the family. (time mark 3:19–4:32). Over the course of the episode, the audience watches as Stinkmeaner/Tom disrupts Tom's professional and personal lives. As Granddad prepares for a date, Stinkmeaner/Tom attacks the Freeman family. After the Freemans eventually subdue Stinkmeaner/Tom, Huey and Riley tie him to Riley's bed in the boy's bedroom. After regaining consciousness, Stinkmeaner/Tom ruins Granddad's date by verbally insulting him from the bedroom, forcing the elder Freeman to call for an exorcist.

The only person whom Granddad can reach is Uncle Ruckus. Uncle Ruckus tells the assembled Freemans that "we must use these tools that the great God has given us to fight n*****s: a whip, a noose, a nightstick, a branding iron. These things strike fear into a n*****'s heart. A job application" (time mark 16:16–16:28). As Ruckus enters the boys' bedroom to confront Stinkmeaner/Tom, he declares "In the name of white Jesus and all great white men who have come thereafter, I command thou Black n****r soul back to the depths of Hell!" (time mark 17:00–17:09). Following Ruckus's example, Granddad and Riley begin beating Stinkmeaner/Tom for hours. Huey, knowing that this is the wrong approach, refuses to join them. "This isn't an exorcism. It's a beating," Huey says, to which Ruckus replies, "There's very little difference" (time mark 17:58–18:03). Having failed to exorcise and/or beat the ghost of Stinkmeaner out of Tom, Huey has an epiphany and engages a risky gambit.

"Stinkmeaner, you hate Black people, don't you?" the ten-year-old asks. Stinkmeaner/Tom replies, "I sure do. I mean, I hate everyone in general, but Black people especially." "And, and, Ruckus, you hate Black people too," Huey says over his shoulder. "I wouldn't exactly call 'em 'people,' but yeah, yeah, I have a deep distaste for negroids," Ruckus retorts. Quickly seizing the moment, Huey turns back to Stinkmeaner/Tom and asks, "And, Stinkmeaner, I bet you hate Rap Music?" Stinkmeaner/Tom answers, "If you can call that ol' stinky booty, gorilla noise 'music,'" a remark that brings a chuckle out of Ruckus. "Stinky booty, heh, heh, heh. I must say that's a brilliant observation, 'meaner.'" As Ruckus and Stinkmeaner delight in their mutual hatred of hip-hop, Huey's voiceover reveals the strategy: "I forgot that a n***a moment cannot be resolved with violence. But where there's harmony and peace . . . (Stinkmeaner's soul begins to leave Tom's body) a n***a moment cannot exist" (time mark 18:47–19:40). Hip-hop is central to the execution of this story in wonderful and, possibly, unexpected ways.

Although it might be tempting to connect *The Boondocks* to the small subgenre of "Comedy Rap," such a connection misses the mark. The comic strip and animated series are typically humorous and thought-provoking but have more in common with politically conscious rap groups like Public Enemy and X-Clan, with satirical rap groups like De La Soul or with the mockumentary *Fear of a Black Hat* (1993), than they do with Zack Fox (of *Abbott Elementary* fame), Fu-Shnickens, or the Odd Future offshoot group "I Smell Panties." The comedy is built into *The Boondocks*' DNA, so hip-hop serves other purposes.

The appearance of Ghostface Killah in apparition form to Huey suggests that hip-hop is a source of wisdom and guidance. Ghost's opening voiceover establishes the premise for, and tension within, "Stinkmeaner Strikes Back." Ghost's witty banter with Huey matches the comic sensibilities of the show without making a dark subject feel even heavier. Not only does Ghost confirm the validity of Huey's dream, he also leads Huey to a resolution of the problem. On both occasions of his appearance to Huey, Ghost concludes his remarks with "Think about it. Peace!" This was not just a salutation but encouragement to ruminate on the threat.

In addition to the framing done by the theme song, hip-hop beats serve to punctuate certain moments in the animated show. Just before Tom witnesses his parking space stolen, we hear hip-hop beats that signal an impending confrontation. As Huey meditates on the meaning of his dream about Stinkmeaner's return from death, the audience hears a hip-hop track, then Ghostface Killah appears. A different set of beats marks the conclusion of the show as day breaks and Tom wakes to find himself bruised, battered, and chained to Riley's bed. This differs from the music that plays at other times in the episode.

McGruder also uses hip-hop for its history. Recall that Ghostface Killah—perhaps the least likely member of the Wu-Tang Clan to engage in de-escalation of a dispute—is the only person who confirms Huey's premonition. And that character is the only one willing to guide Huey to a reasonable resolution. In contrast, Granddad repeatedly rejects Huey's entreaties. Even when the boys have Stinkmeaner/Tom taped to Riley's bed, Granddad admits that he hadn't taken seriously Huey's warning, then ignores Huey's pleas to forget about his date and focus on resolving the issue with Stinkmeaner. Granddad also ignores Riley's pertinent questioning: "Why we gotta put the n****r in my bed . . . my bed ain't the only bed up in here. What if he pees in the bed, or vomits or shoots a deuce?" (time mark 13:09–13:25). Hip-hop's history of emerging from the marginalization of and disinvestment in Black/Brown communities is littered with examples of adults (usually, but not exclusively, those in power) refusing to listen to youth. In this context, hip-hop reinforces the ease with which adults can dismiss or overlook the concerns of young people and children (Chang, 2005, pp. 89–107; Orejuela, 2015, pp. 9–16).

In terms of storytelling, McGruder's take mirrors the "rags to riches" trope of many hip-hop songs. Typically, these rap music stories involve a protagonist struggling against insurmountable odds or the dismissiveness of broader society, only to triumph in the end. (Chang, 2005, pp. 26–28, 99–107, 184–87; see also Kendrick Lamar, "Swimming Pools [Drank]"). In "Stinkmeaner Strikes Back," Huey tries to warn Granddad to no avail, but eventually finds a way to defeat a supernatural force. This story arc is not unusual. "The Fund-Raiser," episode 7 of Season 3, illuminates Riley's efforts to use a school fundraising project to enrich himself, reflecting the ethos of "get rich or die trying" (50 Cent, 2003). Beyond the storytelling, hip-hop's influence on The Boondocks is evident in how some of the characters adorn themselves and their living spaces, or how they speak.

As previously mentioned, the hairstyles of Huey and Riley are similar to youth culture styles worn by artists like Craig Mack (afro) and Snoop Dogg (cornrows). In other episodes throughout the series, the character Thugnificent wears his hair in two Afro puffs, similar to a style worn by Ludicrous at an early stage in his career. Huey and Riley's bedroom prominently features a poster of Malcolm X, a bit of iconography enjoyed by Black Power advocates and political rappers alike. (McQuillar, 2007; see also the album cover for "By All Means Necessary"). When the episode under current examination first reveals Stinkmeaner, he says his name, then shouts "Holla at'cha boy! I gets money," something that makes no sense in a spiritual plane, but that, in the world of hip-hop, marks him as a serious person. And all of Stinkmeaner's insults and one-liners sound more like those of a contemporary rap artist or rap consumer instead of the dated references and sayings that might be used by an octogenarian.

Hip-hop also encouraged McGruder to mix and match references and styles, much like a 1980s DJ crew. In addition to layering references to The Exorcist (1973) over the "n***a moment," McGruder also invoked the Kung

Fu movies that inspired generations of breakdancers, graffiti artists, and rappers like Wu-Tang Clan and Digable Planets (Chang, 2005, pp. 109–25). The "sports montage" of Stinkmeaner in Hell actually opens with a stylized rendition of the title sequence of a Shaw Brothers Hong Kong film. And many of the characters in *The Boondocks* fight in a martial arts style or aspire to do so. It also bears mentioning that Asian American artists like Seung Eun Kim help draw the characters in a style similar to the artwork in the current Netflix animated series *Ninja Kamui*. The existence of hip-hop almost acts like a form of permission to create these layers within the story. Importantly, an underlying message throughout the series appears to be that Black cultural expression can be enhanced by Afro-Asian solidarity (Orejuela, 2005).

## IV. CONCLUSION: U.N.I.T.Y.? THE POWER/LIMITS OF MC MCGRUDER OR HUEY FREEMAN'S NARROW PATH TO "FREEDOM"

Not unlike the prototypical hip-hop DJs of the 1970s and '80s, McGruder brings to bear numerous styles and pop culture references to his animated television show. The characters in "Stinkmeaner Strikes Back" use hip-hop in its various manifestations to chart a course to freedom. However, the absence of Black women constrains their vision and, ultimately, could derail their quest.

In McGruder's hands, a "n****r" is not a permanent identity. Indeed, it is not even part of a dialectic. Thus, the episode is a rejection of the Chris Rock binary from his famous stand-up comedy routine: "It's like a civil war going on with Black people and there are two sides: there's Black people and there's n*****s" (*Chris Rock: Bring the Pain* [1996]). This view of the identity as transitory and impermanent—in this case, Tom became a n****r because Stinkmeaner's ghost possessed him—is reminiscent of the lyrics of MC Lyte, Lauryn Hill, Stetsasonic, Dead Prez, and Ms. Melody, rappers who aimed to help Black people redeem themselves. McGruder foreshadowed this story arc in the first season's "Return of the King" (episode 9, aired January 15, 2006).

In that episode, McGruder creates an alternate American future in which Rev. Martin Luther King Jr. had not been killed by an assassin's bullet, simply placed in a coma. King regains consciousness nearly thirty years later and is barely able to recognize the America he left. Prodded by Huey, the revived MLK aims to create a political party to renew the nation's commitment to justice. But when the plan goes awry—because a serious political event was marketed as a party—MLK loses his patience with the crowd he sees and offers a scornful assessment, which includes referring to those in attendance as "n*****s" (time mark 18:18–19:48).

In short, a n****r is a Black person whose soul is hungry. This soul hunger, like white supremacy, is insatiable and can only be addressed through the dominance of other Black people, conspicuous consumption, reflexive violence, and a propensity to seek an individual accommodation with white power instead of the collective struggle for freedom that is the hallmark of Black movements for freedom, among other things. But since Black women largely are absent in "Stinkmeaner Strikes Back," the audience may be missing other behaviors that surface from the n****r persona, as well as other methods of transformation back to Black. Interestingly, Black women were part of the audience that the revived MLK addressed in "Return of the King." So it would seem that their absence from "Stinkmeaner Strikes Back" is not an accident. Perhaps their absence is an indication that McGruder feels ill-equipped to talk about how n***a moments might manifest themselves in family violence, drug abuse, date/marital rape, child/family abandonment, or infidelity. And, as a result, perhaps the artists cannot suggest other methods of creating harmony aside from two old Black men relishing in a shared hatred of hip-hop. And this absence is unfortunate because it was lyricists like Queen Latifah who demanded the creation of a truly harmonious community, even as Black men often acted as the most proximate tormentors of Black women (Collins, 1999; Davis, 1990; hooks, 1994; Morgan, 1999; Wynter, 2022).

The disappearance of Black women from the narrative is troubling in multiple ways. First, it is an act of symbolic annihilation that contributes to the disempowerment and social isolation of Black women (Howard, 2013, p. 165). Moreover, this disappearance tells the audience that Black women are not problem-solvers. The more profound implication is that, if they are not problem-solvers, Black women could be a source of problems. This dynamic is reflected in, among other places, in the early 1990s conversation between rapper Ice Cube and radical activist/educator Angela Davis. When their conversation turned to the matter of gender, Ice Cube justified his masculinist approach to Black communal restoration by saying "[b]ut the Black woman can't look up to the Black man until we get up." Davis shot back, "[w]ell why should the Black woman look up to the Black man? Why can't we look at each other as equals?" Ice Cube simply shrugged off the recommendation: "[i]f we look at each other on an equal level, what you're going to do is have a divide. It's going to be divided" (Chang, 2005). The experiences of Black female rappers, especially after the rise of so-called Gangsta Rap, further demonstrate this hierarchical notion of community-building.

The corporate reordering of the music industry that quickly followed on the heels of Gangsta Rap saw music industry executives making bigger financial bets on fewer artists and fewer projects. This narrowing of the diversity of ideas and sounds also led to a narrowing of voices. Celebrated female rappers of the 1980s like MC Lyte, Roxanne Shante, and Salt-n-Pepa vanished, and the most resonant hip-hop feminist voices emerged from the neosoul genre. Although music fans associate neosoul with artists like Erykah Badu, Jill Scott, or Lauryn Hill, perhaps the best exemplar of this transition was Angie Stone. Stone had been a member of the pioneering, all-female rap group The Sequence. With little to no room for a heavy-set, dark-skinned Black woman to maneuver in hip-hop (Missy Elliott being a notable exception), Stone resurfaced in the realm of neosoul as a singer (Chang, 2005, pp. 443–47; see also Bogle, 1996, p. 291). Hip-hop's marginalization of Black female artists parallels their ostracism in *The Boondocks*.

In an episode about overcoming "n\*\*\*a moments" and creating peace in the Black community, the absence of Black female problem-solvers diminishes the potential analyses of issues and the development of solutions. It is as if to say that silencing Black women is fundamental to achieving "harmony" in the Black community. Yet, real-world events demonstrate that this phallocentric approach is nothing more than a pyrrhic victory. Although airing a decade before the eruption of Black Lives Matter protests, "Stinkmeaner Strikes Back" anticipated the devolution of Black protest movements in the new millennium. Although three Black women created the phrase "Black Lives Matter—then built an international movement with a horizontal leadership structure—mainstream media focused on Black male leaders and demonized the founders. And now, in the second Trump era, the nauseating attacks on DEI initiatives and so-called "woke culture" go unchallenged by any visible Black Left political formation, leaving many of us to fear the return of Jim/Jane Crow to every aspect of Black life (Cullors et al., 2020).

Despite these limitations, *The Boondocks* stands as a thought-provoking show that seems like an heir to the tradition begun by *The Richard Pryor Show* (1977) and carried on by shows like *In Living Color* (1990–94). Given the racial history of television, *The Boondocks* is a critical antidote to a culture of "the middle" that celebrates mindless consumption, endless competition, and obedience to authority (Marc, 1989, pp. 26–28, 177). As Whaley points out, "[i]f, as McGruder muses, his younger audience members are not reading newspapers for information on a daily basis, his Afro-Anime satire is ever more vital in serving as the medium through which they might find encouragement to raise their consciousness to a critical level" (2013, p. 201). In addition to incisive content, the television series is a perfect example of storytelling in the twenty-first century that exists on multiple media platforms and is multicultural in its performance. *The Boondocks* reveals how a multilayered critique can be conveyed through the creative use of anime-style art, seasoned comedic writers, and the inventive casting of celebrity voice actors. It also reveals the narrow path forward that its characters identify for their audience.

What McGruder is driving at in "Stinkmeaner Strikes Backs" is both the results of succumbing to white supremacy as well as a means to navigate it. The unmistakable conclusion is that in McGruder's visual art, hip-hop is both a source of chaos and a means of salvation. But Black women are missing in this art, unnecessarily limiting its vision and constraining its offer of repair and redemption. Sadly, this invisibility also is reflective of some of the worst aspects of hip-hop and its history. Despite McGruder's shortcomings (Forman & Neal, 2004, p. 309), Arrested Development reminds us that there "can't be a revolution without women/can't be a revolution without children" (Genius, Arrested Development, "Mama's Always On Stage," 1992).

## REFERENCES

Alexander, M. (1996). *The shock of arrival: Reflections on postcolonial experience.* South End Press.

Allen, H. (2000) Foreword. In A. McGruder (Ed.), *The Boondocks: Because I know you don't read the newspaper.* Andrew McNeel Publishing.

Amidi, A. (2004, August 31). *The John Kricfalusi interview, part 2.* Cartoon Brew. https://www.cartoonbrew.com/old-brew/the-john-kricfalusi-interview-part-2-434.html

Asheru (2006). Judo flip [Song]. On *Hip-hop docktrine: The official "Boondocks" mixtape.* Guerilla Arts Ink.

Bailey, C. (2012). Fight the power: African American humor as a discourse of resistance. *Western Journal of Black Studies, 36*(4), 253–63.

Barnes, R. (Writer), McGruder, A. (Writer), Taylor, Y. (Writer), Horne, J. (Director), Hathcock, B. (Director), & Thomas, L. (Director). (2005, December 4). A date with the health inspector (Season 1, Episode 5) [TV series episode]. In A. McGruder, R. Hudlin, & R. Barnes (Executive Producers), *The Boondocks.* Rebel Base Productions; Sony Pictures Television.

Bennetts, L. (1987, August 9). Theater; the pain behind the laughter of Moms Mabley. *The New York Times.* https://www.nytimes.com/1987/08/09/theater/theater-the-pain-behind-the-laughter-of-moms-mabley.html

Bogle, D. (1996). *Toms, coons, mulattoes, mammies, & bucks: An interpretive history of Blacks in American films.* The Continuum Publishing Company.

Bonilla-Silva, E. (2006). *Racism without racists: Color-blind racism and the persistence of inequality in the United States.* Rowman & Littlefield.

Boogie Down Productions. (1988). *By all means necessary* [Album]. Jive Records; RCA Records.

Boogie Down Productions. (n.d). *My philosophy lyrics.* Genius Lyrics. https://genius.com/Boogie-down-productions-my-philosophy-lyrics

Braxton, G. (2004, April 25). He's gotta fight the powers that be: Aaron McGruder's in-your-face cartoon strip, "The Boondocks," takes no prisoners—Black or White. How did this nice young man from the suburbs get so mad? *Los Angeles Times.* https://www.latimes.com/archives/la-xpm-2004-apr-25-tm-mcgruder17-story.html

Bruchey, S. (1999, June 9). Ironic or insulting? *Los Angeles Times.* https://www.latimes.com/archives/la-xpm-1999-jun-09-cl-45492-story.html

Carpio, G. (2008). *Laughing fit to kill: Black humor in the fictions of slavery.* Oxford University Press.

Chang, J. (2005). *Can't stop/won't stop: A history of the hip-hop generation.* Picador.

Coleman, R. & Cavalcante, A. (2013). Two different worlds: Television as a producer's medium. In B. Smith-Shomade (Ed.), *Watching while Black* (pp. 33–48). Rutgers University Press.

Collins, P. H. (1999). *Black feminist thought: Knowledge, consciousness, and the politics of empowerment* (2nd ed.). Routledge.

Cullors, P., Bandele, A., & Davis, A. Y. (2020). *When they call you a terrorist: A Black Lives Matter memoir.* St. Martin's Griffin.

Davis, A. (1990). *Women, culture & politics.* Vintage Books.

50 Cent. (2003). *Get rich or die tryin'* [Album]. Shady Records; Aftermath Entertainment; Interscope Records; G-Unit Records.

Forman, M., & Neal, M. A. (2004). *That's the joint! The hip-hop studies reader.* Routledge.

Genius Lyrics. (n.d.). Mama's always on stage by Arrested Development [Lyrics]. https://genius.com/Arrested-development-mamas-always-on-stage-lyrics

hooks, b. (1994, February). Misogyny, gangsta rap, and "The Piano." *Z Magazine.*

Howard, S. C. (2013). Gender, race, and "The Boondocks." In S. C. Howard & R. L. Jackson (Eds.), *Black comics: Politics of race and representation* (pp. 89–104). Bloomsbury Academic.

Ibrahim, S. (2016, January 8). An ode to Jalessa Vinson: The unsung hero of "A Different World." The Root. https://www.theroot.com/an-ode-to-jaleesa-vinson-the-unsung-hero-of-a-differen-1822521726

IMDB. (n.d.). *The Boondocks.* IMDb. https://www.imdb.com/title/tt0373732/

Jeffries, L. B. (2010, January 18). The film noir roots of "Cowboy Bebop." PopMatters. https://www.popmatters.com/cowboy-bebop-film-noir-roots

Lamar, K. (2012). *good kid, m.A.A.d city* [Album]. Top Dawg Entertainment; Aftermath Entertainment; Interscope Records.

Marc, D. (1989). *Comic visions: Television comedy and American culture.* Unwin Hyman.

McGruder, A. (2000). *The Boondocks: Because I know you don't read the newspaper.* Andrews McMeel Publishing.

McGruder, A. V. (Executive Producer). (2005–2014). *The Boondocks* [TV series]. Rebel Base Productions (seasons 1–3), New Line Cinema, & Sony Pictures Television.

McQuillar, T. L. (2007). *When rap music had a conscience.* Thunder's Mouth Press.

Morgan, J. (1999). *When chickenheads come home to roost: My life as a hip-hop feminist.* Simon & Schuster.

Orejuela, F. (2015). *Rap and hip-hop culture.* Oxford University Press.

rboylorn. (2015, September 10). *Love, hip-hop, and ratchet respectability (Something like a review)*. Crunk Feminist Collective. https://www.crunkfeministcollective.com/2015/09/10/love-hip-hop-and-ratchet-respectability-something-like-a-review/

Reynolds, M. (2004, October 14). Bush "not concerned" about Bin Laden in '02. *Los Angeles Times*. https://www.latimes.com/archives/la-xpm-2004-oct-14-na-osama14-story.html

Scheinin, R. (2013, October 8). *The complete Nicholas Payton interview with Richard Scheinin*. Nicholas Payton. https://nicholaspayton.com/the-complete-nicholas-payton-interview-with-richard-scheinin/

Smith-Shomade, B. E. (Ed.). (2013). *Watching while Black: Centering the television of Black audiences*. Rutgers University Press.

Watkins, M. (2005). *Stepin Fetchit: The life and times of Lincoln Perry*. Pantheon.

Whaley, D. E. (2013). Graphic blackness/anime noir: Aaron McGruder's The Boondocks and the Adult Swim. In B. E. Smith-Shomade (Ed.), *Watching while Black: Centering the television of Black audiences* (pp. 187–204). Rutgers University Press.

white, g., jr. (2017). "Say what one mo' time": Transmedia storytelling and racial violence in the 21st century through the lens of The Boondocks. *The Projector: A Journal on Film, Media, and Culture, 17*(1), 53–83.

white, g., jr. (2013). "I may not know nuttin' about history but I ain't stupid:" Using "The Boondocks" to teach about slavery, resistance, and the creation of usable pasts. *FIRE!!!: The Multimedia Journal of Black Studies, 2*(1), 26–59.

Williams, E. A. (1995). *The humor of Jackie "Moms" Mabley: An African American tradition*. Garland.

Wynter, S. (2022). *We must learn to sit down together and talk about a little culture: Decolonizing essays 1967–1984*. Peepal Tree Press.

CHAPTER 11

# "I'M MICHAEL JORDAN, I'M NOT MALCOLM X"

Performing Black Masculinity in *The Boys*

COLLIN M. BRIGHT, KATHRYN HOBSON, LEA BEKA, AND DANIEL SILVER

*This chapter includes spoilers for all four seasons of* The Boys; *proceed cautiously.*

## INTRODUCTION

*The Boys* (2019–present) is a satirical television series developed by Eric Kripke for Amazon Prime about a world where supes (superheroes) and nonsupes (ordinary people) coexist in a world much like ours. In the series, notions of traditional superhero tropes from what we have always known them to be—selfless, brave, and driven to the higher calling of justice—become more complex, human, and ultimately flawed. Almost all supes are selfish, egotistical, and image-driven, while a few are power-hungry narcissists and violent killers.

In the show, seven superheroes (named "The Seven") work for Vought, a pharmaceutical, entertainment, and defense corporation that licenses and attempts to make and control superheroes. The plot unfolds when A-Train (Jessie T. Usher), a member of The Seven and the fastest man on Earth, runs through the protagonist, Hughie's (Jack Quaid) girlfriend, Robin (Jess Salgueiro), killing her in front of Hughie's face. Rather than stopping to help

Hughie, the tall, incredibly fit Black man, in his tight blue unitard, sporty sunglasses, and shaved head, looks to Hughie and, between exasperated breaths, says, "I can't stop, I can't stop" and zips away, leaving a wake of chaos, as Hughie holds his girlfriend's dismembered arms.

Vought tries to bribe Hughie and buy his silence with an NDA, but he refuses the offer and joins forces with the Boys—a ragtag group of misfits who aim to destroy Vought. While Robin's death is a catalyst for the events that follow, every one of the Boys hates Vought, and these stories converge, creating a domino effect that slowly chips away at Vought's perfect image and exposes the corruption infiltrating the institution.

Our chapter begins by reviewing and connecting scholarship on speculative fiction and hip-hop culture. Next, we justify the use of the text *The Boys* as rife with political-satirical examples for many of our modern-day culture wars, like abortion, LGBTQ+ rights, defunding police, and confronting the threat of global warming. Then, in our analysis, we draw on critical perspectives of power and performativity as we critique the performances of three primary Black characters, A-Train (Jessie T. Usher), Sister Sage (Susan Heyward), and Mother's Milk (Laz Alonzo; referred to as MM from here), specifically, explicating the latter two's influence on A-Train's racial and gendered performance transformation. Although our culture gives us a homogenous view of what it means to perform Blackness, *The Boys* demonstrates that there is no one way to be a Black person in our culture. For Collin, this offers hope for his performance of Black masculinity, and for Hobson, Lea, and Daniel, this critique problematizes the monolith of representations of Blackness as overwhelmingly negative.

## POSITIONALITY

But who are The Others, and what are we doing here? We are an unlikely group of cultural critics, but, like the OG four characters in *The Boys*, here we are: First author, Collin Bright, is a young, Black, PhD student and hip-hop lover; second author, Kathryn Hobson, is a white, middle-ish-aged queer, enby, femme faculty member; third author, Lea Beka, is a white, queer, Kosovan filmmaker and musician, undergraduate student; and fourth author, Daniel Silver, is a white, Christian, cishet man, and recent undergrad graduate. As such, through our reflexive scholarship, we are committed to self-reflection, acknowledging our points of privilege and places of marginality.

So, let's get started, shall we? As Butcher would say, "You just want to kick back, drink a few Mai Tais, and let us do all the work, is that it?"

On that note, bottoms up from The Others.

# WHY *THE BOYS*

*The Boys*, a popular streaming show, premiered in 2019 on Amazon Prime, and over six million viewers watched its first episode (Porter, 2019). The first season was favorably reviewed, with critics praising the show's willingness to "engage in heavy, relevant themes" (Rotten Tomatoes, n.d.a). The second season started with a viewership of 891 million minutes viewed in its first week (Porter, 2020a) before shooting up to over 1 billion minutes viewed in the next week (Porter, 2020b). The Internet Movie Database (IMDb) gives the series an overall rating of 8.7 out of 10.[1] The show's second season was nominated for five Emmys, including Outstanding Drama Series (IMDb, n.d.). Season four of *The Boys* held steady at just over a billion minutes of views in the first week it aired (Porter, 2024). The viewing numbers of seasons two and three put *The Boys* above other streaming shows like *The Office* and *Friends*, therefore being culturally impactful.

We chose *The Boys* because it serves as a metonymy of contemporary America, a metarepresentation depicting the pervasiveness of white supremacy through satirical fiction. As viewers, we watch a superhero show about egotistical and licentious supes who center their needs above all because it provides an eerie critique of present-day Fascist GOP leaders and the cult of MAGA that blindly follows this leadership without critical inquiry.

## LITERATURE REVIEW

### Speculative Fiction

Speculative fiction is a genre set in something other than the ordinary world, frequently including science fiction or supernatural elements. Its global popularity has produced prevalent work involving superheroes (i.e., *The Avengers* [2012]). In media, we see superheroes as comforting characters who can persevere through obstacles (Smith, 2009; Tilley, 2018). Speculative fiction uses superheroes to make audiences feel more hopeful and empowered in their frustrations by "providing a fantasy of having the supernatural capability to overcome those barriers" (Smith, 2009, p. 132).[2]

The newest developments in this subgenre use superheroes to reflect the changes in the current society and push the audience's boundaries. Moreover, some of the more recent examples of superheroes present power abuse and "the violation of human rights," not seen "as problematic by the state in and of themselves," but instead a public image/relations problem that could hinder their power (Jenkins & Secker, 2021, p. 222). However, we note that even within the more progressive stories, superhero characters are still created within a normative white supremacist cishet patriarchal and capitalist system, which consequently "muzzles" rather than empowers them [superheroes] to execute their own "radical promise" (Kirkpatrick, 2023, p. 20).

Moreover, there are often two competing visions of masculinity presented in comics: hypermasculinity, represented by the traditional muscle-bound superhero in a skin-tight suit that shows every muscle and vein, versus the nerdy, everyday man who is often more cerebral but seen as physically soft and weak, usually feminine (Brown, 2021). Brown (2000) states that for superheroes, traditional masculinity is usually "defined by what it is not, namely 'feminine'" (p. 168). Beyond that, the masculine "Other" is weak, soft, and feminine. For example, the gay man is effeminate, the Jewish man is weak, and the Asian man is small (Brown, 2000). Unsurprisingly, in comics, representations of Black masculinity have often been separated into stereotypical binaries of "authentic" and "inauthentic" or "real" and "fake" (Rodriquez, 2018), which mirrors hip-hop culture (Máthé, 2019).[3]

### Hip-Hop, Black Masculinity, and Authenticity

Hip-hop began in the summer of 1973 in the Bronx, New York, and has since given a voice to Black people to share their stories as a means to fight against systemic oppression and police brutality. For our chapter, we are drawing on Forman's (2004) definition, who writes, "Hip-hop can be seen as a series of practices with an evolved history and the ongoing potential to challenge both social norms and legal stricture; in hip-hop, there are always stakes of crucial importance" (p. 1).[4]

Like comic books featuring black superheroes, the representations of Black masculinity in hip-hop culture are often framed around similar binary logics of real/authentic vs fake/cosplay. As Forman (2002) suggests, "[authenticity combines] aspects of racial essentialism, spatial location, and a fundamental adherence to the principles and practices of the hip-hop culture" (p. xviii). Often, we see this dichotomy formed by discourses of struggle, violence, poverty, location, gang affiliations, and gendered performances (Boyd, 1997). While authentic/inauthentic is a prominent binary discourse in most hip-hop, it is overwhelmingly a trope for Black men's representations in hip-hop (Rodriguez, 2018).

Hip-hop music has roots in political revolution; however, hip-hop does not exist in a cultural vacuum; neoliberal ideologies have influenced it. With the commodification of hip-hop music by corporations like Clear Channel and UMG, politically conscious hip-hop was suppressed for a "gangsta" image that was selling to a predominantly white audience that was fascinated by this supposedly "authentic" portrayal of complex, rebellious Black masculinity within hip-hop. However, authenticity is a performatively constructed notion born from the influence of discourse, socio-political institutions, and material conditions. Authenticity is paradoxical, fortifying socio-cultural tenets while cementing class and racial subordination. (Boyd, 1997). For instance, MCs often adopt this hegemonic performance of "authenticity" by calling out "inauthenticity" as a discursive strategy to sell more records, which produces racial and class subservience and discrimination at the hands of wealthy, white male corporate executives (Wright, 2004).

Because "authenticity" concretizes through a series of discourses and performances, it shifts with the change of location, a multiracial MC, or a middle-class origin story; it is too simplistic of a frame for the entire community of Black men's masculinity. The notion of authenticity is not a biological imperative but is couched in a white supremacist performance of authentic Blackness and inauthentic Blackness. Rather than an essential part of Black manhood, "authenticity" has been used as a discursive tool to police Black masculine performances while simultaneously reinforcing hegemonic ideologies of masculine and feminine performances and expressions. To illustrate the tension between the gendered binary, we turn to the relationship (differences) between a "rapper" and "singer" within hip-hop as an analogous representation.

Often, when some male hip-hop artists attempt to sing on records (i.e., Biz Markie or Ol' Dirty Bastard), it is done satirically and/or out of the appropriate registers. The purpose, and the subsequent effect, is to idolatrize one's lyrical ability over one's vocal delivery. "Undoubtedly, the male hip-hop artists' disarticulation of sincere singing from skilled rapping is tied to notions of black masculinity that are not directly challenged when Lauryn Hill, Queen Latifah, or Eve sing *and* rhyme passionately in their songs" (Jackson Jr., 2005, p. 187).

While there are material benefits to performing "authentic" Black masculinity (i.e., cultural currency), "inauthenticity" is likened to "cosplaying" or trying to seem a part of hip-hop culture while never facing the challenges of growing up Black and working-class (Hodgman, 2013). This is the case in several famous hip-hop, specifically rap rivalries, like Drake/Kendrick Lamar and Kanye West/Jay-Z (Máthé, 2019). By focusing our attention on the individual behaviors and aesthetics of Black men, we take our collective eye off the ball of systemic inequalities.

However, The Others believe that this is a shortsighted vision of both hip-hop and Black masculinity, and we advocate for more wide-ranging representations of Black masculinities that are firmly rooted in "the culture"—an expression used in hip-hop parlance to refer to the Black community- while also being relational and emotional. The relationship between A-Train, MM, and Sister Sage gives us hope for Black masculinities as we collectively run toward the future—embracing hip-hop as a pedagogical tool for consciousness-raising that does not rely on outdated authentic vs. inauthentic discourses.

## CRITICAL AND PERFORMANCE METHODS AND THEORIES FOR STUDYING "THE CULTURE"

In a super world where the threat of bodily harm via the fascist leaders of Vought International is ever-present, The Others use intersectional performance criticism as a heuristic for examining how Black masculine supes and nonsupes perform their identities in a neoliberal Vought society. As Perry (2016) explains, performance criticism "analyzes and practices certain kinds of communication, specifically repeated behaviors for an audience" (p. 21). There is no formal procedure for performance criticism, so The Others relies on Johnson's (2003) view of performance, which considers physical spaces, relationships, and contexts. Johnson (2003) calls us to pay attention to who says what, what is said, *how* it is said, where, and for what purpose because Hamera (2018) explains that our identity performances "do cultural and political work" by excavating a text's underlying, embodied meanings.

To accomplish this analysis, The Others streamed every episode of *The Boys* seasons 1–3 several times, paying particular attention to the scenes involving A-Train and his performances. However, season four of the other was released in the summer of 2024, which required us to go consider the new "data," which are the episodes of season four, and this required us to consider not only A-Train and Mother's Milk's performances of Black masculinity but also the new supe character of Sister Sage, a Black woman who is the "Smartest Person in the world," to consider what this satirical show is accomplishing. As performance critics, when we watch, we attend to the linguistic interactions and relationships between characters, the context, bodies, staging, props, and costumes on our screens.

The Others also use various critical perspectives to analyze the intersectional performances of Black characters. As Ono (2011) notes, a critical perspective must scrutinize how power shapes social life, which we examine through Ehlers's (2012) analysis of racialized performance. By applying

Foucault's (1991) concepts of "discipline," "punishment," and "power," Ehlers suggests that the purpose of disciplining the racialized body, often through coercive means, is to increase productivity through the labor force and minimize political engagement, resulting in the docility of the subject.

However, along with Foucault (1991), Ehlers utilizes Butler's (1990) idea of "performativity." Ehlers (2012) suggests that "Race is performative because it is an act—or, more precisely, a series of repeated acts—that brings into being what it names" (p. 6). Considering race as performative suggests that performances are not inherent but can shift and change depending on context and time, in which characters can develop a political consciousness around various inequities within social systems and choose to perform resistance.

We examine various character performances within the metaverse of the "Vought-Industrial Complex" and how those performances satirically embody various positions within contemporary socio-political discourse—analyzing how those performances uncover underlying power dynamics and systemic inequities. Similarly, we use Crenshaw's (1991) concept of intersectionality, which highlights the complex interplay of structural and dynamic factors in discrimination, illustrating how individuals can experience privilege and marginalization.

At its core, the series is a conduit to critically explicate the political climate within America, demonstrating the daily operations and antagonistic conduct of white sovereign institutions. *The Boys* illuminates Foucauldian notions of coercion and disciplining of bodies trapped within institutions that are discursively and physically edified to present and perform as docile bodies. However, if we focus only on disciplining the subject, we flatten the agency of various characters within the show. Thus, we use the lens of performance criticism to open up multiple possibilities of resistance to disciplinary regimes within the show and the real and present danger of fascism in the US, given the current presidency of Donald Trump and Project 2025. Performance criticism allows The Others to analyze the show as a medium depicting resistance by marginalized people against fascist Vought International (which serves as a hyperrepresentation of the United States of America).

Various Black characters in the show, including A-Train, Mother's Milk, and Sister Sage, epitomize overlapping and contradictory performances of both hegemonic compliance and liberatory resistance. In the following analysis, we examine the character of A-Train and his interactions with two other significant Black characters to illuminate the resistance possibilities within their performances.

## ANALYSIS

This analysis uncovers the deeper meanings within A-Train's story to see how he shifts from the stereotypical "baller" performance to a subjectivity imbued with agency. A-Train's performances shift to relationally engaging with those in his community, especially other Black men. This new performance of Black masculinity offers us the possibility to expand what it means to be a Black man performing Black masculinity in this culture. However, we must also acknowledge women's roles in the show regarding authenticity, race, and gender. In the following analysis, we examine two primary themes: A-Train prepolitical consciousness, akin to Michael Jordan and during his process of decolonization, akin to Malcolm X.

### A-Train as Michael Jordan and Malcolm X

A-Train is the perfect antihero as he is not well known for putting his speed to good use on "saves" or heroism, but rather for running foot races with other men in tights to drum up good publicity for Vought. A-Train's superspeed is a supe embodiment of a "natural" athlete racial stereotype that affects many Black men (Azzarito & Harrison Jr., 2008). A-Train's compulsion to run over and over again with no concern for others keeps pushing forward to remain relevant because he "cannot escape" his environment and the expectations he must meet (Ehlers, 2012, pp. 55–56).

Returning to A-Train's opening scene, the audience is pulled into the narrative, wondering what "Can't stop; can't stop" means. A-Train's first words eerily resemble the hip-hop phrase "can't stop, won't stop" that was popularized by Sean "Puff Daddy" Combs (Kripke, 5:40). Rhetorically, this expression is used in hip-hop to highlight a person's determination for success, but, just like the person who popularized the phrase, if one is unable to control their impulses, a catastrophe is bound to be left in the wake.[5] According to Brown (2000), "In contemporary culture, black men are often seen more as beasts, rapists, gangsters, crack heads, and muggers—literally as bodies out of control—than as fathers, scholars, statesmen, and leaders (p. 173)." A-Train's literal inability to stop running is his hubris because his body becomes an out-of-control accidental killing machine under Compound V (a drug that enhances/elicits superabilities).

In *The Boys*, Vought uses A-Train's body as an economic and political tool to promote their social in/justice initiatives. A-Train's hegemonic dependence upon the Vought corporate machine to take care of his flawed image and grant him access to Compound V makes him the perfect "docile" subject, according to Foucault (1991). Rather than being able to assert his agency and say no to the gross injustices he and his community have suffered at the hands of Vought and Homelander, A-Train becomes complicit in the Vought corporate machine so that he can continue leveraging his flawed image into financial stability. Thus, when A-Train cannot perform at top speed due to the side effects of his excessive use of Compound V, his core sense of self unravels as he is emasculated and desperately searches for ways to remain significant in the public eye.

At the beginning of season three, A-Train attempts to increase his marketability by reconnecting with the Black community. He strives to "get back in touch with [his] roots, like in *Roots*," and rebrands himself as a social activist for "the culture" (Kripke, 2022, 20:20; Smith & Lacy, 2024). A-Train changes his blue uniform to a stereotypically African black, red, and green Kente cloth pattern to "show the community [he is] down with the cause" (Kripke, 2022, 31:30). Through his disingenuous attempts to reconnect with the Black community, A-Train reinforces his self-proclamation that he is more akin to "Michael Jordan [and not] Malcolm X" (Kripke, 33:08).

A-Train's comparison highlights a turn away from militant social activism and community engagement toward financially lucrative performances of stellar individualism, prioritizing fame, status, and notoriety over the well-being of his community (Boyd, 2008). Moreover, he allows Vought the power to devalue his body and identity when the company creates "A-Train content" through a right-wing conservative lens, negatively depicting Black culture as the dominant culture's entertainment. Wanzo (2015) describes this as the conservative tendency to preserve the status quo by failing to question how our history has shaped us.

A-Train is drawn to Vought's homogenizing web and, thus, deemed powerless. For example, after A-Train's brother, Nathan (Christian Keyes), is assaulted and paralyzed by a white supremacist supe terrorizing his hometown, it is when he is personally affected by the injustice at the hands of those in power that A-Train demands that Vought take action to contain the chaotic violence of Blue Hawk (Nick Wechsler). However, the CEO of Vought tells A-Train that while the members of Vought are "heartbroken over [his] brother's tragic accident," she has scheduled the racist supe to twelve weeks of sensitivity training as punishment (Kripke, 10:30).

Even when A-Train finally gets the gumption to make demands of Vought, the Vought Industrial Complex buries his demands in bureaucratic red tape and "racial sensitivity" training. This scene mirrors the real-world consequences or lack thereof that law enforcement officers and vigilantes often experience after assaulting and murdering unarmed Black people, i.e., George Zimmerman, Daniel Pantaleo, Darren Wilson, and many more, by not holding them accountable for their actions (Vera & Krishnakumar, 2022). Realizing that if he wants Blue Hawk to be held responsible for his excessive use of force, he must take matters into his own hands, A-Train murders Blue Hawk as a way to resist Vought, which systematically works to disenfranchise and marginalize those with less access to power. It is his now-paralyzed brother who reminds him that Black youth deserve to see justice and not more death—a cycle that even the fastest man in the world struggles to outrun.

In seasons 1–3, A-Train attempts to avoid the socio-political effects of the racial caste fracture in his relationship with the Black community. Instead of seeking validation and kinship from his community, A-Train embodies a "hypercommodified affect" whereby he serves the institutions he believes empower him. Still, in reality, he is being bought and sold as a racialized product of Vought (Judy, 2004, p. 113). Through A-Train's choice to kill, although violent and illegal, he is finally resisting docility. It is not until season four that we see A-Train's redemption arc as he leans toward a politically active Malcolm X archetype. However, the entrance of Sage (Susan Heyward ) into the cast in season four complicates A-Train's journey toward redemption even further.

### Sage and A-Train's Conflicting Relationship

The etymology of sage is derived from "sage" (Middle English) and "sapium" (Latin), tacitly translated to "wise." In *The Boys*, Sage *is* a Black woman from Detroit whose superpower is being the most intelligent person alive. However, the running gag around Sage is that people refer to her as the "Smartest woman in the world," to which she always calmly corrects and says, "Smartest person."

Homelander discovers Sage in the fourth season's first episode, in her small, crowded apartment, bursting at the seams with books reading *Naming and Necessity*, a book of lectures by Saul A. Kripke (1970), while listening to a different audiobook on the toilet. The book *Naming and Necessity* reflects Kripke's philosophy of language and the relationships between naming objects, truth, and identity. In a humorous familial nod, Saul A. Kripke is the second cousin of the Producer and Writer of *The Boys*, Eric Kripke. As Eric Kripke says of Sage: "Many superhero worlds have that character. Whereas most of them are usually really reedy white dudes, we wanted a Black woman who was raised in a low socioeconomic area, so no one f----ing listens to her. It's both commentary and satirical that you have literally the smartest person in the world that could cure all of society's ills, but she just can't get anyone to listen to her. So then she becomes a bitter misanthrope" (Romano, 2024).

When Sage opens the door to Homelander, unphased, she says, "I am almost never surprised" (34:37). Sage's character is performatively complex because, as a Black woman, she challenges stereotypes of Black women, and also, what intelligence looks and acts like in the white supremacist world of *The Boys* and the world of the home viewer; however, she is enmeshed in the web of Vought's hegemonic dominance.

For example, when Homelander calls her "Sister Sage," she explains that Vought added "Sister" to her name because Vought "Cannot have one of us without a racial qualifier" (35:12). Johnson (2019) suggests that the use of the term "sis" in the modern era is a callback to Black American cultural and linguistic oral traditions, i.e., Br'er Fox from the Uncle Remus folktales. Vought still has control over essential aspects of her identity via her name, even though she is more intelligent than all the supes and nonsupes combined. Ironically, Kripke's (1970) *Naming and Necessity* suggests a theory of naming where names are "rigid designators" like Aristotle or Nixon, which hold essential properties and are not simple labels or descriptions but directly connect to the object they refer to.

The relationship between Sage and Homelander is enigmatic, as she is one of the few people on the show who does not overtly proclaim or show a sense of fear towards Homelander. This is not to say that she is not afraid of him, but she possesses the intellect to waltz past his psycho-sadistic machismo, puppeteering the strongest supe alive as her chess piece. Further, the relationship between the two complicates the presence and enactment of white supremacist ideologies throughout the basic operations of Vought.

Before Sage, Vought was what West (1992) would see as a corporate market institution, a capitalistic, money-hungry machine concerned only with turning a profit. After the introduction to Sage, Vought is still this. However, Vought's actions are no longer being spearheaded by a tyrannical man-child suffering and showing clear signs of an Oedipus complex. Instead, it becomes a socio-political machine secretly run by a Black woman who does not have the agency to determine her name.

However, it is not just Sage and Homelander's newfound dynamic that complicates the viewer's understanding of racial performativity. Sage and A-Train have a complex and multifaceted relationship. Specifically, they find camaraderie because of their shared racial identity; for example, we see them greet each other and exchange annoyed looks at one another in the face of Vought's racial micro and macro aggressions. However, tensions brew as these two antipodes compete for attention in Vought's hierarchical order. For instance, during Ezekiel's memorial service (S4 E5), Vought representative Cameron Coleman (Matthew Edison) shares with the audience Vought's newest DEI initiative, "Black At It," with Sage as the figurehead for the campaign and Noir (Nathan Mitchell) and a bitter A-Train in supporting roles behind her.

In the scene, The Deep remarks: "For the first time in Vought's history we have Two Black superheroes and one unspecified; Vought proudly supports and amplifies BIPOC voices; am I right?" (22:27) Cameron Coleman replies, "which is why these *articulate* heroes will lead Vought's diversity initiative; 'Black At It'" (emphasis ours) (22:39). The Deep adds, "As part of our campaign, they're debuting a new feature which is custom digital product placement" (22:55). This is, essentially, product placement in movies that will change depending on the audience's racial identity. For example, white Vought fans will see a Vought-sponsored IPA beer through this new feature, while Black Vought fans will see Vought Imperial Peach cognac.

The camera pans to Black audience members who shift slightly uncomfortable in the stands, and A-Train and Sage exchange a knowing glance about these ridiculous microaggressions being hurled from the main stage of Vought programming. From the outside, we are left wondering, what happens if there is a group of people watching something from multiple racial groups, or what if someone is multiracial? Can the Vought algorithm detect specific product placements for those racial groups? Instead, custom digital product placement is meant to not only target specific racial groups but also meant to produce well-behaved, docile racialized subjects who have their every whim catered to in hopes of displacing justified outrage at racial injustice and targeting it instead toward consumption of stereotypical consumer goods. Docile bodies are instrumental because they may be "improved" through the systems of power they have to navigate (Foucault, 1991, p. 136). Like the Vought algorithm, bodies are improved as they interface with various power structures, but neither are ever outside of those power structures.

In season four, Sage is *the* vital piece to Homelander's plot to have the ultimate power. Thus, she is inducted into The Seven, where she meets the other supes, including A-Train. Sage devises a maniacal plan to have members of The Seven, including A-Train, murder three civilians to set up members of the Starlighters as martyrs for Homelander's "Hometeamers." This is when we begin to see a definite shift in A-Train's consciousness as he stands idly by until one of the civilians tries to get away and A-Train cuts him off at the door, but before A-Train can act, Black Noir beats the civilian to death. As A-Train sighs in disgust, Sage orders, "Stay here and wait for further instruction" (46:04).

As Sage becomes more integrated into the Vought corporate machine via Homelander, she becomes more emboldened to assert her authority over the "morons" Homelander works with. In season four, episode two, A-Train gives up stolen security cam footage of the two Starlighters who supposedly committed the murder of the three innocent civilians to *The Boys*' Hughie and Starlight. At face value, finding how this stolen security footage got into *The Boys*' hands becomes Sage's mission; however, through dramatic irony, the audience is at least somewhat clued into the fact that Sage knows precisely how the footage ended up with them.

This is no more evident than in the Sage and A-Train's interaction at the memorial for Ezekiel. In a side conversation, A-Train and Sage converse, and Sage says: "Still searching for this leak.... That footage didn't just *run* itself out of crime analytics, am I right?" (11:07, emphasis ours). Their eyes meet as they are both aware that Sage knows the truth, yet Sage never lets Vought or The Seven know the truth about A-Train, ultimately leading to her being fired from Homelander's army when he learns of this deception. However, as we learn from Sage's last scene of season four, this has all been a part of her plan from the beginning as she tells Homelander, "Buckle up for phase two" (57:27). The Others are eagerly awaiting phase two, but until season five airs, we cannot know what that refers to.

Unlike Homelander's overt narcissism and bloodlust, Sage disciplines Vought and The Seven via subliminal coercive forces, slowly manipulating situations into her control. Simultaneously, to an inevitable end, Sage is still serving Homelander, even though it's her brain running the operation the whole time. Ehlers (2012) suggests that the constant threat of bodily violence of tyrannical rulers shifted during the modern and postmodern eras to a more relational and often more subliminal form of power via "coercion to modify and manipulate the body" (Ehlers, 2012, p. 4).

This coercion, which Foucault (1991) names "political anatomy," is "Defined [as] how one may have a hold over others' bodies, not only so that they may do what one wishes, but so that they may operate as one wishes with the techniques, the speed and the efficiency that one determines" (p. 138). This is Sage's modus operandi, whereby she disciplines all of those around her, including Homelander, through subliminal means, whereby she holds back some pertinent information, leaks other information, and stays calm during egregious acts of violence, like the murder of Coleman for leaking the security footage, which she knows was not his doing.

Is this to maintain A-Train's innocence? Is she doing it for the culture? Most likely, this is to keep her newly acquired power under the auspice of ignorance, which the audience knows she is not. However, Vought, Homelander, and A-Train underestimate Sage because of her unsuspecting presence, her Detroit skyline T-shirt, and, of course, her identity as a Black woman, which was intentional by Eric Kripke. Sage appears neutral in her expressiveness, which is not the normative stereotypical performance of Black womanhood or megalomaniacs, which, to Foucault, makes her the perfect disciplinarian, not overt, callous, or unhinged in outward affect, but manipulative, lurking behind the scenes in the shadows. A-Train eventually realizes he cannot trust Sage and instead turns to Mother's Milk for redemption.

### The Paternal Relationship of Mother's Milk and A-Train's

In season four, we see a notable shift in A-Train as he develops a friendship/allyship with MM; MM's influence on A-Train is vital to his evolution. When Nathan appears out of the blue and accuses A-Train of lying about his heroic "saves" and "cosplaying" as a superhero to impress his nephews after his family leaves, a heartbroken A-Train ponders the moment and speeds away. With neither Vought's support nor his family, A-Train finds a friend in an unlikely place with The Boys and MM.

Like A-Train, MM is also performatively complex. MM is a large Black man, nonsupe with cropped hair and a signature leather bomber jacket, hailing from Harlem. His identity is performatively grounded within hip-hop culture through material artifacts like his gold Cuban link chain, hip-hop t-shirts, and direct communication. In an interview with Alonso, he remarks, "hip-hop t-shirts as an ode to where M. M. is from, with most of the tees being rappers from New York" (Watson, 2022, para. 3). Having lost his grandfather and father to racial violence at a young age by Vought, MM's worldview is shaped by his childhood trauma and oppression which resulted in a harsh and often vindictive performance of Black masculinity. Those traits find a welcome home amongst the vengeance-seeking Boys, who also perform brash and hyperversions of masculinity.

However, MM is also "the moral compass" of the show (Watson, 2022, para. 1), and he often performs his Black masculinity similarly to a strong Black father, combining tough love, empathy, and dependability, qualities he experienced and then was deprived of as a child. Through his familial relationships, like with his daughter, we witness his vulnerabilities, which are his most excellent motivators. The Public Enemy chain clock is a significant hip-hop artifact he gives his daughter as a gift to instill social justice and morality. MM's performance challenges monolithic representations and essentialized notions of Black masculinity by demonstrating there is more than one way for Black men to vibe with "the culture."

In seasons 1–3, A-Train's attempts to avoid the socio-political effects of the racial caste fracture his relationship with the Black community. Instead of seeking validation and kinship from his people, A-Train remains subservient to an institution he believed granted him authenticity or what Judy (2004) calls a "hypercommodified affect." In their first interaction in season four, MM uses his complex performance to challenge A-Train and express concern for him. MM says: "You spent so much time wearing that stupid ass Black power suit, pretending to give a shit, that something stuck. You may have that racist white boy's heart in you, but you got a second goddamn chance actually to give a shit. So what you going to do with it, man?" (Kripke, 20:30).

A-Train's desire to be a part of "the culture" has further pushed him away from it. When A-Train takes MM to the hospital after he has a panic attack, a young Black boy witnesses the save and watches in admiration. In a later scene, A-Train tells MM that there "were no screaming fans. No cameras. Nobody even knew. Except for this one kid. That felt better than anything I ever did at Vought. Because for once, I didn't hate myself. That's on you" (Kripke, 23:00). Since A-Train's "saves" up until this point were manufactured products by Vought, the moment between the young Black boy and A-Train illustrates an essential connection to one another, giving A-Train cultural belonging in a way he has not experienced. A-Train saving MM was his first "real save"; however, the moment between A-Train and the young Black boy may prove to be another. If a young Black boy can see a different, vulnerable performance of masculinity between two Black men, it may inspire him to embody this performance for a lifetime. In this tiny moment, The Others see the potential for significant changes in the negative perceptions of Black men.

## CONCLUSION

*The Boys* continues to push the boundary of speculative fiction through a radical depiction of superhuman coexistence with nonsupes in the digital age. In this chapter, we began by discussing speculative fiction, hip-hop, and the genre's problematic ties to discursive and material shows of "authenticity," which, in the end, produce constrained performances of Black people and Blackness that are ideologically meant to continue serving white supremacy, often to their detriment. However, if racial performativity is a series of repeated acts not innate to the bodies that interpolate them, critical performance theories offer marginalized folks the possibility to perform resistance to oppressive structures.

In our analysis, we conducted a performance criticism of A-Train's performance of Black masculinity as it shifts through his interaction with MM, Sister Sage, and hip-hop culture. There are myriad ways to read the character of A-Train. Still, he frames himself comparably to Michael Jordan, who reigned during an era where "it was *political* to be Black, wealthy, and empowered by one's own image," and the polemical revolutionary Malcolm X (Boyd, 2008, p. 104).

Throughout the series, A-Train runs back and forth between the two poles of Jordan and X when, ostensibly, A-Train is both of these transcendent and enigmatic historical figures simultaneously. Using intersectionality, we can see how A-Train operates within a "matrix of domination" from which he cannot remove himself. The speedster spends the majority of seasons 1–3 in an embodied stasis invoked by Vought's discursive, and at times physical, violence, molding him to function at their will. A-Trains submission is paramount to the betterment of Vought as docile bodies are instrumental, both materially and functionally, because they may be "improved" through the systems of power they have to navigate (Foucault, 1991, p. 136). However, starting in season four, we begin to see A-Train challenge Vought's discursive and material construction of his Black masculinity through his intricate relationship with MM and Sister Sage, who oppugn his cosplaying.

Thinking of media conglomerates as disciplinary structures that promote neoliberal ideologies rather than simply entertainment, *The Boys* provokes questions about Black masculine performances in the superhero genre, specifically when these performances are extrinsically linked to monetary values. In this chapter, we explicated the authentic component of A-Train's Black masculine performances concerning his involvement with Vought and "the culture" existing outside of his institutional relations. We recognize authenticity as a slippery slope, a socially constructed sign concretized through hegemony and institutional forces that attempt to organize and classify subjects into social hierarchies. A sentiment shared by Wright (2004), who opines that "In many ways, hip-hop may try to *keep it real*, but that voice is often silenced because oppressors control hip-hop's *image* (p. 18). At this intersection between hip-hop and the superhero genre, future areas of inquiry should consider how race and identity, more broadly, are constructed as performative objects via governing institutions, questioning biological essentialism, and considering how factors such as time, space, and intersectionality shift our performances.

## NOTES

1. IMDb ratings are done by registered users who vote on a scale 1–10 and then the votes are summarized into a singular IMDb rating on the title page.
2. For a detailed account of the speculative fiction see Soares (2020) and Tilley (2018).
3. For example, Luke Cage is a large, Black, Harlem-born gang member with superstrength and powerful skin, falsely imprisoned and with superstrength and titanium-powered skin. He wears chains to conjure up images of slavery Cage gained his superpowers through a prison experiment gone wrong.
4. For a more detailed history of hip-hop, see Harris et al. (2022).
5. For example, see Roundtree & Dillon's (2024) detailed account of the effects of Sean Combs's tyranny over time.

## REFERENCES

Azzarito, L., & Harrison Jr, L. (2008). "White men can't jump": race, gender and natural athleticism. *International review for the sociology of sport, 43*(4), 347–64. https://doi.org/10.1177/1012690208099871

Boyd, T. (1997). *Am I Black enough for you? Popular culture from the 'hood and beyond.* Indiana University Press.

Boyd, T. (2008). *Young, Black, rich, & famous: The rise of the NBA, the hip-hop invasion, and the transformation of American culture.* Bison Books.

Brown, J. A. (2000). *Black superheroes, milestone comics, and their fans: Milestone comics and their fans.* University Press of Mississippi. https://ebookcentral.proquest.com/lib/jmu/detail.action?docID=619210

Brown, J. A. (2021). *Love, sex, gender, and superheroes.* Rutgers University Press.

Butler, J. (1990). *Gender trouble: Feminism and the subversion of identity.* Routledge.

Crenshaw, K. (1991). Mapping the margins: Intersectionality, identity politics, and violence against women of color. *Stanford Law Review, 43,* 1241.

Ehlers, N. (2012). *Racial imperatives: Discipline, performativity, and struggles against subjection.* Indiana University Press. http://www.jstor.org/stable/j.ctt16gh861

Forman, M. (2002). *The 'hood comes first: Race, space, and place in rap and hip-hop.* Wesleyan University Press.

Forman, M. (2004). Introduction. In M. Forman & M. A. Neal (Eds.), *That's the joint: The hip-hop studies reader* (1st ed., pp. 1–8). Routledge.

Foucault, M. (1991). *Discipline and punish: The birth of the prison.* (A. Sheridan, Trans.). Penguin. (Original work published 1975).

Hamera, J. (2018, February 26). Performance Studies in Critical Communication Studies. *Oxford Research Encyclopedia of Communication.* Oxford University Press. https://oxfordre.com/communication/display/10.1093/acrefore/9780190228613.001.0001/acrefore-9780190228613-e-640

Harris, T., Woods, S. "lyfestile," Horton, D., Horsley, N. M., & McGregor, S. (2022). Funk what you heard: Hip-hop is a field of study. *Journal of Hip Hop Studies, 9*(1). VCU Scholars Compass. https://doi.org/10.34718/vqdm-jv58

Hodgman, M. R. (2013). Class, race, credibility, and authenticity within the hip-hop music genre. *Journal of Sociological Research*, 4(2), 402. https://doi.org/10.5296/jsr.v4i2.4503

Internet Movie Database. (n.d.). *The Boys*. https://www.imdb.com/title/tt1190634/?ref_=ttawd_ov_i

Jackson, J. Jr. (2005). *Real Black: Adventures in racial sincerity*. The University of Chicago Press.

Jenkins, T. & Secker, T. (2022). Conclusion: The American way, "The Boys," and the wrong message? In T. Jenkins & T. Secker (Eds.), *Superheroes, movies, and the state: How the U.S. government shapes cinematic universes* (pp. 211–34). University Press of Kansas.

Johnson, E. P. (2003). *Appropriating Blackness: performance and the politics of authenticity*. Duke University Press.

Johnson, P. (2019). "You ok sis?": Black vernacular, community formation, and the innate tensions of the hashtag. In A. De Kosnik & K. P. Feldman (Eds.), *#identity: Hashtagging Race, Gender, Sexuality, and Nation* (pp. 57–67). University of Michigan Press.

Judy, R. A. T. (2004). On the question of nigga authenticity. In M. Forman & M. A. Neal. *That's the joint: The hip-hop studies reader* (1st ed., pp. 105–17). Routledge.

Kirkpatrick, E. (2023). *Recovering the radical promise of superheroes: Un/making worlds*. Punctum Books. https://library.oapen.org/handle/20.500.12657/75787

Kripke, E. (Producer). (2019–present). *The Boys* [Television Series]. Canada. Prime Video.

Kripke, S. A. (1970). *Lecture 1: Naming and Necessity*. [Written]. https://uh.edu/~garson/NamingandNecessity.pdf

Máthé, N. (2019). Representations of Black masculinity in the 2010s hip-hop. *Studia Universitatis Babeş-Bolyai Philologia*, 64(1), 65–80. https://doi.org/10.24193/subbphilo.2019.1.06

Ono, K. A. (2011). Critical: A finer edge. *Communication and Critical/Cultural Studies*, 8(1), 93–96. https://doi.org/10.1080/14791420.2011.543332

Perry, P. S. (2016). What is biblical performance criticism? In M. A. Powell (Ed.), *Insights from Performance Criticism* (pp. 21–72). 1517 Media.

Porter, R. (2019, October 21). *Nielsen releases first ratings for Amazon: "The Boys" draws 4m viewers*. The Hollywood Reporter. https://www.hollywoodreporter.com/tv/tv-news/nielsen-releases-first-ratings-amazon-boys-draws-4m-viewers-1249040/#:~:text=Live%20Feed-,Nielsen%20Releases%20First%20Ratings%20for%20Amazon%3A%20'The%20Boys'%20Draws,in%20its%20first%2010%20days.

Porter, R. (2020a, October 1). *"The Boys," "Mulan" break Netflix stranglehold on streaming top 10 (exclusive)*. The Hollywood Reporter. https://www.hollywoodreporter.com/tv/tv-news/the-boys-mulan-break-netflix-stranglehold-on-streaming-top-10-4069432/

Porter, R. (2020b, October 8). *"The Boys" stays in Nielsen's streaming top 10*. The Hollywood Reporter. https://www.hollywoodreporter.com/tv/tv-news/the-boys-stays-in-nielsens-streaming-top-10-4073810/

Porter, R. (2024, July 11). *Streaming ratings: "The Boys," "House of the Dragon" return to charts*. The Hollywood Reporter. https://www.hollywoodreporter.com/tv/tv-news/streaming-ratings-the-boys-house-of-the-dragon-return-to-charts-1235946573/

Rodriguez, N. S. (2018). Hip-hop's authentic masculinity: A quare reading of Fox's "Empire." *Television & New Media*, 19(3), 225–40. https://doi.org/10.1177/1527476417704704

Romano, N. (2024, May 17). "The Boys" season 4 introduces world's smartest supe and alt-right Firecracker to the Seven. *Entertainment Weekly.* https://ew.com/the-boys-season-4-sister-sage-firecracker-details-exclusive-8647433

Rotten Tomatoes. (n.d.a). *The Boys season 1.* https://www.rottentomatoes.com/tv/the_boys_2019/s01

Roundtree, C. & Dillon, N. (2024, May 28). Bad boy for life: Sean Combs' history of violence. *Rolling Stone.* https://www.rollingstone.com/music/music-features/diddy-friends-bad-boy-artists-abuse-violence-1235028178/

Smith, G. M. (2009). The superhero as labor: The corporate secret identity. In A. Ndalianis (Ed.), *The comic book superhero* (pp. 126–43). Routledge.

Smith, D. L., & Lacy, N. B. (2024). Til death do us part: Kendrick Lamar, "The Heart Part 5," and Black male vulnerability. *Howard Journal of Communications, 35*(3), 359–73. https://doi.org/10.1080/10646175.2023.2264218

Soares, M.A. (2020). Superman v. Specialman: Rhetorical border crossings of unlicensed superheroes. *The Journal of Popular Culture, 53,* 600–625. https://doi.org/10.1111/jpcu.12922

Tilley, C. L. (2018). Superheroes and identity. In E. Wesseling (ED.), *Reinventing Childhood Nostalgia: Books, Toys, and Contemporary Media Culture* (1st ed., pp. 51–65). Routledge.

Vera, A. & Krishnakumar, P. (2022). From Trayvon Martin to Ahmaud Arbery: How images have changed a movement. *CNN.* https://www.cnn.com/interactive/2022/02/us/travyon-martin-10-year-death-anniversary/

Wanzo, R. (2015). It's a hero? Black comics and satirizing subjugation. In F. Gatewood & J. Jennings (Eds.), *The blacker the ink: Constructions of Black identity in comics and sequential art* (pp. 314–32). Rutgers University Press.

Watson, E. C. (2022, July 13). *Laz Alonso explains why Mother's Milk wears hip-hop tees in "The Boys."* Okayplayer. https://www.okayplayer.com/interviews/the-boys-mothers-milk-hip-hop-shirts.html

West, C. (1992). Nihilism in Black America. In G. Dent (Ed.), *Black Popular Culture* (pp. 37–47). Bay Press.

Wright, K. (2004). Rise up hip hop nation: From deconstructing racial politics to building positive solutions. *Socialism and Democracy, 18*(2), 9–20. https://doi.org/10.1080/08854300408428395

CHAPTER 12

# REMEMBERING DANIEL DUMILE

"The Classic Conception of Death"
Through Dr. Victor Von Doom née MF DOOM

JOHNNY JONES

This chapter honors the transition of hip-hop artist Daniel Dumile (1971–2020) via his appropriation of Marvel Comics' supervillain, Dr. Victor Von Doom (est. *Fantastic Four* #5, 1962), into the masked MC persona, MF DOOM. Dumile's resistance to traditional hip-hop narratives generated his masterful lyrical and absurdist performance that fueled his transformation throughout his life of loss, grief, and untimely death while exiled in England due to immigration deportation. MF DOOM's absurdity, or "vomitspit" of non sequitur, allusive, and hilarious poetry, often reflects a world that is an existential ghetto of fatalistic atrocities imposed on individual and collective humanity. As an artistic witness, Dumile channeled Victor Von Doom, Marvel's greatest villain, whom creator Jack Kirby called "the classic conception of death," and cast a ridiculous shadow that helped him face life's tragedies. I honor Dumile for becoming MF DOOM and utilizing Dr. Doom's character narrative to transform grief into a hiatus, then a superhuman return to claim the classic hip-hop legacy of "The MC in the Iron Mask." This chapter merges MF DOOM and Dr. Doom's narratives to reveal how Dumile is hip-hop's classic conception of death, who made us laugh after having cried on earth for a considerable time.

Both Doom narratives are read "against the grain" to craft a narrative textual analysis that emphasizes how comic book life and real life might intersect and to uplift how Dumile navigated a self-reflexive, resistant, culturally heroic, folkloric remix between his real life, Dr. Doom's fantastic narrative, and MF DOOM's art (Church, 2022; Jones, 2017). Moten's (2003) and Hartman's (2019) close readings of Black life, aesthetics, narratives, and performance inform this interpretation of Dumile's life and catalog paralleled with von Doom's Marvel narrative throughout comic books, cartoons, and cinema. By "remixing" these texts, this chapter will highlight how MF DOOM subverted the glorification of death, hypermasculinity, and exploitation in commercial hip-hop because Daniel Dumile embodied grief, Dr. Doom, and absurdity and equipped it with sonic, cultural, and lyrical armor (pun intended) to navigate life.

## KAUZIN' MUCH DAMAGE, ZEV LOVE X-ITS [*SIC*] TO DOOM

> "It's like this: the physical body is not us anyway," Zev continues, equating visiting a grave to worshipping graven images." Subroc's presence is numinous, he tells me. "So the whole 'physical form' shit is mad wack." He pauses, toking on the blunt. He knows Subroc will live on through his music and in people's loving memories. But still the pain is deep. After a second, he stares into his lap, shakes a Newport out of his pack and says, "I feel like a fucking piece of bullshit." His face is a mask of torment.
>
> —RO, 1994

Daniel Dumile transitioned from his first MC persona, Zev Love X, via the death of his younger brother Dingilizwe Dumile a.k.a. DJ Subroc (1973–1993), the second half of their 1990s Afrocentric adolescent group, KMD, a.k.a. Kauzin' Much Damage.[1] The epigraph captures the grief and torment spurred by the loss of Subroc and embodied by Zev Love X. Moten's "sentimental avant garde" (2003) cites aesthetics of the Black radical tradition in which modern expatriate jazz, literary, and visual artists function as instruments that "play" to establish unities amidst despair, expand Black performance, and evoke nostalgia that inspires creative value in surplus (Moten, 2003). In hip-hop, that surplus in the music "brings the noise" that helps us remember spaces, times, and bodies lost, i.e., "to reminisce over you." Subroc's body lost premeditated Zev Love X's transformation to Doom.

The tragedy that triggered Dumile's torment ensued on April 23, 1993, when nineteen-year-old Dingilizwe was found unconscious on an exit ramp of the Long Island Expressway and died from blunt force trauma to the head. At the time, the Brothers Dumile were completing their second album with Elektra Records. Shoutout writer Ronin Ro (1994), who interviewed Zev Love X one year after Subroc's death and captured Dumile drowning in his sorrows, darkened in dress, tone, booze, and smoke. A deeper reading of the interview reveals what Moten calls "voices/forces" speaking to/ pushing through to Zev Love X, who expressed a desire to talk about his brother. Subroc's absence, Zev said, generated an unknown creative being within him: "It's like him-and-me-combined-as-one type shit" (Ro, 1994). The album provided a sonic portal of memory, creativity, value, and unity, materializing Sub's voice to Zev as the album was one of the last things that the two brothers did together when the younger Dumile died: "It seems like one point in time, stuck there, can't change" (Ro, 1994).

Dr. Victor von Doom (1962), who possessed mind transference and the ability to summon, among his many powers, was a well-established supervillain in the Marvel Comics universe during the Dumiles' tragedy.[2] So, while Dumile was trapped in a cycle of grief about Subroc's transition, von Doom could also speak to Dumile and evoke Subroc. Nicknamed "Doom" by his mother as her firstborn, Daniel Dumile occupied his grief with an imagination that included Dr. Doom. Both brothers were avid comic book fans, and von Doom's reign in Marvel rose during the Dumiles' youth. By the 1990s, von Doom was believed to have died alongside the X-Men, Avengers, and Fantastic Four at the hands of Onslaught, Professor X's (and a catatonic Mangeto's) psionic entity (*Onslaught: Marvel* #1, 1996). However, von Doom and the others were hidden inside a Counter-Earth. And when it was safe to return to primary Earth-616, Dr. Doom remained, explored, and conquered the Counter-Earth and used its source of power for his ends (Doom #1, 2000; Fantastic Four #23–25, 1999).

Vanguard von Doom, trekking the frontlines of Counter-Earth, informed Zev Love X's need to *counter* as he mourned Subroc. After producing half of KMD's album physically with Subroc, he finished it with his brother in spirit. Titled *BL_CK B_ST_RDS* (pronounced *Black Bastards*), the album's cover art featured Zev Love X's drawing of a hangman sketch of a lynched Blackface sambo, which called out the American entertainment industry that exploited derogatory images of Black folk. After criticism from Black *Billboard* writers who misjudged the art, Elektra Records deemed the image offensive. They dropped KMD from the label on April 7, 1994, two weeks before the one-year memorial of Dingilizwe's death. Elektra paid Dumile $20,000 severance and gave him the album's masters. That was the counter. Although he was terminated, *BL_CK B_ST_RDS* was a meal ticket and an exit portal for Dumile. Inspired by The Last Poets alum Gylan Kain's spoken-word album, *The Blue Guerilla* (1970), *BL_CK B_ST_RDS* sampled avant-garde Black Arts Movement jazz and blaxploitation films during a time when rap music was selling (out) more to the mainstream. Within his torment, Zev Love X exited the industry with the sonic/phonic memory of Subroc operating as a creative entity within Zev, minus living flesh. As Ro defined it, the *numinous* presence of Subroc is amplified throughout *BL_CK B_ST_RDS* but particularly on Subroc's sole solo track, "It Sounded Like a Roc."[3] The song sampled Cecil McBee's upright bass on jazz saxophonist Pharoah Sanders's album title track "Thembi" (1971), which means "love, faith and hope" in the South African language, Xosa. Subroc rapped wittily about being lyrically and physically "hard" and affirmed his eternal presence in the song's last line: "If I be ghost, expect me back to haunt." Dingilizwe spoke eternal devotion over his brother Daniel as he proceeded towards the way of von Doom and teleported from the industry.

This is the Doom origin story, told with narratives of how superheroes and supervillains activate their superpowers. Zev Love X's weapons were public disappearance with enough money to live on, a classic album, an uncanny lyrical technique, and a mystical imagination. Combined loss and subsequent grief produced torment and an obstacle for Zev Love X to accept. Victor Von Doom originated from similar gifts, circumstances, and stakes. As a young man, he accepted his torment as a child, lying in the arms of his dying father after his sorceress wife, Victor's mother, Cynthia, was murdered and banished to Hell (*Fantastic Four*, vol. 4, #9, 2013). Victor inherited his parents' science and mysticism, and he acquired and mastered skills like illusion. Dumile's embrace of his torment empowered his prequel to an unprecedented underground hip-hop zenith, particularly when he embraced Dr. Doom. Despite "disappearing," Zev Love X's first reappearance was only a few months after Elektra's termination and KMD's disbandment. Like von Doom's voice communicating telekinetically to his enemies, a voice was activated during the twilight hours of the classic *Stretch Armstrong and Bobbito Show* on Columbia University's 89.9 FM. DJ Bobbito Garcia introduced a song titled "Gas Drawls" by an MC who "is down with KMD," whose "name is Doom" (Armstrong & Garcia, 1994). The voice rapped at a slightly slower pace and lower pitch. He referred to himself as "the supervillain" and "Doom with the metal face." Then, he slightly evoked the name attached to "X the Antisocial," "X the Unemotional," "the Unseen," and "X The Unannounced I'm out" for the last line. The voice seemed unheard again for years until Stretch and Bobbito greeted one called "MF Doom" live on their show in 1997 (Lopez, 2021). Like a Doombot appearing to misdirect an enemy from Dr. Doom's true scheme, MF Doom was playful like Zev Love X and switched the speed of his freestyle flows rapidly over multiple beats. He also spoke more like Zev, which was different from the lower-pitched, huskier tone and slower pace for 1994's "Gas Drawls." The joy in MF Doom's voice as he joked obnoxiously with Bobbito, Stretch, and DJ compatriot (now Shade 45's) Lord Sear was different from the "X" that Ronin Ro encountered in their "dark interaction." The freestyles were improvisations of eventual *Operation: Doomsday* (1999) tracks "Go with the Flow," "Hey!," and "Red and Gold." MF Doom, who signed off as "Mad Flows," "Metal Fingers," and "Metal Facin'," had activated superpowers in his names and poetry cut with edge and an enhanced skill to rhyme constantly and shift flows. Referring to himself as "Sci.Fly the odd Merlin" and comparing his MC'ing to *The Twilight Zone* creator Rod Serling, MF Doom appeared to infiltrate space with his voice incorporated with imagination and characteristics parallel with Dr. Doom's invasion of Marvel Comics.

1994's "Gas Drawls" was the first song to mark Zev Love X's reappearance and transition to the Doom-von Doom appropriation. It also revealed Doom's method of creating multiple versions of songs with shifting deliveries and allusions that illustrated his transformation. "Gas Drawls" was an offshoot to Zev's first-ever appearance on 3rd Bass's "Gas Face" (1989), an industry diss track calling out industry deception, anti-Blackness, and wackness to be destroyed on sight via lyrical knowledge of self, echoing the Dumile's relationship with the Ansaaru Allah Community, an offshoot of the Nation of Islam. "Gas Drawls," however, is "murder rap." Dumile depicted himself disappearing from scenes in a dark, oversized T-shirt, jeans, Tims, and a stocking cap half-covering his face as he smoked L's that induced a mystical stye in the corner of his eye. The lyrical villain anticipated opportunities outside on street corners or sitting in a room cleaning guns or bagging nickel bags. Listening closer, "Gas Drawls" describes itself as "massive versatile," displaying multiple deliveries in its multiple iterations and speaking as a battle rap challenging all sucka MCs to "master" their craft. Furthermore, as von Doom's rap incarnate, "Gas Drawls" warns the competition: do not fuck with him. Shouting out KMD third member Onyx alongside Subroc, Doom summoned the living and dead and displayed physical and spiritual powers gathered and obtained to, as old folk in the South put it, *send yo' ass to hell with gasoline drawers on*. Like Victor von Doom's origin story that did not appear until after he was an established villain in Marvel, Zev Love X + DJ Subroc = MF Doom manifested a lyrical gift to counter the torment of death and to build a unique destruction on the industry world.

## SUPERVILLAIN VAUDEVILLE HIP-HOP POETICS OF THE ABSURD

> Your life hangs on a thread to be cut short on Doom's command! [. . .] death shall be your only reward.
> —DR. VICTOR VON DOOM[4]

The section title references the performativity of MF Doom during his creative zenith and how Victor von Doom's presence loomed within Marvel's universe and influenced MF Doom. A dirty audio recording titled "MF DOOM—Doomsday (First Live Performance—Nuyorican Poet's Cafe)" (2021) surfaced on YouTube. Samples of Sade's "Kiss of Life" and Boogie Down Productions' "Poetry" percolated an old-school mood, followed by the revelation of MF Doom on the tiny stage of the spoken word cultural mecca, the Nuyorican Poets' Cafe in Lower East Side, New York. It was a September Saturday night in 1998, and the intimate crowd close to the tiny stage witnessed MF Doom perform in the sacred underground space where poet Saul Williams (*Slam*, 1998), pre–*Def Poets*' Mos Def (a.k.a. Yasiin Bey), Erykah Badu, Eminem and others sharpened their performative crafts (Mlynar, 2018). Performing the "Operation Doomsday" title track from his unreleased debut album, MF Doom mounted underground hip-hop theatre to "destroy rap." His key costume piece and prop were a stocking cap to cover his face and the mic. "Supervillain Vaudeville," we can call it, was a specialty of hip-hop poetics appropriating the modern age of comic books (1985–present) when Victor von Doom focused more on battles between allies and cosmic forces whose powers he coveted. For MF, cosmic forces KMD-Subroc had transformed Zev Love X in physical flesh to "Metal Fingers" in sonic form and the voice of "Metal Face Doom" driven by the core element of poetics: *language*. MF Doom had tapped into *nommo*—the West African concept that Paul Carter Harrison (1972) called the life force we contribute to the world through *words*. Appropriating von Doom's iron mask later, he molded to his face an acquired element of mystique that completed the cipher of his Supervillain Vaudeville DOOMiverse: "Hip-hop is dominated by the spiritual and revolutionary belief that we make our own world through the performativity of our words and thoughts" (Banks, 2011, p. 10). From 1999 to 2009, the merging of MF Doom and Von Doom became comics/hip-hop poetics, producing one of the most prolific runs in hip-hop history.

*Operation: Doomsday* (1999) revealed MF's mission to disrupt rap's focus on commercial image and identity. Although he revealed himself and evoked

Subroc throughout *Doomsday* (the "Dumile" name/"Doom will lay"), MF still activated von Doomish disguise, illusion, and misdirection with the mask, low-pitched vocals, and other tactics as he reentered the industry. The *MF EP* (2000) cover alongside MF Grimm was the only time Doom did not wear the mask for his album art, but he sported a baseball cap low over his eyes and tilted his face away from the camera. The voiceless *Special Herbs* instrumentals (2001–2006) used *Fantastic Four* comic pages for cover art, which caused a cease-and-desist letter from Marvel (Fernando, 2024). Additionally, "Metal Fingers" used his MPC 2000XL beat machine to flip samples and then hide them from major record labels with obscure names of herbs and spices for song titles under another moniker and distributed by independent labels. Production was, therefore, a complementary weapon to MC'ing, like Dr. Doom's secret weapon, a hypersound piano used to distract and attack enemies (Fantastic Four #87, 1969; #236, 1981). *Mm..Food* (2004) is an anagram for "MF Doom," who titled each song after food mixed with metaphors that expressed his desire to devour toxic parts and people in mainstream rap that he also compared to the toxic food industry. Von Doom, a master at potato au gratin and of world domination, has used a range of tactics like surprise dinner party attacks against enemies. Or, as Emperor Doom, he stopped war and world hunger and only became bored with it because he also restricted people's free will. This coincides with MF's *Mm.. Food* critique of food's dominant presence in our lives that can help and harm us and protect us from hunger but also take our free will to eat what we want or overcome bad eating that plagues us.

During this period, von Doom's mastery of illusion and focus on mysticism remained central to Marvel Comics' character narrative. But unlike MF Doom's transformation into the new millennium, Dr. Doom's Marvel poetics descended. Victor sacrificed his one true love, Valeria, in exchange for demonic power. He then used her skin to create a mystical armor and tried to use his new powers to send his Four nemeses to Hell (*Fantastic Four*, vol. 3, #67, 2003). Von Doom's narrative evolved into a predictable cycle of god complex, sympathy, and antiheroics a few years later. This version of Victor collaborated with heroes but remained resistant to considering superheroes his peers due to his pursuit of omnipotence (*The Books of Doom*, 2005–2006). He was accused of war crimes and then exonerated (*Dark Avengers*, #1, 2009). He helped the Avengers invade Wakanda, maimed T'Challa, and destroyed its vibranium (Incredible War #606, 2010). Trapped by The Beyonders, he made amends with The Four, but his desire for omniscience bested him as he pursued it to make supercontemporaries his servants (*FF*, #23, 2012).

Although it made sense that Marvel's greatest supervillain would resist traditional superhero narratives, the cycle limited von Doom's arc. Unlike MF Doom, who resisted traditional rap narratives through his relentless pursuit of craft (*nommo*), Victor von Doom enlivened death to the poetic death.

Listen to hip-hop and read comics long enough, and you will recognize absurd acts by rappers, heroes, and villains. As death functions at the intersection of both Doom narratives—MF grieving death and von Doom conceiving death—so does life and laughter. Shoutout beloved critic of da kulcha [*sic*] Greg Tate (1957–2021), who highlighted the absurdity of rappers' exaggerated gangsterism, death wishes, and hypermasculinity. Tate (2016) crowned MF Doom "hip-hop of the Absurd" for his resistant language that borders on profound meaninglessness: "The lyricist known as MF Doom is perhaps our most uncanny contemporary purveyor of that [Absurdist] style. [. . .] Doom's sort of absurdism piles on so many silly in-jokes and obscure references that you may at first easily feel fan boy brilliant for catching them until you realize the joke's on you. Being able to footnote Doom's roll call of cultural waste products we've come to realize is, though mad fun, no sign of intelligent life" (Tate, 2016, p. 325).

Tate highlighted MF Doom's absurdism, borne from necessity and his intention to resist the mainstream with grotesque performance and lyricism. Subsequently, this fanboy sees MF Doom expounding on absurdism's three ("3-times dope") hilarious, existential, and fatalistic points. The hilarious nature of Doom includes his stream of consciousness jokes, rapping about himself in the third person, and laugh-out-loud lyricism coinciding with goofy cartoon interludes. Additionally, the mask with Doom's throwback appearance was a dig at studio gangsters and drug dealers who snitch on themselves as they become flashy, murderous commercial rappers: "Doom's music was revanche, and the Doom persona felt like it had emerged from the graveyard of rappers murdered by glam-hop. Onstage, Doom looked the part. He cultivated a disheveled aspect—ill-fitting white tees or throwback Patrick Ewing jerseys. His paunch gently rebelled against the border of his shirt. He was visibly balding. His manner suggested a retired B-boy tossing off the trappings of domesticity for one last boisterous romp" (Coates, 2009).[5]

MF Doom's albums proceeded with an existential absurdist tone as the Supervillain Vaudeville DOOMiverse expanded rhyme, sampling, alter-ego, and folklore. *Take Me to Your Leader* (2003) was produced by and featured King Geedorah, the mythologized three-headed dragon rap god summoning MF Doom to summon young whipper-snapper *Vaudeville*

*Villain* (2003) Viktor Vaughn teleporting through time from 1990s samples like Biggie's "Warning" (on "Lickupon") to open-mic stage dates with 1990s fly girls Rae Dawn Chong ("Raedawn") and Apani B./Nikki ("Can I Watch"[6]). Doom remixed his humor with Adult Swim's twilight cartoon food munchies characters, Aqua Teen Hunger Force, and with fellow Marvel remix Tony Stark/Ghostface Killah, underground backpack rapper Talib Kweli, and eccentric Cee-Lo as he merged with superproducer Danger Mouse as DANGERDOOM (*The Mouse and the Mask* [2005]). And his supreme collaboration with Madlib manifested Madvillain to create the supervillain exposé, *Madvillainy* (2004), which continues to expand in legend and popularity (Skelton, 2024). The hallmarks of MF Doom's absurdist technique were hookless songs, continuous rhyme schemes replete with nothingness, and shifting into living creative entities. For "nothingness" enters a poetic, existential context that made MF Doom a (Black) pop culture icon: "Doom's raspy baritone weaves an intricate web of allusions drawn from comic books and metaphysics, along with seeming nonsense and non sequiturs. [...] To read Doom's lyrics is to relinquish the need for certitude. His lines often defy paraphrasing" (Bradley & DuBois, 2010).

He became the revered supervillain devouring rappers and candidly "jerking" promoters out of money when he ghosted concerts and fans that seemingly forgave him for substitute Doomposters, who performed shameless lip sync performances donning the mask as he sat backstage, in the audience, or "St. Elsewhere" (Coates, 2009). Like von Doom's Doombots, MF indulged supervillain status, gaining a cult following of respect (like von Doom's Servo-Guards), because he dedicated himself to *nommo*: his craft and mask as a life force portal that fed life and reimagined a world beyond: "I wanted to get onstage and orate, without people thinking about the normal things people think about. Like girls being like, 'Oh, he's sexy,' or 'I don't want him, he's ugly,' and then other dudes sizing you up. A visual always brings a first impression. But if there's going to be a first impression I might as well use it to control the story. So why not do something like throw a mask on?" (Coates, 2009).

In the Fantastic Four's 2000s movies, Von Doom's mask evolved into a permanent fixture integrated with Victor's face. Through MF Doom's masked performance/repertoire, he countered the industry, cornered a market, and sustained artistic integrity. His absurdist, allusive rhyming aligned with alter egos inspired by "Supervillain Muse von Doom" created a metamorphosis that manifested the supervillain MF DOOM—ALL CAPS when you spell the man's name—into a complicated, absurdist cultural dynamic.

## APPROACHING THE CLASSIC CONCEPTION OF DEATH

> Dr. Doom was the classic conception of Death, of approaching death. I saw Dr. Doom as The Man in the Iron Mask, symbolizing approaching death. It was the reason for the armor and hood. Death is connected with armor and inhuman-like steel. Death is something without mercy, and human flesh contains that element of mercy. Therefore I had to erase it, and I did it with a mask.
>
> —JACK KIRBY (VIOLA, 1987)

Dr. Victor von Doom's sixty-year-old narrative arc includes some humanity, despite creator Jack Kirby's imagining him as the classic conception of death. By the 2010s, at the height of MF DOOM's appropriation of Kirby's character, Marvel Comics seemed to favor a more empathetic Doom character. Despite his invasion of Wakanda in the *Dark Reign* (2009) and *Doomwar* (2010) series, he was humbled elsewhere. He suffered from brain damage and underwent surgery as he sought to be reborn and abdicated Latveria's throne (*Fantastic Four's Future Foundation*, 2010–2012). He created the Parliament of Doom for peace across the multiverse. He atoned for misdeeds and reversed past enemies' deaths (*Avengers World* #16; *Secret Wars* #9). Archnemesis Reed Richards healed von Doom's face and cleansed his soul, and he earned Tony Stark's respect and became Iron Man when Stark fell into a coma (*Civil War II*; *Invincible Iron Man* #3; *Infamous Iron Man* #12). These humanistic von Dooms coincided with 20th-Century Fox's *FANT4STIC* (2015). Victor, genius protégé of scientist/father figure Franklin Storm, was consumed by a lava substance on foreign Planet Zero. While the substance gave him and The Four their superhuman powers, Victor was left behind on the planet, forever transformed with ironclad human frailty armored with inhuman trauma.

The 2010s "human-washed" approach to "Classic Conception of Death von Doom" might have been influenced by multiple factors, including MF DOOM. First, the rise of the *other* MCU (Marvel Cinematic Universe) attracted a PG-13 audience in which themes of death and destruction were carefully curated before premiering in movies made for families with kids. Simply put, the MCU was not ready for Dr. Doom. Additionally, MF DOOM's appropriation became popular circa 2010, as he had spent the previous ten years becoming an underground rap cult figure associated with absurdist pop culture stereotypes of stoners and sippers indulging in the dark humor of Adult Swim. Whether the MCU paid attention to the ALL

CAPS's remix of Marvel's greatest supervillain or not, Victor von Doom was not ready for the cinematic universe as bookwriters humanized him and MF DOOM reintroduced him to an alternative audience. Dumile had remixed the classic conception of approaching death, as Kirby put it, through his unique embodiment as a response to his own needs and talent.

Furthermore, we have mercy on Dumile for his embodiment, because we consider the inevitability of death for all human life and the fact of life connected to dying for all mere mortals: *living*. Although von Doom and other superhumans can teach us lessons about truth and life (e.g., "with great power comes great responsibility"), the comic book legend ripe for endless re-creation does not have to endure real life. Dumile created MF DOOM to overcome suffering and to approach death unlike any human ever or how any supervillain could never. The one hero that comes close that should be briefly evoked here is King T'Challa née Chadwick Boseman (1976–2020). Von Doom's 2010s archenemy and Dumile's hip-hop pop culture contemporary parallels Dumile DOOM's transformation of Marvel's classic conception of death. After he also died with Dumile in 2020, *Wakanda Forever* (2022) blessed us with tears to collectively mourn "Numinous Boseman" via King T'Challa's silver screen presence.

Meanwhile, social media geeks speculated von Doom's unseen presence in the same film. This was never confirmed. But during the July 2024 Comic-Con, Marvel introduced their upcoming series, *Avengers: The Secret Wars* (2027), and its first film, *Avengers: Doomsday* (2026), MCU's first Dr. Doom film. A row of Doombot actors wearing iron masks and green, caped suits lined up onstage. When Robert Downey Jr., a.k.a. Iron Man, unveiled his mask and revealed that he would play the next Dr. Doom, the crowd geeked. This suggested that the cinematic MCU finally resolved the challenge of bringing Marvel's greatest supervillain to film. But seeing Downey Jr. as von Doom also hinted that Marvel might have been perplexed about presenting the Classic Conception of Death onscreen without a proper remix of sympathetic fodder for Victor, including his reformed images cited above. Additionally, casting *The Avengers*' antiheroic superhero "greatest actor" is an approach to death that deflects Dr. Doom's destructive, self-serving powers as he approaches death by way of Disney.

Evoking MCU's transition from T'Challa to von Doom with a safe, popular approach uplifts the transition of MF DOOM. For this is not the "unsung" story or "the mask behind the music." Just sixty-four days after Boseman's untimely passing and four years before announcing the revival of *Avengers: Doomsday*, Dumile approached death one last time quietly on Halloween 2020. This chapter has remixed Dumile's remix of his and von

Doom's archive/repertoire to tell you, Dear Reader, a story of "how a man dies," i.e., the journey of a Black man approaching death, becoming the classic conception of death. Like both MCU's, MF DOOM's narrative rose to prominence, overcoming antiheroic supervillainy that created joy, heroism, commercial appeal, and critical acclaim. After a ten-year zenith run of MCs, alter-egos, villains, classic albums, collabs, and special herbs, *Born Like This* (2009), titled under the moniker DOOM (minus the MF), became the most personal culmination of DOOM's run. It revealed supreme lyrical craft, trilling with allusions that revolutionized rap's most overused device of rhyme spoken in DOOM's trademark, lower pitch, and written with a balance of absurdity undermining listeners with the new. And what of Death? DOOM remixed his classic conception of death that impacted his singular legacy on hip-hop and comics.

*Born Like This* was never announced as DOOM's final solo album. But it was, and this chapter reads it as the backdrop to recognize DOOM's life's work from the late 1990s to the early 2010s, beyond the given circumstances of Dumile's mortality. *Born Like This* is a testament to the relentless craft borne from living, i.e., human suffering. Although the form and content are in step with DOOM's previous classics, the stakes are higher. He collaborated with crate-digging masters ("Numinous J. Dilla" [1974–2007]) and crossover superhero MCs (Ghostface Killa and Raekwon The Chef/Lex Diamonds) who deepened the album's sound and content. But above this classic lineup of the numinous and nommo is the sample from poet "laureate of lowlife" Charles Bukowski (1920–1994) reciting his poem, "Dinosauria, We" (1992) and approaching death apocalyptically. For the song "Cellz," DOOM did not alter Bukowski's voice with a "chop up" or loop; he instead blended "Dinosauria, We" over a "Superfriends" (1973) sample of bombs crashing in the background that created an ominous tone. Bukowski repeated the line "born like this" and warned listeners of our world in warfare with an all-consuming force aided by mankind's villainous, inhumane assistance. DOOM reinforced this message with two verses, and the whole album lit with his dark, absurdist tone that makes Marvel's *Secret Wars* read like a kid created it, which is convenient to compare here if you consider the *Secret Wars*' premise: the Beyonder, a cosmic, childlike entity, created a Battleworld then "called" heroes and villains to battle for power to their destruction of continuous warfare (*The Beyonder* [Earth-616]). Created in 1984 and rebooted in 2015, *Secret Wars* is Marvel's current cinematic focus (*Avengers: Secret Wars*, 2027), to be preceded by "Archvillain von Doom" in *Avengers: Doomsday* (2026). While Disney has commercialized its narrative for a widespread audience, DOOM upped his supervillain status in *Born Like This* beyond von Doom's narrative in *Secret Wars*, which tended to trap him in the narrative cycle of self-destruction, often considered his strongest weakness. Although *Secret Wars* might offer lessons on self-destruction, *Born Like This*'s Metal Face spoke to the perils of the world, getting money to care for family and taunting sucka MCs with language that hinted at conspiracy and homophobia that Dumile denied and justified as his allegiance to his character's supervillain and his committed resistance to the industry as a literary artist: "DOOM's a villain. I'm a writer, I touch on all topics. DOOM happens to talk shit about everyone; regular street n****s, punks, fat n****s, queens, and kings. I talk shit about every facet of life" (Ma, 2018).

As DOOM's grotesque lyrical and character transformation approached death with the element of mercy for Dumile's human life, the morbidity of *Born Like This* foreshadowed the mercilessness of life, and approaching death was amplified when Dumile was disallowed reentry into the US in 2010. Although he recorded music until his death, deportation marked the end of DOOM's creative zenith and the start of an inadvertent "Sister Souljah moment."[7] You cannot help but ponder the absurdity: The first US presidential administration of African (Kenyan) descent flexed its nation's anti-immigration muscle and refused reentry to a third-generation Trinidadian-Zimbabwean born in Hounslow, West London, while his immigrant American citizen mother was visiting her sister; this forty-year-Long Beach, Long Island-New Yorker-raised b-boy all-star and thirty-year hip-hop genius was disallowed reentry into the states where he created culture, community, and taught knowledge of self.[8] This is even more absurd when we listen to *Doomsday* samples of *The Fantastic Four* (1968) cartoon, where Victor von Doom teleported between Long Island and Latveria, wreaking world havoc for world domination. Meanwhile, Dumile, who was posthumously honored with a street named after him and Dingilizwe in Long Island, was denied permanent residency and deemed an "unlawful presence" due to a short list of misdemeanors that ultimately rendered him "inadmissible" in the country where he had spent his life up to that point. Dumile, also an Atlantan transplant who had moved Black creative culture from state to state and in and out from Canada to Jamaica, received no mercy from a nation of immigrants with a border crisis problem. Unlike the genius Latverian transplant von Doom, Dumile was deemed illegal for immigration travel.

During deportation, the mask of torment returned. Hardly a sound was heard amid a few collaborations and an Instagram post under the handle @gasdrawls, featuring the DOOM mask as the profile photo. Inside the post is a photo of two Black fingers holding a small 3 × 5 photo of a Black boy looking directly at the camera without a smile but without suspicion. "ALL

CAPS" evoked *Thembi* ("love, faith and hope") over his son: "KING MALACHI EZEKIEL DUMILE 2/22/03–12/18/2017 THE GREATEST SON . . ."
The pieces for the sacrament were staged: deportation over teleportation, villainizing over supervillainy, sporadic collaboration amid the death of a son, all revealed pieces of a man seemingly experiencing the erasure of mercy. Play an MF DOOM song: "Rapp Snitch Knishes" (2004), which journalist Mike Lupica quoted to explain Trump & Co. snitching on themselves about Russian collusion (Yoo, 2018). Better yet, play that song's special herb instrumental, "Coffin Nails" (2003), which was listed on President Biden's inauguration playlist to celebrate defeating Trump, not deporting Dumile. Or play "Strange Ways" (2004) only if we also play "Notebook 04" (2017) and reference Trump reviving his presidency on immigration reform promises based on the mass deportation of "illegals." Then, play back "Coffin Nails" and go back, *way back* to its original sample: David Matthews's 1977 rendition of "Space Oddity," David Bowie's 1969 anthem about von Doomish space journeying and MF DOOMish psychedelic trips. Because Zev Love X has exited, Metal Fingers is at rest for eternity. MF DOOM was deported. Daniel Dumile has died, dearly departed, mask never to be removed, unlike Downey Jr.'s at Comic-Con, hilariously shouting, "new mask, new task," to the crowd's roar.[9] Suppose it could all be so simple. Von Doom forever roams the multiverse, retells his story, and avenges his mother and father's glory. Actors can leave the hero and return the doom. But Dumile faced death inside a COVID-restricted white room furnished with a metal desk on Halloween night 2020, with no supervillain spell to conjure against angioedema. With his wife/manager, Jasmine, at his bedside, he joined the numinous spirit of Brother SUBROC that led him back to Dr. Doom myths they read as young boys and that he used to create the hero DOOM that he invoked for his son, Numinous Malachi Ezekiel, his wife, and other children. Through the life force of word—*nommo*—an Instagram post from Jasmine Dumile on New Year's Eve 2020 sent a shockwave through our lives, as "Hip-Hop's Classic Conception of Death, of Approaching Death" was revealed to us with uncanny absurdity that we've grown accustomed to. Jasmine opened her tribute by giving thanks to "THE ALL" and honoring Dumile as "the greatest husband, father, teacher, student, business partner, lover and friend" she could ever ask for. She expressed deep gratitude for the lessons Dumile taught about love, forgiveness, and personal growth, as well as the love he provided to their family. "My world will never be the same without you," she wrote, as the letter closed with an invocation for "THE ALL" to continue to bless their family and the planet.

If the erasure of mercy was Kirby's goal with the mask, and von Doom was the classic conception of death, Daniel Dumile became the supervillain's mediated symbol who transformed through him MF DOOM with numinous presence, Shakespearean command of the word to wield the life force of living and overcoming, and an absurdist tone of creativity and humanity as he approached death against bullshit terms.

## CODA DUMILE VON DOOM

In the *Days of Doom* (2024), Dr. Victor von Doom sampled the lyrics of MF DOOM from *Madvillainy*'s "Accordion": "Livin' on borrowed time, the clock ticks faster" marked the first time von Doom had spoken from the cosmos through MF DOOM. Marvel honored DOOM only once before with 2015's hip-hop variant cover of Thor referencing *Madvillainy* (Turner-Williams, 2024; Gonik, 2015). As Victor lives on traveling the multiverse, protecting Latveria, starring in the movies, and thirsting for new worlds, he also has a hip-hop arsenal that MF DOOM built and left for von Doom writers. Daniel Dumile created sacred material to overcome the despair that the world wrought upon him, and Victor von Doom's narrative could be improved by it.

Howard and Jackson (2013) are good to consult here because if "[c]omics represent imagination and inspiring people to imagine things beyond their realities" (Jefferson, 2018), then Dumile remixing von Doom and creating a cult classic persona who critiqued the commercial rap industry and intersected pop culture is the epitome of forging representation in comic book culture via hip-hop culture. Dumile's sheer skill to masterfully sample his source material is a testament to his imagination and his deconstruction of comic book narrative history—a history that Howard and Jackson argue needs further expansion opposite previous representations of Blackness. Through MF DOOM, Dumile inserted himself and therefore Blackness into Marvel's narratives without ever being asked to guest edit a comic book or appear in a Marvel movie. Although Marvel never prominently acknowledged MF DOOM as a possible component of Dr. Doom's popularity, Dumile modified how hip-hop cultural citizens look at Dr. Doom with humanity and with a soundtrack that we can all *bump to death*. This makes Dumile a profoundly significant indirect representation of the history of Black folk, hip-hop, and comics (Howard, 2017).

# NOTES

1. KMD also stood for "a positive Kause in a Much-Damaged society," according to Fernando's unauthorized biography of MF DOOM, *The Chronicles of DOOM: Unraveling Rap's Masked Iconoclast* (2024), which includes details that informed this book chapter.

2. Series and publication dates for all comic book narratives were obtained from the Marvel Database at marvel.fandom.com and Dr. Doom's page on Wikipedia.org. The Marvel Database was created by Marvel Comics fans and enthusiasts, who provide character bios and synopses, comic issues, special editions, etc. The resource was the most reliable in navigating and managing Dr. Doom's shifting multiverse narratives. Endnotes on the database include issue names and numbers that readers can click on for a breakdown of the specific issue. This chapter lists the issue name, number, and publication year provided via the Marvel Database. See also the Marvel Database citation on the reference page.

3. Titles of songs and one-liners from songs reveal a hidden playlist in the book chapter. Google it and enjoy.

4. An epigraph created from two Dr. Doom quotes, one from the Marvel Database and the second from the Marvel vs. Capcom Wiki (marvelvscapcom.fandom.com), combined here, proves von Doom's got bars.

5. See Coates's description of MF Doom in De La Soul's euphoric live performance of Rock Co.Kane Flow on Carson Daly's "Last Call" on NBC, 2003, https://youtu.be/XWiUeU6VCso?si=1E58CX2-Cg9Skndo.

6. Apani B. (Apani Smith) is a good place to acknowledge women MCs' similar use of DOOM-like reinvention of skill, image, and identity performativity in hip-hop. In MF DOOM's biography (2024), "Nikki" is Apani B.'s featured alias alongside DOOM's Viktor Vaughn alter-ego, on "Can I Watch" (2003). The song was rare because DOOM rerecorded new lyrics multiple times after hearing Nikki's verses. She and DOOM essentially battled each other on the flirtatious song, one of the few that included a feature. A diligent, anticommercial MC, DOOM rarely used features or choruses but usually included one female voice at least once on most of his albums. The "femcee" usually rapped (some sang) and used extra aliases with superheroine twists such as Pebbles the Invisible Girl ("The Mic," 1999) or Empress Stahhr the Femcee née Kimberly Richardson, who aliased herself Angelika after Angelica Jones, the love interest on *Spider-Man and His Amazing Friends* (1982) animated series. Stahhr was DOOM's primary female collaborator ("Next Levels" and "Guinnessez," 2003) who studied his process and applied it.

Angelika's adopted persona coincides with DOOM and other artists who create reinventive performances to undermine or confront industry standards. Femcees have a history with these techniques, including the use of superheroes. Jean Grae (Tsidi Ibrahim), DOOM's mid-1990s contemporary, adopted her moniker from Marvel's X-Men character to highlight her supreme lyrical prowess and knowledge of self. Lauryn Hill did not use a super alias. However, *The Miseducation of Lauryn Hill* (1998) is still a superhuman masterpiece for marginalized voices that teaches the pursuit of wisdom and love, and to never be afraid to resist industry demands or exit altogether. While some artists like Nicki Minaj have remained in the industry, she still uses characters (Roman Zolanski, Barbie, and Chun-Li) to demonstrate the play and power of transformation. Even Minaj's and other women's hypervisibility and sexual images can push back against rigid constraints in hip-hop, similar to DOOM. Lastly, classic women MCs like Queen Latifah and Sister Souljah embodied noble and militant personas that they used to expand their messages socially and politically. By expanding the conversation beyond masculinity, we can see how hip-hop's culture of transformation is equally—if not more—urgent for women, who continue to shape their mythologies as a means of resistance.

7. According to Wikipedia, A Sister Souljah moment is "a calculated public repudiation of an extremist person, statement, group, or position perceived to have some association with the politician's party." The phrase was named for 1990s rapper, activist, and *New York Times* bestselling novelist, Sister Souljah née Lisa Williamson (b. 1964), when her comments about racial violence after the Los Angeles Riots of 1992 were weaponized by then President Bill Clinton to prove to voters that he was tough on race issues considered divisive.

8. Pitchfork provides two of the most thorough accounts of the two poignant events of Daniel Dumile's life: his immigration injustices and the malpractice during his last days. Please see Noah Yoo's (2021) "Untangling MF Doom's lifelong struggle with the immigration system" and Jazz Monroe's (2023) "MF Doom's Wife sheds light on the circumstances of his death."

9. Google this viral moment announced on Saturday, July 27, 2024, at Comic-Con.

## REFERENCES

Armstrong, S. & Garcia, B. (1994, December 15). *Stretch Armstrong and Bobbito Show*. 89.9 WKCR FM.

Banks, D. (2011). *Say word! Voices from hip-hop theater, an anthology*. University of Michigan Press.

Bradley, A., & DuBois, A. (Eds.). (2010). *Anthology of rap*. Yale University Press.

Church, S. H. (2022). *Turntables and tropes: A rhetoric of remix*. Michigan State University Press.

Coates, T. (2009, September 14). Catch me if you can. *The New Yorker*. https://www.newyorker.com/magazine/2009/09/21/the-mask-of-doom

Fernando, S. H. (2024). *The chronicles of DOOM: Unraveling rap's masked iconoclast*. Astra House.

Harrison, P. C. (1972). *The Drama of nommo and totem voices: Plays from the Black world repertory*. Grove Press.

Hartman, S. (2019). *Wayward lives, beautiful experiments: Intimate histories of riotous Black girls, troublesome women, and queer radicals*. W. W. Norton & Company.

Howard, S. C. & Jackson II, R.L. (Eds.), (2013). *Black comics: politics of race and representation*. Bloomsbury Press.

Jefferson, J. (2018). *Black comic books and to long journey to positive representation*. VIBE. https://www.yahoo.com/entertainment/Black-comic-books-long-journey-153844609.html

Jones, J. (2017). Narrative Blackness, Treme, and the great American television drama. In D. Gendrin, S. Roberts, & C. Dessinges (Eds.), *Treme and Post Katrina catharsis: The mediated rebirth of New Orleans* (pp. 257–86). Lexington Press.

Lopez, B. B. (2021, December 24). *MF DOOM—Strech & Bobbito freestyle 97* [Video]. YouTube. https://youtu.be/XOb2Rx_3ICY?si=eDFmezWPve2hSU5y

Marvel Database. (n.d.). *Marvel Database*. Fandom. https://marvel.fandom.com/wiki/Marvel_Database

MF Doom. (2015, August 9). *MF Doom—Gas drawls (1994 demo)* [Video]. YouTube. https://www.youtube.com/watch?v=LgVAK9FBBXQ&list=RDLgVAK9FBBXQ&start_radio=1

MF Doom. (2021, December 21). *MF Doom—MF DOOM—Strech & Bobbito freestyle 97* [Video]. YouTube. https://www.youtube.com/watch?v=XOb2Rx_3ICY&list=PLt66S96TziyRGSyfWyGofWoociNdun3cW&index=14

MF DOOM. (n.d.). *Apple Music*. https://music.apple.com/us/artist/mf-doom/3864756

Mlynar, P. (2018). *The Nuyorican Poets Café, a DIY hip hop incubator*. Red Bull Music Academy Daily. https://daily.redbullmusicacademy.com/2018/11/nuyorican-poets-cafe-feature/

Moten, F. (2003). Voices/forces. In F. Moten (Ed.), *In the break: The aesthetics of the Black radical tradition* (pp. 31–40). University of Minnesota Press.

Ro, R. (1994, June). "Life After Death." *The Source*, pp. 82–85.

Skelton, E. (2024, March 23). *MF DOOM and Madlib's Madvillainy is getting more popular every year. Here's proof*. Complex. https://www.complex.com/music/a/eric-skelton/mf-doom-madvillainy-streams-increasing-madlib

Tate, G. (2016). "Black modernity and laughter, or how it came to be that ni***s got jokes." In *Flyboy 2: The Greg Tate reader* (pp. 322–29). Duke University Press.

Turner-Williams, J. (2024, April 6). *Here's the release date for MF DOOM biography "The Chronicles of DOOM."* Complex. https://www.complex.com/music/a/jaelaniturnerwilliams/mf-doom-biography-the-chronicles-of-doom

Viola, K. (1987). Jack Kirby: The master of comic book art. *Jack Kirby Collector*, 7. TwoMorrows Publishing. https://twomorrows.com/kirby/articles/07violaint.html

CHAPTER 13

# HEARING COMICS IN HIP-HOP

Leikeli47 as Black Feminist Superhero

BREA M. HEIDELBERG AND JUSTIN D BURTON

The video for Leikeli47's "OMC" (2017) is definitely set in New York. Specifically, it seems to be shot on a rooftop in Brooklyn, around where Bushwick is about to turn into Williamsburg. This location can be triangulated from Figure 13.1—a still from 0:49 in the video. In this still, the following landmarks are visible: 1) in the middleground at Leikeli47's 10 o'clock, the spires of Most Holy Trinity church sit alongside the Bushwick Houses; the shot comes from a low enough angle that the Bushwick houses block our view of Manhattan's downtown, 2) in the background at Leikeli47's 12:30 rises the Empire State Building, and 3) in the foreground at Leikeli47's 2:00, a water tower perches atop 239–41 Varet St.

The thing is, "OMC" is definitely set in New York, except something's kind of . . . *off* about the city. For starters, we only see it in black and white, a visual aesthetic that often conjures a different time and place. There are also a number of upside-down shots, which can challenge the viewer's perspective or else can convey the point-of-view (pov) of an erratic first-person perspective. Finally, the least New York thing about "OMC" is that *there's nobody there*. Aside from Leikeli47—masked, as she always is—and her compatriots, the city is empty. There's no sign of zombie or environmental apocalypse, though, so it's not immediately apparent why "OMC"'s New York is vacant.

To understand what's happening in "OMC," we read hip-hop and comics alongside each other in this chapter. Though Leikeli47 doesn't directly

**Figure 13.1** Leikeli47 raps atop a Brooklyn rooftop.

reference comic books in her music or interviews, we argue that she's legible as a street-level Black feminist superhero, carving out protective spaces for her people and using her abilities to capture resources that she funnels back into her community. In this framework, the visual cues in "OMC" combine with the song's lyrics and sounds to place us in what we're theorizing as a pocket universe, a space next to but separate from the viewer's universe. By listening to "OMC" alongside other Leikeli47 songs and videos, we demonstrate how hip-hop and comics can be understood together, even when one medium is only a subtext to the other.

## LEIKELI47 AS A STREET-LEVEL HERO

The primary comic subtext in Leikeli47's work is her mask. She's never seen without it, and she guards her anonymity closely. The opening sequence of "OMC" seems like an unmasking, as the camera grants the viewer close-ups of Leikeli47 cutting through her wool balaclava with fabric scissors while the eight-measure instrumental intro cranks up (Figure 13.2). At the end of that intro, Leikeli47 pulls off her mask to reveal . . . another mask. It's a bandana with eye/mouth holes identical to the ones in her original mask. "I don't rock wit you, homie . . . I don't go out my circle," she tells us as she launches directly into the song's hook. Like any comic book superhero (or villain, for that matter), Leikeli47 prioritizes protecting her identity and refuses to show her face outside her circle. And since "ain't nobody vouching for you," that face stays covered.

One of the undercurrents of *Hip-Hop and Comics* is that both hip-hop and comic books, though rooted in (and still drawing from) underground and marginalized cultural communities, have grown into mainstream forces

**Figure 13.2** Leikeli47 cuts off her top layer of mask.

that permeate all manner of media in the twenty-first century. The chapters in this volume trace significant moments of crossover and cross-pollination between the two art forms. In this final installment, though, we want to acknowledge the supercharged influence of hip-hop and comics by thinking about them together even when there is no explicit connection. Leikeli47 could wear a mask for any number of reasons, but when we see it, our reaction is to think "hey, that's real superhero coded" and then to ask, "what does it mean for her to be a Black female superhero, anyway?" This chapter takes that reaction seriously, considering what sort of superhero Leikeli47 is and what kind of work she does. It's one possible avenue of Leikeli47 analysis, and it's a gambit that we take with the belief that it can deepen our understanding of comics, hip-hop, and the way Black women move in the world. We'll start with what kind of hero Leikeli47 is.

The "OMC" video suggests that Leikeli47 is a street-level superhero. Having surveyed a number of online sites where fans discuss the different levels of superhero, we define the street-level superhero according to the following seven criteria:

1. Geography: The street-level superhero operates primarily in the area where they reside. Think of "your friendly neighborhood Spider-Man."
2. Scope of Care: The street-level superhero's primary scope of care is the people they live near and interact with on a daily basis when they are not being a superhero.
3. Humanity: The street-level superhero is typically human. This can include "peak human" (Daredevil) and "enhanced human" (Spider-Man), but the street-level superhero is not typically a god, demigod, alien, or mythical creature.
4. Resources: The street-level superhero is not usually well-resourced.

5. Modus Operandi: The street-level superhero often works solo.
6. Relatability: The street-level superhero is usually more realistic and faces moral dilemmas that their readers may struggle with, too.
7. Power/Demolition: A street-level superhero fight is likely to destroy things like cars, lampposts, and other street-level objects, but not buildings, cities, or planets.[1]

There are, of course, street-level superheroes who will be exceptions to these rules, as well as superheroes who aren't entirely street-level but who hold several characteristics of one. Kamala Khan/Ms Marvel, for instance, is descended from a line of supernatural alien beings (criterion 3), travels through time and space (criteria 1, 7), teams up with the other Marvels (criterion 5), and finds herself involved in intergalactic kerfuffles (criterion 1). Despite missing so many criteria, though, Kamala Khan is written as a relatable character (criterion 6) who is primarily navigating family and community (criterion 2). As described by *Spider-Man* writer Dan Slott, "she's a teenage superhero, juggling her life, making mistakes, trying to do everything right" (Ching, 2014). The comparison to Spider-Man, perhaps the best-known street-level superhero, is apt, as Spider-Man also finds himself pulled into a team for global and galactic fights (criteria 1, 5, 7) and gifted a suit he wouldn't otherwise have the resources to acquire (criterion 4). But Ms Marvel and Spider-Man feel like street-level superheroes who are sometimes plucked from the street into something bigger. They side hustle at the global and uni/multiversal levels, but their main job is in the streets. Meanwhile, a character like Batman is a human (criterion 3) who tends to fight street-level fights (criterion 7) but is massively resourced (criteria 4, 6) and a key member of the Justice League (criterion 5) who seems to hate the people of Gotham about as much as the villains he fights (criterion 2). Batman cosplays as a street-level superhero, but he operates primarily at the city level when working solo and on the national and global level when working with the Justice League.

For the most part, though, street-level heroes stay on the streets. And New York is crawling with them: Luke Cage and Jessica Jones in Harlem, Spider-Man in Queens, Daredevil in Hell's Kitchen, and the Punisher also in Hell's Kitchen as well as, well, your nightmares (Figure 13.3 shows a humorous rundown of these heroes in a page from *The Astonishing Ant-Man* #8, as a low-level villain called the Magician who is contemplating a visit to New York is warned about the city by his colleagues). The grounding of street-level heroes in the streets is integral to what makes them compelling characters. Because they are human and fighting to protect their neighbors while navigating everyday moral dilemmas, the stakes can feel more immediate to a reader than, say, a supervillain with a ray gun pointed at the Earth. Street-level superheroes operate at the same level where their readers live, so they tend to feel familiar and also aspirational ("*You* could wear the mask," Miles Morales reminds us).

We're adding Brooklyn's Leikeli47 to the New York map of street-level heroes. Criteria 1 (geography), 3 (humanity), 4 (resources), 5 (modus operandi), and 7 (power/demolition) are all evident in the "OMC" video. Though Leikeli47 refuses to show her face, she makes no attempt to hide where she is, providing visual cues to her location in Brooklyn (criterion 1). She reads as clearly human (criterion 3) with no particular superpowers or resources (criterion 4) that lift her any higher than a 3-story building at the edge of her borough (this suggests criterion 7, as we're not dealing with the kind of superstrength or biotech that could raze a city). And though she's joined by trusted people from her neighborhood in the video, she's the only one who is masked, marking her as a superhero who works alone (criterion 5).

That's all well and good, but criterion 2 (scope of care) is integral to understanding a superhero, as the work they do helps us understand their moral compass and general sense of justice. "OMC" speaks to criterion 2 (scope of care), but to really understand what's happening in this video, we need to visit some of Leikeli47's other videos to establish what work she does on behalf of her community.

Leikeli47's day job is rapping. "Money" (video released November 2016) is structured like a straightforward luxury rap song, where an emcee brags about their riches. The hook, which is the first thing the listener hears, is simple: "Money, I got money." But the video isn't rife with the trappings of wealth, nor are the lyrics. Instead, Leikeli47 once again embeds herself in her borough (criterion 1), mentioning Brooklyn at the beginning of the first verse and accompanying it with a visual of the street-level view of buildings projected onto her mask. Instead of flaunting the money she says she's got, Leikeli47 spends the song talking about her work ethic. After a secondary hook that ends with people telling her that she got famous overnight and changed, she sarcastically retorts, "sho, you right" and then segues into a verse about how she rehearses for her tour in her kitchen. In terms of criterion 4 (resources), Leikeli47 may have money, but the ducats she's stacked by grinding in the studio and on tour aren't being spent on Bugattis, Balenciagas, or Bottegas.

If "Money" poses the mystery of where Leikeli47's ins are going, the video for "Miss Me," released a few months later in July 2017, offers an answer. Here, Leikeli47 works the register at a bodega on Nostrand Ave in Crown Heights, Brooklyn. It's a quotidian video, with shots of everyday transactions in the shop and people walking on the sidewalk outside. But if we keep "Money"

**Figure 13.3** Stick to Midtown!

in mind while watching the video, two details shine through. First, intercut with indoor bodega scenes are sequences of Leikeli47 posted up in a lawn chair next to a cooler on the sidewalk outside the store. In the first of these sidewalk scenes (0:33 in the video), a teenage boy taps Leikeli47 on the shoulder, and she hands him some cash and then makes direct eye contact with the camera. Second, lining the shelves of the bodega are canned goods—food staples—branded with Leikeli47's name: hot sauce, peanut butter, beans, soup, cereal. Street-level superhero Leikeli47 grinds for resources in order to funnel them back to her borough: she feeds her people.

## LEIKELI47 AS BLACK FEMINIST STREET-LEVEL HERO

It's hopefully obvious at this point that Leikeli47 doesn't always do things in the most straightforward manner. In the same way that she feints luxury rap with the song "Money," she also sidesteps one of the expectations of street-level superheroes: she doesn't fight (criterion 7). She isn't, as the villains in Figure 13.3 put it, webbing people up or handing out concussions. One of the reasons criterion 7 (power/demolition) is a thing is because street-level superheroes are constantly fighting "bad guys"—ranging from pickpockets to crime lords—and leaving busted windows, alarmed cars, and spewing fire hydrants in their wake. So while we're arguing that Leikeli47 is a street-level superhero, the fact that she doesn't fight marks her as a fairly anomalous hero.

It's because she's not just a street-level superhero but a Black feminist street-level superhero. We mean this to be inclusive of but not reduced to the fact that Leikeli47 is a Black woman. Beyond her identity and lived experience of race and gender, Leikeli47 is a Black feminist because of how she operates in her community. Consider her actions in "Money" and "Miss Me" against the backdrop of the Combahee River Collective's statement of 1977: "We realize that the liberation of all oppressed peoples necessitates the destruction of the political-economic systems of capitalism and imperialism as well as patriarchy. We are socialists because we believe the work must be organized for the collective benefit of those who do the work and create the products and not for the profit of the bosses" (Combahee River Collective, 1979, p. 366).

The Combahee River Collective (CRC) is not the first group of Black women to work for their freedom, but their statement—drafted by Barbara Smith, Demita Frazier, and Beverly Smith—is generally received as a germinal declaration of contemporary Black feminist politics. At the heart of the CRC's analysis is what they call "interlocking" systems of oppression and what Kimberlé Crenshaw (1989) would later call "intersectionality." That is, the CRC worked from the idea that their experiences of race, gender, and class could not be separated from one another, meaning that in order to achieve their liberation, they had "to combat the manifold and simultaneous oppressions that all women of color face" (1979, p. 362). This means that Black feminists consistently find themselves working with theoretical concepts and alongside activist groups—those fighting for racial freedom, sexual freedom, class freedom—even if "no other ostensibly progressive movement has ever considered our specific oppression a priority or worked seriously for the ending of that oppression" (1979, p. 365). The CRC acknowledges that Black feminists may be the only ones interested in the liberation of Black women but that Black feminists, in order to be successful, must be about the business of the liberation of all people.

Angela Davis employs a metaphor to explain why this is:

> ... try to visualize a simple pyramid, laterally divided according to the race and social class of different groups of women. White women are situated at the top—the bourgeoisie first, under which we place the middle classes and then the white working-class women. Located at the very bottom are Black and other racially oppressed women, the vast majority of whom come from working-class backgrounds. Now, when those at the very apex of the pyramid achieve victories for themselves, in all likelihood the status of the other women remains unchanged... On the other hand, if those at the nadir of the pyramid win victories for themselves, it is virtually inevitable that their progress will push the entire structure upward. The forward movement of women of color almost always initiates progressive change for all women. (1990, pp. 30–31)

Davis is focused specifically on feminist movements here (and she mixes in race and class), but her point can be scaled if we think of a pyramid that includes all genders. The forward movement of Black women and others at the bottom of the pyramid would still mean improvement for everyone above, too. As the CRC puts it, "if black women were free, it would mean that everyone else would have to be free since our freedom would necessitate the destruction of all the systems of oppression" (1979, p. 368).

Unsurprisingly, Black feminism tends to be at the root of ambitious, all-encompassing movements like harm reduction and prison abolition. "The history of harm reduction in this country," Shira Hassan chronicles, "is about the radical revolutionaries who believed that we, as all of those who were and still are disproportionately impacted by HIV and AIDS, deserved to survive"

(Hassan, 2022, p. 114).² Harm reduction has included things like syringe exchanges, safe injection sites, protection, and advocacy for sex workers. Resonating with Davis and the CRC, harm reduction has developed strategies for survival and thriving for those most vulnerable in society. Tourmaline notes that "trans women of color were developing [harm reduction]'s best practices," which happen "in the pockets of exquisite care we show our loved ones, without questioning or judging their life choices, or imagining that we know better than they do" (2022, xvii–xviii).

Prison abolition operates similarly, advocating for the creation of a society without police and prisons. It's a "transformative justice movement led by Black, Indigenous, and people of color survivors"—those situated at the bottom of Davis's pyramid—that isn't simply a negative thesis (Kaba 2021, p. 3). As Mariame Kaba describes it, prison abolition is "a vision of a restructured society in a world where we have everything we need: food, shelter, education, health, art, beauty, clean water, and more things that are foundational to our personal and community safety" (2021, p. 2). Abolition is a huge project, as aptly captured by the title of Ruth Wilson Gilmore's book on the subject: *Change Everything* (2024). Black feminism ends up undertaking massive projects like harm reduction and prison abolition because of what CRC observes in their 1977 statement: if Black women are to be free, then everyone has to be. So while we may move slowly toward reshaping the world, the goal can never be anything less than that, and it starts with caring and providing for one another.

Leikeli47 doesn't fight the "bad guys" because that's not how Black feminist projects work. Her time and energy is instead dedicated to caring for the people in her community, harnessing resources through rapping and then redistributing them to her Brooklyn neighbors. While other street-level heroes tend to either work with cops (even if it's just the "good" ones) or place themselves in the role of the cops, Leikeli47 steers clear of state violence and of employing tactics of control and punishment that the state does. She's engaged in practices of harm reduction and abolition, working entirely outside of notions of criminality.

Leikeli47's Black feminist work helps to explain her anonymity, too. While many superheroes protect their identities by wearing a mask (though, interestingly, in New York, Luke Cage, Jessica Jones, and the Punisher primarily operate without a mask), Leikeli47 goes to further lengths than just her mask to shroud her identity. While in some songs—like "OMC," "Money," and "Miss Me"—Leikeli47 is physically centered throughout most of the accompanying video, in others, she obscures herself from sight.³ She has a few strategies for achieving obscurity. In "Fuck the Summer Up" (March 2015), "Drums II

Clean" (May 2015), and "Girl Blunt" (October 2018), a variety of people who aren't Leikeli47—including people who read as masculine, femme, white, Black, Latinx, and, in one case, a child—wear masks and take turns lip syncing for the camera. In each of these videos, as well as "LL Cool J" (March 2022), Leikeli47 doesn't seem to appear at all. For "LL Cool J," no one wears a mask, and a viewer unfamiliar with Leikeli47 would likely believe that one of the lip syncers (though it would be difficult to determine which one) is Leikeli47. In "Tic Boom" (January 2019), Leikeli47 appears throughout the video and is the only person in a mask. However, she moves in and out of an assembly of people, and in many wide shots, she isn't centered, forcing the viewer to search her out in the crowd. Moreover, her music appears on licensing sites as registered to "Hasben Jones," an alias that allows her to receive "Money" for her music but that says "Miss Me" to anyone trying to track her down. When a journalist asked her her real name in 2022 (a question that the journalist felt certain wouldn't be answered), Leikeli47's publicist interjected, "I want to know, too, because even *I* don't know" (Rocque, 2022).

Leikeli47's careful guarding of her identity is unsurprising when we recognize that her Black feminist work places her at odds with the state. When Angela Davis was arrested and put on trial working to free people from prison, James Baldwin published an open letter decrying her prosecution and enumerating the ways that "we know" that the American system brutalizes Black people, ending with this: "If we know, then we must fight for your life as though it were our own—which it is—and render impassable with our bodies the corridor to the gas chamber. For, if they take you in the morning, they will be coming for us that night" (Baldwin, 1971).

Baldwin's sentiment is the harrowing inverse of the idea that "if black women were free, it would mean everyone else would have to be free." Baldwin suggests that, if black women *aren't* free, it's only a matter of time until no one is. One of the principles of prison abolition is that the system isn't broken; it's operating just as it was designed to, sucking up and dehumanizing those in its path. And while Black and Latinx people are disproportionately affected by the system, they aren't the only ones in harm's way. And when there are no more Black and Indigenous and people of color and poor and disabled and queer and and and for the system to grind up, it won't stop grinding. As a Black woman engaged in practices that don't feed that system, Leikeli47 needs her mask to protect a vulnerability that few street-level superheroes have to navigate.

"Surveillance is nothing new to black folks. It is the fact of antiblackness," writes Simone Browne (2015) in *Dark Matters* (p. 10). From plantation overseers to stop-and-frisk laws, the history of the United States is pockmarked by regulations that insist that Black bodies must be watched at all times. Leikeli47's city's history includes colonial "lantern laws," mandating that Black and Indigenous enslaved people must carry a candle after dark to illuminate themselves, to facilitate surveillance of them: "We can think of the lantern as a prosthesis made mandatory after dark, a technology that made it possible for the black body to be constantly illuminated from dusk to dawn, made knowable, locatable, and contained within the city" (Browne, 2015, p. 79).

Browne's book engages the long history of the surveillance of Black, Indigenous, and people of color, as well as the countersurveillance strategies that Black people have employed against their surveillance in order to claim autonomy. Leikeli47, in keeping her face always covered and her name always redacted, practices what Browne calls "dark sousveillance." If *surveillance* is observation from above, then *sousveillance* is observation from below; it's the people watching the watchers, the less powerful monitoring the movements of the powerful (think of the filming of police violence). And dark sousveillance "charts possibilities and coordinates modes of responding to, challenging, and confronting a surveillance that was almost all-encompassing" (p. 21). Dark sousveillance isn't just the precarious keeping watch over the powerful. It also includes the refusal to be surveilled. Leikeli47 certainly refuses her own surveillance, but returning to "OMC," we can see that she extends her dark sousveillance tactics to her community, as well.

## THE STREET-LEVEL BLACK FEMINIST WORK OF "OMC"

We began the chapter with the observation that the New York City of "OMC" is uncanny: it's filmed in black-and-white, includes a number of upside-down and erratic first-person shots, and depicts a city—"the city that never sleeps," no less—that's empty except for Leikeli47 and her comrades. With the understanding that Leikeli47 is a Black feminist street-level superhero, let's return now to that Brooklyn rooftop to better understand the dark sousveillance of the video. The song's refrain tells us a good deal about the position of the listener in relation to the singer: "I don't rock wit you, homie. I don't go out my circle." We are outsiders to wherever Leikeli47 is, and she's turning us away.

And where is she? In comic book terms, we might call it a pocket universe, a space tucked inside of our own universe—that's why it looks so familiar—but cordoned off.[4] Sometimes pocket universes are prisons or detention centers, like the one the Time Trapper uses to trap the Legion of Superheroes or the town in *Wandavision* that Agatha uses to hold the Scarlet Witch. In "OMC," though, Leikeli47 creates a pocket universe that shields and protects those inside it from the universe surrounding them. The off-kilter elements of the video, from the upside-down shots to the black-and-white aesthetic to the city's emptiness, signal that we're on the edge of a space that operates according to a different logic than the world the viewer is positioned in. The listener's and viewer's inability to discern color, to delineate up from down, to see the population of the space, to orient oneself at all, signal a transitional space. Standing before Leikeli47 on the Brooklyn rooftop, we are likely surrounded by a proletariat that we simply can't discern beyond the veil that separates us from them. Out of sight from the surveilling forces of this universe, Leikeli47 works dark sousveillance so that her people can move in and out of the shadows, sometimes accessing this universe and sometimes taking refuge in the shadows of the pocket universe.

Leikeli47, as we've observed, guards her appearance in a manner that underscores the fact that we will not be privy to what happens in the pocket universe's sanctuary space that she guards. Beyond shielding her face, Leikeli47 uses sonic techniques to evade detection, too. Her vocals are processed so that her voice can't be recognized by surveillance technologies. What sounds like an overdrive effect produces a buzzy edge to the low end of her range, while the high end takes on a metallic quality that sounds like it comes through a formant filter. The signal also sounds split and delayed so that the vocals fill the stereo field, spreading across the listener's soundscape. These techniques make it hard not only to detect whose voice this is but also to discern what direction the voice travels from. The motif that opens the song and loops almost without interruption shares some timbral similarities with the vocals; this synth has a buzzy low end with bright overtones that come from what sound like a square and a saw wave stacked on top of each other. The volume envelope sounds like a gate message, meaning the sound immediately hits peak volume and sustains there, then immediately falls to silence upon release. The synth is also layered with a higher warbling synth that sounds like a ringtone. This synth layer seems to perform a scrambling function that makes it difficult to hear what's happening beyond the vestibule of the pocket universe. Figure 13.4, for instance, shows the drumline that Leikeli47 brought as backup, but we can't hear what they're playing, which suggests that there are likely other sounds reverberating in the pocket universe that remain inaudible from our vantage point.

In *Let This Radicalize You* (2023), Mariame Kaba demonstrates the importance of care as refuge with a scene from the George Floyd protests in Chicago. On May 30, 2020, Mayor Lori Lightfoot announced at 8:25 p.m. a curfew that would start at 9:00 p.m., then lifted the Chicago River's bridges, trapping many protestors in the city. Those protestors' mere existence in the space was

Figure 13.4 Leikeli47 and the drumline we can't hear.

now criminalized, and one of the country's most notoriously violent police departments was sanctioned to deal with them as they saw fit. The Chicago Freedom School (CFS), a space cofounded by Kaba in 2007 and dedicated to educating youth of color about organizing and activism, became a place of refuge for protestors—many of them suffering the effects of police pepper spray—who were unable to get themselves out of the city.

When the police arrived at CFS later that night, Tony Alvarado-Rivera, the executive director of the school, and Jaxx Hamilton, who oversaw wellness, culture, and action at the school, met them at the door. As the police escalated their threats to arrest the two adults, it became clear they would have to let the cops in or else risk being cuffed and dragged away, leaving the young people inside vulnerable. Communicating wordlessly, it was decided that Hamilton would go lead the remaining youth out a back exit while Alvarado-Rivera stalled for a few more minutes. By the time the police breached the entrance, no one was left inside for them to find (pp. 64–70).

Or, in Leikeli47's words: "I don't rock wit you, homie." Sometimes you can care and provide for your people right where you are, funneling resources captured from a capitalist system back to those "who do the work and create the products" (CRC 1977/1979, p. 366). Other times, it requires a vanishing act. And in "OMC," Leikeli47 lets us walk up to the transitional space of refuge where she's ferried her people before demanding "Gimme 50 feet or better. Matter fact? Gimme better." The viewer of "OMC" can be privy to what she's done, but will not be granted entrance to her pocket universe.

Here, at the end of this volume that brings together hip-hop and comics, we direct your attention to Leikeli47, a street-level Black feminist superhero rapper whose only connection to comics is the subtext of her mask. We offer this speculative rendering of her as a street-level superhero because we can hear in her music and see in her videos possibilities that come to life when we listen and see with comic books in mind. We can also take her Black feminist work back to comic books to think more deeply about how other street-level superheroes operate. And we can do all of this while centering the ethos of Black feminist thought and work, striving in each place it takes root to grow a universe where, because Black women are free, everyone is free.

## NOTES

1. The fandom sites we read include the following: https://marvel.fandom.com/f/p/4400000000003558747, https://comicvine.gamespot.com/profile/shroudofsorrow/lists/marvel-and-dc-street-level-characters/42405/, https://comicvine.gamespot.com/forums/gen-discussion-1/what-do-you-mean-by-street-level-1637807/, https://cadabattles.fandom.com/wiki/Street_Tier.

2. Importantly, Hassan uses the term "liberatory harm reduction" or "radical harm reduction" to delineate the street-level practices of the original activists and organizers—many of them queer BIPOC folks—from the co-optation the term "harm reduction" has suffered in its uptake into state-run systems of social work.

3. In "Money," Leikeli47's face is manipulated so that it's oversized, and it isn't clear whether the body her head is attached to is her own or a stand-in's.

4. Elsewhere, Burton has theorized a similar space as a "posthuman vestibule," a space that "allows for insurgency and apartness," a space carved out by those who are most vulnerable so that they can both gain relief from the world while also imagining a new one (2017, p. 35).

## REFERENCES

Baldwin, J. (1971, January 7). An open letter to my sister, Miss Angela Davis. *The New York Review of Books*. https://www.nybooks.com/articles/1971/01/07/an-open-letter-to-my-sister-miss-angela-davis/

Browne, S. (2015). *Dark matters: On the surveillance of Blackness*. Duke University Press.

Burton, J. (2017). *Posthuman rap*. Oxford University Press.

Ching, A. (2014, October 12). NYCC: Marvel's "Spider-Verse" Panel, "Spider-Gwen" and "Silk" ongoings announced. *Comic Book Resources*. https://web.archive.org/web/20141016073838/http://www.comicbookresources.com/?page=articar&id=56244

Combahee River Collective. (1979). The Combahee River Collective: A Black feminist statement. In Z. R. Eisenstein (Ed.), *Capitalist patriarchy and the case for socialist feminism* (pp. 362–72). Monthly Review Press.

Crenshaw, K. (1989). Demarginalizing the intersection of race and sex: A Black feminist critique of antidiscrimination doctrine, feminist theory and antiracist politics. *University of Chicago Legal Forum*, 1(8), 139–67.

Davis, A. Y. (1990). *Women, culture and politics*. Vintage.

Gilmore, R. W. (2024). *Change everything: Racial capitalism and the case for abolition*. The MIT Press.

Hassan, S. (2022). *Saving our own lives: A liberatory practice of harm reduction*. Haymarket Books.

Hayes, K. & Kaba, M. (2023). *Let this radicalize you: Organizing and the revolution of reciprocal care*. Haymarket Books.

Kaba, M. (2021). *We do this 'til we free us: Abolitionist organizing and transforming justice*. Haymarket Books.

Rocque, S. (2022, April 20). *For Leikeli47, privacy is preference and access is a privilege*. MIC. https://www.mic.com/culture/leikeli47-shape-up

Tourmaline. (2022). Introduction. In S. Hassan (Ed.), *Saving our own lives: A liberatory practice of harm reduction*, xvii–xix. Haymarket Books.

# AFTERWORD

THE DARRYL MAKES COMICS TEAM
(SPENSER NELLIS, AMY CHU, AND RIGGS MORALES)

Hip-hop and comics are intrinsically tied-together art forms. Beginning with our tradition of oral and musical storytelling passed down for generations that tell the legends of myths and heroes through rhyme and sequential cave drawings depicting our earliest struggles, both mediums are evolutions of our most basic forms of communication and catapulted onto the biggest stages humanity has.

From sold-out concert venues to billion-dollar silver screen franchises, both mediums have become bedrocks of global culture from humble beginnings. Both were fostered by and exploded in popularity from here on the streets of the Big Apple. Leaping off spinner racks at your local grocery store and blasting out of mixtapes shared with your friends, these art forms awakened creativity in those who had eyes to see and ears to hear. From legends like MF Doom to my hometown Shaolin heroes Wu-Tang Clan wearing their comic love on their sleeves, to Marvel lovingly curating an entire line of hip-hop album tribute variant covers, documenting hip-hop's history via Marvel superheroes recreating the most iconic album art, hip-hop and comics share a long-standing respect and love for one another that continues to this day.

I've been privileged to work alongside Darryl McDaniels in crafting his comic book universe for the past few years. As he'll tell you at the drop of a Kangol hat, Darryl's love of comics ran deep in his bones and shaped him into the master of the mic he is today. Comic books gave him a framework to shape his sense of identity, hero status, and announce to the world his name's "DMC in the place to be." Peter Parker was from Queens, and so was he.

I'm proud to work on the Darryl Makes Comics universe with Darryl and an ever-growing roster of all-star and soon-to-be all-star creators from across the comics industry. We all come together for a love of the craft of both mediums. The universe itself is bursting with creativity and a celebration of both worlds that raised Darryl. It's a graffiti-splattered, sci-fi-fantasy epic where space aliens and school teachers from Queens can meet and fight for a better tomorrow. It's the world outside your window and the unfathomable edges of the universe all within the four-color pages. It's the perfect fusion of both worlds that we hope will inspire the next generation of comic creators and hip-hop artists. Everyone is celebrated here and welcomed to the table.

To explain, in his own words, a bit about the universe and how the worlds of hip-hop and comics collide, is one of the original architects of the DMC universe, as well as a key player in the music industry, Riggs Morales (Executive Vice President, A&R, Def Jam Recordings):

Whether its Sugar Hill Gang referring to Superman on rap's first major hit, "Rapper's Delight" or Bill Sienkiewicz penning classic album covers for EPMD, TI and Kid Cudi or Denys Cowan's work on GZA's Liquid Swords, the relationship between hip-hop and comics is that of two creative cousins who show up to the family gathering and never separate. One is an exercise in creativity the other an exercise in performance; both an expression of the arts that is engrained at a young age.

Where they both meet is DMC, the comic fan who grew up in comics and became a hero to an entire generation because of the heroes he read about in the comic pages. Name a rap icon on your playlist and he'll likely name DMC on his/ hers. Name a comic icon, and he's likely to be embedded into DMC's personality as one half of the rock hall of fame inductees, RUN-DMC.

When he launched Darryl Makes Comics in 2014, it was as natural as picking up a microphone and yelling "Now we crash through walls, cut through floors, Bust through ceilings and, knock down doors," which we found out later came from his upbringing as a Marvel fan reading The Incredible Hulk. These days, DMC is a fully devoted comic book publisher releasing graphic novels and activating the fanboy hidden through years of making music. As a publisher of color, DMC has made it his company's mandate to work with or provide opportunities to creatives of color. To encounter DMC at a comic con is encountering a hero, inspired by heroes. The same inner child that makes us read is the same inner child that finds him devoted to making Darryl Makes Comics a playground for the creative.

On the comics side of things, hear from one of the driving creative forces behind the DMC universe, comic book writer superstar Amy Chu (*Carmilla:*

*The First Vampire, Poison Ivy, Sea Sirens*), about her time working with Darryl at the crossroads of hip-hop and comics: "It's a joy working with DMC. Not only does he respect the medium and craft, but he understands the collaborative nature of what we do. Like music, comics has pacing, rhythm, and beat, while also telling a story."

Looking back on Darryl Makes Comics' ten-year anniversary and looking to the future, we're excited to continue this longstanding history between the two mediums and inspire the next generation to greatness.

I'm happy such a scholarly work like this book can exist and not only celebrate this connection but truly dig deeply into it and trace the higher concepts that go along with it. Thanks so much to Dr. Sheena Howard for inviting me and the Darryl Makes Comics team along for this; we hope this book continues one of the longest and coolest collabs in history.

# ABOUT THE CONTRIBUTORS

**Lea Beka** (they/them) is an undergraduate student at James Madison University, double majoring in Media Arts and Design (in Digital Video and Cinema) and Music (in Music Studies). Their work primarily focuses on fiction/documentary films and research that uses these mediums to share stories for LGBTQIA+ and other marginalized communities. They are planning to continue their higher education with a master's degree in Communication Studies.

**Collin M. Bright** is a communication PhD student at the University of Utah. He holds an MA in Communication & Advocacy with an emphasis in Environmental Studies from James Madison University. His work is currently focused on critical-cultural approaches to creative inquiry and textual analysis of Black aesthetics, media studies, and music.

**Justin D Burton** is a scholar of popular music and culture, with expertise in hip-hop studies and sound studies. They are the author of *Posthuman Rap* and coeditor of *The Oxford Handbook of Hip Hop Music*, exploring music through the filter of gender, race, and class.

**John P. Craig,** PhD, is a dedicated academic and educator with a profound expertise in Africology and African American Studies. He earned his doctorate from Temple University and holds a Master of Arts in Africana Studies from SUNY Albany, along with a bachelor's in History with a concentration in Secondary Education from Morehouse College. Dr. Craig is currently a tenure-track continuing instructor at Portland Community College, where his research delves into African American history, Afrofuturism, the history of race, and the representation of Black people in popular culture and sequential art. He has a robust teaching portfolio, having taught a variety of courses ranging from introductory Black Studies and Ethnic Studies to detailed historical surveys of Africa and African American history.

**Michael B. Norton Dando** is an associate professor of Communication Arts and Literature and Director of the Secondary Language Arts Education Program at St. Cloud State University in St. Cloud, Minnesota. An award-winning author, artist, educator, and scholar with two decades of classroom experience, his research and writing explore ways teachers and schools collaborate with communities to build collective, civically engaged, democratic opportunities and speculative systems for social justice education. Particularly, his research examines ways youth employ various cultural forms, including hip-hop and comics, to construct social, cultural, and political identities and literacies that generate educational opportunities for sustained, critical, democratic engagement for social justice.

**Jayanti Datta** (MA in English Literature, Calcutta University) is an associate professor of English at Sivanath Sastri College. Datta's original novel in English, *Yearning*, writers workshop, was nominated by the publishers for the Commonwealth Prize for first-time authors. Datta's English translation of Sahitya Academy Award–winning Bani Basu's Bengali novel, *The Enemy Within*, was published by Orient Longman. Datta also has a published book of short stories, *Churning*, and a novel titled *Until the Rains Come*. Datta has been conducting independent research on rap music in India for the past few years, and Datta's articles have appeared in prestigious journals, such as *The Journal of the Indian Anthropological Society*.

**Brea M. Heidelberg** is a scholar and arts management consultant specializing in cultural policy and organizational behavior in the creative industries. Her work bridges academia and practice, focusing on equity in the arts and entertainment sectors.

**Kathryn Hobson** (they/them) is an associate professor in the School of Communication Studies at James Madison University. Their research is located at the crux of intersectionality, performance, and popular culture. Their current work focuses on Futurism, social change, and building queer kinship networks for surviving the zombie apocalypse.

**Sheena C. Howard** is an Eisner Award–winning author, filmmaker, and scholar known for her work at the intersection of representation and comics. She is the first Black woman to win an Eisner Award and has written and edited numerous books, including *Black Comics: Politics of Race and Representation*, *Why Wakanda Matters*, and *Encyclopedia of Black Comics*.

**Johnny Jones** currently teaches at Simmons College of Kentucky, the 107th Historically Black College/University, where he also serves as chair of Cross-Cultural Communication. Johnny has taught at multiple universities in multiple disciplines, including Theatre Arts, African American Studies, Modern to Contemporary African American Theatre, and Composition. A native tongue of the Arkansas Delta, Johnny's writing focuses on Black narratives in modern and contemporary African American theatre and media. He has published work in *NORMA—International Journal of Masculinity Studies* as well as book chapters for *HBO's Treme and Post Katrina Catharsis: The Mediated Rebirth of New Orleans, Popular Culture in Perspective, Black Women's Portrayals on Reality Television,* and *Gender Actualized,* and *Routledge Companion of African American Theater*. He has also directed theatre productions at the Smithsonian Museum of American History and the National Black Theatre Festival.

**Spenser Nellis** is a lifelong comic book fan and is happy to give back to the medium he loves as the marketing manager at Papercutz Graphic Novels and the editor at Darryl Makes Comics, where he helps introduce the next generation of readers to their next favorite comic.

**Patrick A. Reed** is a New York City–based pop culture historian and journalist. He is the founder and organizer of the *Hip-Hop and Comics: Cultures Combining* series of conferences and programs; curator of *The Hip-Hop and Comics Show*; and cocurator of the Skirball Cultural Institute's Jack Kirby exhibition and international touring exhibitions *Marvel: Earth's Mightiest Exhibition, Spider-Man: Beyond Amazing,* and *Marvel: Universe Of Super Heroes*. He has been published by Black Dog/Hachette, MTV, TwoMorrows Publishing, Sony Music, and numerous other entities. He can be found on social media at @djpatrickareed and @HipHopComicsCC.

**Michael Sales** is a writer who focuses his work on hip-hop, art, and spirituality. His writing has been featured in *Charlotte Magazine*, the *Salt Collective*, and *Medium*. He has also contributed to *Black Comics: Politics of Race and Representation*, edited by Sheena Howard.

**Daniel Silver** (he/him) is a recent graduate of James Madison University. He graduated with a BS in Individualized Studies. His research projects include his undergraduate thesis, *The Inescapable Ideology: How Third Cinema and Afrofuturism Can Change the Future* and *Reinforcing Dominant Narratives: The Hegemony of White Culture in Genre Filmmaking*.

**Matthew Teutsch** is the director of the Lillian E. Smith Center at Piedmont University. He is the editor of *Rediscovering Frank Yerby: Critical Essays* (UPM, 2020), and he maintains Interminable Rambling, a blog of literature, culture, and pedagogy. He has published articles and book reviews in various venues, including *LEAR*, *MELUS*, *Mississippi Quarterly*, *African American Review*, and *Callaloo*. Follow him on Twitter @SilasLapham.

**Stephen J. Tyson Jr.** (a.k.a. Ellect) is a musician, educator, and documentarian. He is the founder of JusListen Entertainment LLC, a multimedia arts company that encourages critical thinking and freedom of expression through hip-hop music and culture. In addition to songwriting and music production, Dr. Tyson also teaches at the undergraduate and graduate levels about the history of hip-hop culture and its role in international peacebuilding efforts. With over twenty-plus years of experience in youth development and education, his work in diverse communities around the globe includes providing professional development and leadership in various nonprofit organizations, school districts, summer camps, and college access programs.

**george white jr.** is a professor of history and Interim Dean of the School of Arts & Sciences at York College, CUNY. He teaches and writes about African American history and culture, the history of US foreign relations, and Black military history. He has been married for thirty-five years and is the father of three adult children, all of whom enjoy Black speculative fiction and anime.

**Laith Zuraikat** is an assistant professor of Radio, Television, and Film at Hofstra University. He holds a bachelor's degree in Art & Technology from Allegheny College, a master's degree in Higher Education Administration from Upper Iowa University, and a PhD in Communications Media and Instructional Technology from Indiana University of Pennsylvania. He is a multidisciplinary researcher whose interests span a wide range of areas in the field of communications. His previous research has focused on such topics as the parasocial nature of the podcast, the educational benefits of comics, and the public relations strategies of professional athletes.

# INDEX

Page numbers in **bold** indicate figures.

Aarey Forest (Goregaon, India), 59–60
AAVE. *See* African American Vernacular English (AAVE)
absurdism, 235
*Across the Spider-Verse* (film), 161
*Adventures of Mr. Obadiah Oldbuck, The*, 71, **71**
aesthetic sensibility, 160–61
African American Vernacular English (AAVE), 148
African Americans, 46, 196; artists and listeners, 4; community admiration of Badman trope, 162–63; media's portrayal of, 150; medical and military exploitation of, 158; middle-class, 152–53. *See also* Black community
Afrika Bambaataa, 15, 25, 110
Afro-Latino identity, 153, 155
*All or Nothing* (album), 151
Alvarado-Rivera, Tony, 258
Amar Chitra Katha, 55
Ambedkar, B. R., 50, 51, 55–57
Ansaaru Allah Community, 232
Apani B. (Apani Smith), 236, 243n6
Aqua Teen Hunger Force, 236
*As Nasty as They Wanna Be* (album), 4
*Astonishing Ant-Man, The* (comic series), 249
*Astroworld* (album), 134
A-Train (character), 8, 209, 210, 214, 215–18, 219–24
authenticity, 98

*Avengers* (franchise), 142
*Avengers: Doomsday* (film), 238
*Avengers: Infinity War* (film), 131
*Avengers: The Secret Wars* (TV series), 238
*Azadi Bachao Andolan* (Save Freedom Movement), 51
Azadi Records, 50

"Baby Got Back" (song), 133
Badman trope, 161–64; African American folklore, 161; antihero masculinity, 146; influence in hip-hop, 162; superhero connections, 161–63
Baker, Kyle, 114
Bantai, Emiway, 54–55
Barthes, Roland, 76
Basquiat, Jean-Michel, 73, 78, 83
*Batman* (film), 127
*Batman, The* (film), 141
*Batman Returns* (film), 141
Bechdel, Alison, 73, 82–83; "Bechdel Test," **82**, 83; *Dykes to Watch Out For*, **82**
Beck, Robert (Iceberg Slim), 92, 95
*Beerbongs & Bentleys* (album), 134
Bhim Army, 51, 56
*Bhimayana* (Natarajan & Anand), 48, 55–57, 64; attacks on hegemonic structures, 55; colors and metaphors used in, 56; Gond folk art employed in, 56–57; protagonist of, 55
Bhoir, Prakash, 60
Billson, Janet Mancini, 174, 185
Black Arts Movement, 151; jazz, 231
*BL_CK B_ST_RDS* (album), 230–31

269

Black bodies, 157, 158, 256
Black books, 14–15, 22
Black characters: *The Boys*, 210, 214–15; female, 148; historical representation in mainstream comics, 100; male, 148; stereotypical images of, 97–98
Black comedic tradition, 192, 194, 195–98
Black community, 175, 193, 195, 200, 205, 214, 217, 218, 223; cultural narrative, 157, 160, 203; struggle for identity, 153. *See also* African Americans
Black culture, 21, 150, 197, 199, 217
Black Eyed Peas, 111, 119, 120
Black feminism, 8, 253, 254
Black feminist superhero, 246–59; street-level, 247, 252–56; work of "OMC," 256–59
Black identity, 164, 165; media construction, 146–47; storytelling and cultural symbolism, 154–55; in superhero narratives, 153
Black Lives Matter, 157, 205
Black manhood, 147, 154; authenticity and, 213
Black masculinity: binary of authentic/inauthentic, 212–14; *The Boys*, 210, 212–15; in hip-hop and Marvel comics, 154–61; hip-hop influence, 145–47, 151–52; multifaceted nature depicted in hip-hop, 152
Black men: aesthetics of, 213; identity, 164; joblessness, 174; patriarchal, 185; solidarity, 8, 193
*Black Noise* (Rose), 149, 173
*Black Panther* (film), 131, 157, 161; Black identity and resistance, 159; cultural movement, 164; soundtrack, 6, 7, 126, 140
*Black Panther and the Crew* (comic series), 148
Black Power Movement, 147, 151, 161
Black superheroes, 163; complexities of, 159; development of, 147; hip-hop's cultural language with Marvel's, 147; masculinity and, 159–60; Marvel's first, 153; narratives of, 145–46

Black women, 204–6; absence of in *The Boondocks*, 203–6; in *The Boys*, 219–22; challenging oppressive systems, 163; exclusion in McGruder's framework, 193; in hip-hop and Marvel, 146–47, 151–52, 205; struggles foregrounded through Tupac's music, 154; in superhero narratives, 153; symbolic annihilation of, 204
Blackness, 193, 198, 242, 255; authentic, 213; Blaxploitation cinema and, 104; in *The Boys*, 210, 213, 223; inauthentic, 213; in Lamar's work, 155
*Blade* (film), 139, 160
Blaxploitation cinema, 91–92, 147, 153, 157, 161, 163, 231; Cage's character influenced by, 153; characters, 148; critique of oppression and capitalism, 92; mirrored in Marvel's commercial strategy, 92; portrayal of heroes, 92
*Blue Beetle* (film), 130
*Blue Guerilla, The* (album), 231
*Blueprint, The* (album), 155
*Boondocks, The* (TV series), 5, 84, 192–206; Black comedic tradition, 192, 194, 195–98; Black male solidarity, 193; censorship in newspapers, 195; critique of Black masculinity, 198; critique of racial fascism, 195; "A Date with the Health Inspector," 194; depiction of white privilege, 194; exclusion of Black women, 193; hip-hop influence of, 199–203; history of, 195–99; political and pop culture mash-ups, 194; racial stereotypes, 198; "Stinkmeaner Strikes Back," 193, 195, 196, 199–206; toxic masculinity satire, 193; youth-centered storytelling, 202
*Born Like This* (album), 239–40
Boseman, Chadwick, 238
*Boys, The* (TV series), 209–24; analysis of, 216–23; A-Train as Michael Jordan and Malcolm X, 216–18; authenticity in, 212–14; Black characters in, 210, 214–15; Black masculinity, 210, 212–15; culture wars, 210; hip-hop in, 212–14; IMDb rating, 211; methods and theories,

214–15; metonymy of contemporary America, 211; paternal relationship of Mother's Milk and A-Train, 222–23; Sage and A-Train's conflicting relationship, 218–22; superhero tropes, 209
*Break the Chain* (comic book), 114–17, **116**, 120, 124
Bright, Mark: collaboration with Priest, 92; narrative critique of constructed personas, 98; racial themes in narrative, 99
Browne, Simone, 255–56
Buck Wild (character), 104–5, **106**, 107, 108n5
Budget Printing, 19, 20
Bukowski, Charles, 239
Bush, George W., 195
*By All Means Necessary* (album), 195

Cameron, James, criticism of DC and Marvel films, 129–30
Camp, Bob, 110
Cardi B, 134, 151; Badwoman trope, 163
CCA. *See* Comics Code Authority (CCA)
CFS. *See* Chicago Freedom School (CFS)
*Change Everything* (Gilmore), 254
*chapri*, 55
character graffiti, 70
"Cherchez La Ghost" (song), 184
Chess, Marshall, 114
Chess Records, 114
*Chetavani (Warning)* (album), 50
Chicago Freedom School (CFS), 258
Chu, Amy, 262–63
Citizenship Amendment Act (CAA), 50
civil rights movement, 95, 96, 158, 161, 197
"Coffin Nails" (song), 241
*Cold Rock Stuff, The* (Simmons), 15
Coles, David. *See* Ghostface Killah
Colter, Mike, 160
Combahee River Collective (CRC), 252–54
Combs, Sean "Puff Daddy," 216
Comics Code Authority (CCA), 5, 72
"Coming of the Super-Predators, The" (story), 175, **176**
*Cool Pose* (Majors & Billson), 174–75

Cool Pose: artists embodying, 155–57; definition, 174–75; hip-hop and superheroes, 146; implications for character development, 159–60; in media, 160
Cope2, 70
Coppola, Francis Ford, criticism of superhero film, 130
*Cosby Show, The* (TV show), 39
Crenshaw, Kimberle, 215, 253
Crew, The (comic characters), 148
"Crush On You" (song), 186
Cultural Materialism, 49
Cultural Prism Theory (CPT), 13–22

Dark Horse Comics, 23
*Dark Knight, The* (film), 131
*Dark Knight Rises, The* (film), 141
*Dark Matters* (Browne), 255–56
*Dark Reign* (comic series), 237
dark sousveillance, 256
Darryl Makes Comics (DMC), 34, 261–63; graphic novel cover, **31**; graphic novel line, 35; graphic novel panel, **36**; legacy of comic book line, 36; types of images, 39–40
Davis, Angela, 194, 204, 253–54
Davis, Blair, 93, 94
"Daytona 500" (song), 184
DC Comics, 178; characters from, 177; superheroes of, 42
De La Soul, 38, 201, 243n5
DEI (diversity, equity, and inclusion) initiatives, 205, 220
*Delhi Calm* (Ghosh), 48, 55, 57–59, 64; critique of "Emergency of 1975," 57; protagonist of, 57–58
Dharavi, Mumbai, 52–55, 64; festival celebration in, 53; *Gully Boy* based on, 54; issues of religion, caste, and patriarchy, 53; rap groups functioning in, 54
Dharavi Redevelopment Project, 53
Dharavi United, 54
diegetic sound, 138
*dignas* (art pattern), 57
DiIulio, John J., Jr., 175
DJ Subroc (Dingilizwe Dumile), 229–34

DMC. *See* McDaniels, Darryl (DMC)
DMC universe, 39, 262–63
Dole, Bob, 175–76
*Doomwar* (comic series), 237
Downey, Robert, Jr., 238
Drake, 134, 213; Badman trope, 162; and Black masculinity, 154, 155–56; embodying Cool Pose, 155; emotional vulnerability, 146
Dumile, Daniel. *See* MF Doom

Ehlers, Nadine, 214–15, 221
Eisner, Will, 70
Elektra Records, 230
Eminem, 40, 111, 233
*Eminem Show, The* (album), 134
Englehart, Steve, 92
*Enter the Wu-Tang* (album), 182
environmental activism, 59–64; *River of Stories*, 61–64; by Swadesi, 59–61
"excluded cultures," 72
*Ex-Con, Voodoo Priest, Goddess, and the African King, The* (Jones), 158–59
*Exorcist, The* (film), 202

Fairey, Shepard, 70
*Falcon and the Winter Soldier, The* (TV series), 159
*Fantastic Four* (comic series), 153, 234
*Fantastic Four* (franchise), 139–40, 142, 236, 237
Fat Joe, 111, 118, 151
"Father Time" (song), 188
fatherhood, in superhero narratives, 190
*Fear of a Black Hat* (mockumentary), 201
female hip-hop artists, 205; contributions to superhero films, 141; integration with music, 142; marginalization of, 205; redefining gender norms, 151
50 Cent, 151, 183
*Fight*, 117, 124
5Pointz, 74
Forbidden Planet, 20
Foucault, Michel, 217, 222; "discipline," "punishment," and "power," 215; heterotopia, 79; "political anatomy," 221

*4:44* (album), 189–90
Foxy Brown (character), 163

gangsta rap, 197; artists influence, 152; Badman trope, 150; criticism of, 128–29; industry restructuring, 204–5; Jay-Z glorifying, 155; rise of, 152
Garcia, Bobbito, 231
"Gas Drawls" (song), 231, 232
"Gas Face" (song), 232
gatekeepers, 133; comic creators bypassing, 24; cultural, 55; in radio industries, 134–35
gender norms: female graffiti artists challenging, 83; female hip-hop artists challenging, 146, 151–52, 163
Genter, Robert, 179
"Get Money" (song), 186
*Get Rich or Die Tryin* (album), 134
*Getting Ugly* (comic issue), 99, 105. *See also Power Man and Iron Fist* (comic series)
Ghosh, Vishwajyoti, 57, 58–59
"Ghost Deni" (song), 184
Ghostface Killah, 37, 44, 151, 182–85, 199, 201, 236; alter ego, 110; criticism of new hip-hop generation, 129; *Ironman*, 5, 140; "Slept on Tony," 140; *Supreme Clientele*, 184
"Girl You Know It's True" (song), 133
"Go with the Flow" (song), 232
Godwin, Archie, 92
Goines, Donald, 91, 93; Kenyatta novels, 93
graffiti, 67–70; art form of resistance and survival, 173; artistic expression, 69; character graffiti, 70; connection to comics aesthetics, 149; designs and practice lettering, 22; dialogue between comics and, 75; element of hip-hop, 149; growing recognition of, 26–27; and hip-hop culture, 3–4; ignoring physical boundaries, 79; implications of, 85; negative perceptions of, 26; New York City and, 23, 26; notebooks, 74; origins of, 69; political culture, 26–27; public access, 73–75; public marginalization and refusal of, 72–73; public mediation, 75–76; self-expression of,

79; "Slaps," 69–70; spatial arrangement of, 78–79; Stencil Art, 70; "street art" versus, 69; synthesis of, 84; "Tags," 69; visual rhetoric of, 78–80; Wildstyle, 70
Graham, Billy, 92
Grandmaster Caz, 37
Grandmaster Flash & the Furious Five, 3, 34, 174
Grandwizard Theodore & the Fantastic Five, 3, 34
Graphic India, 55
Greene, Sanford, 39, 107
*Gully Boy* (film), 50, 54
GZA/Genius, 150; *Liquid Swords*, 182

Hall, Stuart, 72–73
Haring, Keith, 16, 18, 19, 78; Orr meeting with, 26; as judge in Swatch Watch show, 17
Harvey, Eric, 150
Hassani, Shamsia, 83
"Heart Part 5, The" (song), 188
*Heist, The* (comic), 118, 124
"Hey!" (song), 232
Hill, Lauryn, 146, 151, 203, 205; Badwoman trope, 163; Black female character inspired by, 148; Black masculinity and singing and rapping, 213; challenging hypermasculinity, 146; *The Miseducation of Lauryn Hill*, 243n6
Holloway House, 95; Kenyatta novels, 93; *Pimp: The Story of My Life*, 92; pulp fiction publishing by, 91
"Homeboy Cosmopolitan" concept, 155
Homelander (character), 218, 219, 220–22
hooks, bell, 194; concept of city, 72–73; concept of cultural identity, 73; cultural criticism and transformation, 84; on sexism, 185

Ice Cube, 95, 176, 204
Iceberg Slim, 91; *Pimp: The Story of My Life*, 92, 95
Ice-T, 95, 120, 152
*Icon* (comic series), 92, 99; cover and initial splash page, 105; pages from, **106**

IMDb. *See* Internet Movie Database (IMDb)
Indian hip-hop. *See* 7Bantai'Z; Swadesi
Indian Independence Movement, 51
Internet Movie Database (IMDb), 211, 225n1
intersectionality, 215, 224, 253
*Into the Spider-Verse* (film), 160, 161; hip-hop-heavy soundtrack, 140–41
*Invasion of Privacy* (album), 134
*Iron Man* (comic series), 178–82; "Demon in a Bottle," 179, **180**; pages from, **179–82**
*Iron Man* (film), 140
*Ironman* (album), 5, 140, 183

Jackendoff, Benjamin, 119
Jay-Z, 7, 183, 213; Badman trope, 162; and Black masculinity, 154, 155; clothing styles, 160; as cultural parallel to street-level heroism, 153; debates on Black empowerment, 157; embodying Cool Pose, 155; entrepreneurial masculinity, 145; *4:44*, 189–90; fusion of music and storytelling, 151; glorifying gangsta rap, 155
Jazzy Jay, 15, 16, 25; logo, **16**; Orr working with, **19**
Jennings, John, 95; creating Black Kirby, 95–96; interactive "illabus," 96, 108n3
Jones, William, 158–59
Jordan, Michael, 148, 216–18, 224
"Judo Flip" (song), 195
*Jungle Action featuring the Black Panther* (comic series), 92

Kaba, Mariame, 254, 257
Kain, Gylan, 230–31
Kid 'N Play, 111–12, **113**, 124
Kim, Seung Eun, 203
King, Martin Luther, Jr., 194, 203–4
King Geedorah, 235
Kirby, Jack, 95, 237; "classic conception of death," 228; creation of T'Challa (Black Panther), 92; introducing Black Panther, 147

KMD (Kauzin' Much Damage), 229–32, 243n1; Afrocentric adolescent group, 229; *BL_CK B_ST_RDS*, 230–31; relationship with MF Doom, 229–32
Kramer, Ronald, *Painting with Permission*, 27
Kripke, Eric, 209, 222; *The Boys*, 209–24; *Naming and Necessity*, 218, 219
Kripke, Saul A., 218, 219
KRS-One, 111, 120; *By All Means Necessary*, 195

"Ladies First" (song), 185–86
Lamar, Kendrick, 6, 7, 95, 126, 164, 213; anthem of resistance, 157; Badman trope, 162; and Black masculinity, 154–55; curating Black Panther soundtrack, 140; embodying Cool Pose, 155; "Father Time," 188; "The Heart Part 5," 188; introspection, 146; introspective lyricism and social commentary, 156; "Mother I Sober," 188; *Mr. Morales and the Big Steppers*, 187–88; Pulitzer Prize, 187
Larocca, Salvador, 110
Lee, Stan, 33, 35, 37; creating T'Challa (Black Panther), 92; definition of superhero, 130; introducing Black Panther, 147
Leikeli47, 8, 246–59; as Black feminist street-level hero, 252–56; and drumline, **258**; guarding identity, 255; as masked performer, 247; "Miss Me," 252, 254; "Money," 250, 252, 254; "OMC," 246–47, 248, 250, 254, 256–59; rapping at Brooklyn rooftop, **247**; as street-level hero, 247–52
*Let This Radicalize You* (Kaba), 257–58
Lil' Kim, 111, 118, 151, 163, 186
Liquid Comics, 55
*Liquid Swords* (album), 182
LL Cool J, 38, 148, 178, 255
*lok shayar* (people's poet), 51
*Lovecraft Country* (TV series), 164
Luke Cage (character), 91–94, 95–100, 102–7, 108n4, 225n3; "Am I not a Cage and a brother?," **103**

Luke Cage (Netflix series), 157, 159
*Luke Cage, Hero for Hire* (comic series): cover of, 93; splash page, **94**

Mabley, Jackie "Moms," 198, 199
*Madvillainy* (album), 236, 242
Majors, Richard, 174, 185
Malcolm X, 8, 194, 196, 202, 216–18, 224
*Mark of Zorro, The* (film), 127
Marley, Bob, 196
Martin, Travon, 159, 161
Marvel Cinematic Universe (MCU), 129, 154, 159, 178, 237–39; *Avengers: Doomsday*, 238; Doom's first solo film buildup, 238; limits on death themes, 237; transition from T'Challa to Doom, 238–39
Marvel Comics, 178, 230; addressing social issues, 35; AR and VR technology, 120, 123; Black cultural moment being exploited, 91–92; Black Panther and the Crew, 148; *Break the Chain*, 114–17, **116**, 120, 124; character narrative, 234; covers inspired by classic hip-hop albums, 150–51; The Crew, 148; *Eminem/The Punisher*, 118–19; employment practices in the 1970s, 98; featuring hip-hop artists in comics, 111; *Fight*, 117, 124; *The Heist*, 118, 124; hip-hop artists being empowered, 111; influence on DMC, 35; intersection of hip-hop and, 7; *Masters of the Sun*, 119–22, **121**; "pulp authenticity," 91; pursuit of "genre money," 92; *Secret Wars*, 239–40; superheroes of, 42; *Ultimate Spider-Man*, 81
Marvel Unlimited, 120, 272
Marvel Variant covers, 40
*Massacre, The* (album), 134
*Masters of the Sun* (comic series), 119–22, **121**, 124; AR/VR experience, 120; companion album of, 120–21; hype related to, 122; setting, characters, and action of, 122
*matti* (clay), 57
M.C. Hammer, 133
MC Lyte, 151, 203, 205

McCloud, Scott, 74, 104–5; definition of comics, 70; "Understanding Comics," 76

McDaniels, Darryl (DMC), 6, 29–47; addressing social issues, 35; on alter egos, 21; being a hero in hip-hop, 37–38; Catholic school upbringing, 33; comic book universe, 261–62; comic books as confidence source, 33, 34; comic books helping define identity, 33; devastating mic controller, 33–34; ethos of comic book superheroes, 42; identity construction, 42–44; interview with Sheena C. Howard, 31–41; introduction to Marvel Comics, 32; journey of, 46–47; love for comic books, 32–33, 42; observer of early hip-hop pioneers, 34; Symbolic Interaction Theory, 30–41; *Ten Ways Not to Commit Suicide*, 47; Wu-Tang logo, 4

McDuffie, Dwayne, 83, 92; *Icon*, 92, 99, 106; Milestone Media, 83; use of satire to address systemic racism, 92

McGruder, Aaron, 192–206; Afro-anime satire, 205; analytical focus on Black male experience, 195; Black comedic tradition, 192, 194, 195–98; commitment to candor in comedy, 196; creation of *The Boondocks* comic strip, 195; critique of racial violence and white privilege, 194–95; exclusion of Black women critique, 193; exploration of Black masculinity, 198; hip-hop-inflected storytelling, 192; pop culture references, 203; racial satire and social critique, 195–96; vision of Black solidarity, 192; visual art and hip-hop, 206

*Medical Apartheid* (Washington), 159

Megan Thee Stallion, 151; Badwoman trope, 163; cameo in *She-Hulk: Attorney at Law*, 142; female hip-hop artist, 141; music featured in TV series, 142

Melle Mel, 37, 174, 175

"Message, The" (song), 174

Method Man, 36, 182; alter ego, 110; fusion of music and storytelling, 151; in Netflix series, 157; rapper with comic-book title, 151

MF Doom, 8, 36, 150, 228–42, 261; *Born Like This*, 239–40; classic conception of death, 237–42; *Days of Doom*, 242; honored by Marvel, 242; inspired by comic book characters, 5; *Madvillainy*, 236, 242; mask as performance strategy, 233–36; mastery of illusion and focus on mysticism, 234; *MF EP*, 234; *Mm..Food*, 234; *The Mouse and the Mask*, 236; *Operation: Doomsday*, 232, 233–34; "Rapp Snitch Knishes," 241; relationship with DJ Subroc, 229–34; relationship with KMD, 229–32; *Special Herbs*, 234; "Supervillain Vaudeville," 233–36; *Take Me to Your Leader*, 235; transition from Zev Love X, 229–32; *Vaudeville Villain*, 235–36; Viktor Vaughn, 235–36

Milestone Comics, 5; Black and brown characters by, 83–84; characters dealing with contemporary issues, 84

Milestone Media, 83–84

Miranda-Rodriguez, Edgardo, 73

*Miseducation of Lauryn Hill, The* (album), 243n6

misogyny: female hip-hop artists against, 151; Tupac's lyrics exhibiting, 152

Missy Elliott, 141; Badwoman trope, 163; challenging hypermasculinity, 146; genre-bending artistic expression, 151

Mizell, Jason "Jam Master Jay," 47

Monie Love, 151, 185

Moore, Tradd, 78; *Ghost Rider*, 80; *Spider-Man*, 80

Morales, Riggs, 262

Morris, Bentley, 95

Mos Def, 96, 233; "The Boogie Man Song," 104; "Fake Bonanza," 107

"Mother I Sober" (song), 188

Mother's Milk (character), 210, 214, 215, 222–24

*Mr. Morales and the Big Steppers* (album), 187–88

*Ms. Marvel* (comic series), 84

Munby, Jonathan, on Blaxploitation complicity and critique, 92
"My Philosophy" (song), 195

*Naming and Necessity* (Kripke), 218, 219
Nas, 151; debates on Black empowerment, 157
New Jack Swing (NJS), 133, 147–48
New York City, 172–73; political culture of, 27; Vandal Squad in, 22
*Ninja Kamui* (Netflix series), 203
*nommo* (life force), 233, 241
*Noughts and Crosses* (TV series), 164

OBM Records, 19
*Only Built 4 Cuban Linx* (album), 182–83
Onyx, 111, 117, 232
*Operation: Doomsday* (album), 232, 233–34
Orr, Eric, 11–28; fear of Vandal Squad, 26; Jazzy Jay logo, **16**; *Rappin' Max Robot*, 4, 6, 11, 149; transition to comic books, 4
Owsley, Jim. *See* Priest, Christopher

*Painting with Permission: Legal Graffiti in New York City* (Kramer), 27
Parents Music Resource Center (PMRC), 4
"performativity," 215
*Pimp: The Story of My Life* (film), 92; command to recall promotional material, 95; memoir by Iceberg Slim, 95
"Planet Rock" (song), 15, 173–74
*Please Don't Hurt 'Em* (album), 133
Post Malone, 134
*Power Man and Iron Fist* (comic series), 92, 96–99; *Getting Ugly* issue, 99, 105; pages from, **97**, **101**, **106**; used to confront racial themes, 99; visual references to panels in, 105
Priest, Christopher, 92, 108n1; addressing white creators' stereotypes, 96–98; critique of racism in comics, 99; *Power Man and Iron Fist*, 92, 96, **97**, 99
prison abolition, 254
Pryor, Richard, 198, 199
Public Enemy, 35, 38, 150, 196, 201, 222

Quayle, Dan, 4
Queen Latifah, 120, 151, 185–86, 244n6; Badwoman trope, 163; Black masculinity and singing and rapping, 213; challenging hypermasculinity, 146; "Ladies First," 185; "U.N.I.T.Y.," 186; "Wildflower," 185

radio industry, restricting early hip-hop access, 134–35
Raekwon, 120, 182, 183
Rakim, 120, 178; criticism of new hip-hop generation, 129
"Rapp Snitch Knishes" (song), 241
"Rapper's Delight" (song), 173, 178
*Rappin' Max Robot* (Orr), 4, 6, 11–28; Bronx setting, 149; cover page, **12**; cultural impact, 25–26; Cultural Prism Theory, 13–22; economic impact, 24; historical impact, 23–24; political impact, 26–28
*Reasonable Doubt* (album), 155
"Red and Gold" (song), 232
*Reflections* (album), 95
*River of Stories* (Sen), 48, 55, 61–64
Ro, Ronin, 230, 231, 232
Robinson, Stacey, 95; creating Black Kirby, 95–96; interactive "illabus," 96, 108n3
Rose, Tricia, 149, 173
Roundtree, Richard, 92, 97
Roxy, the, 16, 17, 25
Run-D.M.C., 29, 38, 47; clothing styles, 160

Sanders, Pharoah, 231
satire: Afro-anime, 205; in comics, 78; racial, 195; of transgression, 55
Scott, Damion, 39, 74; defining comics, 70; "Understanding Comics," 76; work in *Masters of the Sun*, 119, 122
*Secret Wars* (comic series), 239–40
Sen, Orijit, 61, 63–64
7Bantai'Z, 48, 54, 64
Shakur, Tupac: Badman trope, 162; bald aesthetic influence, 148; and Black masculinity, 154; clothing styles, 160; as cultural parallel to street-level heroism,

153; fusion of music and storytelling, 151; socially conscious lyricism and activism, 145–46
Sharma, Dub, 50–51
*She-Hulk: Attorney at Law* (TV series), 142
Simmons, Joseph "Run," 47
Simmons, Russell, 15, 25
Sister Sage (character), 210, 214, 215, 218–22, 224
Sister Souljah, 240, 244n7
*Slumdog Millionaire* (film), 52
Snoop Dogg, 120, 202; and criticism of new hip-hop generation, 129; gangsta rap, 152
*Soul Rebels* (album), 196
sousveillance, 256
speculative fiction, 107; *The Boys*, 211–12, 223; scholarship on, 210
*Spider-Man* (comic series), 249
*Spider-Man* (film), 131
*Spider-Man* (TV series), 178
*Spider-Man and His Amazing Friends* (TV series), 243n6
*Spider-Verse* (film franchise), 153–54
Spiegelman, Art, 82–83
Stencil Art, 70
stereotypes: internalized inferiority, 99; in perceptions of hip-hop culture, 128–29; propagation of caricatured Black characters, 98; racial, 198; superpredator stereotype, 175–76; white creators', 96–98
"Stroke of Death" (song), 184
Strong City Records, 18, 19
Sugar Hill Gang, 262
"Sunflower" (song), 141
*Super Friends* (TV series), 178–79
superhero films: areas for growth, 141–42; box office earnings of, 130–31, **132**; commercial restrictions on death, 237; critics or criticism of, 129–30, 142; growth of, 130–31; hip-hop music versus, 135–37; history of, 127; MCU narrative redesign, 238; music shaping narrative and emotional arc, 137–38; number per year, **131**; and scrutiny over violent content, 129–30; top grossing, 131; use of hip-hop soundtracks, 137–38; with and without hip-hop songs, 139
superhero media: Black identity and, 146, 164; Black women contributing in, 146; redefining Black storytelling, 164–65; representation of Black masculinity, 145, 164
superheroes: Cool Pose and, 146; of DC Comics, 42; ethos of comic book, 42; hip-hop artists personas as, 150; human-rights violations, 211; power abuse, 211; traditional masculinity, 212
*Superman* (film), 127, 130, 131
*Supreme Clientele* (album), 184
surveillance, 256
Swadesi, 48, 50–52, 55, 64; *Chetavani (Warning)*, 50; collaborating with Bhoir, 60; environmental activism by, 59–61; focus on working-class people, 52; members of, 51–52
Swatch Watch, 16, 17
Symbolic Interactionism, 30–41; identity construction, 42–44; meaning and language, 44–45; self, social interaction, and agency, 45–46; significance of, 43; symbols and language in, 30, 32
*Symbolic Interactionism and Cultural Studies* (Denzin), 30
systemic oppression, 8, 92, 161, 164; addressed through hip-hop narratives, 154–55; Badwoman and Badman tropes resisting, 163; fight against, 212; hip-hop and dialogue exploring, 57; in Lamar's work, 162; Tupac's music addressing, 154
systemic racism, 92, 153, 162

*Take Me to Your Leader* (album), 235
"Take Your Mask Off" (song), 189
Tate, Greg, 235
*Teenage Mutant Ninja Turtles* (film), 139
*Ten Ways Not to Commit Suicide* (McDaniels), 47
*Thembi* (album), 231, 241
T.I., 111, 118, 150, 151

*To Pimp a Butterfly* (album), 140, 154
Töpffer, Rodolphe, 71
Torre, Sigmund, 122
toxic masculinity, 155
toxic patriarchy, 185
Trick Daddy, 111, 118, 151
*Truth: Red, White & Black* (comic series), 157, 158
Twista, 111, 118, 151
2Pac. *See* Shakur, Tupac
Tyler, the Creator, 164; "Take Your Mask Off," 189

*Ultimate Fallout* (comic series), 153
*Uncaged: Hero for Higher*, 96
"U.N.I.T.Y." (song), 186
Urban Renewal Movement, 172–73

Vandal Squad, 17, 22, 26
*Vaudeville Villain* (album), 235–36
*Views* (album), 134
Vought International, 214, 215

*Wakanda Forever* (film), 164, 238
War on Drugs, 175
Washington, Harriet A., *Medical Apartheid*, 159
Wedgwood, Josiah, 100
"What's Up Danger" (song), 141
"white patriarchal universalism," 100
white supremacy, 96, 100, 107, 185, 204; confronting, 161; psychological impact of, 92, 99, 102; resistance to, 150; structural issues of, 91
*Who Got the Camera?* (Harvey), 150
"Wildflower" (song), 184–85, 186
will.i.am, 111, 119; interest in technology, 122
Wilson, G. Willow, 84
Wu-Tang Clan, 8, 36, 50, 150, 181–83, **183**, 201, 203, 261

*X-Men* (franchise), 142

*Yo! MTV Raps*, 37, 40

www.ingramcontent.com/pod-product-compliance
Lightning Source LLC
Chambersburg PA
CBHW030103170426
43198CB00009B/477